# SHOUTING
# FIRE

Also by Alan M. Dershowitz:

*Psychoanalysis, Psychiatry, and Law*
(with Jay Katz and Joseph Goldstein)

*Criminal Law: Theory and Process*
(with Joseph Goldstein and Richard D. Schwartz)

*The Best Defense*

*Reversal of Fortune: Inside the Von Bülow Case*

*Taking Liberties: A Decade of Hard Cases, Bad Laws, and Bum Raps*

*Chutzpah*

*Contrary to Public Opinion*

*The Advocate's Devil: A Novel*

*The Abuse Excuse: And Other Cop-Outs, Sob Stories,
and Evasions of Responsibility*

*Reasonable Doubts: The Criminal Justice System and the O. J. Simpson Case*

*The Vanishing American Jew:
In Search of Jewish Identity for the Next Century*

*Sexual McCarthyism: Clinton, Starr, and the Emerging Constitutional Crisis*

*Just Revenge: A Novel*

*The Genesis of Justice: Ten Stories of Biblical Injustice That Led
to the Ten Commandments and Modern Morality and Law*

*Supreme Injustice: How the High Court Hijacked Election 2000*

*Letters to a Young Lawyer*

# SHOUTING
# FIRE

*Civil Liberties
in a Turbulent Age*

Alan M. Dershowitz

LITTLE, BROWN AND COMPANY
BOSTON NEW YORK LONDON

*This book is dedicated to the victims of terrorism — and to those seeking to combat its horrors while preserving our civil liberties.*

First Edition

For information on AOL Time Warner Book Group's online publishing program, visit www.ipublish.com.

Library of Congress Cataloging-in-Publication Data

Dershowitz, Alan M.
    Shouting fire : civil liberties in a turbulent age / Alan M. Dershowitz. — 1st ed.
      p.  cm.
    Includes bibliographical references and index.
    ISBN 0-316-18141-2
     1. Civil rights — United States.   2. Civil rights.   I. Title.
JC599.U5 D47 2002
  323'.01 — dc21                          2001034453

10  9  8  7  6  5  4  3  2  1

Q-FF

*Design by Interrobang Design Studio*

Printed in the United States of America

# CONTENTS

✳

## PART V: THE RIGHT TO LIVE

## PART VI: THE RIGHT TO A ZEALOUS
## AND ETHICAL LAWYER

## PART VII: THE RIGHT TO AN HONEST JUDGE

## PART VIII: CAN RIGHTS BE SUSPENDED FOR EMERGENCIES?

# ACKNOWLEDGMENTS

It is impossible to acknowledge by name all those who contributed to the nearly forty years of research and writing that comprise this volume, and so I will limit my expression of gratitude to those who helped in the final phases of completion and editing, especially my research assistants Howard Anglin and Matthew Stein. My continuing thanks to Maura Kelly, who typed the manuscript flawlessly and always with a smile. I could not have completed this project without the advice and assistance of my agent, Helen Rees; my editor, Geoff Shandler; and my assistant, Peggy Burlet. Also, a word of appreciation to Peggy Leith Anderson for her always professional and pleasant assistance. My family all contributed their usual insights, criticisms, and love.

# INTRODUCTION

✳

# A PREFERENCE FOR RIGHTS

*Experience is more forceful than logic.*
— ISAAC ABRAVANEL (1437–1508),
*Commentary on the Bible*

THIS BOOK SEEKS TO MAKE A COMPELLING CASE FOR RIGHTS in the new millennium, based on the tragic experiences of the past millennium. In doing so, it necessarily confronts the oldest and most persistent of jurisprudential and moral dilemmas: if rights are "natural" — that is, external to the law itself — then what are their sources? Does natural law actually exist outside of positive law? Or have we simply made it up to satisfy an enduring human need?

If rights are merely positive — that is, a creature solely of human-made law — then why should the "rights" of some individuals who cannot garner the support of the majority outweigh the preferences of those in the majority?

In this book, I challenge the approach to rights taken by both classic natural law and classic legal positivism. I propose a third way, which I call an "experiential" approach to "nurtural" rights. My suggested approach builds a theory of rights from "the bottom up," by examining the history of injustices, inducing certain experiential lessons from them, and advocating rights based on those historical lessons.

I believe that because we can never have anything approaching consensus regarding what constitutes perfect justice, any attempt to derive a perfect theory of rights from an ideal of justice will inevitably fail. There is, however, widespread consensus regarding perfect injustice. Virtually every thinking person today regards the Holocaust, the Stalinist mass murders, the Cambodian genocides, the Rwandan massacres, slavery, the Inquisition, and the Crusades as instances of perfect injustice, never to be repeated. While there is no complete consensus regarding the lessons — especially as to rights — to be drawn from this history, our collective experiences with injustice are a fruitful foundation on which to build a theory of rights.[1]

In my view, rights are not "out there" waiting to be discovered, deduced, or intuited. They must be consistently advocated, based on the experiences of humankind with the injustices of those societies that have denied individual rights in general and certain fundamental rights in particular.

The theory of rights that I present in this book is, in a nutshell, the following:

- Rights *do not come from God*, because God does not speak to human beings in a singular voice, and rights should exist even if there is no God.
- Rights *do not come from nature*, because nature is value neutral.
- Rights *do not come from logic*, because there is little consensus about the a priori premises from which rights may be deduced.
- Rights *do not come from the law alone*, because if they did, there would be no basis on which to judge a given legal system.
- Rights *come from human experience*, particularly experience with injustice. We learn from the mistakes of history that a rights-based system and certain fundamental rights — such as freedom of expression, freedom of and from religion, equal protection of the laws, due process, and participatory democracy — are essential to avoid repetition of the grievous injustices of the past. Working from the bottom up, from our *experiences* with *perfect injustice*, rather than from the top down, from a *theory* of *perfect justice*, we build rights on a foundation of trial and error.
- In a word, *rights* come from *wrongs*.

In this book, I elaborate this experiential approach to nurtural rights and try to make the case for rights in a world so full of wrongs. Indeed, I use these wrongs as the building blocks for rights. Since I do not believe that rights exist outside of human experience — they are not God-given, natural, or eternal — I can do no more than advocate them. The burden of proof should be on those who advocate limitations on the power of the majority. I willingly undertake that burden and seek to satisfy it in the remainder of this book.

This book also documents the development of my own particular approach to rights over nearly four decades. Although the specifics of my views have changed since I began writing about rights in the 1960s, my general approach has remained relatively consistent.[2] I have always believed — and continue to believe — that the best defense of rights is active and persistent advocacy rather than a passive recourse to "higher authority." Every day poses new challenges to entrenched ideologies and new opportunities to advocate rights. The most recent of these challenges arises from the threat of terrorism, especially state-sponsored, religiously inspired global terrorism and the easy availability of weapons of mass destruction. Such terrorism not only denies its direct victims the most basic of civil liberties but also provides governments with justifications for curtailing the civil liberties of those suspected of complicity with terrorism as well as of other individuals and groups. This new experience with terrorism will surely inform our approach to rights in the future. That is why I have included a section on rights during emergencies.

This book presents the record of my persistent — often controversial — advocacy of civil liberties and human rights.[3] It is an invitation to join in the eternal struggle against the all-too-natural human tendency toward accepting tyranny and authority as the seductive alternatives to liberty's burdens. It is an invitation to become an advocate for rights as well as a doer of rights.

# ONE

# WHERE DO RIGHTS COME FROM? GOD? NATURE? POSITIVE LAW?

*The greatest menace to freedom is an inert people.*
— LOUIS D. BRANDEIS

INDIVIDUAL RIGHTS HAVE BEEN THE GREAT HISTORICAL counterweight to governmental authority, control, and tyranny. Though human experience has taught us that rights are indispensable to democracy, such rights are — at least in theory — quintessentially undemocratic, since they constrain the state from enforcing certain majoritarian preferences. If the claim of the aggrieved individual is deemed to be a right, it will generally trump the will of the majority.

What, then, are these things we call rights? Why are they accorded such a special status in comparison with other strongly held preferences? Why should rights trump the will of the majority? From where do these checks on majoritarian power emanate? From God or human beings? From nature or nurture? Do they exist outside of the law? Or are they merely creations of the law? Are they inherent and inalienable? Or are they merely a self-imposed and repealable majoritarian check on itself? Who should be empowered to enforce rights against governments and majorities? Are rights absolute? Or must they be balanced against other considerations? What if rights clash? Who decides which one should prevail? Do rights change over time — for example, during emergencies? Or are they eternal and universal?

Of all these questions, the most challenging — both theoretically and practically — is, Where do rights come from? The *source* of rights determines their *status*. If rights come from God, then they are truly "unalienable," as our Declaration of Independence baldly asserts.[1] If they derive from nature, then they are as immutable as the natural laws of physics and astronomy.[2] But if rights are solely the product of human lawmaking — if they are inventions rather than discoveries — then they are subject to modification, even abrogation, by the same source that devised them in the first place. Accordingly, a great deal turns on the answer to the question, Where do rights come from? I will address that intriguing question in considerable detail. But first we must understand what we mean when we use the term *right*.

The word *right*[3] is of relatively recent origin, although the ideas embodied in it trace their roots to biblical times.[4] Nor is the term without its ambiguities, multiple meanings — and, indeed, deliberate misuses.[5]

At the very least, a right must be somewhat different from a mere preference or interest. It should be something more enduring, more entrenched — something that those in positions of authority should not be able to take away, at least not without a compelling reason. Even in a democracy, the majority should not be empowered to trample the rights of minorities, whatever those rights might be.

Sometimes we use the word descriptively, as in "the constitution gives me a right not to be censored by the government." This is the traditional legal positivist definition of *right* — a claim grounded in enacted law.[6] The right may be statutory, common law, constitutional, or based on other accepted sources of authority, such as a treaty, a convention, or a contract.[7] But it is entirely a creature of humanly devised law, with no necessary external sources in God, nature, or objective morality.[8]

Sometimes the term *right* is used prescriptively, as in "I (should) have the right to do anything I want unless it hurts somebody else."[9] But unless the right has been codified, it lacks the status of positive law. As Oliver Wendell Holmes Jr. once quipped about a claim of right grounded in the philosophy of a writer popular in his day: "The Fourteenth Amendment does not enact Mr. Herbert Spencer's *Social Statics*."[10]

Often there is confusion as to whether a claim of right is descriptive or prescriptive, since not everybody knows the actual content of the law, but nearly everybody has opinions about his or her rights.

While legal positivism grounds all law — and thus all rights — in humanly enacted rules, natural law grounds the content of rights in external sources, such as God, nature, reason, or objective reality.[11] Put colloquially, natural law posits that we don't just make it up as we go along — that there is something beyond human invention that determines the content of morality, law, and rights.[12] Blackstone, whose *Commentaries* have had enormous influence on Anglo-American jurisprudence, asserted that human laws may not contradict God's laws, and if they do, they have no validity.

To be sure, positive law can be in conflict with natural law, as it often is to advocates of the latter. For example, the decisions of the United States Supreme Court recognizing a woman's right to choose abortion are seen by many as in violation of the natural right to life of the fetus. Some natural-law proponents take the position that although the Supreme Court's decisions have the status of positive law under our constitutional system, they are not really "the law" as mandated by God, nature, or reason and hence should not be followed by just people. As my colleague Lloyd Weinreb put it: natural law asserts "that a rule of positive law that fails to conform to overriding, fully general moral principles, and is for that reason not obligatory, is not truly *law* at all."[13] Others say that the positive law should be followed — for either prudential or democratic reasons — but that efforts should persist to bring it in line with natural law. In condemning human embryo cell research, the Vatican recently declared it "a gravely immoral, and thus gravely illicit act."[14]

The traditional case for "natural rights" is an uncomfortable one to make in a religiously and philosophically diverse democracy, since the claimed external "sources" for natural rights seem ill suited to such a society.

## GOD AS THE SOURCE OF RIGHTS

The first claimed external source of natural rights is God. But experience has demonstrated that the natural rights of the Bible and other holy books can be cited by the devil as well as by conservatives and liberals. "Like a harlot, natural law is at the disposal of everyone. The ideology does not exist that cannot be defended by an appeal to the law of nature."[15]

Those who claim to speak in the name of God have often used natural rights as a tactic — to serve partisan, religious, or personal agendas. For example, in 1873 the United States Supreme Court, in denying a woman the right to be admitted to the bar, relied on a divine concept of natural law: "God designed the sexes to occupy different spheres of action," and "It belonged to men to apply and execute the law." Women's divinely assigned role was in the "domestic sphere." God's law has also been cited as the source of justification for slavery, serfdom, monarchy, anti-Semitism, genocide against Native Americans, terrorism, and many other evils.[16] Apologists for divine law argue that these were misreadings or misapplications of God's true will. But how are we to be sure that today's "correct" reading of God's law will not be subject to tomorrow's correction? Indeed, the history of divine law is a history of repeated corrections of yesterday's lethal misreadings and misapplications.[17] To be an advocate of divine law is to always have to say you're sorry for the mistakes of your predecessors, as your successors will inevitably have to apologize for the mistakes you are now making when you claim to know God's true intentions. It insults God to believe that it was he who mandated eternal inequality for women, execution for gays, slavery, animal sacrifice, and the scores of other immoral laws of the Bible, the Koran, and other books that purport to speak in God's name. Humans are to blame for these immoralities, just as humans must be credited with the hundreds of morally elevating laws of these holy books. And it is humans who must continue to change law and morality so as to remain more elevated than the animals who indeed cannot rise above the law of nature and of the jungle. In a diverse world where many claim to know God's will, and where there is consensus about neither its content nor the methodology for discerning it, God should not be invoked as the source of our political rights.[18] In any event, for the millions of good and moral people who do not believe in God, or in an intervening God — or who are agnostic about these matters — there must be other sources of morality, law, and rights.

## NATURE AS THE SOURCE OF RIGHTS

The second traditional source for natural rights is that they somehow derive from "the nature" of human beings.[19] But human beings have no singular nature. We include the best and the worst. We are creatures of accidental forces who have no preordained destiny or purpose. We must make our own destiny and define our own purposes. To attempt to derive normative rights from descriptions — even if accurate — of human nature is to indulge in a variation on the "naturalistic fallacy."[20] There is no necessary correlation between what is and what ought to be in a world capable of constant improvement and increasing aspirations.

Of course, there have always been some who believe that we cannot improve upon nature. The idea that nature is inherently good — that it contains a positive moral component or leads in a positive moral direction — goes back a considerable time. Cicero believed that "whatever befalls in the course of nature should be considered good." Juvenal agreed: "Never does nature say one thing and wisdom another," as did Augustine: "All nature is good." John Florio called nature "the right law."[21]

For those who believe that nature is "the image of God," as did Blaise Pascal, or the "art of God," as did Dante,[22] the conclusion that nature is good is little more than a tautology that flows from the premise that God is good and omnipotent. But that conclusion cannot follow for those who share Spinoza's more skeptical view that "nature has no goal in view, and final causes are only human imaginings."[23] Even Einstein, who famously quipped that "God does not play dice with the universe," did not believe that the immutable rules of nature were directly translatable into eternal laws of human morality.[24]

The reality is that nature is morally neutral. It is full of beauty and wonder, but it thrives on violence and predation. Nature is a mother animal nursing her helpless cub and then killing another helpless animal to survive. Nature is life-giving sunshine followed by death-dealing floods. Human nature is Albert Schweitzer and Adolf Hitler, Jesus and Torquemada, Kant and Nietzsche, Confucius and Pol Pot, Mandela and bin Laden, the early Martin Luther, who reached out to the despised, and the later Martin Luther, who advocated rounding up the Jews and making them "miserable captives" in forced-labor camps.

In constructing a moral code — or a system of rights — one should not ignore the varieties of human nature, or their alleged commonalities. But neither can the diverse components of nature be translated directly into morality, legality, or rights. The complex relationship between the *is* of nature and the *ought* of morality must be mediated by human experience. The history of rights illustrates this complexity. A rights-based system is certainly not the natural human condition. If there is any natural condition, it is closer to tyranny. The history of humankind has been a history in which the norm has almost always been authoritarianism, elitism, censorship, arbitrariness, and denial of what we have come to call due process of law.[25] Dostoyevsky's Grand Inquisitor saw the surrender to tyranny as necessary to deliver human beings from "their present terrible torments of personal and free decision." He predicted that people will come to understand that "they can never be free, for they are weak, vicious, worthless and rebellious," and that in the end even the most rebellious "will become obedient." For those, like Jean-Jacques Rousseau, who believe that "man is born free," the question arises, Why then is he everywhere "in chains"? Why, as Thomas Hobbes famously observed, is the "life of man, solitary, poor, nasty, brutish, and short"? The answer is because *that* is closer to the natural human condition, at least descriptively, than any system based on rights. The function of rights, indeed, of law and morality, is to change that natural condition for the better — to improve upon nature, to domesticate its wild beast, and to elevate us from the terrible state of nature into a state of civilization. It is a never-ending challenge. If the advocates of rights fall asleep at the wheel for even one historical moment, there is danger that the natural human condition will rear its ugly head, as it has so many times over the millennia.

Yet from the beginning of recorded history, a relatively small number of liberty-loving individuals have struggled against the deeply ingrained human need for authority, control, domination, paternalism, and, indeed, tyranny. They have lived and died for rights. It is too early in the annals of humankind to know with any degree of certainty whether the entrenched forces of authoritarianism will once again prevail over the recurrent but episodic demands for liberty. What is certain is that the struggle for liberty — and for rights — never stays won.[26]

It is precisely because rights are not natural — that it is not in the nature of most human beings to value the rights of others above their own immediate interests — that we need to entrench certain basic rights, continuously advocate them, and never grow complacent about them. If rights were as natural as some claim, we could expect them to be far more popular than they have ever been among the general public.[27]

We need rights to offset the natural instinct of most human beings to take what they can get, with little concern for the interests of others, particularly strangers. It should not be surprising that among the first rules of religion, civility, and community are Love your neighbor as yourself and What you would not have done to yourself, do not do to others. Listen to a portion of John Adams's argument in defense of the British soldiers who were accused of participating in the Boston Massacre and who claimed the right of self-defense against rock-throwing provocateurs:

> The first branch [of human duty] is self-love. [God] has implanted it there. . . . Blackstone calls it "the primary canon" in the law of nature. That precept of our Holy religion which commands us to love our neighbor as ourselves . . . enjoins that our benevolence to our fellow men, should be as real and sincere as our affections to ourselves, not that it should be as great *in degree*.[28]

The secular Oliver Wendell Holmes Jr. echoed Adams's religiously based views when he declared that "in the last resort a man rightly prefers his own interest to that of his neighbor."[29] This recognition of the natural selfishness of most human beings has formed the basis for much religious, economic, political, and philosophical doctrine. John Rawls's influential "original position" is a variation on this recognition of inherent selfishness. The "veil of ignorance" is designed to preclude those in the original position from acting on their selfishness by denying them knowledge necessary to make self-serving decisions. Kant believed that our first political duty is to leave the state of nature, where selfishness is the first rule of survival, and submit ourselves along with others to the rule of a reasonable and just law.[30] These religious and philosophical approaches are striking examples of human beings recognizing the natural *is* of selfishness and aspiring to the less natural *ought* of altruism.

## THE NEW NATURAL LAW AND ITS VARIANTS

If rights do not come from God or from nature, where else could they come from? For traditional legal positivists, the answer is simple: from the human beings who write the laws. But what if these human beings decide that there should be no rights in general? Or what if they refuse to enact specific rights deemed by many to be fundamental, such as freedom of speech, equality under law, or due process? Would those rights cease to exist? Or would people still be able to claim those rights based on some authority outside of existing positive law?

These questions have daunted legal philosophers for generations. In recent times, a new genre of thinkers has sought to occupy a middle ground between the "metaphysics" of traditional natural law and the "reductionism" of traditional legal positivism. Perhaps the most influential of these thinkers is Ronald Dworkin (whom I count as a colleague and friend). Dworkin rejects simple legal positivism, insisting that "plainly, any rights-based theory must presume rights that are not simply the product of deliberate legislation or explicit social custom but are independent grounds for judging legislation and custom." Rights are, to Dworkin, "political trumps held by individuals," which necessarily exist outside of the positive law, because people have "moral rights against their governments."[31] Nonetheless, Dworkin is suspicious of rights that purport to come from God,[32] or are "to be found in natural law or locked up in some transcendental strongbox."[33] He seems equally suspicious of "ghostly entities like collective wills, or national spirits."[34] Nor does he accept John Rawls's "intuitionistic" assumptions about "innate categories of morality common to all men, imprinted in their neural structure,"[35] noting that the majority of citizens, even in the United States and Britain, "do not exercise the political liberties that they have, and would not count the loss of these liberties as especially grievous."[36]

Yet Dworkin agrees with traditional proponents of natural law that rights must be "discovered" rather than invented or created.[37] Discovery connotes an existing entity waiting to be found, if only we look in the right places.[38] And Dworkin tells us where to look: he suggests that "we discover what rights people actually have by looking for arguments that would justify [certain] claims." He locates such natural rights within a "constructive model," which human beings build "as if a sculptor set himself to carve the animal that best fits a pile of bones he happened to find together."[39] The "bones" from which Dworkin constructs his model of rights consist of principles related to equality of human beings.[40] His core principle is that governments must treat all their citizens with equal concern and respect. This principle is a fundamental "postulate of political morality" to which all reasonable people must adhere. Other basic rights flow from this egalitarian postulate. Dworkin believes that a rights-based system constructed from the promise of equality promises "the best political program." Dworkin acknowledges the compatibility of his approach with "a fundamental goal that underlies various popular utilitarian theories."[41] Yet Dworkin rejects one important criterion of classic utilitarianism:

> It is no answer to say that if individuals have these rights [speech, religion, political activity] then the community will be better off in the long run as a whole. This idea — that individual rights may lead to overall utility — may or may not be true, but it is irrelevant to the defense of rights as such, because when we say that someone has a right to speak his mind freely, in the relevant political sense, we mean that he is entitled to do so even if this would not be in the general interest.[42] If we want to defend individual rights in the sense in which we claim them, then we must try to discover something beyond utility that argues for these rights.[43]

But in the absence of any reliance on God, nature, or positive law, is there anything "beyond utility" that is out there waiting to be discovered and that can justify a minority's claimed rights trumping the will of the majority? Though Dworkin believes that a rights-based approach is "best," he would presumably insist on it even if it turned out to be worst! Otherwise, he would be submitting his moral conclusions to the very consequentialist test he eschews.[44] But in the absence of God's voice or nature's mandate, how can we evaluate the claim of rights in general or of any right in particular without weighing them against some utilitarian end — without insisting on some empirical assessment of what is best, as judged by agreed-upon criteria?[45]

Dworkin's logic is impeccable. Yet it leaves me incompletely satisfied about the source of rights over time and place and the criteria for evaluating their contribution to governance. I find myself accepting his egalitarian postulate, following the logic of where it is supposed to lead me, but then disagreeing — or finding it reasonable for others to disagree — with some of his conclusions, and wondering whether the postulate is unduly ambiguous, the logic too one-directional, or the conclusion preordained. Like other brilliant legal philosophers, Dworkin does a better job in criticizing other sources of rights than in coming up with a compelling, stand-alone theory of his own.[46]

Perhaps a completely satisfying theory of the source for natural law is not so necessary for a legal philosopher writing about the American system, since — as Dworkin notes — in America we have "certain moral rights made into legal rights by the Constitution."[47] Because many of our "natural rights" have been entrenched by positive law,[48] there is less of a practical need to deconstruct our rights and obsess about their sources.[49]

Of course, not all our claimed moral rights have been made into legal rights. We must still consider the sources of those claimed rights that do not qualify as *both* moral and positive. Even the most ardent advocate of natural rights will have to acknowledge that the vast majority of "rights" claimed in any society, including our own, have no basis outside of positive law. There can be no rational claim to a natural right not to have troops quartered in one's home except during wartime.[50] But absent an abrogation of the Third Amendment, such compelled quartering would violate the positive-law constitutional rights of the homeowner (or renter).

Were the Fifth Amendment's requirement of a grand jury indictment as a prerequisite to federal prosecution to be abrogated in favor of a preliminary hearing requirement, no one's natural rights would be violated (indeed, it would be *better* for the rights of defendants). But at the moment, every federal defendant has a positive-law constitutional right to a grand jury.[51]

Nor does the warrant requirement of our Fourth Amendment constitute a natural right. Perhaps the general right to privacy, or even the more specific right to be protected against unreasonable searches may lay claim to being fundamental or even natural. But the warrant requirement grows more out of our unique colonial experiences as a nation[52] than out of any sense that the warrant procedure provides some talismanic guarantee of reasonableness or privacy.[53]

Some might argue that the right to a jury trial in a serious criminal case is fundamental *in the United States*, but it is surely not a natural right, as evidenced by the fact that few other countries accept it.[54] Indeed, it would be difficult to make the case that any *particular* right of criminal defendants is natural. The most that might be claimed is that basic fairness — by whatever means it is achieved — is a fundamental right that some may wish to characterize as natural. Such basic fairness might include independent decision makers (whether judge, jury, or some combination), the right to present a defense with the assistance of counsel, placing a burden on the prosecution to prove its case, some avenue for appeal, and protection against excessively cruel punishments (which might vary over time and circumstances).

The right to private ownership of property was certainly deemed fundamental and perhaps even natural by the framers of our Constitution. They entrenched a provision into the Bill of Rights precluding the government from taking property without just compensation. Since that time, however, many good and decent countries — along with some bad and indecent ones — have expropriated some private property for public uses without paying just compensation.[55]

Even the right to transfer wealth from one generation to another — a right once deemed fundamental to my friend and colleague Robert Nozick — is hard to characterize as natural or inalienable. A decent society could, in my view, decide that the fairest way of dealing with wealth is to require each generation to start anew, be free to accumulate wealth during that generation, and then return all (or some, or most) to the state upon the death of all members of that generation. This may be a foolish, unworkable, or even wrongheaded approach, but if it were to prove, over time, to constitute an improvement — by agreed-upon criteria — over our current approach, it would be difficult to call it unnatural, even if a court were to find it unconstitutional.[56]

The National Rifle Association regards the Second Amendment — which says, "A well-regulated Militia, being necessary to the security of a free State, the right of the people to keep and bear Arms, shall not be infringed" — as entrenching a broad-based natural right. Gun-control advocates read the preamble to the amendment — especially the reference to a "well-regulated militia" — as limiting the right to the possession of weapons for military use.[57] They also argue that the words *well-regulated* suggest reasonable regulation of gun ownership, such as licensing, waiting periods, and mandatory gun locks.[58] The constitutional issue — what the framers "intended" more than two hundred years ago by their somewhat confusing choice of language — will never be resolved to the satisfaction of all sides. But the claim of private, unregulated gun ownership as a natural right is difficult to defend, since it is a uniquely American right, growing out of our colonial experiences.[59]

If the right to bear arms is narrowed to include only the right to defend oneself and one's family — thus excluding the right to hunt, collect guns, and possess them for other reasons — a stronger case can be made for its near-universality.[60] But the right to self-defense is generally limited to specific threats and requires that there be no reasonable alternative. It does not extend to the private possession of guns for use in the hypothetical event of lethal aggression, and it certainly does not extend anywhere near where the National Rifle Association would locate it.

It would seem clear, therefore, that many of the rights contained in our Constitution are simply positive, homegrown rights with roots in the unique American experience, rather than natural rights with legitimate claims as transcending positive law. The opposite is also true. The "right" of the fetus to live, though deemed natural and universal by many, is not recognized by our Constitution. To the contrary, the Supreme Court, in purporting to construe the Constitution, has given the pregnant woman the "right" to abort — that is, to end the life of — the fetus, at least during certain stages of the pregnancy. According to some natural-law advocates, this ruling (*Roe v. Wade* and its progeny) *is not* and *cannot be* the law, since the natural right of the fetus transcends any positive-law enactment.[61]

There are those on the opposite side of the political spectrum who make a similar point with regard to the right of a pregnant woman to reproductive freedom, including the choice to abort "her" fetus. They argue that if the Constitution were amended to guarantee the right to life to every fetus, such an amendment would violate the natural right of the woman to control her body.[62] Similar arguments have been made on behalf of the right of homosexuals to engage in "illegal" activity with other consenting adults. It is still a crime in some states (and countries) for homosexuals to have sex with each other. A closely divided Supreme Court upheld "sodomy" laws in 1986. The Louisiana Supreme Court upheld its sodomy law as recently as 2000. Many gays, claiming a fundamental right to sexual privacy and autonomy, argue that these anachronistic statutes are not the law and they willingly disobey them with a clear conscience. (They generally stay away from invoking "natural law," since that phrase has so often been used against gay rights, especially by religious groups; indeed, sodomy is called a crime "against nature.")

Thus, despite Dworkin's correct observation that in America we have "certain moral rights made into legal rights by the Constitution," there are many instances of moral rights that did not make the positive-law cut and of other rights that did make it into our Constitution but that can more fairly be characterized as experientially based rights of Americans than as universal or natural rights that transcend positive law. It follows, therefore, that even a legal philosopher writing about American law has some burden of pinpointing the source of his or her claimed rights that are not part of the positive law of our Constitution. No one, in my view, has ever convincingly discovered, discerned, constructed, or demonstrated a secular source for his or her theory of natural rights.

## A PREFERENCE FOR RIGHTS

What, then, do I mean by *rights*, and what are the claimed sources for my concept of rights? In sum, my view is that rights are those preferences that experience and history — especially of injustice — have taught are so fundamental that the citizenry should be persuaded to entrench them and not make them subject to easy change by shifting majorities. If I am correct, then we must constantly defend our choice of rights by reference to the slowly changing forces of history and experience. We cannot merely claim that the rights we espouse came from an eternal God, from the immutable nature of human beings, or even from the logic of democracy. Rights cannot be discovered, since they are not anywhere to be found. Nor can they be logically deduced or constructed, since the premises on which any such deduction or construction may be based are themselves the product of differing experiences and perceptions. They must be advocated, based on experience, especially our long collective experience with injustice.

## "NURTURAL" RIGHTS

If rights grow out of the experiences and histories of human beings, then they are more a function of nurture than of nature. The term *nurtural rights*, though a bit clumsy, is apt. In this respect, rights — like morals — are somewhat situational, not in the sense that there is no commonality in their application to differing situations, but in the sense that they reflect the differing histories and conditions in which people have found themselves when they have articulated and ranked rights.

It should not be surprising, therefore, that I fundamentally disagree with the approach espoused by those who wrote that oft-quoted paragraph of our Declaration of Independence which invoked "the Laws of Nature and of Nature's God" as the source of their rights.[63] They declared certain "truths" to "be self-evident," among them that human beings "are endowed by their Creator with certain unalienable Rights," and that "among these are Life, Liberty, and the pursuit of Happiness." The Declaration then moved from God-given natural law to man-made positive law based on social contract by asserting that "to secure these rights, Governments are instituted among Men, deriving their just powers from the consent of the governed."

There are numerous problems with this formulation. If the truths contained in these laws are so "self-evident," why did the British authorities, and American Tories, not also recognize all of them? How are conflicts among self-evident truths to be resolved? What if there is a conflict between the law of "nature's God," as defined by some elites, and "the consent of the governed?" Who are the governed whose consent is required? Consider, for example, slavery, which many whites believed was consistent with the law of nature's God but surely was inconsistent with equality, liberty, consent, and the "unalienable rights" of the enslaved, who were regarded as property rather than citizenry. And what about the rights of disbelievers, skeptics, and agnostics? From whom or from where do *their* rights derive — if they indeed have rights?[64] Did God give human beings the right not to believe in him? If so, why do his ministers threaten eternal damnation for its exercise? Does the nature of human beings require belief in God? If so, which God? The Declaration of Independence does not answer these and numerous other vexing questions raised by its deistic formulation of the source of rights.[65] As a consensus-building document advocating a course of action, it sought to cover all bases by writing at a level of abstraction and generality designed not to offend anyone whose support was being elicited. It should not be misread as presenting a coherent — or authoritative — theory of the sources of our rights. Rather, it is part of the genre of political "midrash,"[66] or mythology, akin to the religious midrashim of God giving Moses the Ten Commandments at Sinai, of Allah dictating the Koran to Muhammad, and of Joseph Smith discovering the buried tablets.[67] Yet, because it forms an important rhetorical basis for one of our most important foundational documents, it is often cited as part of our positive law.

A careful reading of the entire Declaration of Independence — not just its quotable rhetoric — supports my experiential approach to rights. The centerpiece of the Declaration is a catalog of wrongs — of "abuses and usurpations" — which made it the "right" of the Americans "to institute new Government," in order to provide "new Guards for their future security." Thus, the signatories of the Declaration invoked both the laws of nature and their own experience with injustice to justify their demand for rights. Their claims based on experience were, in my view, far more compelling than those based on God, nature, and other "self-evident" propositions.

## WHEN DO PREFERENCES BECOME RIGHTS?

If rights do not come from "the laws of nature and of nature's God" and if they are not "self-evident," then what gives certain personal preferences the special status of "rights"? Put another way, when does a preference have "the right" to call itself a right? Surely the answer cannot simply be when an individual feels strongly enough about it. This would make the concept of rights entirely subjective and individualistic and would rob it of all meaning.

For positivists the answer is relatively simple. Those preferences, and only those preferences, that are entrenched in the law as rights are to be accorded that elevated status. But this reductionistic formulation tells us nothing about which preferences *ought* to be entrenched and which left to shifting majoritarian determination. For advocates of divine natural law, the answer may be a bit more complex. A right is anything God has decided is a right. How to discern God's intention in this regard may be somewhat problematic. For biblical fundamentalists, that intent may be manifested in the text of various holy books. In this respect, such fundamentalists are close — at least structurally — to some legal positivists, with the former looking to the Bible and the latter looking to more secular law books.

The secular natural-law advocates have a heavier burden in distinguishing rights from strongly held preferences. They must derive such rights from human nature, reason, or other such phenomena. Or they must construct rights from the raw material of agreed-upon first principles. In this respect, they are not much different from some nonfundamentalist religious advocates of natural law and natural rights. Contemporary Catholic thinkers, who reject both biblical fundamentalism and legal positivism, have contributed a brilliant, if not always entirely satisfying, literature to the debate over natural law and natural rights.[68] They — like Jewish and Muslim nonfundamentalists — have designed institutional processes for interpreting biblical texts. These processes — referred to as "reading the Bible within the church," or "Halakah" (the Road) or "Shari'ah" (the Broad Path) — are akin to secular common law, with authoritative interpreters. In the end, the preferences these religious interpreters choose to call rights often seem to reflect result-oriented thinking that generally comes out in favor of preordained doctrinal positions. Lawyers and legal scholars, especially good ones, are experts at shifting the level of analysis of a question so that the answer comes out the way they want it to. Like a good chess player, a clever advocate always thinks several moves ahead. If an abstract, rights-based, Kantian analysis will eventually lead to the conclusion sought by the advocate, he will frame the question so that it is amenable to precisely that kind of analysis. If a more utilitarian analysis will bring him where he wants to go, he will frame the question in that manner and then invoke case or rule utilitarianism,[69] depending on which is more likely to lead him to his desired outcome.

Most, though not all, jurisprudential theorists construct elaborate frameworks of principle that just happen to lead them to the promised land of policies that they favor on political, religious, or personal grounds. I am not suggesting that is always deliberate or conscious. Principles and policies are related, of course, and it should not be surprising that "liberal" or "conservative" principles — to use imprecise but familiar terms — will often lead to liberal or conservative policies.[70]

The arguments made by Southern intellectual and religious leaders in defense of slavery before and during the Civil War provide a perfect example of the human capacity to construct after-the-fact arguments in order to justify almost any morally disputed practice. Brilliant and honest intellectuals invoked natural law, biblical law, the rules of political economy, and virtually every other method of reasoning known to humans. They defended slavery as a "right" — a right not only of the slave owner but also of the slave!

Invoking divine law, they pointed to the biblical description of the patriarch Abraham's family. In the words of historian Eugene Genovese, "Abraham was, in their oft-expressed view, simultaneously a slaveholder and God's favorite patriarch of a household that included many slaves."[71] Even John C. Calhoun, regarded by many as a moderate, cited "Hebrew theocracy" as the greatest government man had ever experienced and "held up the extended household under the firm authority of its male as the model for its organization."[72] This concept of "Christian slavery" was designed, according to these arguments, to save the souls of the black slave. Hence, the right to be a slave in order to be saved.[73]

Slavery, it was claimed, was the "natural and proper condition of all labor" and the foundation of all freedom. But what of the civil and political rights of the slave? "Led by Calhoun, the Southern theorist overwhelmingly accepted natural law but vehemently rejected the attempts to deduce natural rights from it," especially civil and political rights. Some did argue for natural rights but limited them to certain statuses: "the rights of the father are natural, but they belong only to the father." The same was true of the right of property; it belonged "only to those who had property" — namely, the slave owner, not to the property itself, namely, the slave. Even for those who regarded slaves as more than property, the only right the slave had was the right to be treated decently, the way slaves were supposed to be treated in the Bible. "Slaveholders are responsible . . . for the humane treatment of their fellow human beings whom God has placed in their hands."[74]

Ironically, some Southern religious writers even made arguments that sounded suspiciously like evolutionary claims. One such writer jumped from Genesis to Darwin with hardly a pause. He asserted that God created white people "after the image of the Creator."[75] He then pointed to the continuum of intelligence between "the ape tribes" and lower humans. Finally, he postulated a time in the future when apes would have progressed to the point where they "should learn to speak," and he asked, rhetorically, whether they should then "be placed on an equality with whites, as they indicate somewhat of a human form and intelligence so as relates to the performance of labor!" His answer — a resounding no — was supposed to resolve the issue of equality between the white race, which was created in the image of God, and the black race, which was created "for subordinate works."[76] (For some, this time in the future has arrived. There are now proponents of human rights for great apes. In 1999, New Zealand became the first nation to adopt a law guaranteeing certain rights to great apes. Several years earlier, scientist Carl Sagan had posed the following question: "If chimpanzees have consciousness, if they are capable of abstractions, do they not have what until now has been described as 'human rights'?"[77])

Southern intellectuals also invoked economic and political arguments in support of slavery. They pointed to the dreadful situation of "free laborers" in the North and throughout Europe, and the exploitative nature of industrial capitalism. The slave owner felt a moral obligation toward the slave and had an economic stake in his continued welfare, since the slave was valuable property. The capitalist treated his worker as disposable and replaceable. Southern intellectuals rejected socialism and its variants as an alternative to capitalist exploitation, since it could not be brought about without the instabilities seen throughout Europe in the mid–nineteenth century. For Southern intellectuals, the only real alternatives were pure exploitative capitalism or pure paternalistic slavery. The choice for them was clear.

Finally, there was the political argument, which rejected the natural-law claims made by Northern abolitionists against secession and slavery. Pointing to the contractual nature of our constitutional system — a "political compromise between two sectionally based social systems"[78] — they argued that the North had no right to impose its system on the South. Invoking the rhetoric of the founding fathers, they cited the Declaration of Independence as the source of their right to secede and maintain their slave-based social system. As far as the right of every slave to be a free laborer, they mocked this argument as the right to be "free to beg, steal and starve."

In reading these arguments, which sound so lame to the contemporary ear, one cannot help but be struck by their sincerity. These people actually believed what they were saying. They believed that slavery was right, and they believed in the arguments they were making in justification of this institution.

This process of justification also illustrates the complex relationship between a priori and experiential reasoning. Some of the arguments offered in favor of slavery derive directly from external sources — the Bible, natural law, or some logical construct. Others are based on observations and experiences. Each type of argument is invoked in support of the other, and it is never clear which comes first. It is as if a certain number of "argument cards" were distributed to each player in this game of advocacy. Some cards trump others. Some types of cards lead the player down one path or another. A good player knows how to think ahead several moves and anticipate the countermoves of his or her opponent. Experienced advocates have heard it all — every conceivable argument made in favor of every conceivable practice. They have heard them made with sincerity, passion, consistency, authority, and other tools of advocacy. They have seen every card played. They cannot avoid a certain degree of cynicism regarding the human capacity to persuade oneself and others about the virtues of a particular point of view at a particular point in time.[79]

For true advocates of liberty's agenda, the continuing struggle represents a genuine and deep-seated commitment to civil liberties and human rights, without regard for the political agendas of the day. For such authentic civil libertarians, a rights-based system is essential regardless of who or what it happens to benefit at any particular moment in history. Thus, freedom of speech is as desirable in the newly liberated nations of the former Soviet Union, where it may immediately benefit racists and anti-Semites, as it is in China, where the beneficiaries would be democratic dissidents.

But for many apparent advocates of liberty's agenda, the demand for civil liberties is merely a temporary tactic designed to support their immediate political goals. For example, the hierarchy of the Polish Catholic Church was in the vanguard of liberty when Soviet Communism was in control of Poland. The church advocated freedom of speech, conscience, educational choice, and other fundamental freedoms as a tactic to undercut the totalitarianism of Communist rule. But once communism crumbled, and the church itself became a dominant political force in Poland, the agenda of liberty was generally forsaken, and the agenda of authority — its own authority — was once again advocated by many in the church hierarchy. Civil liberties had been little more than a convenient tactic in the overall strategy of church domination. A similar phenomenon has been at work in Israel, where the fervently religious minority has employed democracy as a tactic for enhancing its power, while eschewing democracy when it conflicts with its theocratic goals.

This story of the tactical use and abuse of civil liberties to serve other agendas has been a recurring theme in modern history. Even Thomas Jefferson was guilty of the double standard. Before he held high office, he famously quipped, "Were it left to me to decide whether we should have a government without newspapers, or newspapers without a government, I should not hesitate a moment to prefer the latter." But after twenty years of public service, his views changed. In 1807, he said the following about his formerly beloved newspapers: "The man who never looks into a newspaper is better informed than he who reads them, insomuch as he who knows nothing is nearer the truth than he whose mind is filled with falsehoods and error." Likewise with Václav Havel, whose Velvet Revolution in Czechoslovakia demanded a free press, but who, after serving as president, wondered out loud whether the press was "too free" to criticize him. Some might argue — in defense of the church, Jefferson, Havel, and others — that their own experiences tempered their perspective on rights. Because the change occurred so quickly, however, it is difficult to avoid the charge of the self-serving double standard. The kind of historical and experiential change to which I have referred occurs over a more sustained period of time and relates to a broader segment of society than to the individual (or elites) who have ascended to power. Beware of those whose advocacy of individual rights changes too quickly when these same rights curtail their own recently acquired power.

Throughout history we have also seen the courageous struggle for liberty's agenda, often led by lonely advocates with no personal or partisan stake in liberty's triumph, but with an abiding commitment to liberty for liberty's sake and for the sake of human dignity. This book celebrates that struggle.

Consider once again the "right to life." Reasonable, intelligent, and moral people fundamentally disagree about whether, when, and to what extent a pregnant woman or girl should have the right to choose abortion rather than to choose to give birth. There is nothing in the nature of man or woman that definitely resolves this issue. Nor is there any definitive logical argument that leads inexorably to one or another approach. Neither is there an unequivocal biblical commandment, as evidenced by the fact that believers in the Bible disagree about the abortion issue.[80]

There are some who arrogantly proclaim that if people simply thought more clearly and morally, they would understand that abortion violates the natural right of the living fetus. Others argue, equally persuasively, that if people thought more logically, they would all understand why compelled birth violates the natural rights of the mother. Both are demonstrably wrong, since clear-thinking, moral people come to diametrically opposite conclusions, based on their differing worldviews, values, upbringings, experiences, and assessments of the future.[81] Both sides may well be right, if one accepts the premises of their arguments. Some of the premises are plainly empirical, for example, easy abortion promotes sexual promiscuity. Others are plainly faith based, for example, God has ordained that no abortions — or only some abortions — may be performed. Still others purport to be based entirely on moral claims without regard to facts but upon analysis turn out to have a significant empirical component, for example, if abortion is permitted, it will diminish the value we place on human life and make it easier for us to justify other takings of human life. This sort of subtle, slippery-slope argument is premised on facts that may be difficult to establish, but they are facts nonetheless.

Consider as well the debate over the morality of the death penalty. Religious abolitionists cite the commandment "Thou shall not kill." Proponents read the commandment differently: "Thou shall not murder," arguing that execution of the guilty is not murder. They distinguish between the killing of an innocent fetus and the killing of a guilty criminal. Abolitionists point to the reality that any system of capital punishment will inevitably include some innocent defendants who were falsely convicted. Capital-punishment supporters respond that there is a difference between the deliberate killing of a person known to be innocent (like a fetus) and the inadvertent killing of a person erroneously believed to be guilty. They invoke the religious-moral concept of the "unintended effect," which allows an action to be taken if no immoral result is specifically *intended*, even if it is statistically inevitable.[82]

Those who oppose the death penalty but favor a woman's right to choose abortion offer yet another distinction: an executed defendant — even a guilty murderer — is a human being, whereas a fetus is not a human being. For them, innocence or guilt and willfulness or in-advertence are not the determinative issues. The issue is the humanity of the person executed versus the nonhumanity of the fetus.[83]

My point here is not to resolve either the capital-punishment or the abortion debate. It is to demonstrate how the terms of these debates can be influenced by how the issues are framed, how the premises are articulated, and how the level of discourse is selected.

For those who believe in the inerrancy and absoluteness of natural law, both sides cannot be right.[84] But the reality is that there may indeed be both a right to life and a right to choose, just as there may be a right to life and a right of individual or societal self-defense. Why is it supposed that rights may not be in intractable conflict?[85] This conflict may require an agreed-upon *process* for reaching a workable resolution within a pluralistic democracy.

An old story about a wise Eastern European rabbinical judge illustrates this reality. The rabbi was hearing a dispute between an estranged husband and wife. The wife argued that her husband had violated her marital rights by sleeping with other women and refusing to give her enough money for necessities. The rabbi listened and ruled, "You are right, my daughter." Then he heard her husband's claim that his marital rights had been violated by his wife's refusal to sleep with him and to cook his meals. The rabbi listened and ruled, "You are right, my son." The rabbi's student interjected, "But, rabbi, they can't both be right" — to which the rabbi responded, "You are right, my student." But the husband and wife *can* both be right — and wrong. Life is more complex and nuanced than language. There may be multiple "rights" in any complex situation, and they will sometimes be in conflict.

Fyodor Dostoyevsky — one of the great propounders of moral and legal hypothetical cases — posed a wonderful moral dilemma to which there is plainly no single right answer. Mikhail, a highly regarded town official who is married and has children, confides in Zozima that fourteen years earlier he had killed a woman in a well-planned act motivated by jealousy. The peasant who had been suspected of the crime died before he could be brought to trial. No one would materially benefit from Mikhail's belated confession, but his innocent wife — whom he married after the killing — and his young children would suffer grievously: "My wife may die of grief"; "My children, even if they are not stripped of rank and property, will become a convict's children, and that forever"; "And what a memory I shall leave in their hearts." Mikhail and Zozima cite conflicting scriptural and philosophical sources in support of confessing or remaining silent.

Kant would surely argue that truth is all that matters, regardless of the consequences. Jeremy Bentham would point to the accumulated unhappiness that would result from a selfish confession — selfish because, according to Dostoyevsky, it would be designed to bring salvation to Mikhail's conscience at a high cost to his family. Other philosophers would invoke principles pointing in different directions, some arguing that consequentialist thinking would produce great evils in other cases (e.g., killing a "worthless" witness in order to spare innocent family members the grief of their breadwinner's being caught), with others arguing that suffering in silence or even suicide would be a more noble and moral act for Mikhail than shaming his family to assure himself paradise. The question is not which of these solutions — or others — is preferable. The question is whether there is only one right solution, and if so, what is its authoritative source and how shall we deal with powerful and persuasive counterarguments? I believe that reasonable people — moral, religious, and good — can and should disagree about this and other complex moral conundrums and that we should not presume that there is a single, perfect answer to be discovered if only we could access the proper source.

A somewhat counterhypothetical, inspired by Dostoyevsky's Grand Inquisitor poem, also tests the principle that truth is absolute. Imagine being on a visit to Qumran caves outside Jerusalem and coming upon a previously undiscovered Dead Sea scroll that contains the account of a meeting of religious leaders deciding how to deal with rampant disbelief, lawlessness, and violence. They come up with the idea to stage a "revelation" on a mountain called Sinai from which God will "give" ten commandments carved on two tablets. They argue about the content of the commandments and finally compromise on the ones we know. The scroll contains considerable details about the staging necessary to persuade the common folk that the revelation is genuine. A second idea is to stage a crucifixion and resurrection of a man who they will claim was God's son. Someone suggests that he be born to a virgin, as is common in Greek mythology, and that he be crucified and resurrected. Calvary is selected as the site for this final miracle.

I mean no disrespect by these hypotheticals, because that is exactly what they are — made-up scenarios. But they are designed to test principles. You, the finder of the scroll, are a deeply religious person, equally committed to truth. You also believe that organized religions, particularly the Judeo-Christian faiths, are extremely valuable and central to the lives of millions, including your own parents and grandparents, whose faith would be shaken by the disclosure of your findings. You are convinced beyond any doubt that the scroll is authentic and that the events reported by Scripture to have taken place at Sinai and Calvary were completely fabricated by people of utter goodwill — they were truly "pious frauds." Do you disclose your findings? Remain silent? Destroy the scroll?

A more mundane variation on this unrealistic hypothetical probably occurs every weekend somewhere in the world, when a religious leader — on the eve of delivering a major sermon on the importance of believing in God — suddenly begins to believe that there is no God. This surely happened to many rabbis, priests, and ministers during the Holocaust — and perhaps after the destruction of the World Trade Center. Does truth require cancellation of the sermon, revelation of the new belief, a change in tone, or simply a crossing of one's fingers as the original sermon is delivered?

These are daunting questions — and there are so many others — to which a singular correct answer would be insulting to the complexity and diversity of the human mind and experience. It is the brilliance of great literature — such as that written by Dostoyevsky, Shakespeare, Kafka, and Bellow — that it is never satisfied with a single, correct answer to a complex and often ambiguous human dilemma. Its characters — through their internal dialogues as well as their external conflicts — reflect the diversity of human experiences and emotions. A truly great philosopher must have the insights of a poet!

Even simple hypotheticals — carefully crafted for their single-dimensional simplicity — defy singular answers. The famous "railroad track" hypotheticals are designed to show there is no right answer: You are a train conductor whose brakes have failed. You see a fork in the rails ahead. If you turn right, your train will hit a group of children playing on the tracks; if you turn left, you will hit a single old drunk lying on the tracks; if you fail to choose, random forces will choose for you. A complicating variation would be to have a straight track leading directly to the children. But there is a turn you could make that would lead you toward the drunk. Under this variation, if you do nothing, the children die. You must choose to kill the drunk. Countless variations on these "tragic choice" dilemmas are imaginable, including the one generated by the hijacking of airplanes to destroy densely occupied buildings: Would it be morally justifiable to shoot down a passenger jet being flown toward such a building? Each has multiple "right" and "wrong" answers. That's the point.

The difficult issue — of morality, legality, and practicality — is how to devise an acceptable process for resolving such conflicts in a pluralistic democracy committed to balancing the preferences of the majority against the rights of minorities.

The reality is that there is no absolutely perfect resolution to these and other right-to-life conflicts.[86] They reflect deeply felt moral concerns, intuitions, historical experiences, and worldviews that may and do differ over times and cultures. Recall that as recently as two centuries ago — a blip on the time line of recorded history — most thoughtful and decent people honestly believed in the moral inequality of whites and blacks, men and women, Christians and "heathens," heterosexuals and homosexuals, as well as other dualities. Who can know which of our contemporary moral beliefs — for example, the distinction between the value of human and animal life — will seem unacceptable to our progeny in generations to come based on new experiences and histories.

Law, morality, even truth, are ongoing processes for resolving conflicts in a democracy comprising people with differing histories, experiences, perceptions, value hierarchies, and worldviews. To expect singularly "correct" or even singularly "true" moral answers to emerge from such different experiences is to devalue our diversity. We respect our heterogeneity when we construct democratic processes for compromise and for accommodating and living with the inevitable differences — even about rights — that are inherent in such a diverse society.

It should not be surprising that the United States has served as the great laboratory for constructing these conflict-accommodating processes, since our population is the most diverse in the history of the world. We began as a community of immigrants and dissenters with a relatively common ethnic background. By the end of the nineteenth century, our ethnic backgrounds had diversified, along with our religious differences. Unlike some other countries, which share a more common worldview about the *substance* of morality, law, and rights,[87] we have developed a consensus about the *processes* for resolving our substantive differences. Our system of checks and balances may often result in deadlock or gradual change, but it is a system designed to accommodate differences. Compromise has been the essence of the American experience, even in areas as difficult to compromise as religion.[88]

When I was a child, I once asked my father why the mezuzah — the religious object that adorns the doorpost of a Jewish home — is always placed on a slant. My father asked our rabbi, who explained: "There were two schools of thought: one believed that it should be placed horizontally, the other vertically. Each was convinced it was correct but could not persuade the other. Finally, they split the difference by agreeing that it should be placed at a slant halfway between horizontal and vertical." What a wonderful symbol for a home, in which compromise is always required. It is also a symbol for how America, at its best, has sometimes compromised and avoided the religious and political polemicism of other nations.

We should not strive for the uniformity and singularity of one correct morality, truth, or justice.[89] The active and never-ending processes of moraliz*ing*, truth search*ing*, and justice seek*ing* are far superior to the passive acceptance of, or quest for, a static Holy Grail of the one truth, the singular right, or even the solitary source of all rights. The right*ing* process, like the truth*ing* process, is ongoing.

# TWO

# RIGHTS COME FROM WRONGS

THE ONGOING NATURE OF THE RIGHTING PROCESS DOES NOT require that we ignore the wrongs of perfect injustice or allow those who advocate or inflict them to fall back on moral relativism as a justification for absolute immorality. There is no possible moral justification for genocide, as evidenced by the fact that no reasoned argument has ever been attempted on its behalf — certainly none has succeeded in the marketplace of ideas over time. Even Hitler and his henchmen tried to hide what they were doing behind euphemisms and evasive rhetoric. Today we have Holocaust deniers but few if any Holocaust justifiers. Indeed, the Holocaust serves as the paradigm of perfect injustice.

Slavery, too, serves as a paradigm of injustice. Yet it had its moral defenders — at a certain time and place in history. The arguments made by these defenders have been soundly rejected by the verdict of history, and not only because the slaveholders lost on the battlefield. Even had the South been victorious, the institution of slavery would not have long survived. Economic and moral considerations would have doomed slavery, as it has been doomed in nearly every part of the world.

Slavery, viewed through the lens of experience, has proved to be a paradigm of injustice despite the contemporaneous arguments of its practitioners and defenders. There is no consensus about what perfect justice would be for those who work for others: A fair wage? A share of the profits? Various types of insurance? Reasonable people can and do disagree about perfect economic justice for employees. But every reasonable person now recognizes that slavery was perfect injustice.

## THE BOTTOM-UP APPROACH

In one important respect, therefore, my theory of rights is really a theory of wrongs. It begins with what experience has shown to be absolute injustices: the Crusades, the Inquisition, slavery, the Stalinist starvation and purges, the Holocaust, the Cambodian slaughter, and other unquestionable abuses. It then asks whether the absences of certain rights contributed to these abuses. If so, that experience provides a powerful argument for why these rights should become entrenched. This bottom-up approach builds on the reality that there is far more consensus about what constitutes perfect injustice than about what constitutes perfect justice. If there can be agreement that certain rights are essential to reduce the chances of perfect injustice, that constitutes the beginning of a solid theory of rights. We can continue to debate about the definition of, and conditions for, perfect justice. That debate will never end, because perfect justice is far too theoretical and utopian a concept. But in the meantime, we can learn a considerable amount about rights from the world's entirely untheoretical experiences of injustice. Building on this negative experience, we can *advocate* and *do* basic rights that have been shown to serve as a check on tyranny and injustice. Perhaps someday we will be able to construct a complete theory of rights designed to lead to perfect justice. But since we have had far more experience with perfect injustice than with perfect justice, the bottom-up approach seems more grounded in reality than any top-down approach. It is more modest in its scope, but if it can contribute to a slowing down of the kind of perfect injustice we have experienced in the twentieth century, it will have accomplished a great deal.[1]

## SEPARATION OF CHURCH AND STATE

Consider the relationship between church and state. Reasonable people can and do disagree about what the ideal relationship between these institutions ought to be: Should governments be entirely neutral toward all religions and toward religion in general? Should the state discriminate against religious speech in the public forum? Should government agencies work with religious institutions on such common goals as the elimination of poverty and the reduction in teen pregnancy and sexually transmitted diseases?

The lessons of history tell us little about the ideal relationship between church and state, though they are relatively clear about what the worst relationship between church and state has been over the years:

When the state establishes one particular religion and backs the religious ideology of that church with the military and police power of the government, the experience of history has shown that this relationship corrupts religion and denies citizens freedom of conscience and the free exercise of religious choice. The end results have been crusades, inquisitions, and state-sponsored religious terrorism.

This historical experience has led to a broad consensus — among church leaders, government officials, civil libertarians, and moral philosophers — that government should not establish a particular church and support its particular religious ideology by force; nor should it deny individuals the free exercise of their own religion, even if that religion is deemed to be a "false" one by the majority of the state's citizens.

From this bottom-up conclusion, arguments can and have been made about the content of the rights that should derive from the experiences of the world with the relationship between church and state. Building on these experiences, some argue that a high wall of separation must be placed between the "garden" of the church and the "wilderness" of the state. This powerful metaphor has animated much of the debate about freedom of religion and freedom from religion, which are two sides of the same coin. Strict separationists argue that the wall of separation should preclude governments from supporting religion in general over secularism, even if they support no particular religion. Some believe that it is wrong, in and of itself, for a state to place its imprimatur on religion as such, while others believe that to do so is the first step down the slippery slope of establishing, or preferring, a particular religion. Lurking in the background of this debate are the powerful images of Joan of Arc being burned at the stake, Galileo being imprisoned, Jews being expelled from Spain, Jesus being crucified. These terrible experiences produce a consensus that every person should have the right to choose a particular religion, or no religion, without fear of state-supported persecution. They also inform the debate over how high to build the wall of separation on this basic foundation of experience. This bottom-up approach has the virtue of beginning with a baseline consensus, grounded in the experiences of injustice, and leaving room for reasoned debate beyond that consensus. It need not await the development of a fully articulated theory of the right at issue. It is always a work in progress, building on core experiences and evolving with new experiences.

## THE RIGHT NOT TO BE CENSORED BY GOVERNMENT

Another right that can be constructed bottom-up from the injustices of the past is freedom of speech. There is considerable controversy over the positive theory of free speech: Does the so-called marketplace of ideas really work, especially in a world in which the marketplace is heavily skewed in favor of those who can afford to buy time in the media? The experiential case *for* freedom of speech is not nearly as compelling as the case *against* governmental censorship. Societies in which citizens do not choose to speak out publicly on a range of issues can be good and decent, if somewhat boring, places. There is far less public controversy in some Scandinavian countries than in the United States and some other European countries. Yet there is no less freedom, justice, or fairness in these "quiet" places than in more "noisy" venues.

The same cannot be said about societies in which a system of governmental censorship determines what a citizen may say, write, read, or hear. It has been said that governments that begin by burning books end up by burning people. This may overgeneralize the historical record, but it makes an important point: a regime of governmental censorship often entails other evils, such as informers, searches, loyalty oaths, coercion, and torture.

Even without these additional adverse consequences, the dangers inherent in governments' dictating what their citizens can read, see, and hear have been demonstrated by the historical record. The road to perfect injustice has often been paved by governmental control over all sources of information. Based on this experience with injustice, we have developed a consensus, not necessarily regarding the *virtues* of free speech but concerning the *vices* of a regime of governmental censorship, especially prior restraint. Our Bill of Rights does not entrench a general right of free expression: corporations, universities, churches, families, and other nongovernmental entities need not allow their members to speak freely. Only the government may not "abridge" the freedom of speech by state censorship. Building on that core right, which grows out of our experiences with injustice, we are involved in a never-ending debate about the appropriate scope of that right: Should it be permissible for a government to impose spending limitations on the exercise of free speech by the wealthy in order to level the playing field for the less affluent? Should it be permissible for a government to censor certain specified genres of speech — for example, pornography, racism, and historical untruths — in the interests of promoting equality? These and other proposed exceptions are debatable among reasonable people. Some opponents of such exceptions argue, in similar fashion to those who argue for a high wall of separation between church and state, that any governmental power to censor is wrong in and of itself, while others contend that it is the first step toward a full regime of censorship. Again, we need not await the development of a fully articulated positive theory of free expression. We can build from the bottom up, based on the widespread consensus against governmental regimes of censorship that have contributed to the experiences of perfect injustice in the past.

The late justice Robert Jackson, in the middle of the horrors of the Second World War, drew some basic conclusions about rights from these experiences, in words with which few will disagree:

> If there is any fixed star in our Constitutional constellation, it is that no official, high or petty, can prescribe what shall be orthodox in politics, nationalism, religion, or other matters of opinion or force citizens to confess by word or act their faith therein.

This is a solid experiential foundation on which to build a more complete theory of expressive rights, as well as other fundamental rights.

## SOME OTHER EXPERIENTIAL RIGHTS

To illustrate the experiential basis for valuing particular rights, consider the right to emigrate from — to leave — a country and to move elsewhere. Many people would not rank the right to leave very high among basic human rights. Some would not consider it a right at all, since they would deem the obligation to remain in one's homeland more important. In the nineteenth century, the right to emigrate would have seemed almost treasonous to a nationalistic Frenchman.

To be sure, some malcontents chose to emigrate to America or Canada, but they were not "real" Frenchmen.

To the Jew, however, the right to emigrate has always been of transcendent importance because of the history and experiences of the Jewish people. The "wandering Jew" has escaped persecution by moving from country to country, sometimes voluntarily, other times as a result of being expelled. Because they had no homeland (during the nineteen hundred years between their expulsion from Palestine by the Romans and the reestablishment of the State of Israel) and because they were generally not considered first-class citizens in their adopted countries, they felt little nationalistic obligation to remain in the face of persecution. If so many Jews had not exercised their right to emigrate from Europe to America (particularly at the end of the nineteenth and beginning of the twentieth centuries), even more of the Jewish community would have been murdered during the Holocaust.

Nor are Jews the only people who have experienced the need to exercise the right to emigrate. The United States is composed of groups that exercised a similar right, in the face of famine, religious persecution, and other forms of tyranny. Moreover, the vast majority of us who have exercised that right have benefited enormously from its exercise. We have been treated well by our host nation and have become an important part of it. As a nation of generally successful immigrants, we tend to recognize the importance of the right to leave one place and move to another. People who have never experienced the need to exercise that right, or who have exercised it less successfully, have a lesser appreciation of its importance. On the other hand, people who have been expelled from their homeland may value "the right to return" more highly than the right to leave, especially if they have been treated poorly by their host countries.

One reason the Arab-Israeli dispute has proved so intractable is that the Palestinians, who believe that they were expelled from their homeland, and who have often been treated badly by their host nations, claim the right to return. The Israelis, who were denied the right to a Jewish homeland for so many centuries, claim the right to remain a Jewish state. The law of return, which entitled any Jew in the world the right to apply for Israeli citizenship, is regarded as one of the most fundamental laws of the Jewish nation. Its perceived importance cannot be understood without the historical and experiential background of the Jewish people, especially the refusal of virtually every nation in the world — even the United States and Canada, which boasted of their status as nations of immigrants — to accept Jewish refugees during the Nazi era. Had the gates of other nations been open to Jews, millions could have been saved from Hitler's ovens, since the initial goal of the Nazis was merely to rid Europe of Jews. Many Jews believe that if the State of Israel had been in existence during the Holocaust, its open doors would have saved many Jews. Following the end of the war, England — which controlled Palestine — imposed rigid quotas on the number of Jewish refugees from the Holocaust who would be allowed into Palestine. Many Jews died or were imprisoned trying to evade these quotas. It is entirely understandable, therefore, that the very first law enacted by the new State of Israel was the law establishing a right of return. As Oliver Wendell Holmes Jr. observed, "The life of the law has not been logic: it has been experience." The experience of the Jewish people led them to elevate the right of return for every Jew in the world to asylum in the Jewish state over the right of Palestinians to return to the land from which they were expelled or they left. Now some young Israelis, who have never experienced the need to leave a hostile nation but who have observed the suffering of Palestinians, are seeking to abolish or limit the law of return. This is not surprising, since historical experiences are generational even within a given society.

The point here is not to argue the Israeli-Palestinian conflict but to illustrate how the unique experiences and memories of a people influence the way in which they perceive and value particular rights. The right to leave a country or return to it does not come from God or nature, despite competing biblical claims to the contrary. It cannot be deduced from the logic of democracy. It grows out of the specific experiences of particular people over time.

An example from American history can also be used to illustrate how rights change with experience and context. In 1776 most high-minded and moral New Englanders believed that among the most basic political rights was the right to separate from the mother country and establish an independent nation. Less than a century later, the grandchildren of these high-minded and moral New Englanders supported waging a bloody war to prevent Southern states from exercising a similar right.[2] The circumstances were, of course, very different, but that's the point. Different circumstances and experiences generate different conceptions of rights. Moreover, the arguments about rights tend to be made at levels of abstraction that maximize their persuasiveness and minimize their inconsistency. For example, some of those who favored secession focused on the right of self-determination rather than on the right to own slaves, whereas most of those who opposed secession argued about its consequences for slavery.

Or consider homosexuality. The Bible deems male homosexuality an abomination. Many modern religious conservatives consider it abnormal, deviant, or sick. Many liberals consider it genetically determined. Some regard it as a morally neutral life choice. Thus, the moral evaluation of homosexuality has changed, and continues to change, over the years. The law, too, has changed. The Bible punishes men who have sex with other men by death. In the twentieth century, it was first a felony punished by imprisonment and then a misdemeanor rarely punished in practice. Now few Western societies regard private, consensual homosexual conduct between consenting adults to be the appropriate concern of the criminal justice system, though some anachronistic laws remain on the books. This change did not result from a change in God's wishes or from a different logical deduction or from some alteration in human nature. It has been a consequence of our changing experiences in regard to homosexuality and homosexuals over time.

## COMMON-LAW DEVELOPMENT

Building a system of rights from the bottom up, based on the experiences of injustice, is consistent with the common-law approach to the development of legal doctrines. Injustice provides the occasion for change. The history of the common law has been a history of adapting legal doctrine to avoid or minimize injustice. When all parties to a dispute believe that justice has been done, there is no occasion for litigation, no need for dispute resolution, and hence no stimulus to change the law. The case reports are not about instances of perceived justice, they are about injustices in search of remedies. Even Aristotle's theory of corrective justice recognized the close relationship between wrongs and the need for corrective laws to restore equilibrium.

The same is true of the history of rights. Where the majority does justice to the minority, there is little need for rights. But where injustice prevails, rights become essential. Wrongs provoke rights, as has been evidenced by the Declaration of Independence, the American Revolution, the post–Civil War amendments, and the broadening interpretations of the Bill of Rights following the evils of the Palmer Raids, McCarthyism, and Jim Crow.

If rights develop from our experiences with perfect injustice, it is fair to ask the following questions: In the absence of a theory of perfect justice, how can we recognize its polar opposite, perfect injustice? By what standard are we to judge perfect injustice in a world without perfect justice? These are theoretical questions that may have no perfect theoretical answer. But the fact remains that experience has taught us to recognize, if not *perfect* injustice, then certainly types of injustice that no one — at least no one today — would try to justify. What constitutes perfect justice remains debatable among decent and intelligent people today, but no such people would debate the injustice of the Holocaust or other instances of deliberate, mass genocide. We have seen perfect injustice and we now know it, even if some did not know it at the time it was being perpetrated. It is remarkable to me that some people today do not acknowledge the perfect injustice of terrorism, arguing that some forms of terrorism are justifiable or that some noble ends justify the use of terrorism as a means. Even these people seem to agree that at least certain acts of terrorism — such as those directed against the World Trade Center — constitute perfect injustice. Perhaps if we were ever to experience perfect justice, we would know that too, but as of now we have never come close to that experience. Indeed, even the utopian philosophers failed to achieve consensus over what a perfectly just society would be like, even in theory. It has been easier for writers to describe perfect injustice — as in Orwell's *1984*, Huxley's *Brave New World*, and Kafka's *The Trial* — than to imagine perfect justice.

# THREE

# THE CHALLENGE OF RIGHTS BASED ON HUMAN EXPERIENCE

MUCH OF JURISPRUDENCE HAS BEEN DEVOTED TO TRYING TO resolve the intractable conflict between those who advocate natural law (and its variants) and those who espouse legal positivism (and its variants). At the extremes, it is a false dichotomy between one illogical approach that seeks to derive moral content from the morally neutral operation of nature and another equally illogical approach that seeks to ascribe morality to humanly enacted laws that may, or may not, be moral.

There are no divine laws of morality, merely human laws claiming the authority of God. Nor are there any moral laws that derive from the nature of man, merely human efforts to control the evils of human nature. Any attempt to build a jurisprudence on the word of God or the workings of nature must fail, because neither God nor nature speaks with one voice capable of being heard or understood by humans. Nor can a jurisprudence be built on legal positivism, since that approach to law is bereft of substantive moral content. It is merely descriptive of what the law is, rather than prescriptive of what it ought to be.

In an age when we better understand the randomness of nature — that it has no externally mandated "purpose" — we cannot continue to abdicate our human responsibility to construct a morality that elevates us above our natural instincts. My friend and colleague Stephen Jay Gould has put it this way:

Homo sapiens may be the brainiest species of all, but we represent only a tiny twig, grown but yesterday on a single branch of the richly arborescent bush of life. This bush features no preferred direction of growth, while our own relatively small limb of vertebrates ranks only one among many, not even *primus inter pares.* There is nothing special about us. The world is not there for us. We are not the object of creation, but rather the product of random forces.[1]

If he is correct, then the randomness of the universe poses the greatest challenge to human morality. If we are here alone, with no preordained destiny, then it is we — as individuals and as community — who must determine our destiny. We are responsible for our future, as we have been for our past. It is we who must improve upon nature and repair the world. It is we who create morality, for better or worse, simply because there is no morality "out there" waiting to be discovered in the "ether" or handed down from some mountaintop. It is because I am a skeptic that I am a moralist. It is because there is no morality beyond human invention that we must devote so much energy to the task of building morality, law, and rights. We cannot endure without morality, law, and rights, yet they do not exist unless *we* bring them into existence by inducing the proper lessons from our experiences. It is we who must write and rewrite the laws. We must not abdicate our own decision making to other human beings who alone claim to hear the silent voice of God or to understand the unknowable moral implications of nature. A great Hasidic rabbi was once asked whether it is ever proper to act as if there were no God. He replied, "Yes. When a poor man asks you for charity, act as if there is no God — act as if only you can save him from starving." I would extend the rabbi's answer to other moral decisions about repairing the world. Further, in an age when we have seen the worst abuses of morality done in the name of positive law, we cannot accept the existence of law as an argument for its morality. One can, of course, agree with Socrates that a citizen has a moral obligation to obey laws that were properly enacted by a fair society, though few would extend that principle to the racist laws of Nazi Germany.

The time has come to recognize the intellectual bankruptcy of both traditional natural law and traditional legal positivism and to seek a different approach to the relationship between the *is* of nature and the *ought* of morality, as well as between the *is* of existing law and the *ought* of what law should be. This approach must rest on the experiences of human beings.

It is beyond the scope of this essay to offer a complete and comprehensive new approach. My goal is to begin a process of constructing such an approach, which rests neither on the shadowy metaphysics of natural law or the empty tautology of legal positivism. I recognize how much easier it is to attack the traditional schools than to construct and defend a new one. Perhaps it is impossible to come up with a completely unassailable theory of rights. If that were so, it would be an argument in favor of, not against, my process-oriented, advocacy approach to rights. Doing rights, while advocating a continuous process of right*ing* — of exploring the possible sources of rights outside of natural and positive law — is entirely consistent with an acceptance of the possibility, indeed the likelihood, that we will never devise a perfect theory of rights. This would not undercut my continuing advocacy of a world that recognizes the importance of certain rights based on the experiences we have had with worlds in which rights have been subordinated to power, even in the recent past. Advocating rights without a perfect theory is far better than silently accepting wrongs until such a theory can be perfected.[2]

The development of rights is an ongoing human process, because changing experiences demonstrate the need for changing rights. Rights once "discovered" or "revealed" do not remain immutable. The process of "righting" must always adapt to the human capacity to do wrong (as we are learning in the age of innovative terrorism).

The experiences of the twentieth century include some of the worst abuses of human rights ever committed by governments, including the Holocaust, the deliberate starvation of Ukrainians, the massacres by and of Cambodians, and others. These cataclysmic events challenged conventional theories of religion, law, and morality. How could an intervening, omniscient, omnipotent, and good God have permitted the Holocaust?[3] Did Jews have any rights in Nazi Germany when the vast majority of Germans strongly supported laws depriving them of all rights? How could so many great philosophers — from Heidegger to Heisenberg — have accepted the morality of Nazism?

For a lawyer who rejects natural law, the challenge is particularly acute. What is the alternative? The Germans were scrupulous about enacting their laws with great attention to procedural niceties and formalities.[4] This raises, for legal positivists, the challenging question: Were the Nuremberg racial laws — which denied Jews and others basic rights — "the law"? Did Jews actually lose all of their rights, or did there continue to exist, outside of enacted German law, a set of legal and moral rights that the victims of the Nuremberg laws could claim and seek to enforce? The answer is a complex one that gives no more solace to supporters of natural law than to advocates of positive law. The reality is that the victims of Nazism had no legal rights in fact — and certainly no legal remedies — while in Germany and Nazi-occupied Europe.[5] They and their supporters urged those who could still exercise some power or influence over Germany — religious, moral, economic, military, diplomatic, or other — to do so in a moral way so as to try to save them. But these appeals to morality generally failed, because self-serving practical considerations were deemed more pressing.

An interesting postwar prosecution in Germany illustrates the dilemma of dealing with positive law that is later deemed immoral. Toward the end of the Nazi regime a woman who wanted to be rid of her husband turned him in to the Gestapo for insulting Hitler. The husband was punished under the law. After the war was over the wife was prosecuted for illegally depriving her husband of his liberty. She defended by pointing to the fact that her husband's deprivation of liberty was pursuant to German positive law and thus could not be deemed criminal. The appellate court affirmed the wife's conviction, ruling that the statute under which her husband was punished was "contrary to the sound conscience and sense of justice of all decent human beings." This reliance on natural law to trump positive law was clearly a reaction to Nazi positivism, which declared *Gesetz als Gesetz* (law as law) and demanded compliance with the most immoral of laws. Legal philosophers who were positivists before the war became proponents of natural law after experiencing the legal abuses of Nazism.[6]

But natural law did little to prevent the abuses of Nazi positive law when it might have mattered — during the war itself. Though the Catholic Church has traditionally been the most articulate exponent of a transcendent, divinely based natural law, the Catholic Church, as an institution, did little to articulate natural law in opposition to Nazi law. Indeed, the "infallible" pope failed in his role as moral leader. In *Christian Antisemitism: A History of Hate*, William Nicholls writes: "Asked by the Berlin correspondent of the Vatican newspaper, *L'Osservatore Romano*, if he would not protest against the extermination of the Jews, Pius replied, 'Dear friend, do not forget that millions of Catholics serve in the German armies. Shall I bring them into conflicts of conscience?'"[7]

If it is not the job of the chief spokesman for natural law and morality to create "conflicts of conscience" in those who were violating such law and morality in the most fundamental way, what is his role? And if it is not the role of natural law to serve as a check on the barbarity of the laws of Nazism, then what function is natural law supposed to serve? Nor was the failure of the Catholic Church limited to its passive silence. It was actively complicit in some of the most egregious violations of natural law, including the employment of slave laborers allocated to German Catholic institutions by Nazis.[8] Natural law, especially divine natural law, cannot excuse its failures by claiming that it cannot be expected to work during periods of crisis or emergency. These are precisely the situations in which natural law makes its greatest claims to superiority over human law.

In the pope's defense, some have pointed to pragmatic concerns, such as preventing the victory of communism, preserving church property, and even saving the lives of priests. But it is the claimed virtue of natural law and morality that it does not employ cost-benefit analysis or situational ethics. Yet that is precisely what is claimed on behalf of Pope Pius XII, who is on the road to becoming a saint. Elevating Pius XII to sainthood would send a message to future generations that tactical silence in the face of immorality will be rewarded — even decades after the crisis has passed — by those who claim to champion natural law. Others argue that the fact that *this* particular embodiment of natural law failed to live up to its demanding and uncompromising standards does not mean that natural law, as an ideal concept, is bankrupt. But those who advocate natural law as a check on positivism at least have the burden of demonstrating that it has worked during times that test the souls of men and women. The experiences of humankind do not appear to satisfy that burden.

Events such as the Holocaust raise questions not so much about the *sources* of the law as about the *scope*, power, and *reach* of the law. I believe that the Nuremberg racial laws, which were properly enacted within Germany, violated positive international law and the norms of human morality. Indeed, the entire Nazi legal system elevated proper form over improper substance to a degree that it could well be argued that it violated positive law. All civilized nations condemned what the

Nazis were doing in the name of German law (though few acted on that condemnation). They simply could not enforce their more elevated notions of international law and morality until after the war was over and the Nazi leaders were tried, ironically, at Nuremberg.

But what if all the nations of the world agreed that it is permissible to kill the Jews, to enslave blacks, or to eat children? Would that make it "law" and deny these victims any claim of right? To what source of authority could the victims then point? The postwar Nuremberg tribunal sought to answer these questions by recognizing and imposing a set of fundamental rules designed by human beings to transcend the positive laws of individual nations.[9] This effort has not been without its difficulties, conceptually and practically, especially when the "new" positive law has been applied retroactively to acts that occurred before its articulation. But it has made a difference. There have been some trials and convictions of those who acted in violation of international positive law, though their actions were in accord with their own domestic positive law.[10] Thus, *Nuremberg* stands for both ends of the legal and moral continuum. The very laws that were enacted at Nuremberg during the Nazi regime were placed on trial at Nuremberg immediately after the war. The original Nuremberg laws proved to be no defense to the higher positive law imposed by the victorious nations at Nuremberg, and this now serves as a positive-law precedent throughout the world. Although the precedent is often difficult to enforce, the world of international human rights is in a different place today than it was a century ago.

For those who share Jeremy Bentham's skeptical view of individual human rights — "nonsense on stilts" he called all moral rights — my answer is that he may have been correct as a matter of descriptive fact, especially at the time he was writing. This means that we must try harder. It is our responsibility as advocates of international human rights to persuade the world community that it is better to live in a world governed by rights than one ruled by force, just as it is better to live in a nation governed by rights rather than power. This is our challenge, especially in an age of globalized communication, where no one can any longer plausibly present the excuse claimed by most decent people during the Holocaust: "We did not know." Many of them did know, or should have known, or could have found out but just did not want to know. As Supreme Court justice Felix Frankfurter told the great Jan Karski after listening to Karski's detailed account of the Warsaw ghetto and the death camps, "A man like me talking to a man like you must be totally honest. So I am. So I say: I cannot believe you."[11] He did not say that he *did not* believe it was true but rather that he *could not* and *would not* believe it. He, and others like him, *chose* not to know, in the interests of self-serving pragmatism. *That* was nature at work. Our efforts to avoid the recurrence of the Holocaust is nurture at work.

Denial is no longer possible in an age of instant communication, and so we must confront directly the difficult issue of how to advocate, implement, and enforce the kinds of basic human rights — most especially the right not to be killed on account of one's race, religion, or ethnicity — that elevate us above species that act only on the "natural" instincts of self-preservation and genetic propagation. In this era of state-sponsored terrorism based on race, ethnicity, and religion, this imperative has taken on a new urgency.*

---

*The recent terrorism is the kind of "experience" that changes philosophies. Consider President George W. Bush's uncriticized conclusion to shoot down hijacked passenger jets about to crash into occupied buildings. Now philosophers have to fit this *conclusion* into existing *theories*. John Rawls will have little difficulty, since anyone behind a veil of ignorance would favor saving thousands of full lives over hundreds of additional seconds of life. Nor would Jeremy Bentham hesitate under his utilitarian calculus. But Immanuel Kant would have difficulty, since it would be using one group to save another. A clever Kantian might argue that the passengers would *will* their own deaths rather than become the instruments of death of so many. But that would not solve the problem for theologians for whom willed death is suicide. If a terminally ill person in pain cannot will his own death before God decides to end his life, then how can a passenger hasten his demise to save others?

Theologians will find justifications. They might see an analogy to soldiers who know they will die performing their duty. But what if some of the passengers prefer to try to regain control of the plane, even if the odds are low? Perhaps there is an analogy to a person being used as a human shield by a criminal firing his gun. The certainty is that the Bush order will be found religiously, philosophically, and legally correct, since no one who wants to be taken seriously will say that the plane should not be shot down. The *constant* is the answer; the *variable* is the reasoning. Our experience with evil (terrorists using jets as bombs) has given us the right *answer* to what once was a debatable tragic choice. Now we must figure out how to *frame the question* so as to ensure arriving at this answer.

# FOUR

# WHY WE SHOULD
# PREFER RIGHTS

IN THIS BOOK I WILL TRY TO DEFEND MY STRONG PREFERENCE for a society based on fundamental rights. That is all I can do — defend my *preference* for *rights*. I will argue that based on our experiences over time, we should prefer to live in a society in which the government is denied certain powers, such as the power to censor speech, even deeply offensive speech, as well as the power to restrict or promote religion. I will also argue that we should all prefer to live in a society in which no citizen can be imprisoned, executed, deported, or otherwise deprived of basic freedoms without "due process of law." Finally, I will argue that we should all prefer to live in a society where all people are deemed equal and are treated as equals by the government.

I believe that experience demonstrates that a democratic society that recognizes and enforces these basic rights — uncensored expression, freedom of conscience, due process, democracy, and equal protection of the laws — is preferable to a society that does not.[1] That is my case for rights. That is why I have a strong preference for rights. That is why I would leave, if I could, any society that did not protect rights in general and these rights in particular, believing as I do that the right to leave an oppressive country and settle elsewhere is among the most basic of rights.[2] If I could not leave, I would be willing to fight, and perhaps even die, for these fundamental rights. But I make no claim for these rights beyond my ability to persuade you to agree with me that history — especially the history of wrongs — has shown these rights to be important enough to be given a special status in the hierarchy of preferences. It may surprise you to learn that for me there is no sharp line — certainly no natural or inherent line — separating rights from strongly held preferences. Rights are those fundamental limitations on state power that should be accepted by those who govern and those who are governed on the basis of human experience. Their authority may be explicit, as in a written constitution, or implicit, as in an unwritten consensus developed over time.

If rights have no authority beyond some kind of social or political agreement, then what distinguishes rights from preferences? That is a profound question that is rarely answered honestly. I will try to answer that question in this book. In the pages to come, I will try to persuade the reader that these basic rights — first accepted widely in the eighteenth century, elaborated and extended in the nineteenth century, and applied more broadly in the twentieth century[3] — should continue to constrain governmental action in the twenty-first century, despite technological innovations and threats of mass destruction unimaginable even a few years ago. In the conclusion, I will argue that certain old rights — refined to meet current conditions — must remain the basis for controlling new wrongs. The goal of this book is to convince the reader to share my strong preference for rights.

I agree with Dworkin and others that individual rights should serve as trump cards against the power of the state, but for me these trumps must be consistently advocated, not merely discovered or discerned. My approach is more activist in regard to rights. It requires constant reassessment and recommitment. It is less confident that others will simply recognize the eternal logical truth of its premises and conclusions.

The major conceptual difference between Dworkin's approach and mine is that his methodology is largely deductive: he reasons logically from the premises of the liberal, egalitarian, democratic state and deduces certain rights that naturally flow from the premises that a government must treat all of its citizens with equal concern and respect. My methodology is largely inductive: I look around at the experiences of people and nations over time and place — especially the experiences of injustice — and try to persuade that, based on these experiences, people should conclude that entrenching certain rights into the positive law will, in the long run, produce a less unjust society.[4]

I reject Dworkin's view that the "rights" of the minority should trump the will of the majority "even if this would not be in the general interest," broadly defined and extended over time. Unless the community "will be better off in the long run as a whole"[5] by entrenching certain rights, it will be impossible to persuade people to do so, and my advocacy will fail — as it should in a democracy. My approach requires me to persuade by a variety of arguments — self-interest, doing the right thing, being consistent, adhering to one's own expressed values — that a system that entrenches and vindicates certain fundamental rights is preferable to one that does not. I will often fail in this effort, because the case for the long-term benefit of rights is a difficult one to make in a world in which short-term advantage is easier to see and understand. But this is an argument in favor of, not opposed to, my approach of continuous and persistent advocacy of inconvenient rights in a world impatient to get where it wants to go without the interference of countermajoritarian headwinds, which inevitably slow down the progress of the will of the majority.

At bottom, the ultimate source for Dworkin's nonpositivist rights is the fierce logic of his brilliant argumentation. He believes that he can persuade the world that the very logic of the liberal, egalitarian, democratic state demands a system of rights outside of the law and transcending — trumping — the power of the state. Accepting his source of rights requires accepting the brilliance of his logic rather than persuading people that experience demonstrates the utility (broadly defined) of rights. He has succeeded in persuading me, and many others, as to much of his reasoning and many of his conclusions. But what about those whom he fails to persuade? Are they all necessarily wrong? Is there really only one right answer? And must it be Dworkin's? I might be happy if that were the case, but I must acknowledge that there are other reasonable positions that do not require complete acceptance of Dworkin's rigorous logic. The life of the law, as well as of morality, is, after all, experience, not logic — not even Dworkin's powerful and persuasive logic. And experience, unlike logic, rarely points inexorably toward a singular truth. It is the virtue, as well as the limitation, of logic that it points unerringly in one direction (if its original premises are accepted). It is the vice, as well as the richness, of experience that it may be perceived differently by different human beings with different backgrounds, value systems, and types of intelligence.[6] It is truly in the eye of the beholder.

That is why I believe that my approach is somewhat more democratic and less elitist than Dworkin's: because it depends on continuing advocacy and it acknowledges that it may be rational and moral for a citizen to stick to his or her differing viewpoint, as distinguished from Dworkin's assertion that logic leads to only one rational and natural conclusion, regardless of the experiences, values, and intelligence of the particular person. While Dworkin relies on abstract and often technical philosophical analyses designed to persuade the academic, my approach relies on commonsense arguments growing out of the experiences of the people and an assessment of what will lead to a better society for them and others.

Sometimes I wish there were natural rights that I could invoke as external trumps. How much easier it would be if I could call upon God, nature, reason, a categorical imperative, a mythical social contract, a heuristic original position, or some inexorable Dworkinian logic in support of my preference for a legal system that recognizes the right to free speech. But to do so would not be faithful to my belief system or my experiences. Jeremy Bentham once quipped that people invoke natural rights "when they wish to get their way without having to argue for it."[7] Well, I have to argue for rights. All I can do is continue to advocate the right of free speech, based on the comparative experiences of nations that have accepted or rejected this risky and uncomfortable approach to governance. For me, rights come from the human experiences of injustice in societies without basic rights. The source of rights is, in a word, wrongs.

In one respect, the very question Where do rights come from? assumes an erroneous conclusion. To ask about the source of rights is to assume that such a source exists. Implicit in this assumption is yet another: that the source of any right (or rights-based system) is outside the structure of the humanly constructed legal system. Under my approach, the "source" of rights is in the experiences of humankind, most particularly our experiences with injustice. Yet it is somewhat imprecise to characterize our history of injustice as the "source" of our rights. The word *source* generally carries a somewhat different connotation. An analogy from biology might help to clarify the way in which I am using *source*. It can perhaps be said that the source of antibodies is infection. In one sense that may be true, but it is an incomplete account. Similarly, it is somewhat imprecise to say that the history of injustice caused by the merger of church and state is the source of the right to the free exercise of religion. This experience may be the *stimulus* for that right, but the *source* is the human ability to learn from experience and to entrench rights in our laws and in our consciousness. It is in that composite sense — experiential stimulus plus human reaction — that I use the term *source* in this discussion.

## PHILOSOPHY AND SOCIOLOGY

There is, of course, a difference between a *philosophy* of rights on the one hand and an *anthropology* or *sociology* of rights on the other. The former is in the nature of a moral inquiry, whereas the latter is in the nature of an empirical search. It can be argued that my approach to rights, being experiential and nurtural, is more akin to the latter than to the former. But that would misunderstand what I am trying to do. I am not seeking a merely descriptive approach to rights. I strongly believe that rights must have a moral component. Though I reject the notion that rights come directly from nature, I also reject the view that they come directly from nurture, without the mediation of morality. Empiricism informs morality, but it does not define it. Nature and nurture both have a vote, but neither has a veto, on the moral component of rights. Even the most stringent legal positivists acknowledge a close historical connection between legal rights and morality: "The development of legal systems had been powerfully influenced by moral opinion, and, conversely, . . . moral standards had been profoundly influenced by law, so that the content of many legal rules mirrored moral rules or principles."[8] Even Holmes, the author of the "bad man" theory of law, recognized that "the law is the witness and external deposit of our moral life."[9]

A right that flies in the face of nature or scientific knowledge — for example, the right to smoke in crowded theaters — will simply not endure. Nor will a right that undercuts the experiences of a people, such as the right to bear arms in postwar Japan or to teach Holocaust denial in postwar Germany. But just as nature alone does not automatically translate into rights, experiences alone do not and should not dictate the content of rights. Rights come from a complex interaction of factors.

The one aspect of rights that must necessarily be governed by experience and empiricism is the evaluation of how effectively rights are working to achieve their stated goals. In order to persuade a democratic citizenry to accept rights (or any particular rights) as a trump on the current will of the majority, an advocate must be able to demonstrate that a world (or a nation, or some other unit of democracy) will be a better place with rights than without them. Rights are not self-justifying (or "self-evident," in the words of the Declaration of

Independence). Nor can they be justified by logic alone. They need to work! — to accomplish something! — in order for the presumption of majority rule to be overcome. Thus, evaluating the success or failure of a regime of rights is largely, though not entirely, an empirical undertaking: agreeing on the ends sought to be served by rights is a moral enterprise, while deciding whether those ends have been achieved — and at what cost — is an empirical undertaking. And the major sources for my moral-empirical advocacy will be the experiences of people over time, especially their experiences with injustice.

In my view, deciding what is moral — what is right — rarely involves the discovery of eternal truths. It is largely an ongoing process of trial and error, evaluation and reevaluation, based on changing experiences over time. Morality is not static. Once discovered, it should not remain unchallenged. It is not enough to deduce it, discover it, and declare it. One must constantly defend it, reconsider it, redefine it, and be prepared to change it.

What appeared to be right, based on the limited knowledge of the past, may now appear to be wrong, based on current information. Indeed, what *was* right for a previous generation may *be* wrong for current or future generations, because of changing experiences.

Morality uninformed by experience is likely to be so abstract as to be incapable of resolving complex dilemmas. This has been the case with Kant's abstract imperatives, which have failed the test of human experience over time. Experience unstructured by morality is likely to be mere narrative. There must be a continuing interplay between morality and experience. Morality does not emerge full-blown from the mind of man or the word of God. Even the myth of Sinai was preceded by the experiences of Genesis. Morality must be honed over time by constant testing against the shoals of experience. But nor should experience alone dictate morality. A subtle and complex relationship necessarily exists between what is and what ought to be. We cannot derive our moral standards entirely from the nature of human beings, but neither can we ignore human nature in formulating and evaluating our values. Constructing a moral system is neither an entirely deductive nor an entirely inductive enterprise. Not unlike much of science, it requires abstract thinking and concrete testing. For some, like Einstein, the imaginings seem to come first and the testing later.

For others, like Darwin, the observations appear to precede the construction of a general theory. For all, there is the constant interplay among imagination, observation, and confirmation. Another point of agreement between science and morality is that for both, all conclusions must be tested against the realities of experience.

It does not confuse philosophy with sociology, or normative with empirical, or deductive with inductive, to acknowledge the interrelationship between the "ought" of morality and the "is" of experience. The difficult task is to assign each its proper role and weight in the process of constructing and evaluating a moral system.

## A TESTING CONFLICT

A contemporary variation on the traditional debate between those who believe that rights and morals exist externally to the law and independent of it and those who deny the existence of any external or independent source of rights and morals was recently played out in a debate between Ronald Dworkin and Richard Posner. Dworkin brilliantly succeeds in demonstrating that without an independent source of rights and morals, all discussion eventually becomes circular, since there needs to be a moral norm against which all consequentialist arguments are judged. But Posner succeeds in demonstrating that there is no moral norm that is, in fact, independent of particular cultures, experiences, and legal systems. Nor does Dworkin persuasively articulate any such universal morality or tell us where it comes from — what its source is, if it is not God or nature. He does tell us what the test of such a universal concept would be: consistency of application to other comparable situations, predictable and unpredictable. But such consistency is often achieved by manipulating — consciously or unconsciously — the level of abstraction of the argument. For example, critics of Dworkin's support of a woman's right to choose abortion argue that it is inconsistent with his opposition to capital punishment and with his demand for equality. Dworkin responds by arguing that a fetus — at least an early fetus — is not a human being and therefore the argument against executing human beings is not inconsistent with his argument in favor of the right of a woman to terminate her pregnancy. Advocates of capital punishment who oppose abortion argue that the fetus is *innocent* life, whereas the person to be executed is *guilty*. Each side believes it is being entirely consistent.

In sum, then, the debate between the moralists and the consequentialists would seem to boil down to a variation on the old saw "You can't live with it, and you can't live without it." Dworkin may be correct when he argues that without an external morality, there can be no basis for evaluating — judging — whether the goals of a consequentialist world are just or unjust. In other words, you can't live without an external morality. But Posner may be right in arguing that no matter how much we may *need* an external and universal source of morality or rights, it just does not exist. The mistake both make, in my view, is in confusing the *desirability* of their positions — an argument that Dworkin wins in my estimation — with the *truth* of their positions. The need for an external source of morality and rights — persuasive as Dworkin is in this regard — is not an argument for the existence of this source. Logic can prove the *need* for an external morality, but it cannot prove its actual existence. Dworkin has the burden of showing us the source and persuading us of its reality.

The most powerful case for natural law and natural rights is that we *need* them! Human beings have proved themselves incapable of governing without some perceived outside source of morality and rights. In the absence of such a source, there are no limits to what we are willing to do, and capable of doing, to each other. We need constraints and we need to believe that these restraints come from some higher authority and are objectively binding on us. We crave "miracle, mystery, and authority," as Dostoyevsky put it in his masterful Grand Inquisitor scene: "Nothing has ever been more insupportable for a man and a human society than freedom. If they begin to build their tower of Babel without us [the church authority] they will end, of course, with cannibalism." Even H.L.A. Hart, a persistent critic of natural law and proponent of a modified version of morally infused positive law, acknowledges the need for some external guarantee of fundamental rights. Citing the horrors of the mid–twentieth century, he observes that "a theory of rights is urgently called for," lest we repeat our tragic history.[10]

The "need" argument for natural law is strikingly similar to the functional argument for God and religion. We *need* God in order to make sense of our existence and to assign us a purpose. We *need* external authority to free us of the internal anxiety of untrammeled choice.[11] We *need* religion in order to deal with life's tragedies and it's inevitable end. We *need* an afterlife to rationalize the injustices of this life. There are no atheists in a foxhole — or on a crashing airplane. Maybe not. But the need argument no more proves the actual existence of God than it proves the existence of an external source (or sources) of natural law or natural rights. Just because we may need something does not prove that this something actually exists. What it may prove is that we need to pretend it exists or to create it or construct it. Hart, who acknowledges the need, has correctly observed that enormous energy has recently been devoted to the quest for a "sufficiently firm foundation" for a theory of basic, inalienable rights.[12] But "need" plus energetic quest do not always produce satisfaction of the need. We need to cure cancer and we are devoting enormous resources to our quest for the cure, but we have not yet satisfied this need, and there is no assurance we will ever do so. Likewise with the quest to satisfy the need for an external source of basic rights: we may never find it, because it does not exist. Just as human beings created God, organized religion, and the afterlife, so, too, have we created divine natural law, secular natural law, and other moral and legal fictions deemed essential to satisfy some of our most basic and enduring needs. As a Dostoyevsky character put it: "The universal and everlasting craving of humanity [is] to find someone to worship. So long as man remains free, he strives for nothing so incessantly and so painfully as to find someone to worship." This is the "fundamental secret of human nature" — that "man is tormented by no greater anxiety than to find some one quickly to whom he can hand over that great gift of freedom with which the ill-fated creature is born."[13]

To the extent that this creative process of need satisfaction is thought to grow out of some inherent human needs, it may be called natural. To the extent that it grows out of the experiences of human beings over time, it may be called experiential or nurtural. The line between the two may not be as sharp as some have asserted, since experiences often reflect inherent or deeply rooted aspects of human nature.

Posner, the economic rationalist, fails to acknowledge the human need for external sources of morality. Dworkin, the rational moralist, recognizes the reality that there are no divine or ghostly sources for this needed external morality, but he is not clear about the sources of his moral trumps.

It is interesting to note that Dworkin and Posner have each constructed theories that play to their own individual strengths. Dworkin has few peers in his ability to formulate general theories, draw apt distinctions, and shift levels of abstraction so as to bring about consistency. Posner has few peers in his ability to use economic analysis to justify his personal and political views. Both approaches have in common their inaccessibility to the general public and their dependence on the esoteric arguments of intellectual elites.

It is also interesting to note that the advocates of natural law and the advocates of more consequentialist and positivist approaches do not divide along traditional liberal-conservative or progressive-reactionary camps. Dworkin is a liberal-progressive who identifies with the left in both politics and constitutional law, while Posner is far more conservative and identifies with the right. Many other advocates of natural law (especially divine natural law) tend to be on the right, while many consequentialists see themselves as closer to the left. Dworkin's natural-law (or more precisely, nonpositivist, nonconsequentalist) approach generally leads him to (some might say follows him from) his progressive views, whereas Posner's more consequentialist approach nearly always leads him to (or follows him from) his more conservative political and economic views.

Neither natural law nor legal positivism has any direct correlation — either in theory or in practice — to either radical or reactionary programs. Each has been employed in the service of revolution, on the one hand, and the status quo, on the other.

Natural law has served as justification for the American Revolution, for slave rebellions, for acts of civil disobedience, and for reformist changes in the law. By invoking a higher authority, radical advocates of natural law have sought to justify the violation of unjust positive law or the overthrow of unjust systems of law. Reactionary advocates of natural law have also invoked higher authority as a justification for religious oppression, denial of positive-law rights (reproductive freedom, assisted suicide, fetal cell transplantation), and the preservation of the status quo (slavery, criminalization of homosexuality).

Legal positivists, too, have been revolutionaries, disobedients, and reformers. Yes, the law is the law, but "the law is a ass" (to use Dickens's phrase) that must be changed, and positive law can be unmade by human beings as easily as it was made by them. Indeed, legal positivism was born of reformist parents such as Jeremy Bentham, John Austin, and John Stuart Mill. It then gave birth to some of the most oppressive systems of legal, political, and military tyranny. "Law as law," said the Nazis, and no one had the right to invoke any higher authority as a justification for disobeying it.

The idea that there are no external sources for law or morality and that human beings create themselves according to their own values has long been associated with the amoral philosophy of Friedrich Nietzsche, whose own values were thoroughly obnoxious. But there is no necessary correlation between the denial of an objective morality and the human construction of any particular subjective morality. The fact that Nietzsche's personal morality was elitist, racist, sexist, and undemocratic simply illustrates the risks of leaving moral choice to individuals. Some will choose badly, as Nietzsche did, while others will create elevated and compassionate moralities that are as good as or better than anything found in natural law or so-called objective morality. I need mention only Mill's and Robert Nozick's as examples of humanly constructed moral systems that are as different from Nietzsche's proto-Nazism as any philosophies can be.

Even if it were true — which it surely is not — that untethering morality from religion or other allegedly external sources would inevitably lead to Nietzsche or "cannibalism" (as the Grand Inquisitor suggests), that would only be an argument in favor of the *desirability of* and *need for* an objective morality derived from an external source. It would not be an argument in favor of its *actual existence*. If no such morality, in fact, exists, we have only a handful of basic alternatives to purely subjective, individualistic morality (or lack thereof):

1. We can *pretend* it exists and act as if it did. We may call this the moral fiction approach.
2. We can try to *derive* an objective morality from sources that do exist, such as human nature. We may call this the derivative approach.
3. We can try to *construct* a system of morality that is so logically compelling that we make a plausible claim of objectivity for it. We may call this the objective-constructive approach.

4. We can look to the *experiences* of human beings over time — especially negative experiences — and draw lessons from them that serve as a basis for an ever changing, humanly created system of morality, law, and rights, and advocate certain rights based on these experiences. We may call this the experiential-advocacy approach.

There is nothing inherently liberal or conservative about any of these approaches. Each is an attempt to *describe* sources of law and rights, and descriptions do not necessarily carry normative implications and certainly do not mandate particular moral conclusions. Each of these approaches can produce good or evil, progress or regress, liberalism or conservatism.

To the extent that some approaches to what has come to be called natural law suggest that its content is universal and eternal, it is — at least in theory — more difficult to change than positive law, which is — also in theory — easily amendable. But natural law has, of course, changed dramatically over the years, and its purported content varies from place to place as well as from time to time. Positive law has sometimes been more enduring than natural law. The United States Constitution, which is positive law, has endured with few changes for more than two centuries, whereas its "natural-law" underpinnings have changed in numerous respects over the same period of time. The durability of positive law is, of course, a double-edged sword, since bad positive laws — such as those enacted in Nazi Germany — may also endure, especially when the positive law deprives citizens of the right to dissent and to seek change in the law.

At an even more fundamental level, the debate between those who seek moral constraints outside of the positive law and those who eschew such external constraints is a disagreement about trusting human beings with freedom. The most powerful case against such trust was made by Dostoyevsky's Grand Inquisitor, who believed that science (or economics) without the authoritative constraints of religion would inevitably lead to the internal anxiety of untrammeled freedom and the external catastrophe of cannibalism (and, by extension, terrorism and nuclear destruction). The case for trust is made by Bentham, Mill, Posner, and others who believe that external moral constraints are nonsense and that human beings must be free, as Oliver Wendell Holmes Jr. liked to say, to make bad choices that lead them to self-destruction: "If my fellow citizens want to go to hell, I will help them."[14]

Among the most compelling proofs that rights grow out of the experiences of humankind and not some abstract, external source is the very history of the epistemology of rights. The nature of the debate over the source of rights has itself been a function of the experiences of the time. Bentham rejected natural law because he had witnessed its abuses. Utilitarianism and legal positivism had their intellectual heydays during a period of great reform. They fell into disrepute following the Nazi era. Now that we have experienced the abuses both of natural law and of positivist utilitarianism, we crave other theories that provide the benefits of each without their difficulties. We search for a utilitarianism that does not sacrifice individuals or small groups to the happiness of the many — that treats individuals as deserving of respect and consideration regardless of the consequences to the many. We seek to discover, create, or construct a natural law that is not dependent on God's word, nature's message, or some other metaphysical source. We know that we need a source of rights beyond the law, the utilitarian calculus, the word of God, or the demands of nature! But we cannot "find" it, for the simple reason that it does not exist outside of human experience. All law and all morality are the constructs of human beings struggling to elevate themselves from the state of nature — without the help of any external forces. All we can do is articulate and advocate those rights that experience teaches us are essential to avoid the catastrophes of the past,[15] recognizing that if we fail to understand the lessons of history, we may be doomed to repeat its horrors.[16]

My approach to rights is located, in one sense, somewhere between the Dworkin-Posner poles, but in another sense, it lies outside the debate as well. It serves as a practical guide to action in the absence of a definitive resolution of the age-old debate between advocates of natural and of positive law. While philosophers continue to refine the esoteric issues of "externality" and "constructivety," practitioners of rights — those who *do* rights — cannot remain on hold. An experientially based, bottom-up approach to rights allows the practitioner to look to history as a guide to which rights could have prevented or slowed down the injustices of the past and might therefore serve as a check on the possible injustices of the future. This is, in fact, an apt account of how many people — even including many philosophers — actually arrive at their approach to rights.

I categorically reject the *program* offered by the Grand Inquisitor — surrender to authority, miracle, and mystery — while agreeing in large part with his *description* of human nature. My program is to struggle against the inherent need of most people for external authority by trying to persuade them not to submit to the seductive Grand Inquisitors of every generation — those who would take away their anxiety-producing freedom of choice and offer them in its place the comfort of believing that others (whether those others be God, the church, the king, the president, the judge, the economist, or the philosopher) have the responsibility of choosing for them.*

Professor Albert Alschuler bemoans the fact — as he sees it — that "the central lyric of twentieth-century American jurisprudence [has been] 'Ain't no wrong, ain't no right.'"[17] To the extent that this lyric suggests there are no absolute rules of morality dictated by God, nature, or reason alone, I agree. But wrong and right (especially wrong) can and must be induced from experience, lest we fail to learn its lessons. Our moral obligation is clear: we must *build* a system of right and wrong precisely because these important moral principles do not exist outside of human experience. We must articulate and advocate rights that will help to prevent recurrence of the terrible wrongs of the past — wrongs so potentially lethal that they now threaten our very existence.

---

*In espousing this continuing advocacy approach, I do not mean to be self-referential. It is certainly not I alone who seek to persuade others of the long-term benefits — the utility — of a rights-based system. Many people throughout history — civil libertarians, human rights activists, and individuals with no particular affiliation — have been part of this process. I employ the first person as a heuristic device to contrast it with the views of others. My approach does not depend on the advocacy skills of any particular individual but, rather, on the collective ability of rights advocates to persuade others that the lessons of history strongly suggest that a rights-based system is preferable to a system based exclusively on power, even the power of the majority. In the pages that come, I draw on the works of rights advocates over time and try to make the case for a rights-based system in general — and certain fundamental rights in particular — in a world so full of wrongs.

*PART I*

❋

# RIGHTS IN GENERAL: THEIR LIMITS AND SCOPE

# FIVE

# OUR ENDURING BILL
# OF RIGHTS

*In 1987 I was asked by* Hadassah Magazine *to celebrate the bicentennial of our Bill of Rights. I used it as an occasion to explore the tension between majority powers and minority rights.*

THE UNITED STATES CONSTITUTION IS IN ITS THIRD CENTURY — and there is much to celebrate. No charter of liberty has been as enduring as our Constitution and its first ten amendments, known as the Bill of Rights.

Although they are called amendments, the Bill of Rights is an organic part of the original document. Without it, the Constitution would not have been ratified, because it created a structure for centralized power without sufficient assurances of liberty. The Bill of Rights struck the balance necessary to alleviate the concerns of those, like Thomas Jefferson, who worried that a constitution without explicit grants of liberty would strike an improper balance between governmental power and individual rights.

Our Constitution, with its Bill of Rights, sought to achieve the appropriate balance. It gave us a strong government without the power to censor newspapers, restrict the free exercise of religion, or otherwise curtail the fundamental rights of its citizens.

The irony — one repeated throughout history — is that it is generally the citizens themselves who want rights curtailed in the name of safety, security, or convenience. Sometimes the reasons are even less compelling: bigotry, xenophobia, and intolerance. The greatest crises for a constitutional democracy occur when the majority demands that minority rights be abridged. The conflict between the power of the many and the rights of the few raises the most profound questions about our theory of government.

How does a democracy justify a Bill of Rights that allows a minority to overrule the majority? Every time one of the first ten amendments to our Constitution — or any of its other provisions — is successfully invoked to strike down a legislatively enacted statute or to constrain a popularly elected official, we have made an uneasy compromise with pure democracy. In that sense, our Bill of Rights is somewhat analogous to the role played by the Ten Commandments or other biblical absolutes. But secular democracy is different from religion.

Throughout our two hundred–year experience with constitutional democracy, efforts have been made to justify minority restraints on majority action. Although no single accepted rationale has emerged, the general consensus has been that the experiment — really a series of ever changing experiments — has worked.

The greatest threats to our liberty have come from transient majorities intolerant of the rights of minorities: the Alien and Sedition laws, white ownership of black slaves, know-nothing nativism and persecution of immigrants, segregation and racism, anti-Japanese hysteria culminating in the detention of more than 100,000 Americans, and the pernicious thought control of McCarthyism.

Our Bill of Rights has provided less-than-perfect protection against the excesses of transient majorities, but it has contributed to the prevention of popular tyranny. The first ten amendments have also occasionally imposed some severe — and in retrospect, perhaps unnecessary — checks on popular majoritarian action. For example, during the early New Deal, some important legislation designed to counter the Depression was declared to be in violation of due process. And today, many Americans believe that the Warren Court may have gone too far in protecting the rights of persons accused of crime. Whether or not one agrees with these assessments, it seems clear that, in general, a workable balance has been struck between the power of the majority and the rights of minorities.

This balance is part of our dynamic system of governing, which eschews too much concentration of power. American sovereignty, unlike that of most other Western democracies, does not reside in one branch of government or even in the majority of the people. Our sovereignty is a process, reflected in such concepts as checks and balances, separation of powers, and judicial review.

But beyond these abstract concepts is a commonsense distrust of untrammeled authority, born of the varied histories and experiences that comprise the American character.

We are different from most other nations, in that most of our forebears chose to leave other places for a better — and freer — life.[1] We are a nation of minorities, dissidents, émigrés, risk takers, skeptics, heretics, experimenters, nay-sayers — distrustful and ornery mavericks. We are a tyrant's nightmare and an anarchist's dream. Our slogans — anachronistic as they may seem — tell us something profound about our individualism: Don't tread on me; Give me liberty or give me death; Show me; Question authority.

Yesterday's quaint slogans have often become today's rude bumper stickers, T-shirt logos, or wall graffiti. Whatever the medium, the American message has been similar for more than two centuries: we need breathing room; we will not submit to regimentation; we demand our liberties.

Against this historical landscape, the Bill of Rights can best be viewed as an insurance policy against tyranny. As with all insurance policies, paying the periodic premiums is no fun. You get nothing material in return — at least, not right away. We pay a heavy premium every time a guilty criminal is freed in the name of the Fourth Amendment, every time a pornographer or a racist is permitted to disseminate filth or poison because of the First Amendment, every time a young girl is allowed to make the "wrong" decision regarding abortion on the grounds of choice, and every time an indigent yeshiva student is denied a subsidized religious education that would violate the constitutional prohibition against the government's establishing religion.

But as with an insurance policy, we pay these premiums in exchange for partial protection against disasters that are specifically unpredictable and generally inevitable. No insurance policy can prevent death or disability, but it can ease their ravages. Sometimes a good insurance policy even reduces risks, by requiring those in control to take precautions.

Likewise, the Bill of Rights cannot by itself prevent oppression. But it can impose barriers to tyranny, especially by transient majorities seeking to entrench their power and extend it over time. It also sends an important message to those who would seek power through dubious means: "We Americans take our rights seriously, and you ignore that message at considerable political risk." The downfalls of Richard Nixon and Joseph McCarthy are eloquent testimony to the American allergy to trashing constitutional safeguards.

Over the past two hundred years, we have paid many constitutional premiums and accumulated much equity in our collective insurance policy. Fortunately, ours is not merely a term policy. It is a whole-life investment in our future as a free country.

There are those today who would turn our Constitution into a narrow sectarian tool for the advancement of particular philosophies, doctrines, and even religions. Evangelist Pat Robertson has called the Constitution a Christian document and has promised to rescue it from "non-Christian" judges who have been misconstruing it in a secular manner. Some politicians view the Bill of Rights as an encumbrance to their political programs. They seek to have it interpreted narrowly to implement its "original intent" — an intent they claim to know. But if there was any original intent of the framers, it was general and broad: to create an enduring charter of liberty capable of responding to changing conditions.[2]

We are a very different nation today than we were in 1787. From an agrarian society composed almost exclusively of English Protestants, we have evolved into the most heterogeneous, multiethnic, multilingual, multiracial, multireligious society in the history of the world. Our Constitution must evolve along with the experiences of the society it governs. And it will, so long as we continue to have confidence in our collective ability to be strong and compassionate, to live by majority rule without compromising minority rights.

# SIX

# A DANGEROUS VOCABULARY
OF NEW RIGHTS

---

*The "victims' rights" movement of the 1990s gave rise to a new vocabulary of rights, which was based on a conception of right quite different from that accepted by the framers of our Constitution and the first ten amendments. This chapter examines and critiques this development.*

---

A NOVEL AND DANGEROUS "VOCABULARY OF RIGHTS" IS being constructed as part of an attempted end run around the Constitution. "Victims' rights," the "right to be protected from pornography," "fetus rights," and the "right not to be exposed to secular humanism" are elements of jargon conceived by right-wing groups to deceive the public into believing that an invocation of governmental power is really an exercise of individual rights.

Rights — especially constitutional rights — exist in relation to governments. The Bill of Rights (and post–Civil War amendments) was designed to limit governmental powers by assuring that certain individual rights could not be taken away by representatives of the government. In the context of criminal prosecutions, it was the criminal defendant or suspect who was given the right to be free from unreasonable searches, self-incrimination, double jeopardy, cruel and unusual punishment, and excessive bail.

There is no provision for victims' rights in the Constitution for a very good and simple reason: it is not the government that is seeking to deny the victim any legitimate claim.[1] The victim was assaulted by a private citizen. The government is on the side of the victim and is seeking to punish the defendant. The Bill of Rights seeks to strike a balance by granting the defendant certain rights.

That is the way the system is supposed to work, in theory. But in practice the government does not always work in the interest of victims, especially when they are poor, unpopular, or powerless. Even middle-class victims are often neglected, inconvenienced, or even abused. Understandably, therefore, victims'-rights lobbies have been formed that seek for victims a greater role in the criminal justice system.

And these groups have become the darling of prosecutors and politicians. How can any decent citizen resist the emotional importuning of victims? Prosecutors no longer claim to be representing the impersonal government (the same one that takes your hard-earned money and doesn't answer your letters). Now they are champions of victims — a group with which every citizen whose home has been burgled or pocketbook snatched can identify!

Legislatures have also jumped on the victims'-rights bandwagon. More than half of our states have enacted victims'-rights laws. Most of these laws are the old wine of law-and-order legislation in a new bottle. Some contain few or no real protections for victims: they simply take rights away from defendants in the name of victims. Other legislation does improve the situation for victims and witnesses by eliminating certain inconveniences and requiring that their interests be taken into account by those who administer the criminal justice system.

Among the most controversial provisions of these new laws is the right of the victim — or the victim's representative — to appear before the sentencing judge and the parole board and to present a victim-impact statement. These statements provide parole boards and sentencing authorities with emotional and highly detailed accounts of how the crime actually affected, and continues to affect, the victim. While there may be some value in humanizing the process by pitting defendant against victim instead of the impersonal prosecution, a victim-impact statement carries with it considerable cost. It invites inevitable class and race biases. When the victim is someone with whom the sentencing authorities can identify, they are apt to see the crime as more serious and deserving of harsher punishment than when the victim is poor, homeless, unemployed, or a member of an unpopular group. It has long been true that the nature of the victim has had a demonstrable impact on the severity of the punishment, but the increasing visibility of the victim in the criminal justice process threatens to exacerbate this discrimination. The concept of victims' rights is clearly a knife that cuts both ways.

The Supreme Court has ruled — by a five-to-four vote — that in cases involving a life-or-death sentencing decision, the victim-impact statement cuts too deeply against the defendant's constitutional rights and has the potential for inflaming the jury in favor of capital punishment. Justice Lewis Powell, writing one of his last opinions for the majority, also pointed out that the degree of suffering experienced by the victims and survivors "may be wholly unrelated to the blameworthiness of a particular defendant."

Notwithstanding the Supreme Court's rebuke of the victim-impact statement in capital cases, the rhetoric of rights is likely to persist in other contexts. So-called victims of pornography will continue to parade through the streets demanding their "right" to have the government remove offending material from their communities. Graphic photographs of "abortion victims" are commonplace at right-to-life demonstrations. Christian fundamentalists are declaring themselves victims of secularism.

Those right-wingers who are using this new rhetoric of rights in an effort to undermine the rights of the individual are misusing words in a deliberately confusing manner. The concept of rights in relation to governmental powers is too important a part of our national identity to be obscured by such faddish rhetoric.

## ADDENDUM OF RIGHTS
## AND COUNTER-RIGHTS

In the course of researching this book, I have come across so many claimed rights that I thought it might be useful to list some of them, along with claimed counter-rights.

| Right | Counter-Right |
|---|---|
| Right to life of fetus | Right to choose abortion |
| Right to life of dying person | Right to assisted suicide |
| Right not to be executed | Right to have loved one avenged |
| Right to pray in public school | Right not to have religion established |
| Right to be well fed | Rights of animals not to be eaten |
| Right to keep and bear arms | Right to safe streets |
| Rights of criminal defendants | Rights of victims |
| Right to free speech | Right not to be offended |

| Right | Counter-Right |
|---|---|
| Right to keep one's money | Right to equitable distribution of wealth |
| Right-to-work law | Right to collectively bargain |
| Right to sexual privacy | Right to a moral society |
| Right to influence elections by voters | Right to equality of all contributions |
| Right to be a free agent in sports | Right of team to continuity |
| Right of employee to a four-day work week | Right of employer to labor of employee |
| Right to privacy and anonymity on Internet | Right to know who is criticizing you |
| Right to confidentiality (lawyer, minister, doctor, rape counselor, etc.) | Right to subpoena relevant information |
| Right of parents to control access to children | Right of grandparents to visit grandchildren |
| Parental right to remove child from school for religious reasons | Right of child to education and to choose different life from parents |
| Right of parent to refuse medical treatment for child on religious grounds | Right of child to live and choose different religion |
| Right of parent to discipline child harshly | Right of child to be free from abuse |
| Connubial rights of husband | Right of wife to refuse |
| Right to smoke | Right not to be subject to secondhand smoke |
| Right to a clean environment | Right to a job that would be eliminated by environmental concerns |
| Right to a bilingual education | Right to linguistic uniformity |
| Right to an organ from a dead person | Right of dead person to be buried with organs |
| Right of parents to know of underage daughter's abortion | Right of daughter to choose abortion without parents knowing |
| Right to choice of doctors | Right to equal medical care |
| Right not to be tested for DNA | Right to evidence of innocence |
| Right to build a church, synagogue, mosque, etc., in neighborhood | Right to residential control |
| Right to integrated neighborhood | Right to live in homogeneous neighborhood |
| Right to proselytize | Right to be free from proselytization |
| Right to treatment | Right to refuse treatment |
| Right to confidentiality of tax information | Right to relevant information |
| Rights of animals | Rights of humans to use animals for medical experimentation |
| Right to genetic privacy | Right of insurer or employer to assess risks |

| Right | Counter-Right |
|---|---|
| Right of defendant to have victim's body disinterred for DNA testing | Right of victim's family to peace for victim's body |
| Right of rape victim to have defendant tested for sexually transmitted diseases | Right of defendant to presumption of innocence and privacy |
| Right of rape victim to have her identity undisclosed | Right of defendant to disclose name of alleged victim in order to elicit challenge to her credibility |
| Right of gay couple to adopt | Right of child to be adopted by heterosexual family |
| Right to quote from and parody any written work | Copyright of author |
| Right of owner to alter art | Right of artist to integrity of his art |
| Right to know of sex offenders in neighborhood (Megan's Law) | Right of privacy after serving sentence |
| Right to your name and identity | Property right in domain names fairly purchased |
| Right to prevent stranger from changing his name to yours | Right to choose an identity |
| Right to express sexist, racist, homophobic, and other bigoted views | Right to be free from a hostile environment |
| Right to jury nullification | Right to equal protection of law |
| Right to procreate without limits | Right to live in an uncrowded world |
| Right to borrow money without interest (or excessive interest) | Right to make profit on risk |
| Right to refuse to testify against your child, parent, spouse, friend, etc. | Right to everyone's testimony |
| Right to a hand recount of machine votes | Right to a final machine vote without "subjective" human recount |
| Right to be free from racial or ethnic profiling | Right to be safe from hijackers and other criminals |
| Right to anonymity | Right to be protected from identity theft by a foolproof national identity card |

# SEVEN

# RIGHTS AND INTERESTS

---

*In 1999 two eminent law professors articulated a provocative theory of rights, growing out of the serious problems confronted by many inner-city African Americans who live in high-crime areas. Focusing on the housing projects of Chicago, Professors Tracey L. Meares and Dan M. Kahan argued that a civil libertarian approach to the Fourth Amendment — which protects against unreasonable searches — endangers the right of inner-city residents to a safe living environment.[1] I was asked to comment on their proposal — which would, essentially, empower a majority of inner-city residents to abrogate the Fourth Amendment rights of the minority — and my response criticizes their concept of rights and seeks to distinguish individual rights from group interests.*

---

PROFESSORS MEARES AND KAHAN PRESENT A PAROCHIAL, Afro-centric view of rights that reminds me of the question my grandmother used to ask when I would joyously tell her that the Brooklyn Dodgers had won the pennant: "Is that good or bad for the Jews?" Professors Meares and Kahan seem to judge every application of legal rights by whether it is good or bad for the majority of inner-city blacks in the 1990s. But rights are not, as Justice Robert Jackson once reminded us, like a limited railroad ticket: good for this train at this day only. They are designed for all people and for an enduring period of time.

The Meares-Kahan essay begins with a historical error. The rights about which they speak did not grow exclusively out of an effort to remedy institutionalized racism. Rights do have histories, and the right of every American to be secure against unlawful police intrusion grew out of a long history of governmental abuse against disempowered people of all backgrounds. The 1960s followed on the heels of Mc-Carthyism and of earlier anti-immigration and nativist abuses. Moreover, there was no revolution of *rights* with regard to police practices in the 1960s. The real revolution of the 1960s involved *remedies*. The rights had long been established, but they were being ignored in practice. By enforcing these old rights with new remedies — most particularly, exclusionary rules and required warnings applicable to state as well as federal cases — the courts were fulfilling promises made earlier. Even back then the majority of blacks, like the majority of whites, did not agree that guilty defendants should go free because their rights had been violated. Meares and Kahan have found nothing new when they tell us, with the breathless enthusiasm of discovery, that the majority of law-abiding blacks — like the majority of law-abiding whites — want the police to have more power, want the courts to stop freeing the guilty, and want civil libertarians to mind their own suburban business.

Nor is there anything new about groups with agendas seeking to undercut inconvenient rights that interfere with their agendas. Recall the impatience many feminists had with the First Amendment's protection of pornography, or that many Jews had with the First Amendment's protection of Nazi marchers and Holocaust deniers. Rights, especially for those suspected of doing or saying bad things, are always inconvenient and rarely garner the support of a majority of any community.

Taken to its logical conclusion, the Meares-Kahan hypothesis would allow a majority of believers in a given community to require Christian prayer in the public schools. After all, in their words, "because these [non-Christian] individuals had every chance to voice their opposition in the political process, and because there is every reason to believe that the majority — whose members were affected in exactly the same way — gave due weight to the dissenters' interests, there's no good reason for courts to second guess the community's determination that [compelled prayer] strikes a fair balance." The same could be said for a community that did not want *Playboy* magazine to be sold in its neighborhood stores, or for Communists or Jehovah's Witnesses to disturb its tranquillity.

Meares and Kahan prefer "group rights"— in this case the right of a majority of law-abiding black inner-city residents — over individual rights: in this case the rights of individuals who do not wish to be subjected to random searches or be told when to go home. But "group rights" is an oxymoron. Groups, especially those with increasing political power, have interests and agendas, but they may not implement them by ignoring the rights of individuals, especially those within these groups who are disempowered and despised.

Throughout their essay, Meares and Kahan use phrases such as "the residents," "the individuals most intimately affected," "the community," "minority residents," "these very citizens," and other group references to make the point that those who are most affected by the challenged police practices, in fact, consent to them. But that is beside the point: if those who are searched are willing to consent, the search is ipso facto lawful. If those who are asked to go home after 11:00 P.M. willingly do so, there is no constitutional violation. The conflict occurs precisely because some individuals refuse to consent. It is their rights that come into conflict with the interests of the majority. It is no answer to say they consented, unless we accept the proposition — rejected by most rights theories — that a majority can consent for an unwilling minority.

The Meares-Kahan approach is part of a dangerous new vocabulary of rights disguised to undercut the traditional approach taken by our Constitution, not in the 1960s, but in the 1790s. Rights are traditionally directed against *governmental* abuses. They are designed to limit the power of the state, especially the police. They are negative rights: "the *state* may *not* . . ." This conception of rights grows out of the lesson of history that teaches that in the long run, abuses by the state are far more dangerous to liberty and democracy than individual criminal conduct, dangerous and disturbing as that is. Now there are those who would introduce a new vocabulary of positive-sounding rights (some of which are cataloged in the previous chapter). The effect of these new positive-sounding rights is to trump traditional negative rights. The implications of this process are limitless. Creative lawyers can come up with an antiright disguised as a positive right to counteract virtually every traditional right. That is why the Meares-Kahan approach is so dangerous, not only to the Fourth Amendment, but to the rest of the Bill of Rights as well.

Meares and Kahan ignore these legitimate concerns, preferring instead to erect the straw man of paternalism. I have never heard a genuine civil libertarian make the absurd and demeaning paternalistic argument attributed to us by Meares and Kahan:

> Civil Libertarians have an answer to these questions too: no. The judgment and "self-respect" of inner-city residents, they maintain, has been deformed by social deprivation. Consequently, they lack the capacity to make critical assessments of curfews, gang-loitering ordinances, building searches, and similar policies.

The argument I make is that civil liberties must not be changed in every decade to serve the immediate interests — legitimate as they may be — of a majority of one particular community. I am prepared to accept the conclusion (unsupported as it may be) that the statutes and regulations advocated by Meares and Kahan are good for a majority of inner-city blacks today. That is surely a factor in assessing their constitutionality. But there are other factors as well, considering the long-term precedential impact of legitimizing such practices and undercutting centuries of development of rights and remedies. I am not siding with white "suburban residents." Indeed, my personal aesthetic favors curfews in my neighborhood (except when they are selectively enforced against minorities, as they often are). But I want these laws judged not by a transient majority of one particular ethnic group but by our long history of abuse of police discretion and the continuing danger of unchecked government power.

If Meares and Kahan are correct that rights established (or remedies strengthened) in the 1960s continue to have an impact (a negative one, in their parochial view) in the 1990s, then it would seem to follow that rights abolished (or remedies curtailed) in the 1990s will continue to have an impact in the twenty-first century. Our framers wrote a Bill of Rights not for one decade or one group of citizens but as an enduring limitation on government. Rights are intended to evolve with changing realities. Meares and Kahan make a compelling case for rethinking the application of rights to certain specific statutes and police actions. But in the process of such rethinking, we must reject their broadside attack on individual rights and their voguish notion that long-entrenched safeguards against excesses of state power should be subordinated to the transient interests of majorities (even majorities within minorities), over the valid objections of minorities (even minorities within minorities).

So let me close with a direct answer to the "real question" Meares and Kahan put to civil libertarians: "Why can't we trust residents of the inner city to decide for themselves?" We can and should (just as we should for all other residents), provided, however, that their decisions recognize the individual constitutional rights of those affected residents who disagree with the majority. That is what distinguishes rights from interests, in a constitutional democracy with an entrenched Bill of Rights.

# EIGHT

# DO GRANDPARENTS
# HAVE RIGHTS?

*In 2000 the Supreme Court decided a case that raised the issue of whether parents had the constitutional right to deny grandparents visitation. In writing about this vexing issue — before the case was decided — I speculated about the natural-law basis of the claimed constitutional right.*

THERE ARE FEW MORE DIFFICULT AND EMOTIONAL FAMILY issues than whether grandparents ought to be able to visit their grandchildren over the objection of the children's parents. That issue was presented in a case challenging the constitutionality of a Washington State statute that empowers the courts to order limited visitation rights to nonparents under specified circumstances. The case arose from the refusal of a woman to allow her son's paternal grandparents reasonable visitation, after the child's father — her late husband, their late son — died and the woman remarried.

Difficult as this issue may be — as a matter of morality — it poses a relatively simple constitutional issue. There is not a word, syllable, suggestion, or innuendo in the Constitution that controls, or even informs, this question. Nor are there any binding constitutional precedents or history on this point. The high court has, of course, talked about "parental rights" in relation to the state, the schools, and other outside institutions but not in relation to grandparents who also claim some parental or family rights. Reasonable people can and should disagree — as a matter of policy — on what the correct answer is. The state of Washington, presumably after considering all sides of this issue, came down in favor of limited grandparental rights, as forty-seven other states have also done. That should resolve the question as a

matter of constitutional law. Where there is no constitutional prohibition on a particular answer and when a state legislature acts reasonably in arriving at an answer, the Supreme Court has no business
second-guessing the state's answer. Only an unreconstructed judicial
activist — a judge who believes in substituting his own personal moral
philosophy for that of duly elected legislators — would even consider
striking down the Washington statute, or the statute of another state
that came to the opposite conclusion and prohibited grandparents
from visiting grandchildren over the objection of parents. Justice
Louis Brandeis, a paragon of judicial restraint, understood that states
must be accorded considerable flexibility so that they can be "labora-
tories" of social experimentation. States should be free to come to differing conclusions on divisive and controversial issues not governed by
the Constitution.

It remains to be seen whether those justices who claim the mantle of
judicial restraint in theory will be able to constrain themselves in practice. It will be especially interesting to watch those judges who are always railing against judicial activism, especially in cases where judicial
restraint reinforces their personal and political views. Newspaper reports of the recent oral argument suggest that Justice Antonin Scalia
may shed the skin of restraint and become a full-blown judicial activist
of the kind he — and most Republican politicians — consistently con-
demns. Getting the issue exactly backward, he asked where "courts get
the power" to intervene in the affairs of families. The answer is simple:
from the Washington State legislature. The real question is: Where
does the United States Supreme Court get the power to intervene in a
pure matter of state law, on which the United States Constitution is
completely silent? Justice Scalia is always asking lawyers who argue before him to point to the words of the Constitution that deny the state
the power to act. He should ask himself that question in this case.[1]

The only honest basis for overruling the state's legislative decision
to strike a proper balance between grandparental and parental rights
lies in the nebulous notion of natural law. But natural law knows no
bounds, and if it were ever to be recognized as a source of authority —
outside the Constitution — for striking down state legislation, then judicial activism would truly become legitimated. "Natural law" is little
more than a matter of personal opinion or belief dressed up as the objective law of nature or God. One judge's notion of what is natural is

another's sense of what is unnatural. Denying good grandparents the right to have contact with their loving grandchildren strikes many as unnatural. But that is beside the point in a nation governed by the Constitution, not natural law.

What else but Scalia's personal view — his sense of natural law — could have led him to make the following categorical statement: "The child does not belong to the courts. The child belongs to the parents." Few will agree with that proprietary concept. A child is not a commodity that *belongs* to anyone. Courts traditionally resolve disputes within the family, and the family has never been limited — as a matter of constitutional law — to the mother and her new husband, without any regard for the dead father's wishes and parents.

A decision striking down the Washington statute — as it applies to grandparents in the situation presented by this case — would find it difficult to ground its reasoning in the language of history or the Constitution. It could only do so by elevating the personal moral views of a majority of the justices over those of a majority of legislators in the state of Washington. If that's not judicial activism, I don't know what is.

# NINE

# DO (SHOULD) ANIMALS
# HAVE RIGHTS?

---

*One way of thinking about issues such as compulsory organ donation after death, and even about the cannibalism of dead bodies, is to ask the question, Does a dead body have rights? Or do only living human beings have rights, including the right to see the bodies of their fellow human beings treated with respect? Thinking about these questions stimulated me to write the following essay, never before published, on the related question of whether animals have rights.*

---

WHEN WE TALK ABOUT ANIMAL RIGHTS, WHAT DO WE MEAN? Do we mean that the animals themselves have rights, such as not to be tortured? Or do we mean that human beings have the right not to experience the torturing of animals? Whose right is it? And does it really matter?

One of the first laws of the Bible prohibits the eating of animals that are still alive (Genesis 10:4). The Bible also prohibits human beings from copulating with animals (Exodus 21:19, Leviticus 17:23). These rules would seem to be designed for the protection of vulnerable animals, but another rule requires the execution of the nonconsenting animal with which a man or woman has copulated (Leviticus 20:15–16). Animal sacrifices are also mandated throughout the Bible, along with humane slaughter laws. Taken together, these rules suggest that they are ritualistic in nature, designed more to keep human beings pure and holy and less to protect the rights of the animals themselves. Indeed, the Bible explicitly declares that humans should "rule over" the animals, and that the animals are "given into" the hands of humans (Genesis 1:28, 9:2).

In theory, a divine- or natural-law approach could include rights that inhere in animals, since rights come from an external source — God or nature — that could bestow them on any being or object. God could grant rights to trees, rivers, forests, or animals. Nature could also be as inclusive as those who purport to interpret it choose to be. Positive law, too, could enact rights for nonhumans, but any such rights would be the product of human decision making. It would be human beings who decided to extend rights beyond their species.

There are other examples — none completely analogous — of decisions by those in a position to create rights to bestow them on others who are not part of the rights-granting process. Benevolent despots have granted limited rights to their nonvoting subjects, as have slaveholders to slaves, male voters to female nonvoters, adults to children, the mentally competent to the incompetent, and so on. Even though the recipients of these rights did not participate in the process that bestowed them, the rights *belonged* to the subjects, the slaves, the females, the children, and the incompetent, who had standing to invoke them, even against their superiors.

We can understand the concept of rights as applied to other human beings, even if we treat them as subordinates politically, legally, and in other ways. But it is far more difficult to think about the concept of rights as applied to nonhumans. When we say, metaphorically, that trees, rivers, and forests have rights, we plainly mean that human beings have rights in relation to the preservation of these natural treasures. Our grandchildren and great-grandchildren, who are not yet here to vote, have the right to be left a planet that is not polluted or otherwise destroyed. That is *their* human right, as it is ours, but it does not belong to any particular tree, river, or forest.

Animals are different. They suffer, they feel, they fear, they remember. At least, some of them do. As Oliver Wendell Holmes Jr. once observed, "Even a dog distinguishes between being stumbled over and being kicked." We can understand the statement "a cat has the right not to be tortured" far more than we can give meaning to the argument that "a tree has the right not to be cut up into small pieces." As sentient beings, we can identify with the pain and fear of a tortured animal. But does that mean the animal has (or should have) a right not to be tortured? Or merely that we, as humans, have the right to live in a society that does not tolerate the torture of animals?[1] (Another, even more pragmatic human-centered approach to the prohibition against torturing animals might be based on the empirical assertion that permitting the torture of animals might encourage violence against human beings, or that those who torture animals are more likely to move on to human victims.)

It does make a difference how we think about this right, perhaps not so much in the context of gratuitous torture — which would be prohibited under any reasonable theory — but surely in the context of eating animal flesh, wearing their skins, and experimenting with their bodies. If the right belongs to the animal itself, then we must ask why we are (or should be) permitted to kill an animal for our culinary or fashion pleasure if others are not permitted to torture them for their more perverse pleasure. If the right belongs to human beings, then there may be a stronger argument for balancing it against human needs and desires, such as good nutrition, a tasty meal, a fashionable coat, or a cure for a human disease. But if the right belongs to the animal itself, how can we, who vote, strike the appropriate balance between our needs and the right of the animal, who doesn't get to vote on it?

There is also the theoretical question of where the rights of animals would come from? Surely there can be no social contract between humans and animals. The Kantian imperative and the Benthamite calculus appear to be limited to humans. How can animals be placed in John Rawls's "original position"? Any reference to nature would immediately deny animals all rights, since the law of the jungle is power based, not rights based. And it was God who ordained man's supremacy over the animals and his right to eat them (or at least some of them) and domesticate them, subject only to certain ritual limitations. Some of these ritual limitations imply a concern for the animal itself: rules of slaughter and the commandment requiring a day of rest for domestic beasts. But the object of these restrictions seems to be the humans on whom the limitations are placed rather than the animals themselves. Indeed, most religious-based rights are human centered precisely because humans are deemed to have souls, which animals lack. Those who advocate a more secular natural-rights theory might substitute the terms *consciousness* or *sentience* for *soul* but would still distinguish sharply between humans and other species in terms of rights.

For those who reject the categorical distinctions ordained by God or by the external mandates of nature, there can be no sharp natural line between humans and animals. We are on a continuum of soulfulness, consciousness, sentience, and capacity to feel fear and pain. There are some animals closer to the human end of that continuum than some human beings. Yet we insist on creating a separate category for *all* human beings. It is murder to willfully kill the most mentally impaired human being, and it is not murder to kill the most educated and feeling primate or dolphin. We insist on maintaining (or constructing) this sharp dividing line because we fear the uncertainties of the continuum. Once we allow any member of our species to be treated as we treat any member of a "lower" species, we empower humans to make their own decisions about the "worth" of other humans.

The dangers of a continuum approach to human worth are well illustrated by the history of our use, and misuse, of animals. In the beginning, animals were used to preserve human life. We needed their flesh to prevent us from starving, their skin and fur to protect us from freezing, and their bones to use as essential tools. Today animals are still used for human survival in some parts of the world, but in most places, they mainly enhance the quality of life. We use them for testing cosmetics and other unnecessary luxuries. We also use them for medical purposes, some potentially lifesaving, others life enhancing. For many people, the lives of animals are simply not important. If we can use animals for *any* purpose, we can use them for *every* purpose — short of the infliction of gratuitous pain. For some, drawing a line about the proper use of animals is crucial to leading a moral life, though they differ as to where the line should be drawn. There are strict vegetarians, who will eat no animal flesh, and even stricter vegans, who will consume no animal products. Then there are those who draw the line at mammals, or primates, or animals with "faces." Some will eat animal flesh but won't wear fur. Others will eat animals but not hunt them, while still others will hunt plentiful animals (deer) but not scarce or endangered ones (whales). Some favor animal experimentation for health but not cosmetic benefits. A small number of people oppose pet "ownership," preferring "guardianship." There are groups opposed to circuses, rodeos, horse racing, zoos, and horseback riding. At the extremes, there are proponents of cock-fighting, bearbaiting, and even animal sacrifices, as well as opponents of clearing rain forests, jungles, and other animal habitats to satisfy human needs. There are even those who argue that great apes should have human rights.[2]

Once we place the worth of animal life on a continuum, everything becomes a matter of degree. There are no natural or inherent criteria for where the appropriate lines should be drawn. It becomes largely a matter of personal taste. Human life can, of course, also be a matter of degree, as evidenced by the debates over when life begins and ends; whether it is proper to take the life of murderers or aggressors; when it is permissible to engage in just wars, proactive self-defense, and other life-and-death issues that have divided humankind over the millennia. But it is the near-universal view that human life has a high value, which may be balanced only against other high values. That is not the near-universal view regarding animal life. We certainly do not want humans to treat other humans in the way that we, as a species, have long treated animals.

To avoid this, we have made the somewhat arbitrary decision to single out our own species — every single member of it — for different and better treatment. Does this subject us to the charge of speciesism? Of course it does, and we cannot justify it except by the fact that in the world in which we live, humans make the rules. That reality imposes on us a special responsibility to be fair and compassionate to those on whom we impose our rules. Hence the argument for animal rights.

The best case for animal rights, in my view, derives from the history and experiences of human beings. Those societies that treat animal life with greater respect tend also to treat human life with greater respect. It is preferable to live in a society that seeks to limit the suffering of animals than in one that does not. This does not necessarily mean that a vegetarian society will always be better than a carnivorous one. Hitler, it is said, was a vegetarian, and the SS surely treated their dogs better than they treated the Jews and Gypsies. Nor is it an argument against necessary medical experimentation on animals, since history and experience have shown that societies that take animal life to preserve human life can be good and caring places in which to live — at least for humans! It is merely a claim that the gratuitous infliction of pain on animals is bad for humans, and its toleration is bad for any human society. This is the soft case for a human-centered approach to animal rights. It requires that when human beings balance their perceived needs against the interests of animals, we must take into account their suffering and seek to minimize it (as we should take into account and try to minimize environmental damage when we create jobs and businesses). This soft case for human-centered animal rights recognizes what decent human beings have been doing for millennia, and it postpones the ultimate decision about how we should relate to animals to a future time when our history and experience no longer make them necessary for human use as food, clothing, or experimental subjects.

Thinking about animal rights also helps clarify the arguments about human rights.

# TEN

# RIGHTS IN A WORLD WITHOUT GOD

*In 1999 the* Harvard Law Review *celebrated the fiftieth anniversary of publication of Lon Fuller's masterful law school hypothetical, the case of the Spelunkean Explorers. In that case, set two thousand years in the future, a group of cave explorers gets trapped in a landslide and they will all starve to death unless they eat one of their number, which they ultimately do after throwing dice. The survivors are eventually rescued and put on trial for murder. As part of the celebration, several law professors were asked to write hypothetical opinions in an appeal from their conviction. My hypothetical "opinion," written by the fictional Justice DeBunker, explores the future of rights in a world without religion or natural law. We have become so accustomed to thinking about law as being natural that in introducing my opinion, Professor David Shapiro found it difficult to credit any view that assumed the eventual rejection of natural law.*[1]

DeBunker, J.

## I. Overview

This case raises disturbing questions about the continuing influence of such anachronistic concepts as natural law, inalienable rights, and other legal fictions of ages past. We have yet to reject these irrational residues of the past even in the present fifth millennium (a system of dating that itself is based on what we now recognize to be a religious myth).

As is well known from the history disks, shortly after the beginning of the third millennium, the world became engulfed in religious warfare between fundamentalist Christians, Muslims, Jews, and others.

Apocalyptic religious extremists obtained access to weapons of mass destruction. The result was the cataclysmic decimation of human life in the name of the various "gods" under whose symbols — crosses, crescents, and stars — the slaughters were implemented. The survivors of this apocalypse began to realize that the religious myths surrounding such deities as the Holy Spirit, Allah, and Jehovah were indistinguishable from those that had surrounded the gods of ancient Egypt, Greece, and Rome. Gradually, a new consensus emerged, at first questioning the existence of any supernatural god (the Agnostic Epoch or AGEP), and then, in the current age, disclaiming any such belief in deities (the Atheistic Epoch or ATEP).[2] Just as the Christian, Muslim, and Jewish primitives of the first and second millennia regarded the Greek and Roman myths of divinity, so too our enlightened age regards the myths of the so-called monotheistic religions — myths such as the divine origin of the Bible, the divine paternity of Jesus, and the claim that Muhammad was a messenger of God.[3] We appreciate the poetry and occasional insights of the Bible and the often wonderful teachings of the so-called Hebrew prophets, Jesus, and Muhammad — much as the monotheists of the first and second millennia appreciated the religious art and literature of their polytheistic forebears — but we now know for certain that they are entirely of human origin.

We know, too, that the world has no "purpose," at least as imposed by some external superior force. Human beings are the product of essentially random processes, such as evolution, genetic mutations, or other largely nonpurposive factors.

We have long understood these self-evident truths, and we apply them to most areas of our lives, such as science, education, and literature. But when it comes to law, we have stubbornly resisted the necessary process of rooting out of our current legal system the anachronistic remnants of the divine mythologies of our past. We persist in speaking about "natural law," as if the physical "laws" of nature carried with them any normative corollaries. We continue to invoke "inalienable rights," as if we believed that they derived from some preexisting, supernatural, nonhuman source.

Because this case raises questions that challenge the very basis of our laws, I see it as an appropriate vehicle for considering the meaning of such concepts as natural law and inalienable rights in a world free of superstitions about divine beings, supernatural forces, and purposive creation.

I am convinced that in such a world — in our world — there can be no such meaningful concepts as natural law or inalienable rights. Natural law presupposes a view of nature — of the nature of human beings and of the world — that is demonstrably false. The nature of human beings is so diverse — ranging from the most amoral and predatory to the most moral and self-sacrificing — that all or no normative conclusions can be drawn from its descriptive diversity.

Inalienable rights presuppose an externally imposed hierarchy that makes no sense in the absence of an external lawgiver. We must now acknowledge that all law must be positive law and all rights must merely be strongly held preferences that we or our predecessors have agreed to elevate over other positive law. This elevated status of particular laws — such as the guarantee of free speech — can be the result of a constitution (written or oral), an entrenched tradition, or another form of superpositive law. It cannot come from any claim of supernatural or natural forces external to the human processes of lawmaking. Thus, the only basis for preferring one set of laws or rights over another is human persuasion and advocacy.

In this opinion, I will try to persuade others to accept my approach, not by reference to some natural or supernatural authority, but, rather, exclusively by reference to human reason and agreed-upon principles. These principles may take the form of preferred imperatives, such as those proposed by ancient philosophers, including Immanuel Kant, or they may take the form of preferred situational rules, such as those proposed by Jeremy Bentham and others. But they are all merely human preferences, even if often articulated in the language of natural law and inalienable rights.[4]

## II. Discussion

How, then, should a supreme court, unencumbered by concepts of natural law or inalienable rights, evaluate the actions that form the basis of this case? First, some preliminary observations are necessary: A civilized society could reasonably legislate either result advocated by my judicial colleagues. The legislature could have, if it had anticipated the current problem, written a clear, positive law explicitly prohibiting starving people from killing one of their number in order to save the rest. The arguments in favor of and in opposition to such a rule are fairly obvious and have been made over the ages.[5] Yet our legislature has never explicitly resolved this millennia-old debate by enacting legislation either prohibiting or permitting such lifesaving killings. My preference in this situation is for the following rule of law: when a tragic choice is sufficiently recurring so that it can be anticipated, and when reasonable people over time have disagreed over whether a given choice should be permissible, the onus must be on the legislature to prohibit that choice by the enactment of positive law if it wishes to do so.

For those who argue that such a positive law would be ineffective because it is against the self-preservatory nature of human beings, there is a simple answer: legislate creative punishments that will be effective. Such punishments might include posthumous shame,[6] deprivation of inheritance rights for offspring, or enhanced painful punishments for survivors. The point is that the argument of ineffectiveness is largely an empirical, rather than a moral, objection to prohibiting the eating of one starving human to save others.[7]

A civilized society could also legislate a positive law permitting (even requiring) the sacrifice of one starving innocent person to save several others. The arguments in support of such a law are also obvious and long-standing. As Oliver Wendell Holmes Jr. reportedly wrote, "All society has rested on the death of men and must rest on that or on the prevention of the lives of a good many." Objections, such as the slippery slope argument, are also commonplace.

The point is that neither approach is more "natural" than the other. Nor can the case be resolved by reference to any inalienable right, such as the right to life. Both approaches claim to be natural and to further the right to life. Both also have considerable moral and empirical advantages and disadvantages, and no one in our society is inherently better suited to choose one over the other than anyone else.[8] Yet a choice must be made. Accordingly, we move the argument from the level of substance to the level of process: who shall be authorized to make such decisions, on what bases shall they be made, and if there are gaps in the primary decision making, who shall be authorized to fill the gaps in particular cases? These issues must also be matters of preference and persuasion.

The problem presented by this case has existed since the beginning of recorded history. There are examples — at differing levels of abstraction — in numerous works of history, religion, and literature. Why then did the representative body that was authorized to enact general laws not specifically address this recurring issue? To be sure, the issue does not occur with the frequency of self-defense, but it is widely enough known to be capable of specific inclusion in any modern code governing homicide. Indeed, one of the most ancient of legal codes — the Talmud — did include specific discussions of this and related questions.[9] Philosophers and legal scholars have also considered these issues over the years. Yet few, if any, criminal codes explicitly tell starving cave explorers, sailors, or space travelers what they may, should, or must do if they find themselves in the unenviable position in which these defendants found themselves. It is to be noted that this case is not unlike one that occurred in the ninth century of the second millennium in a nation then known as Great Britain.[10] Yet even after the divided court in that case expressed considerable difficulty in arriving at a principled decision based upon those facts, the legislature did not enact a positive law to resolve the issue definitively. Nor can the legislature's silence in the face of the nominal affirmance of that conviction be deemed evidence of its intent to demand conviction in this case. The vast majority of comparable cases — both before and after that decision — resulted in acquittal or decisions not to prosecute, and the English case produced a pardon. The law is more than the isolated decisions of a small number of appellate courts.

What does this long history of legislative abdication of responsibility tell us about how we, a court, should resolve this case? It tells us that the people do not seem to want this issue resolved in the abstract by legislation. Our elected representatives apparently prefer not to legislate general approval or disapproval of the course of action undertaken by the defendants here. Our citizens cannot bring themselves to say that eating one's neighbor in the tragic situation presented here is morally just. Nor can they bring themselves to say it is unjust. They would prefer to leave the decision, as an initial matter, to the people in the cave (at least as long as they make it on some rational and fair basis). Then they would have a prosecutor decide whether to prosecute, a jury whether to convict, a court whether to affirm, and an executive whether to pardon or commute. That is the unwieldy process, composed of layers of decision makers, they seem to have chosen.

The question still remains: By what criteria should we, the Supreme Court, decide whether to affirm the jury's conviction (and recommendation for clemency)? The answer seems relatively obvious to me, and I will try to persuade others to agree with the preferences on which it is based. I begin with my strong preference — a preference that I believe and hope is now widely shared — for a society in which any act that is not specifically prohibited is implicitly permitted, rather than for a society in which any act that is not specifically permitted is implicitly prohibited. As Johann Christoph Friedrich von Schiller similarly expressed, "Whatever is not forbidden is permitted."[11] The lessons of history have demonstrated why the former is to be preferred over the latter.

A general preference for freedom of action in the absence of specific prohibition does, however, raise some troubling problems. Innovative harm-doers often find ways to do mischief between the interstices of positive law, and old laws have difficulty keeping up with new technologies. Accordingly, this preference occasionally results in the failure to punish the initial group of creative criminals in any particular genre. Still, I would argue for a strong presumption in favor of freedom in the absence of a specific prohibition — even at the cost of letting some guilty go free.

In any event, the problem outlined above does not describe the situation we face. The actions committed by these defendants were not part of some technological innovation unknowable to the drafters of our positive law. Our drafters could easily have legislated against what the defendants did here. They did not. Why they did not — laziness, thoughtlessness, cowardice, superstition, or an unwillingness to resolve an intractable moral dilemma — is in the realm of speculation. That they did not is not fairly open to doubt. Some may argue, of course, that the general prohibition against willful killing is enough to cover the conduct at issue here because this killing was willful.[12] But I do not believe that it can be reasonably maintained that the absence of an explicit exception to the broad prohibition against killing contained in the positive law must be interpreted as an implicit prohibition against the kind of killing done here. That mode of reasoning would substantially compromise the principle that what is not specifically prohibited is implicitly permitted, especially in the context of a widely reported and debated historical genre of alleged crime such as the killing under consideration here.

Moreover, the law has long recognized justifications for taking actions expressly prohibited by the letter of the law when such actions are "necessary" to prevent a "greater harm." This principle has been summarized by the quip "Necessity knows no law."[13] It is a mischaracterization, however, because there is a well-developed, if imprecise, law of necessity that permits the choice of a lesser harm to prevent a greater harm.[14] Throughout history, philosophers and jurists have debated cases — both hypothetical and real — that tested this difficult principle. During the Nazi Holocaust of the second millennium, a group of Jews who were hiding from Nazi killers smothered a crying baby in order to prevent the Nazis from discovering their hiding places and killing them all. When that terrible dilemma — which occurred in slightly differing contexts throughout the Holocaust — was presented to distinguished religious leaders, the consensus was that the conduct could not be condemned.[15] Nor do I believe that a secular court would have found these desperate people guilty of murder even if they willfully, deliberately, and with premeditation killed the innocent baby.[16]

Necessity as a general defense to crime "seems clearly to have standing as a common law defense."[17] Nearly all jurisdictions recognize the necessity defense for crimes that are short of killing.[18] Thus, if our defendants had found a locked food-storage box in the cave with a sign saying Private, Personal Property, Do Not Open Under Any Circumstances, and they had broken open the lock and eaten the food, no one would deny they were acting lawfully. I doubt that any of my colleagues would convict such defendants of theft even if the words of the theft statute provided for no exception. The general law of necessity provides the requisite exception in cases in which theft is a lesser evil than multiple deaths. However, some jurisdictions have explicitly refused to extend the necessity defense to the killing of an innocent person that is necessary to prevent the deaths of several innocent people.[19] Other jurisdictions have not limited the necessity defense to non-killings.[20] Academic opinion is divided, and the weight of the American Law Institute is on the side of not limiting the defense as long as the killing is necessary and results in the saving of more innocent lives than are taken. "The principle of necessity is one of general validity. . . . It would be particularly unfortunate to exclude homicidal conduct from the scope of the defense."[21] The reason that judicial decisions about this issue are "rare" is that prosecutors almost never bring charges against people who have chosen the lesser evil of taking one life to save many others.

Our jurisdiction has not resolved this debate or even confronted this issue. Our own common law of necessity is thus written in terms as general as our murder statute: "Anyone who commits an act that would otherwise be a crime under circumstances in which it is necessary to prevent a greater evil shall not be guilty." The issue before us, therefore, is whether the legislative silence should be interpreted as acceptance or rejection of the limitation adopted by some jurisdictions and rejected by others. Compounding the complexity of the problem is the fact that in the absence of legislative resolution, these defendants sought authoritative guidance from various sources before deciding what to do — the best they could do under the circumstances. They were denied any such guidance. To hold them criminally liable is to convict them of guessing wrongly regarding what the unpredictable vote of this Court would be. Moreover, to convict them under these circumstances — especially in the face of our legislature's refusal to resolve the debate over the limits of the necessity defense — would be to prefer a rule of judicial interpretation that resolves doubts in favor of expanding the criminal law rather than of resolving "ambiguity concerning the ambit of criminal statutes . . . in favor of lenity."[22] The same rule of lenity must apply, as well, in construing the common law of crime.[23] Where does our Supreme Court get the authority to narrow the law of necessity and thereby to make criminal what the legislature has declined explicitly to proscribe? My brothers and sisters do not answer this question.

Of course, if the legislature had explicitly considered the "choice of evils" presented by the case and expressly foreclosed the action taken, the necessity defense would not be available. But as I have shown, our legislature has not explicitly spoken to this specific problem, despite its prominent place in legal and philosophical discourse.[24] Accordingly, applying the salutary rule placing the onus on the legislature to prohibit questionable conduct by specific, targeted language, it follows that these defendants may not lawfully be punished.

## III. The Views of My Colleagues

Several of my colleagues point to the plain language of the statute, while acknowledging that there must be exceptions, such as self-defense and executions, that are recognized from time to time as common law. But necessity also has been recognized from time to time, and there has been a great debate over the millennia regarding whether necessity can excuse a killing done to prevent greater harm, such as multiple deaths. Renowned authorities have come down on different sides of this debate, and our legislature has refused to resolve it explicitly. It is in this context that the words included in, and omitted from, the statute must be interpreted. That process can be undertaken in different ways.

One of my colleagues proposed an absolute rule of inclusion: unless there is an express exception, the literal words of the statute must apply, regardless of how absurd the result may appear to us. Taken to its logical conclusion, this rule would punish the proper use of deadly force by policemen because the statute does not explicitly exclude such killings.

It is important to recognize that the legislation at issue here is an example of a common-law statute prohibiting a general category of conduct — in this instance, willful killing — in the broadest of terms, while anticipating judicial narrowing. It cannot rationally be argued that the legislature intended the judiciary to recognize certain exceptions, such as self-defense, while precluding it from recognizing other defenses, such as necessity, that are accepted by numerous jurisdictions. Once it is agreed that this Court has the power to decide whether the defense of necessity is part of our law, it surely must follow that it has the power to define its parameters. It is plainly preferable to leave such decisions to the reasoned judgment of disinterested courts than to the unarticulated discretion of adversarial prosecutors.[25]

I am not suggesting that every possible category of crime be specifically mentioned in the statute but rather that widely recognized defenses, such as necessity, cannot be deemed to have been abrogated by legislative silence, especially when the statute seems to invite inclusion of some recognized defenses that are not explicitly mentioned.

Another of my colleagues proposed an "absurdity exception" to the otherwise absolute rule of plain meaning. This would permit prosecution in the following case: A train loses its brakes as it heads toward a fork in the tracks. If the engineer does nothing, the train will hit a school bus full of children. If he takes the fork, it will hit a drunk sleeping on the track. There is no third alternative. He takes the fork, thus killing the drunk. Convicting him would be wrong because his beneficent purpose was to save lives, but it would not be "absurd," because he intended to kill the drunk.[26]

Yet another of my colleagues tells us that all statutes must be interpreted by reference to a "right" whose source is nowhere identified, namely that "all individuals have the right to be protected against violence, including violence that is premised upon the moral calculation that the sacrifice will save more lives than it will take." This rule would permit prosecution not only of the train engineer but also of the hiding Jews who killed the baby in order to prevent their apprehension and murder by the Nazis. Would my colleagues really support their preferred rules in the face of these testing cases?

Another colleague also poses a provocative hypothetical case, which should be troubling to any thoughtful judge or legislator. She asks whether a reversal of this conviction would require the conclusion that a group of people in need of organs to live may properly kill one person in order to harvest his organs so that all in the group might live. It is a good question. One must begin with the conclusion that any general rule of law that would routinely permit the killing of a human being for his organs is a rule of law that should not be accepted by a civilized society. That certainly would be my strong preference. Our case can be distinguished from this one on several grounds. First, there is a universal consensus that killing for organs should be deemed unacceptable. I am aware of no dissent to this proposition in all of jurisprudence, philosophy, or even ancient religion.[27] There is considerable disagreement, however, concerning the Spelunkean case and its sister case involving the crying baby during the Nazi Holocaust. This difference in the level of agreement alone may distinguish the Spelunkean case from the organ case, though the reasons underlying it may bolster the difference in outcome. A second distinction between the organ donor case and this case is that in this case the victim would have died within days even if the defendants had not killed him. In the organ donor case, the murdered organ "donor" could have lived out his life. Thus, the issue in the instant case is not whether the victim would have died but only whether he was to die at the time he was killed so that others could live or whether he would die a few days later, in which case no one would have lived. Quite a difference! The instant case is closer to the situation in which a hijacked passenger jet is shot down to prevent it from crashing into a densely occupied building. Since the passengers would die anyway, it is morally justified — perhaps even mandatory — to deprive them of a few minutes of life in order to save the lives of many others. Third, among the most powerful reasons why we universally reject killing to harvest organs is that organ shortages are a widespread and continuing problem, as Justice West acknowledges.[28] Were we to approve the killing of a potential organ donor, no one would be safe. Everyone with a healthy lifesaving organ would be placed at risk by such a rule. The situation is quite different with our explorers, the crying baby, or the doomed passengers. Although these rare situations recur throughout history, they are unlikely to be experienced more than once in a long period of time. Whatever we decide in these unusual cases will have little or no impact on the future actions of the infinitesimally tiny number of people who may find themselves in the unexpected situation faced by our explorers, the hiding Jews, or the hijacked passengers. These are sui generis cases, about which, in the absence of explicit legislative resolution, we can afford to provide pure retrospective justice, without fear of establishing a dangerous precedent. To be sure, every case contributes to the corpus of precedents, and if the legislature disapproves of our decision, it may announce a rule of law that forbids killing in these situations. The reason the legislature has not explicitly done so for organ donor killing is that no one has ever tried — or, likely, would ever try — to raise a defense of necessity in such circumstances. Such a result would be "absurd," to paraphrase another of my colleagues, and legislators need not explicitly reject every "absurd" defense, especially when no one has ever tried to use it. The defense raised in our case, however, is not absurd and it has been raised and even accepted.[29] These are the differences. Does Justice West believe that smothering the crying baby and killing the person for his organs are really the same case? If not, is not the instant case closer to the former than to the latter?

## IV. CONCLUSION

I believe that those who would punish the conduct at issue here have the burden of acting to prohibit it explicitly and provide for the appropriate punishment.[30] That burden has not been satisfied by the inaction here.

Accordingly, I conclude that the principles expressed above require the conclusion that the killing committed by the defendants in this case cannot be deemed unlawful. The people in the cave could not look to the law for guidance. The statute was not explicit. The precedents cut both ways. They made every reasonable effort to obtain advance guidance from authoritative sources. In the end they had to decide for themselves. They did the best they could under the circumstances, selecting a process that was rational and fair. The end result was a net saving of lives. I cannot find it in my heart — and, more important, I cannot find it in the law — to condemn what they did. If there is disagreement with the preferences stated herein or with the conclusions derived therefrom, let the debate begin. I have an open mind, untrammeled by the "natural" and "supernatural" myths of the past.

---

*The terrorist attacks of September 11, 2001, have made the Spelunkean Explorers case somewhat easier. It is difficult to distinguish that case from the shooting down of a passenger jet that is about to be crashed into a crowded building. The criminal laws relied on by several of my colleagues do not provide an explicit exception for this kind of "homicide." If it would not be legal to remove dozens of life-giving organs from a person who has only minutes to live but who has not consented to the removal, how could it be legal to withdraw life itself from innocent passengers who have not consented to being shot down? Yet there is little disagreement with the pragmatic conclusion that it is legal and moral to shoot down the plane. This conclusion became evident as we experienced the reality of this new kind of terrorism.*

---

# ELEVEN

# THE RIGHT TO YOUR BODY
# AFTER DEATH

---

*In 2000 Nathaniel Philbrick published* In the Heart of the Sea: The Tragedy of the Whaleship Essex *(New York: Viking). Herman Melville based his novel* Moby Dick *on the sinking of the* Essex *by a giant whale. Melville's story ends with the sinking, but Philbrick recounts what happened to the survivors. As in the hypothetical case I wrote about in the previous chapter, the desperate men resorted to cannibalism and eventually to killing each other for food. Unlike in the previous chapter, and the actual British case on which it was based, there was no prosecution of the* Essex *survivors. Reading this book stimulated me to write the following essay, which is published here for the first time.*

---

LAW, RELIGION, CUSTOM, TRADITION, AND MORALITY ALL share in common certain mechanisms for influencing and improving human conduct — for making it less "natural." These mechanisms are premised on the assumption that in the absence of external rules of conduct, most humans would tend to act instinctively, which generally means selfishly (I define *selfish* to include family).[1] The rules are designed to discourage human beings from making individualized ad hoc decisions based on a selfish cost-benefit analysis of the particular situation confronting them. Instead, they impose on individuals the obligation to think more generally, more broadly, more categorically, more altruistically, and more communally — that is, more morally. Such rules prohibit different categories of acts. Some prohibit core evils, such as the killing of innocent people. Others prohibit acts that are not in themselves immoral but that are thought to lead to core evils. Such prohibited acts include driving too fast or while drunk. Yet other rules are designed simply to condition people to accept limitations — even artificial limitations — on their appetites or instincts. These include ritual restrictions on the eating of certain foods or the performance of certain ritually impure acts.

Consider, for example, the issue of cannibalism. Start first with the eating of a human being who has already died. Absent the constraints of law, morality, religion, and so on, any rational starving person — say, a sailor in a lifeboat, a soldier lost in a jungle, an entire city besieged and surrounded — would not think twice about eating the fresh meat of a dead person, any more than he or she would think about eating the fresh meat of a dead animal. Some might argue that it is "natural" for human beings to be revolted by the thought of eating the flesh of fellow human beings, even if they were not responsible for their death. But throughout history and throughout the world, people have eaten dead humans. We are revolted by the thought because law, morality, religion, and so on have conditioned us to become revolted. If we had grown up in a world in which the eating of human flesh was common, we would not be revolted, just as most of us are not revolted by the eating of animal flesh. Perhaps someday in the future when artificial food becomes an easy alternative, our great-grandchildren will become revolted by the prospect of eating the flesh of animals who were once alive, just as my grandparents and parents were revolted by the thought of eating certain dead animals such as pigs and lobsters.

Why, then, do we not eat human flesh? For some, the answer is simple: God has told us not to. But the gods of the Polynesians said it was permissible. What if our God had said it was permissible? Putting the same question at a different level of abstraction: why did our God — or those who have purported to speak in his name — single out the flesh of humans as prohibited food? It seems a waste in a world in which so many are starving. Perhaps the answer lies in the slippery slope. If we would permit the eating of the flesh of someone who was already dead, we might be more inclined to kill them for their food value, just as we do with animals. So we create a prophylactic rule — or, to use the words of the Talmud, we build a fence around the core prohibition. The core prohibition is the killing of human beings. The fence is the prohibition against the eating of already-dead human beings.

Perhaps there is also a core principle behind not allowing the eating of human flesh. Is it that somehow the human body is sacred? That it should never be used as a means toward the end of saving another human life? Surely the answer to those questions must be no, as evidenced by the fact that we encourage the harvesting of body organs of dead human beings for transplantation into live human beings who might otherwise die for lack of a needed organ. In principle, what is the difference between "harvesting" the flesh of dead human beings in order to save the lives of other human beings and "harvesting" their other organs? It cannot be personal preference alone. If it were, I might personally reject the distinction, unless someone could make a persuasive argument in support. If I were dead, I would just as soon have my flesh eaten in order to save the life of another human being as have my heart or kidneys removed for transplant. I make no claim to ownership of my body once dead, as evidenced by the fact that I have signed on as an organ donor. If there were a place to sign on as a flesh donor, I would do that as well — unless a larger principle were at stake.

There is, of course, this difference between transplanting an organ and eating the flesh. The organ is generally needed to save life. There is a one-to-one correlation. Eating human flesh, on the other hand, could become an appetite rather than a necessity. Indeed, we accept the eating of human flesh when absolutely necessary to save life, as in shipwrecks and the famous airplane crash in the Andes. We just don't want it to become routine. We might have the same attitude toward organ transplants if people began to transplant the blue eyes of dead people for purely cosmetic reasons.

Even — perhaps especially — when organs are needed to save lives, we do, and should, worry that transplantation may encourage the killing of some human beings for their organs. It is thought that such practices exist in certain parts of the world even today. And we have built certain fences in order to protect the living from being killed for their organs. No moral, religious, or law-abiding person would order an organ if he knew someone would be killed to provide that organ. If we chose, we could build an even higher fence: namely, prohibit the use of the organs of the dead, just as we prohibit the use of their flesh.

When organ transplantation first became possible, some religious groups made precisely that argument: the human body is sacred; it must be buried with all its organs; removal of any organ is a desecration, even if necessary to save human life. That is no longer the position taken by most mainstream religions, some of which now tolerate, while others encourage, organ donation (some encourage only the receipt of organs, not their donation, but that is an unacceptably selfish moral or religious position). Moral leaders now should encourage their followers to think of their corpses as containing recyclable parts. This change in perspective should be made in the interests of saving human life, thereby enhancing rather than diminishing its value. A dead body whose usable organs have been removed should become a symbol of respect for the living body. It is all a matter of how we view it and what we teach our children. There is nothing "natural" or "unnatural" about cutting up a dead body in order to give life to a live one, whether by using its heart or its flesh.

In order to encourage respect for the living, we mandate respect for the dead. It is a crime to desecrate a cemetery or a corpse. We require our pathologists to perform autopsies in a dignified manner. We dispose of body parts with respect. Soldiers risk their lives to recover the bodies of their fallen comrades. We do all this not because it matters to the dead but because it matters to the living. We have learned the lessons of history, which teach that societies that disrespect the dead bodies and resting places of the deceased tend to devalue the living bodies — the lives — of their contemporaries. What constitutes respect — burying a body *with* its organs or *without* them — is a matter of education and nurture rather than divine law or nature. (In some societies, respect for the dead requires that the body be taken to a remote hilltop so that its flesh may be consumed by birds of prey.)

The same can be said about abortion. Some who argue against abortion say that if we trivialize the "death" of a living human fetus, it becomes easier to devalue the life of a baby, a mentally retarded person, a prisoner, a Jew, a black, an enemy, a stranger. Others who argue for choice say that to compel a woman to bring an unwanted baby into the world devalues the life of the child and the welfare of the mother. Again, there is no one naturally correct answer for all moral people.

Another, less compelling example of a fence around the core violation would be in the prohibition against selling and trading ivory. There's nothing wrong, in principle, with using the tusks of dead elephants. But once a trade in ivory becomes acceptable, live elephants will be killed for their tusks. Accordingly, we try to make ivory an immoral and illegal commodity.[2] Likewise with those who would try to make the wearing of animal fur unacceptable. Again, we can distinguish in principle between stripping the fur from dead animals and killing animals for their fur, but the lesson of history is that permitting the former will encourage the latter. Thus we see the same principle in operation once again: we impose a seemingly irrational prohibition against a harmless use of resources — the flesh of dead people, the tusks of dead elephants, the fur of dead animals — in order to discourage a violation of the core principle, namely, killing in order to secure these same commodities.

The rules of law, religion, morality, and so forth seek to make it more difficult to act on the instinct of selfish preservation of individual and family and to make it acceptable — indeed, obligatory — to act on the basis of a broader principle. The specific principle may vary, depending on whether one is a Kantian, a utilitarian (case or rule), a believer in the Bible, or a follower of any other set of rules, but the mechanism is similar: it requires you to act not as if this were the only situation but as if it were *part* of a principled set of mutually binding obligations.

# TWELVE

# CAN ORGAN DONATION
# BE COMPELLED?

---

*Further on the issue of donating organs, in 2000 the death of a friend, who
had refused to accept a black-market heart, stimulated me to write about the
immorality of those who decline to become organ donors upon death.*

---

A FRIEND OF MINE RECENTLY DIED BECAUSE HE WAS UNABLE
to get a suitable heart for transplant. No healthy hearts were available
at the time he needed his transplant, and so in order to remain alive he
had to settle for the heart of a patient with hepatitis. The heart transplant worked, but soon thereafter my friend died of liver failure.

My friend, unfortunately, is among the large number of Americans
who needlessly die each year because other Americans selfishly refuse
to donate lifesaving organs after their own deaths. In the United
States, there is a presumption against organ donation at death. That
presumption can be overcome only if the potential organ donor has
made an affirmative decision to consent to having his organs removed
upon death. In most European countries, the presumption goes the
other way: all people are presumed to consent to the lifesaving use of
their organs unless they explicitly take action to withhold that consent.
The result is that many more organs are available for transplant patients in European countries than in our own.

I can imagine few more selfish and immoral acts than insisting that
your lifesaving organs must be buried with you so that worms can eat
them rather than their being used by other human beings to save their
lives or to restore sight. Yet many Americans refuse to consent to organ donation upon death. A significant number of such selfish refusers
justify their act of selfishness by reference to their religion. But what

kind of religion would preach that it is wrong to help save lives by donating organs from a dead body? Religious leaders should be in the forefront, urging their followers to overcome their fears and superstitions in order to save lives.

But religious leaders alone will not eliminate the critical shortage of organs. We need to change the law. At the very least, we should move toward the European system of presuming consent in the absence of an explicit withholding of consent. Even this shift of presumption may not produce enough organs. The time has come to raise the question of who owns a person's life-giving organs after that person has died. Do you have a right to have buried or cremated parts of your body that could keep other people alive? Would it be constitutional for a state to pass a statute mandating organ removal and reuse after death? Would there have to be an exception for religious objection? These are questions we ought to begin debating. Improvements in medical technology require us to rethink old attitudes about our bodies after death. These old attitudes will be difficult to shake. Treating the dead body with respect is an important element of humanity, as evidenced by the efforts we make to retrieve dead bodies in military combat and accidents. But the best way of showing respect for the dead, and especially for their bodies, is to retrieve organs that can then be kept alive and given to others.

When organ transplants first became feasible, many traditionalists objected — on moral and religious grounds — to playing God and tinkering with nature. Over time, attitudes changed, and almost nobody today *turns down* a lifesaving organ on religious or moral grounds. The Golden Rule — which is central to Judaism, Christianity, Islam, and other religions — requires that we treat our neighbors as ourselves. Anyone willing to *accept* a transplant must be willing to *give* organs. Religions that permit its adherents to receive transplants *must* permit them to donate organs, lest they be accused of hypocritically violating the Golden Rule. Perhaps an additional encouragement to transplant donation would be a rule excluding all adults who had not consented to donating their organs from receiving the organs of others. At least there should be a preference for those who were willing to donate organs.

Anyone who refuses to sign the box on the driver's license application, which constitutes consent to removal of organs after death, is either a coward, a fool, a knave, or a slave to superstition or religious fundamentalism. There is no softer way of putting this. It is simply wrong to waste the organs of the dead when they can be used to give life. It is understandable that some relatives of a crash or shooting victim would not be willing to consent to the removal of organs from the bodies of their recently deceased loved ones. But it is not understandable for an adult to refuse to consent in advance to the life-giving use of his own otherwise useless organs. We must make such selfishness unacceptable as a matter of morality and perhaps of law.

# THIRTEEN

# RIGHTS AS A CHECK
# ON DEMOCRACY

*This chapter was written especially for this book.*

THE EFFECT OF ENTRENCHING RIGHTS IN A DEMOCRACY IS to eliminate certain issues from majoritarian control. Put another way, it is to take certain entrenched rights and place them outside the sphere of pure democracy. But if one believes, as I do, that rights are not divine, natural, or eternal, and that they are a product of the experiences and history of a people, then there is some burden to justify the antidemocratic character of rights. I do not see rights, properly limited, as antithetical to democracy properly defined. I see rights as the most important check and balance within a democracy.

Rights should not prevent all change, especially if rights themselves are subject to constant reevaluation based on the changing experiences of the people. Rights do slow down certain kinds of change, under certain circumstances. Spiro Agnew, in criticizing liberals who insisted on exercising their rights, once characterized individual rights as a "headwind blowing in the face of the ship of state." It is an apt metaphor, though Agnew did not understand it in its positive sense. It is the function of rights in a democracy to put pressure on government to change course, to move cautiously, to protect important and enduring values from precipitous abrogation. Learned Hand once observed that when liberty dies in the hearts of men and women, "no court can save it; . . . no court can even do much to help it."[1] He was right about the first part of his observation: courts alone cannot save liberty. But he was wrong about the second part: courts can, by properly enforcing rights, slow down the process of tyranny — at least sometimes, as they did during the McCarthy period. Rights work, in part, by taking certain powers away from temporary majorities and vesting the ability to constrain these powers in those who lack traditional political influence or who are otherwise subject to discrimination or marginalization. One genre of rights actually opens up the channels of democracy: free speech, equality in voting, and protection against the establishment of religion.[2] Other genres of rights, while not opening up the channels of democracy as directly as these core rights do, allow democracy to operate more fairly. If Winston Churchill was right when he said that a democracy should be judged by the manner in which it treats its most despised, then the rights of accused criminals, aliens, the mentally ill and other marginalized people, are an important part of the democratic process.

In a democratic system, the unelected judiciary must have only limited power to overrule current majority preferences on the basis of entrenched rights. When the constitution is clear about a particular right trumping a preference — as with the right against compelled self-incrimination overriding our preference for swift conviction of the guilty — then positivism prevails, with little or no need to debate about the source or legitimacy of the right. The plain language of the Constitution governs. The only way to change a clearly expressed constitutional right is by the cumbersome and rarely used process of formal amendment.[3] When the claimed right is not explicitly in the Constitution — as with the rights of parents to forbid grandparents from visiting a child — then process should prevail, accompanied by inevitable conflict over the source and legitimacy of the claimed right and counterright. In the latter instances — when claimed rights are not explicit in the Constitution — which are far more common than the former, those who claim that a right should trump a majoritarian preference have the burden of establishing why their preference deserves to be treated as a right.

The burden rests on them, because in the absence of a compelling claim of right, democracy demands that majoritarian preferences prevail over minority preferences. In seeking to satisfy this burden, the rights claimant can properly point to history and experience in an effort to persuade decision makers that his claim should be treated as a right. As history and experience change, the persuasiveness of a particular claim for status as a right may also change. But history and experience change more gradually than shifting majoritarian preferences. In this respect, rights that are not clearly entrenched are always subject to reevaluation over time. The judiciary, under this approach, is generally limited to slowing down change rather than preventing it. The New Deal is a perfect example of this process at work. The Supreme Court repeatedly ruled that progressive social legislation made necessary by the Depression violated the Constitution's broad requirement of due process. But changing history and experience eventually made it abundantly clear that the high court's conception of property rights (based on substantive due process) was anachronistic and unsuited to the changing realities of American life. It required a change of personnel to finalize the Supreme Court's institutional about-face. Changing personnel — the appointing process — is also part of the mechanism for change, just as the doctrine of stare decisis (deference to precedent) is part of the mechanism for slowing down change and making it more gradual.

Many other examples could be cited to demonstrate the wisdom of Holmes's observation that the life of the law has been experience rather than logic — or God, or nature, or any other universal and immutable truth or external source.

The relatively new concept of environmental rights is obviously a response to the relatively new assaults on the environment growing out of industrialism. Though environmentalist concerns trace their origins to the biblical prohibition against destroying the fruit-bearing trees of a conquered people, the more recent experiences of industrialized nations have turned this concern into a nascent "right." I recall visiting a preindustrial country with high unemployment and low productivity and being told, "What this country needs is a little more pollution!" The history and experiences of *that* nation did not yet reflect the need for environmental rights.

Lesser-developed nations, on the other hand, may have a heightened experiential need for positive economic rights. The Nobel Prize–winning economist Amartya Sen has made a compelling case for the inexorability of the relationship between political and economic rights. He points to the startling fact that no functioning democracy with political rights has ever experienced a famine, and argues that the most basic rights should include a mix of traditional negative political rights (i.e., the government may not restrict freedom of speech, religion, and so on) and positive economic rights (i.e., economic facilities, social opportunities, and protective security).[4]

In the United States, we generally limit our concept of rights to those negative restrictions on governmental power that have their sources in the Constitution. "Congress shall make no law abridging . . . ," is the paradigm. But there are movements from all sides of the political spectrum for a more expansive, positive view of rights. Many on the right, and even the center, favor a constitutional amendment establishing victims' rights. Some on the left advocate a right to affirmative action based on race or gender. Some see health care, education, and safety as rights. Others advocate welfare, or at least a minimum subsistence, as a right.

The difficult question is whether to "constitutionalize" so many areas of what have traditionally been deemed matters of politics and policy. To constitutionalize a preference into a right is to remove it from majoritarian determination and to turn it over to unelected judges (at least in the federal system) for judicial review.

The power of judicial review has itself derived its legitimacy from the experiences of our people over time. It has become an important component of liberty, though — like other components — it is subject to abuse and misuse.

The Supreme Court decision in the 2000 presidential election case is a prime example of the abuse and misuse of judicial review. Invoking the "equal protection" clause of the Constitution, five Republican justices — none of whom had been sympathetic to an expansive view of that clause in previous cases — stopped the hand recount that could have changed the result of the election. In doing so, they have indirectly influenced who will be nominated to serve as their successors on the high court, thereby eliminating an important component of our system of checks and balances.[5] This decision, which has been widely criticized by the experts, neither opened the channels of democracy nor protected the rights of the disenfranchised.

# FOURTEEN

# THE LAW AS MORALITY

---

*This chapter was written especially for this book.*

---

AMONG THE MOST INNOVATIVE AND INFLUENTIAL THINKERS about the proper role of empiricism in the construction and evaluation of morality — especially in the context of law — was the French sociologist Émile Durkheim, who wrote in the late nineteenth and early twentieth centuries. Durkheim saw an intimate connection among empiricism, law, and morality. For him, the law was both the embodiment and the most accurate reflection of the morality of any given society. He believed that any claim for the universality of morality — or rights or law or any other social institution — would have to be proved empirically.[1] That is a descriptive claim: that is, a certain morality or right *is* accepted by all, most, or some cultures. It is possible, of course, to make a claim about the universality of morality or rights that is entirely normative: that is, that a certain universal morality or right is the only just way, and any society that does not accept it — without regard to their experiences or cultural preferences — is immoral. This entirely normative claim can be made, at least in theory, but it will be far less persuasive if a sociologist can demonstrate that many societies, which in all other respects fulfill the criteria of a moral society, reject the particular morality or right asserted to be normatively universal.[2]

Imagine, for example, an isolated society with limited resources that respects life, reveres elders, distributes wealth fairly, and values due process. But it has a rule that when a person gets very old and infirm, he or she is placed on a drifting iceberg and, following a ceremony of respect and love, floated out to sea. All the members of that society understand their ultimate fate and accept it as part of their culture. Anthropologists prove that by employing this approach, the culture improves not only the quality of life but also its average duration. It works — for them! Yet we regard it as barbaric and immoral. It violates nearly every criterion by which we tend to judge morality and rights: innocent people are — let's not mince words — executed. To be sure, they are not being punished for any wrongdoing, but that makes it even worse — comparable, in some respects, to eugenically inspired euthanasia of the "unfit." We cannot bring ourselves to say that what they are doing is just, but can we condemn it as unjust? If we can, we must — at the very least — take into account their differing social mores in *ranking* the seriousness of the alleged injustice. We must also take into account the fact that the system works — for them. It works not only by *their* general standards of morality but by *ours* as well.

This is what distinguishes the iceberg case from the Nazi euthanasia program, which may have "worked" when judged against a racist ideology but not against any widely accepted moral standards. The iceberg case shows a society that is moral by our general standards but that employs a particular technique for allocating scarce resources that is immoral by our universal standards, though it contributes to the overall morality of their society (as judged by our own universal standards). How can such a society be judged by reference to a singular, universal standard of morality or rights? Must not any judgment take into account the sociological realities of the community?

Consider the following testing hypothetical, which elaborates on the previous story of the old people in the isolated society. The entire world experiences population growth incapable of being sustained by diminishing resources. Unless something can be done to curtail population size, the most vulnerable people — the very young, the very old, the very sick, the very poor, and the very weak — will begin to die.

Various proposals are put forward. They include:

- Financial inducements to limit births to one child
- Mandatory birth limitations, enforceable by abortion and sterilization
- Cutting off of Medicare (and comparable financial support) at age seventy-five
- Denial of all medical services and medicines at age seventy-five, regardless of the wealth of the individual

- Cutting off of Medicare for all people with specified chronic conditions, such as Alzheimer's disease, mental retardation, incurable cancer, or serious heart disease
- Denial of all medical services and medicines to the above
- Denial of all medical services and medicines to prisoners sentenced to life
- Cutting off of Medicare to extremely sick babies
- Denial of all medical treatment to the above
- Mandatory life limitation to age eighty, enforceable by execution
- Random execution of 10 percent of the population, selected by lot
- Random killing of 25 percent of the population over sixty-five, selected by lot
- Allowing people selected for random execution to provide a substitute, either by paying for one, getting a loved one to volunteer, or some other "fair" method
- Letting nature take its course

Despite enormous dedication of resources and heroic efforts, there are no "good" solutions to the problem (such as colonization of space, building ocean platforms, cultivating new food sources). The tragic choices are limited to the above.

How would one go about choosing — or thinking about how to choose — among such terrible options? John Rawls's "original position" and "veil of ignorance" fail to provide one right answer. Decent people denied the knowledge of whether, at the operative time, they would be old or young, rich or poor, healthy or sick, would still disagree about the "right" or even the self-serving option. There is no intuition of justice that necessarily leads in one direction. Ronald Dworkin's emphasis on human dignity, equality, and fairness does not provide us with the single right answer he assures us is often possible, since none of the options is completely consistent with these rights, and none is more consistent than several others. Immanuel Kant's categorical imperative would probably lead to inaction, as would most variations on traditional natural law. Traditional legal positivism would simply provide a structure for lawmaking, adjudication, and enforcement, but unless we included substantive institutional components (such as those proposed by H.L.A. Hart and others), it would not in-form as to the substance of the positive rules.

We can articulate some of the considerations that should be fac-tored into any moral and rational decision. They might include the following: a requirement of equality and fairness, which would forbid the use of factors such as money, race, religion, gender, and other such statuses in determining or even influencing the decision as to who shall live and who shall die, or who shall be permitted to procreate freely and who shall have limits imposed; a requirement that the state not ac-tively take the life of innocent people; a requirement that the state not be in the business of mandating abortion or sterilization.

If all of the above propositions — which can be translated into rights — are absolute, then the only moral course of action would be inaction. But doing nothing would produce the most immoral and ir-rational results: the survival of the richest and strongest, the most predatory, selfish, immoral, and conniving. It should not be surprising that the application of natural law would replicate the state of nature that law was designed to overcome.

Some might respond by arguing that natural law would persuade moral people not to kill each other in order to live. That is precisely the point: those who followed such natural law would become the first victims of those who did not. Perhaps natural law would enforce its moral rules forbidding the strong from killing the weak. But how would it enforce such rules in the context of a world where some must die so that others might live? Obviously, by killing or imprisoning those who would kill to save their own lives or those of loved ones. This might produce a just resolution whereby only those who broke the law would be killed. But even putting aside the moral objections to capital punishment, what if this deterrent were to work and an insuffi-cient number of people could be killed for violating the law? The Grim Reaper would remain relentless under my hypothetical, and those who died "natural" deaths would either be the weakest or else they would be people randomly denied food, medication, and other necessities. There are perfectly unjust solutions to our problems — se-lection based on racial, religious, gender, or economic grounds. But there are no perfectly just solutions.

Some might argue with my hypothetical, since it creates a state of emergency, and no system of rights can be expected to work perfectly under such pressures. But "emergencies" are matters of degree. Throughout history, there have been nations in which people have died because of inadequate resources. Even during the Holocaust, decisions akin to those outlined above had to be made. Should a crying baby be smothered to prevent Nazis from discovering the hiding place of a large group? Should a named person be turned over to the Gestapo to prevent the killing of hostages? Should food and medicine be denied the very young or very old to maximize survival of the most survivable? Tragic choices had to be made by moral people who had no morally acceptable options available to them. Some chose immorality, others chose compromise, while still others chose inaction or death. Can we judge them by a single standard of morality?

Oliver Wendell Holmes Jr. once observed that it was the function of governments to cause the death or prevent the birth of some to assure the lives of others. Thomas Malthus made a related observation in a more empirical context. The point is that human life is too complex, too fragile, too unpredictable, too subject to perceived emergencies, to be amenable to a set of simple moral rules that produce singularly right answers. Avoiding absolutely wrong answers may be the best we can do in many circumstances. And that is not trivial.

For those who believe in an absolute morality — a categorical imperative — there can be no balancing of interests or mere avoidance of absolutely wrong answers. There must be a right answer, or else we sink into moral relativism. Dostoyevsky had Ivan put the ultimate test of relativism to Alyosha: "Imagine that you are creating a fabric of human destiny with the object of making men happy in the end, giving them peace at least, but that it was essential and inevitable to torture to death only one tiny creature — that baby beating its breast with its fist, for instance — and to found that edifice on its unavenged tears, would you consent to be the architect on those conditions? Tell me, and tell the truth."

Alyosha replied without hesitation: "No, I wouldn't consent."

Jeremy Bentham, too, would not have hesitated: he would argue that killing the child was the right thing to do — just as he argued that torture was justified if it promoted the greatest happiness for the greatest number.[3] Most of the rest of us would not only hesitate, we would probably not know what we would actually do until confronted with this horrible choice of evils, as we may be if a captured terrorist refuses to divulge the intended imminent target of his fellow terrorists.

Durkheim, while "unashamedly moralistic," believed that philosophy and morality "requires sociology," because "philosophical speculation about moral (including legal) matters must be grounded in comparative study of moral facts."[4] He rejected traditional natural law because he eschewed God (though this scion of a rabbinical family wrote about religion extensively and recognized its importance) and believed that human nature was constantly changing in response to nurture and culture.[5] Yet he also rejected traditional legal positivism. He viewed the law as embodying the morality of a society, in much the same way as religion does. Indeed, he saw striking parallels between the "functions" of law and religion in society. "They are both foci of duty and commitment. They impose obligations on those subject to them, who accept their authority."[6] This comparison may seem bizarre to those who live in societies in which religion — as distinguished from law — lacks the power to enforce its commands. But Durkheim was interested less in the power of a social institution to enforce its views than in its moral authority to persuade. For the law to possess persuasive, as distinguished from coercive, authority it must embody the morality of the society. That, too, is an empirical claim, testable by sociologists, though it, too, can be transformed into a normative claim: only laws that embody morality ought to persuade.

Durkheim was plainly wrong — both morally and empirically — when he asserted that "law is meaningless if it is detached from religion, which has given it its main distinguishing marks, and of which it is partially only a derivation."[7] If Durkheim was referring to traditional organized religions, he may have been right about the sources of many laws,[8] but he was demonstrably wrong about contemporary law, especially in places, like much of Europe, where many people who revere law reject religion. If he was referring to "some shared focus of belief and attachment that is necessary to every society," then he was merely stating a tautology: people will not believe in a legal system unless it reflects their shared beliefs.

Whether or not law must be based on religion (however defined) in order to be meaningful or persuasive, it is clear that Durkheim was groping toward an important insight: namely, that a successful legal system should do more than coerce compliance with its commands through the threat of punishment. It should seek to persuade its constituents to obey the law because that is the right and just thing to do. In order for this mechanism of moral internalization to work, the law must be perceived to be just, and for it to be so perceived it must — according to Durkheim — actually be just, as evaluated against the needs of the particular society.

Durkheim, thus, sought to break down the high walls of separation between philosophy and empiricism, between morality and pragmatism, between religion and law, between what ought to be and what is. He realized, of course, that the primary role of sociology — the discipline he helped create — was to describe existing societies, while the primary role of the normative disciplines, especially moral philosophy, was to prescribe what is right and wrong.[9] But he asked — rhetorically and critically — "By what privilege is the philosopher to be permitted to speculate about society, without entering into commerce with the detail of social facts?" And in a blistering attack on the ivory tower philosopher, he demanded that "moral issues be posed and addressed in the light of systematic study of experience since we are in no way justified in seeing in the personal aspirations that the thinker feels . . . an adequate expression of moral reality."[10]

In my estimation, this gives too much weight to the empirical component of morality and too little to its speculative element. Moral philosophers should be encouraged to speculate freely about the *oughts* of life without being limited by the *is* of any given society, but these speculations must ultimately be tested against the realities of human experience. Durkheim's concept of "moral reality" seeks to bridge the gap between the normative (moral) and the empirical (reality), but it poses the danger of accepting what is without asking what might be. In this regard, it is somewhat reminiscent of those natural-law and morality advocates who believe that "all nature is good." While Durkheim was never so naïve as to believe that all society is good, he gave too much weight to the moral "common sense" of existing society and too little to the abstract, a priori speculations of ivory tower philosophers, such as Kant, Hegel, Bentham, and others.[11]

While I agree with Durkheim's conclusion that "experience alone can decide if [particular abstract moral philosophers] are suitable" to the time and place,[12] I insist that "suitability" is not the only criteria for evaluating the justice of a society's "moral reality." An amoral sociologist would conclude that the moral reality of Nazi Germany was ideally "suited" to its social structure and ideology. That would not make it right or just. Durkheim's response would be that such a society would eventually be destroyed, by either internal or external force.[13] Well, maybe! Just because that happened to the Nazis is no guarantee of its inevitability. There must be an external standard for evaluating a society's morality beyond its suitability to that society. The question is: Does such a standard exist?

Mill disagreed with his mentor Bentham precisely in this regard. Presciently, he postulated an evil society that maximized the happiness of most of its citizens (e.g., Aryans) at the expense of a small oppressed minority (e.g., Jews). Such a society (Nazi Germany) might satisfy Bentham's maximization of happiness principle, but it would not satisfy Mill's requirement of individual rights. Mill sought to reconcile his insistence on individual rights with utilitarianism by postulating "utilities which are vastly more important, and therefore, more absolute and imperative" than the mere promotion of human pleasure.[14] Mill, the moral utilitarian, derived this hierarchy of utilities — what he called primary moralities — from some standard external both to law and to the philosophy of utilitarianism. He is somewhat vague about the source of this standard, beyond the somewhat circular contention that it is necessary for human happiness.

The problem is that no such external standard actually exists in nature or in the word of God. It must be constructed on the basis of the broader experiences of the entire world over time, rather than the limited experiences of one particular society at a single point in its history. The need for, and desirability of, basic universal standards for defining and even enforcing the most fundamental human rights is clear from the experiences of the world in the twentieth century alone. Constructing mechanisms for defining and enforcing these standards, with due concern for the variations made necessary by different cultural and experimental factors, is the great human challenge we face. We cannot abdicate it to God or nature. It is our job, our responsibility, and our challenge to construct such mechanisms. In meeting this challenge, we must look to experience, to nature, and to the a priori speculations of philosophers, moralists, and other thinkers. The difficult question is how each of these elements is to coalesce in the interest of a morality that is both just and workable. Durkheim's contribution to this never-ending quest for the just society is both invaluable and incomplete, especially as it relates to individual rights.

Durkheim tried "implicitly to solve the problems which positivist jurists have long associated with attempts to make law and morality analytically inseparable,"[15] by insisting that law itself — positive law — must have a moral component. He saw the law as something "worth giving loyalty to," because it is the embodiment of society's morality. But he failed to solve the problem of how to evaluate, and whether to comply with, unjust laws that suit an unjust society, or whether basic rights "exist" in a society that has decided that such rights do not suit that society at this time.[16]

Durkheim's concept of rights, and their sources, changed over time. His early writings presented rights as "bestowed by the state on the individual," in order to serve a societal function. They do not attach at birth, do not inhere in the individual, and "are not inscribed in the nature of things." His later works referred to rights and liberties being conferred on man by the "sacredness with which he is invested." This suggests a divine source, but it seems likely that Durkheim was using the term in its broad, metaphorical sense. Durkheim eventually came to believe that certain basic rights — particularly "Freedom of thought" — were moral entitlements as well as societal necessities.[17] But their source or sources, and hence their states as inalienable or merely functional, was never persuasively articulated, beyond his view that morality is — in a general sense — the source of law and religion. As religion evolves into law, it recognizes the capacity of individuals to view rules critically and to challenge them[18] on the basis of experience.[19] Debate and communication then become more important in the formulation of morality and rights, thus leading to the democratic processes of governance that Durkheim believed were essential to the modern state whose primary function is "to liberate individual personalities" and "to provide a realm of basic individual freedoms."[20]

Eventually Durkheim became a zealous advocate of rights, premised on the need for "individualism," which provided "the moral spine" of modern law. The need for these freedoms or rights became clear in Durkheim's later writings, but their source remained obscure, as it does today in the writings of many of our most brilliant secular philosophers and thinkers.

# FIFTEEN

# THE MOST FUNDAMENTAL LIMITATION ON STATE POWER

*Though I do not subscribe to the philosophy of any particular school of jurisprudence — I hope that I think for myself — I am a committed civil libertarian. The classic formulation of civil liberties was articulated by John Stuart Mill a century and a half ago. In 1993 Bantam Books decided to publish a new edition of Mill's philosophy,* On Liberty and Utilitarianism, *and asked me to write an introductory essay on its influence. In that essay, I try to apply Mill's thinking to current issues and to suggest some critiques.*

## THE PRINCIPLE

Few principles of civic morality have had so profound an intellectual influence within Western democracies as John Stuart Mill's "one very simple principle." The principle, governing the proper allocation of state power and individual liberty, was articulated by Mill in his 1859 essay entitled "On Liberty." In Mill's own words:

> That principle is, that the sole end for which mankind are warranted, individually or collectively, in interfering with the liberty of action of any of their number, is self-protection. That the only purpose for which power can be rightfully exercised over any member of a civilized community, against his will, is to prevent harm to others. His own good, either physical or moral, is not a sufficient warrant. He cannot rightfully be compelled to do or forbear because it will be better for him to do so, because it will make him happier, because, in the opinions of others, to do so would be wise, or even right. These are good reasons for remonstrating with him, or reasoning with him, or persuading him, or entreating him, but not for compelling him, or visiting him with any evil in case he do

otherwise. To justify that, the conduct from which it is desired to deter him, must be calculated to produce evil to some one else. The only part of the conduct of any one, for which he is amenable to society, is that which concerns others. In the part which merely concerns himself, his independence is, of right, absolute. Over himself, over his own body and mind, the individual is sovereign.

Mill made it clear that his principle applied only to "human beings in the maturity of their faculties" and granted to the state the power to determine, within reason, the age "of manhood and womanhood." The explicit inclusion of womanhood reflected more than syntactical completeness; Mill wrote eloquently in favor of women's equality in the home, at the ballot box, and in the world at large.[1]

While support for women's rights was uncharacteristic of his circle during the mid–nineteenth century, Mill's implicit acceptance of colonialism was all too typical. He exempted from his principle "those backward states of society in which the race itself may be considered as in its nonage." For such "barbarians," Mill paternalistically concluded, benevolent "despotism is a legitimate form of government," since liberty has no application "to any state of things anterior to the time when mankind may have become capable of being improved by free and equal discussion."

But neither his progressive inclusion of women nor his regressive exclusion of "backward" people is central to Mill's principle and its remarkable influence on Western society. Like other profoundly influential principles, such as the Bible's "Thou shalt love thy neighbor like thyself" and Kant's "So act, that the rule on which thou actest would admit of being adopted as a law by all rational beings," the principle itself is as simple as it is eloquent (at least in conception — Mill was the first to acknowledge its difficulties in application, leaving that to a sketchy final chapter that is among the weakest in an otherwise persuasive essay). The power of the state may not be used to compel a reasoning adult to do or not do anything solely because such action or inaction would be better for that adult.

It is interesting that this principle was, for Mill, based entirely on utilitarian considerations: "It is proper to state that I forgo any advantage which could be derived to my argument from the idea of abstract right [since] I regard utility as the ultimate appeal on all ethical questions." There are, however, persuasive utilitarian arguments in favor of compelling adults to do certain things that would make them happier and better people. Indeed, if a truly benevolent despot really knew the secret of maximizing happiness for everyone, there would surely be many utilitarians who would feel compelled to grant him the power to do what no democracy has thus far succeeded in doing: namely, producing a universally happy society.

In the end, however, Mill is not at his best in attempting to justify his principle solely on conventional utilitarian grounds. Though Mill himself eschews all advantage to his argument from "abstract right," that does not necessarily mean that those who reject utilitarianism and accept abstract rights must reject Mill's principle. Even as an abstract right or as part of a rights-based system, Mill's principle has much to commend it. This is an instance where the power of the principle transcends the strength of the underlying justification offered by its proponent. I think it is true today that a considerable number of non-utilitarians do, in fact, accept Mill's basic principle with as few or as many variations as orthodox utilitarians who accept it.

Indeed, it is fair to say that the fundamentals of Mill's principle have become almost a conventional wisdom of Western society, at least among its intellectuals. It is generally taken for granted as a premise of debate concerning the proper allocation of state power and individual freedom. To be sure, there are some state paternalists, especially among the religious ultraright, who still believe that it is the proper function of government to compel adults to do what is deemed best for them. But the vast majority of contemporary Western thinkers — whatever their philosophical bent — seem to accept the basic Millian principle that it is not the proper function of government to compel conduct solely in order to improve the life of an adult who does not necessarily want his or her life so improved.

Many philosophers reject the rigidity with which Mill stated his thesis. Others have greater difficulty than even he had in clearly distinguishing between actions that affect only the actor and those that have a discernible impact on others. But it is not easy to find many who categorically reject the core concept central to Mill's principle and who would grant the state the power to make reasoning adults take nontrivial actions that they have knowingly chosen not to take but that the state believes they should take in order to better themselves or make them happier. This is especially true in a nation as diverse and heterogeneous as the United States, where it would be difficult to reach a consensus on what constitutes the kind of betterment of happiness that could properly be imposed. But even in more homogeneous democratic nations, Mill's core principle has become the conventional wisdom, at least in theory.

The best evidence of how influential Mill's principle has become — indeed, how it is presumed by most thinkers — may be the repeated efforts of those who would compel a given action against protesting individuals to rationalize such force by reference to the rights of others rather than by reference to the good of the compelled individual. Examples abound, but one will suffice to make the general point. A distinguished colleague of mine would seek to justify mandatory seat belt laws by rejecting the argument that "only the belt-wearer's own welfare [is] at risk." He argues instead that we should recognize that

> refusing to buckle up endangers innocent third parties, not only the dependent children of those who insist on not buckling, and not only those who end up paying higher insurance premiums and higher taxes so that others may enjoy the "freedom" not to buckle, but also those who end up being injured or even killed in avoidable collisions when unbuckled drivers lose control of their cars. Quite simply, the seat-belt law prevents people from becoming loose objects when a car skids or veers into a tree or another vehicle; a belted driver is less likely to become a helpless spectator as his car is turned into an unguided missile. Surely that is a legitimate exercise of society's power to protect the innocent, not the entering wedge of tyranny.[2]

While these observations may all have some small validity, they miss the big picture, namely, that seat belt laws have as their primary object the mandatory protection of the adult belt wearer. I, too, favor mandatory seat belt laws, but I recognize that support for such paternalistic legislation requires a compromise with Mill's principle. And it is a compromise I am prepared to make explicitly rather than uncomfortably try to squeeze seat belt laws into Mill's principle by invoking flying people and leaping logic.

My compromise would establish two significant exceptions to Mill's principle. The first I call the "light pinky of the law" exception. The second I call the "Thanks, I needed that" exception.

The "light pinky of the law" is at the opposite end of the continuum from the "heavy thumb of the law." It refers to regulations carrying minor financial penalties that are calculated to influence the behavior of people who really have no ideological objection to doing something that will help them but who don't care enough to take the step without some gentle nudging from the law. Seat belt laws are a perfect example. Most Americans will wear seat belts if the law requires them to and will not wear them if the law does not require them to. That may seem silly to any believer in rational, cost-benefit analysis. Why, after all, should a fifty-dollar fine work when the compelling statistical and clinical evidence that safety belts save lives does not work? The answer lies in the indisputable fact that most people do not rationally calculate the costs and benefits of their actions, particularly when the benefit is hypothetical, long-term, and statistically quite unlikely to come about. That is so even if the cost is as trivial as buckling up.

For a variety of reasons, the law often works where rational calculation does not. People do not generally want to be perceived — by themselves or others — as lawbreakers even when the penalty is quite trivial. The law does have some kind of moral imperative that moves people to action and inaction more powerfully than the mere economic cost attached to violation. To be sure, if the law is overused, or is used immorally or foolishly, much of that moral imperative may be diluted. But as of now, for most citizens of Western democracies, the law does work, at least in situations where it is used to nudge people into doing something relatively cost-free that promises some potential benefit.

That is why I favor mandatory seat belt laws and other simple self-helping safety rules that are enforced with no more than small fines. But the "light pinky of the law" exception to Mill's principle should not, in my view, be expended beyond the narrow areas in which it is appropriate. To make my point, I will argue that mandatory motorcycle helmet laws — though similar in many respects to seat belt laws — may exceed the narrow bounds of my exception. The distinction may be subtle, but it is real: Most car drivers who would not wear seat belts if the law were silent are not conscientiously opposed either to seat belts or to the legal requirement that they be worn; they are simply lazy, forgetful, or unconcerned; they will do whatever the law nudges them to do. Most motorcycle riders who would not wear helmets in the absence of a law seem to be conscientiously opposed both to helmets and to the legal requirement that they wear them. If I am right about that difference, then mandatory helmet laws are really different from mandatory seat belt laws — at least for those cyclists who care deeply about their freedom to maim and kill themselves. For the conscientiously opposed cyclist — as distinguished from the car driver who couldn't care less whether he buckles up or doesn't — the legal requirement that he wear a helmet will be perceived as a fundamental denial of freedom rather than as a trivial nudge from the state. He will feel the heavy thumb of the law upon him rather than the light pinky that will be felt by the typical car driver who would not buckle up if he did not "have to."

But what about those few car drivers who feel as strongly about seat belt laws as the helmet-free cycle fanatics feel about the helmet laws? There are two ways of dealing with this minority: If we lived in a totally honest society where all defendants always told the truth about why they violated the law, there could be an exception written into the seat belt law for conscientious objectors who could show that they had thought through the issue and had come to an ideological position against buckling up (or against being compelled to buckle up). But because many people who were caught unbuckled would falsely claim that they were conscientious objectors when they were merely lazy, the exception might swallow up the rule. The other way of dealing with the small number of conscientious objectors is simply to regard the fifty-dollar fine as a tax or an insurance surcharge for engaging in behavior that is dangerous to themselves but for which society in general will have to pay. In other words, society would be telling these people that they are not forbidden from driving unbuckled; they must simply pay a small price for doing so.[3]

In no case, under the "light pinky of the law" exception, would I ever put a dissenter in prison — or punish him or her harshly — for refusing to take an action that would benefit only him or her. I would reserve serious penalties for those who squarely fit within Mill's principle.

This brings us to the second exception, which, in my view, sometimes justifies mandatory seat belt laws designed to prevent injuries to those who would not otherwise buckle up, as well as some other limited state force designed to help only the compelled individual. The "Thanks, I needed that" exception derives from the typical scene in old grade-B movies in which one character is out of control and the other character slaps him in the face to restore his control. The slapped character invariably says, "Thanks, I needed that," thus demonstrating his after-the-fact appreciation of his friend's paternalistic assault. Even Mill would permit state compulsion to prevent the mentally ill — those not capable of rational thought — from harming themselves. But my exception would, perhaps, go a bit further. I would justify state compulsion to prevent — at least temporarily — a distraught but rational adult from killing (or otherwise inflicting irreversible serious harm on) himself or herself. I would regard it as morally permissible — indeed, perhaps morally imperative — to try to prevent such self-inflicted harm if I could do so without unreasonable risk to myself or others. I would do so in the expectation that after the person calmed down and thought it through, he would thank me — perhaps not literally but at least in his own mind. If I were wrong in a particular case, I would still not regret what I had done, because the person has an eternity to be dead, and I would not regard myself as having denied him much if I deprived him of several additional hours or even days of death. If, on the other hand, I were to err on the side of not preventing the suicide of a person who would indeed have thanked me for doing so, then I would have contributed to denying him the rest of his life.

As with the motorcycle helmet example, I would not apply the thank-you exception to rational adults who have carefully thought through the issue of suicide over a substantial period of time and have decided to end their lives.

It is somewhat more questionable whether seat belt laws fit comfortably within the thank-you exception as well. The vast majority of car drivers who grumble over buckling up would certainly say thank you if they were involved in an accident in which their lives (or limbs) were saved by wearing the seat belt they would not have worn but for the law. But would they say thank you after each car trip during which they were required to buckle up, or only when — and if — they were involved in an accident?

There is a considerable danger in expanding the thank-you exception to a point where it could swallow up much of Mill's basic principle.

A large number of hypothetical paternalistic compulsions — for example, those directed against smoking, overeating, or not exercising — could be justified by reference to a mirror-image version of the thank-you exception. I can easily imagine angry people on their deathbeds complaining about the lack of compulsion that allowed them to smoke, eat, and couch potato themselves to death. "Why didn't you make me stop smoking? I would be thanking you today if you had!" Well, one response to that hypothetical conversation is: "No, you wouldn't be thanking me if you were up and around and healthy, because you wouldn't appreciate — as you now do — the importance of not smoking. It required you to come face-to-face with death for you to understand why you should not have smoked, and now it is too late." The more persuasive answer is that there is a crucial difference between a brief one-shot act of compulsion such as preventing the distraught person from jumping out the window or taking poison and a long-term, lifestyle-changing compulsion such as that required to make a person stop smoking, overeating, or not exercising. The state should be far more reticent about enforcing long-term, lifestyle-changing compulsions on unwilling adults than it should be to risk not being thanked for a brief one-shot interference with an adult's liberty that may well be appreciated in retrospect.

I offer these two limited exceptions to Mill's principle to suggest that it is far better to argue about the limits of the principle itself than to accept it as an almost biblical (or constitutional) rule of action and then try to find ways to squeeze what are really exceptions into the parameters of the principle.

We live today in a far more interdependent society than the one in which Mill lived. Even in Mill's time and before, there were those who believed that "no man is an island, entire of itself."[4] Mill recognized, of course, that actions that cause harm to the actor often create ripples that touch others.[5] As we shall see later, however, Mill is not at his best in dealing with such matters of degree. Nor is it clear how Mill would have applied his principle to somewhat more complex and multifaceted problems than those he discussed.

Consider, for example, some current controversies on which Mill's principle may bear differently in today's America than it appeared to bear in Mill's England. Mill may or may not have known that smoking harms the lungs and heart of the smoker. But even had he known that fact, he would still not countenance legislation banning smoking. He might, perhaps, have approved of labeling laws designed to give the smoker information necessary to decide whether the present pleasure of the puff was worth the possible pain of the future. Today we know that smoking hurts not only the lungs and hearts of smokers but also the health of nonsmokers. That might well have led Mill to conclude that adults have the right to inhale but not to exhale — at least not in the presence of nonconsenting adults or children. Just as your right to swing your fist ends at the tip of my nose, so, too, your right to puff on a cigarette ends at the edge of my nostrils.

In Mill's day — indeed until quite recently — pornography and obscenity were regarded as "moral" issues akin to masturbation. Both were thought to be bad for the soul, the psyche, and the sexuality of the viewer or reader. As such, Mill would find no basis for preventing adults from indulging in smut in the privacy of their bedrooms. Now, however, we are told by some feminists that those who view or read pornography will be more likely to engage in violent actions against nonconsenting women. This is not the place to rehearse the empirical debate over whether pornography causes rape or other violence toward women. The issue here is a normative one: if it could be shown that pornography did cause harm not only to its consumers but also to others who do not consent to its availability, may the state properly prevent its consumption, even in private?[6]

A similar controversy, but with an interesting twist, surrounds the state regulation of addictive drugs, especially heroin. By criminalizing heroin — a chemical that harms the user but does not itself make him or her more prone to violence — the state increases the cost of obtaining the highly addictive drug. The "market" cost of heroin would be quite low if it were available by medical prescription, but because it is illegal, its cost is many times higher. This increased cost causes most heroin addicts to commit many more acquisitive and predatory crimes against innocent people than they might otherwise commit. (I say "otherwise," because many heroin addicts have long criminal backgrounds.) Accordingly, the criminalization of heroin violates Mill's principle in two ways: first, it employs the power of society to compel (or at least try to compel) the adult user to forbear from doing something because not doing it would be better for him or her; second, by doing so, it causes harm to others.

This may sound like a simplistic analysis, since the causes of crime and the effects of addiction are so complex and varied. Moreover, this analysis is not as clearly applicable to other drugs, such as crack cocaine, which may themselves make the user more prone to violence. But the heroin example makes an important point about the misuses of the criminal sanction.

Mill spoke indirectly to this issue in the context of prostitution and gambling. He concluded that "fornication" and "gambling" must be tolerated, but then he asked whether a person should "be free to be a pimp, or to keep a gambling-house?" He would probably have come to the same conclusion and asked the same question about the drug user (at least those who retain the power of rational thought) and the drug seller. Mill regarded the question of such professional accessories as "one of these which lie on the exact boundary line." It was clear to him, as it remains clear today to most civil libertarians — though not to all feminists — that the case for criminalizing the professional purveyor of vice is far stronger than the case for criminalizing the occasional consumer of vice.[7]

Another controversial set of contemporary issues also demonstrates the limitations of Mill's principle. The whole area of "fetal" rights is not really amenable to solution by reference to Mill's principle because the essential dispute is over a question that Mill did not address; namely, is the fetus a part of the carrying woman and thus beyond the ken of compulsory state regulation? Or is the fetus a "someone else" that the state has the legitimate power to protect against abortion, abuse, or neglect?

Some argue, as the courts have sometimes implied, that the fetus becomes a "someone else" at the moment of viability — that is, when it would be capable of independent life outside the womb. Others argue that the fetus becomes a "someone else" when the carrying woman makes the decision to carry to term rather than to abort. Under this latter approach, the state might have the power to compel a pregnant woman who had decided not to abort to refrain from excessive drinking or other activities that pose significant health risks to the "someone else" she has decided to carry to term.

In the last analysis, Mill's principle does not help us decide whether or when a fetus becomes a "someone else" — that is for theologians, biologists, judges, or perhaps each pregnant woman to decide. But

Mill's rule can help us sort through some complex philosophical issues regarding the relationships between carrying woman and fetus — once it is decided that the fetus has become a "someone else" deserving of some degree of state protection. A wise state may, of course, decline to exercise power — particularly the power of the criminal law — in certain areas where it may well have legitimate authority to act. The relationship between woman and fetus may be such an area.[8]

One more general issue of complexity, alluded to earlier, may warrant brief further discussion. We live in an age in which people have become far more economically interdependent because of insurance, welfare, taxation, and other mechanisms for sharing the risks and costs of individual hardships. Thus, if some drivers buckle up and others do not, and if the cost of insurance or medical care will rise for all as the result of avoidable injuries caused by a driver's decision not to buckle up, then it can be argued that we all have a stake in every driver's buckling up. That argument can be taken, however, to absurd extremes. We nonskiers, non–bungee jumpers, non–hang gliders, also have a stake in preventing daredevils from taking what we regard as undue risks to their limbs and our pocketbooks. We exercising, cholesterol-watching, fat-avoiding, one-drink-a-day consumers have a stake in every greasy hamburger and kielbasa eaten by a couch potato whose clogged arteries will cost us money. Where would a reasonable line be drawn between compelling everyone to live a safe, healthy, moderate life and permitting undue-risk takers to have their destructive lifestyles (and death wishes) subsidized by the rest of us?

One way of dealing with this issue is to impose risk costs on certain clearly dangerous activities. We already do that through differential insurance premiums based on risk factors such as smoking and hang gliding. It would not be unreasonable, in states that make the wearing of seat belts optional, for insurance companies to give drivers who agree to buckle up a discount on the premium. Indeed, the state might even go further, in my view, and impose a tax on those who refuse to wear seat belts or motorcycle helmets. There already are special taxes in many states on cigarettes, the proceeds from which are used to reduce the societal costs attributable to smoking. I doubt that Mill would have had difficulty with a system that imposed the costs of risk taking more directly on the risk takers, so long as the risk taker remained free of state compulsion and could decide for him- or herself whether to incur the risk and the cost.[9]

Mill recognized, of course, the interdependent nature even of his society. Paraphrasing John Donne, Mill wrote:

> No person is an entirely isolated being; it is impossible for a person to do anything seriously or permanently hurtful to himself, without mischief reaching at least to his near connexions, and often far beyond them. If he injures his property, he does harm to those who directly or indirectly derived support from it, and usually diminishes, by a greater or less amount, the general resources of the community. If he deteriorates his bodily or mental faculties, he not only brings evil upon all who depended on him for any portion of their happiness, but disqualifies himself for rendering the services which he owes to his fellow creatures generally; perhaps becomes a burthen on their affection or benevolence; and if such conduct were very frequent, hardly any offense that is committed would detract more from the general sum of good. Finally, if by his vices or follies a person does no direct harm to others, he is nevertheless (it may be said) injurious by his example; and ought to be compelled to control himself, for the sake of those whom the sight or knowledge of his conduct might corrupt or mislead.

Having recognized this interdependence, Mill proceeded to reject it on relatively unsophisticated grounds:

> But with regard to the merely contingent, or, as it may be called, constructive injury which a person causes to society, by conduct which neither violates any specific duty to the public, nor occasions perceptible hurt to any assignable individual except himself; the inconvenience is one which society can afford to bear, for the sake of the greater good of human freedom. If grown persons are to be punished for not taking proper care of themselves, I would rather it were for their own sake, than under pretense of preventing them from impairing their capacity of rendering to society benefits which society does not pretend it has a right to exact.

In the end, Mill merely gives us his preference: "the greater good of human freedom" over what he calls "the inconvenience" of "constructive injury" caused by the exercise of that freedom. It is a preference shared by most libertarians and individualists but not one shared by all communitarians or even utilitarians. This conflict has divided and will

continue to divide people of goodwill who care about both freedom
and responsibility.

## FREEDOM OF SPEECH AND THOUGHT

There is one area of individual freedom that is not neatly amenable to
Mill's general principle. That is the area of "liberty of thought and discussion." In a separate chapter on that subject — a chapter that has
been nearly as influential as the chapter on state power and individual
liberty — Mill makes some of the most powerful arguments for freedom of speech that have ever been expressed. These arguments include historical, empirical, and logical cases both in favor of the virtues
of free expression and against the vices of censorship.

In his ringing defense of free speech, Mill rejects one of the bedrock
arguments of American jurisprudence, namely, that "the marketplace
of ideas" will inevitably produce truth:

> The dictum that truth always triumphs over persecution, is one of
> those pleasant falsehoods which men repeat after one another till
> they pass into commonplaces, but which all experience refutes. His-
> tory teems with instances of truth put down by persecution.

He offers this observation in refutation of the theory, also rejected by
American jurisprudence, that "truth may justifiably be persecuted because persecution cannot possibly do it any harm." Persecution can, in
fact, destroy truths, not only in the short run but forever. How many
truths must have perished forever in the Holocaust? How many with
the genocide against native peoples in America and elsewhere? How
many with the Inquisition, by the Stalinist purges, and on the Cambodian killing fields? Truth is not a piece of matter or a unit of energy
that will survive pummeling and emerge unscathed in one form or another at one time or another. It is a fragile and ethereal aspiration, easily buried, difficult to retrieve, and capable of being lost forever. That
is why every time an idea is censored, a person with an idea killed, or a
culture destroyed, we risk permanent injury to the corpus of human
knowledge. And that is why it is always better to err on the side of more
speech, more expression, more advocacy — even when the benefits

seem distant and the costs immediate. American jurisprudence and Mill's philosophy reach the same conclusion about the benefits of un-fettered exchange, though by somewhat different routes.

Mill argued persuasively even for the freedom to err — the right to be wrong. He offered a utilitarian justification for encouraging false arguments against the received wisdom, because "teachers and learn-ers go to sleep at their post, as soon as there is no enemy in the field."

One of Mill's most compelling arguments has particular applica-tions to the debate over "speech codes" and "political correctness" on contemporary college and university campuses. Mill understood more than a century ago what many proponents of speech codes seem to ig-nore today, namely, that censorship is almost never content-neutral. Codes that purport to ban "offensive" or "intemperate" words are in-evitably invoked selectively against politically incorrect offensive or in-temperate words. Censorship is a weapon wielded by those in power against those who are not. On college and university campuses, those in power — or those who can influence those in power — may be very different from those in power in the outside world, but Mill's point re-mains persuasive:

> With regard to what is commonly meant by intemperate discussion, namely invective, sarcasm, personality, and the like the denunciation of these weapons would deserve more sympathy if it were ever pro-posed to interdict them equally to both sides; but it is only desired to restrain the employment of them against the prevailing opinion: against the un-prevailing they may not only be used without general disapproval, but will be likely to obtain for him who uses them the praise of honest zeal and righteous indignation.

Mill would argue, of course, that even if we could create what I have called "a symmetrical circle of civility" or "ism-equity" — namely, the identical rules of discourse for all, regardless of the content of their views — it would still be wrong to restrict speech based on factors such as offensiveness, incivility, or rudeness.

The hard question for Mill — indeed, for any utilitarian advocate of free speech — is what should happen when freedom of speech clashes directly with Mill's principle authorizing state compulsion "to prevent harm to others." Here Mill is at his sloppiest as a thinker:

No one pretends that actions should be as free as opinions. On the contrary, even opinions lose their immunity, when the circumstances in which they are expressed are such as to constitute their expression a positive instigation to some mischievous act. An opinion that corn-dealers are starvers of the poor, or that private property is robbery, ought to be unmolested when simply circulated through the press, but may justly incur punishment when delivered orally to an excited mob assembled before the house of a corn-dealer, or when handed about among the same mob in the form of a placard. Acts, of whatever kind, which, without justifiable cause, do harm to others, may be, and in the more important cases absolutely require to be, controlled by the unfavorable sentiments, and, when needful, by the active interference of mankind. The liberty of the individual must be thus far limited; he must not make himself a nuisance to other people.

Mill's last sentence — that a speaker may not "make himself a nuisance to other people" — contains the seeds of a system of pervasive state censorship. Mill probably intended the concept *nuisance* to be construed in the narrowest possible way, say by reference to his prior example of inciting an excited mob. But it is surely capable of being applied to almost any manner of offensive speech, ranging from religious proselytization to pornography.

Mill's sketchy utilitarian argument for censorship is, in my view, shortsighted. A larger view would prefer — as the First Amendment to the United States Constitution prefers and as Mill himself seems to prefer elsewhere — the benefits of relatively unabridged speech over the "inconvenience" of tolerating nuisances, even deeply offensive nuisances. One need not agree with the ditty we all learned on the streets — Sticks and stones may break my bones, but names will never harm me — to accept the important distinction between the state regulation of "sticks and stones," on the one hand, and of "names" and other forms of speech, on the other. Justice Louis Brandeis provided wiser counsel than Mill when he argued, in a case involving socialists who trespassed on private property as part of a protest against capitalism, that a free and open society should tolerate a certain degree of nuisance as a price worth paying for free and untrammeled expression.[10] We should have different rules for regulating nonexpressive actions that pose dangers to others, and for censoring expressive speech that poses comparable dangers.[11] A single utilitarian calculus simply will not do in a society that values freedom of expression more highly than freedom of action. Our society is committed to the proposition that freedom of expression is the best guarantor of freedom of action. Our First Amendment expresses a far different calculus for regulating speech than for regulating nonexpressive conduct, and that is as it should be. Your right to swing your fist should end at the tip of my nose, but your right to express your ideas should not necessarily end at the lobes of my ears.

In the end, John Stuart Mill's enduring contribution to the theory of liberty is a remarkable tour de force. Flawed as it is in its applications, it provides no road map for liberty because there can be no road map capable of taking us through the ever shifting terrain of human civilization. But it is an accurate compass of liberty that points us in the proper direction as surely today as it did more than a century ago. Every citizen of the world who aspires to freedom should reread Mill's *On Liberty* periodically and should consistently evaluate and challenge the actions of the state by reference to its simple but profound principle.

# PART II

᠅

# THE RIGHT NOT TO BE
# CENSORED BY GOVERNMENT

IS THERE A RIGHT TO FREE SPEECH? MANY AMERICANS mistakenly believe that our First Amendment grants them a right to say anything they wish without fear of consequences. The reality is that our Constitution grants few *affirmative rights*. What it does do — especially through the Bill of Rights — is to *restrict the power* of government to engage in certain activities, such as censoring speech or the press.

Illustrative of this common mistake was a *Boston Globe* column on February 1, 2000, by Bob Ryan on the decision by major-league baseball to suspend pitcher John Rocker for making bigoted remarks in an interview. This is what Ryan said:

> Has anyone in Major League Baseball ever heard of the United States Constitution, the First Amendment of which, as every high school civics student is supposed to know, pertains to free speech.
>
> This is a wonderful country, not in the least because it allows freedom of expression to all its citizens, drawing the line at such things as advocating the violent overthrow of the government.
>
> [Rocker] is protected by more than just Voltaire's rhetoric. He is — or, at least he should be — protected by the Constitution of the United States of America. What makes America great is that the John Rockers of this world have every right to stand up and reveal their essential ignorance, just as we have every right to rebut each of their outrageously uninformed viewpoints. . . . An acid tongue is protected by the Constitution. . . . Trampling constitutional rights we hold dear is not the answer.

In a *New York Times* op-ed piece the next day, I wrote the following:

> Despite the common myth that we can say anything we please in this country, the fact is that our Bill of Rights does not grant Americans any general right of free speech.
>
> That's why Bud Selig, the baseball commissioner, can suspend and fine John Rocker, the Atlanta Braves pitcher, for expressing bigoted views in a magazine interview.
>
> Indeed, when announcing the suspension on Monday, Selig said

that Rocker "brought dishonor to himself, the Atlanta Braves and Major League Baseball."

But to conclude that baseball has the right to suspend Rocker does not mean that it was right to do so.

The First Amendment prohibits "Congress" and, by modern interpretation, federal and state governments from "abridging the freedom of speech, or of the press." The amendment, then, is a restriction on government power, not a right to say anything without fear of all consequences. The First Amendment says nothing about the power of private employers, universities, or sports leagues to censor or punish speakers who express views with which they disagree.

Thus, Selig was well within his rights as the chief executive of a private corporation to make an independent decision to suspend Rocker.

The problem is that his decision violates the *spirit* of free speech that animates the First Amendment. The Constitution may impose limits only on the government, but the First Amendment is premised on the idea that there should be a free marketplace of ideas. Private universities, for example, are not constrained by the Constitution, but most choose to follow it anyway, because they recognize that the exchange of ideas — no matter how wrongheaded or obnoxious — is good for education.

By accepting this model of open discourse, no university can reasonably claim to be "dishonored" by views expressed by students or faculty members, since they do not reflect the collective thinking of the university.

Baseball is not, of course, a university, and diversity of views is not essential to the enterprise. But trash talking, banter, razzing, and taunting have always been part of the game. However offensive his comments, Rocker had every right to insult New York and New Yorkers. He crossed a line when he moved to racist and ethnic stereotyping, but he is surely not the first player to have expressed such views. Will baseball now need a platoon of speech cops monitoring players in bars and at barbecues? Or will the new rule be limited to published comments? What about taunts on the field? Now that baseball has drawn a line in the sand, it must apply it uniformly.

Selig would have been wiser not to suspend Rocker but to announce that the league is committed to freedom of speech and that the comments of individual players should not be misunderstood as reflecting the opinions of major-league baseball.

Such an approach would deny John Rocker or any other player the power to "dishonor" the game, while allowing major-league baseball to honor the spirit of free speech.

Ryan was wrong about the letter of the First Amendment, but he was certainly right about Voltaire, whose famous statement "I disapprove of what you say, but I will defend to the death your right to say it" reflects the spirit of free speech.

Judicial opinions have interpreted the Fourteenth Amendment — which provides that the states may not deprive any person of "life, liberty, or property, without due process of law" — as a broadening of the First Amendment to include restrictions on the states and on all official governmental actors, such as presidents, governors, public universities, and so on. Still, the First Amendment applies — in its letter — only to what is called "state action," that is, any action by the government or someone acting on its behalf. Even governments are free to censor *some* speech that has been held to fall outside the parameters of "freedom of speech." As we will see in chapter 16, falsely shouting fire in a theater is not protected speech. Nor are obscene words or pictures. There are other exceptions as well, most of which relate to matters of national security, immediate incitements to violence, or words that constitute criminal acts (such as extortion, conspiracy, and transmission of certain secrets). In the following chapters, I explore the scope and limits of freedom of speech under our First Amendment.

# SIXTEEN

# SHOUTING "FIRE!"

*Following decades of listening to people trying to get governments to censor all manner of speech by analogizing it to "shouting fire in a crowded theater," in 1989 I wrote an essay for the* Atlantic Monthly *on the subject.*

WHEN THE REVEREND JERRY FALWELL LEARNED THAT THE Supreme Court had reversed his $200,000 judgment against *Hustler* magazine for the emotional distress that he had suffered from an outrageous parody, his response was typical of those who seek to censor speech: "Just as no person may scream 'Fire!' in a crowded theater when there is no fire, and find cover under the First Amendment, likewise, no sleazy merchant like Larry Flynt should be able to use the First Amendment as an excuse for maliciously and dishonestly attacking public figures, as he has so often done."

Justice Oliver Wendell Holmes's classic example of unprotected speech — falsely shouting "Fire!" in a crowded theater — has been invoked so often, by so many people, in such diverse contexts, that it has become part of our national folk language. It has even appeared — most appropriately — in the theater: In Tom Stoppard's play *Rosencrantz and Guildenstern Are Dead*, a character shouts at the audience, "Fire!" He then quickly explains: "It's all right — I'm demonstrating the misuse of free speech."

Shouting "Fire!" in the theater may well be the only jurisprudential analogy that has assumed the status of a folk argument. A prominent historian has characterized it as "the most brilliantly persuasive expression that ever came from Holmes' pen." But in spite of its hallowed position in both the jurisprudence of the First Amendment and the arsenal of political discourse, it is and was an inapt analogy, even in the context in which it was originally offered. It has lately become —

despite, perhaps even because of, the frequency and promiscuousness of its invocation — little more than a caricature of logical argumentation.

The case that gave rise to the "Fire!"-in-a-crowded-theater analogy — *Schenck v. United States* — involved the prosecution of Charles Schenck, who was the general secretary of the Socialist Party in Philadelphia, and Elizabeth Baer, who was its recording secretary. In 1917 a jury found Schenck and Baer guilty of attempting to cause insubordination among soldiers who had been drafted to fight in the First World War. They and other party members had circulated leaflets urging draftees not to "submit to intimidation" by fighting in a war being conducted on behalf of "Wall Street's chosen few." Schenck admitted, and the Court found, that the intent of the pamphlet's "impassioned language" was to "influence" draftees to resist the draft. Interestingly, however, Justice Holmes noted that nothing in the pamphlet suggested that the draftees should use unlawful or violent means to oppose conscription: "In form at least [the pamphlet] confined itself to peaceful measures, such as a petition for the repeal of the act" and an exhortation to exercise "your right to assert your opposition to the draft." Many of its most impassioned words were quoted directly from the Constitution.

Justice Holmes acknowledged that "in many places and in ordinary times the defendants, in saying all that was said in the circular, would have been within their constitutional rights." "But," he added, "the character of every act depends upon the circumstances in which it is done." And to illustrate that truism he went on to say, "The most stringent protection of free speech would not protect a man in falsely shouting fire in a theater, and causing a panic. It does not even protect a man from an injunction against uttering words that may have all the effect of force."

Justice Holmes then upheld the convictions in the context of a wartime draft, finding that the pamphlet created "a clear and present danger" of hindering the war effort while our soldiers were fighting for their lives and our liberty.

The example of shouting "Fire!" obviously bore little relationship to the facts of the Schenck case. The Schenck pamphlet contained a substantive political message. It urged its draftee readers to *think* about the message and then — if they so chose — to act on it in a lawful and nonviolent way. The man who shouts "Fire!" in a crowded theater is neither sending a political message nor inviting his listener to think about what he has said and decide what to do in a rational, calculated manner. On the contrary, the message is designed to force action *without* contemplation. The message "Fire!" is directed not to the mind and the conscience of the listener but, rather, to his adrenaline and his feet. It is a stimulus to immediate *action*, not thoughtful reflection. It is — as Justice Holmes recognized in his follow-up sentence — the functional equivalent of "uttering words that may have all the effect of force."

Indeed, in that respect the shout of "Fire!" is not even speech, in any meaningful sense of that term. It is a *clang* sound — the equivalent of setting off a nonverbal alarm. Had Justice Holmes been more honest about his example, he would have said that freedom of speech does not protect a kid who pulls a fire alarm in the absence of a fire. But that obviously would have been irrelevant to the case at hand. The proposition that pulling an alarm is not protected speech certainly leads to the conclusion that shouting the word *fire* is also not protected. But the core analogy is the nonverbal alarm, and the derivative example is the verbal shout. By cleverly substituting the derivative shout for the core alarm, Holmes made it possible to analogize one set of words to another — as he could not have done if he had begun with the self-evident proposition that setting off an alarm bell is not free speech.

The analogy is thus not only inapt but also insulting. Most Americans do not respond to political rhetoric with the same kind of automatic acceptance expected of schoolchildren responding to a fire drill. Not a single recipient of the Schenck pamphlet is known to have changed his mind after reading it. Indeed, one draftee, who appeared as a prosecution witness, was asked whether reading a pamphlet asserting that the draft law was unjust would make him "immediately decide that you must erase that law." Not surprisingly, he replied, "I do my own thinking." A theatergoer would probably not respond similarly if asked how he would react to a shout of "Fire!"

Another important reason the analogy is inapt is that Holmes emphasizes the factual falsity of the shout "Fire!" The Schenck pamphlet, however, was not factually false. It contained political opinions and ideas about the causes of war and about appropriate and lawful responses to the draft. As the Supreme Court reaffirmed in *Falwell v.*

*Hustler*, "the First Amendment recognizes no such thing as a 'false' idea." Nor does it recognize false opinions about the causes of or cures for war.

A closer analogy to the facts of the Schenck case might have been provided by a person's standing outside a theater, offering the patrons a leaflet advising them that in his opinion the theater was structurally unsafe, and urging them not to enter but to complain to the building inspectors. That analogy, however, would not have served Holmes's argument for punishing Schenck. Holmes needed an analogy that would appear relevant to Schenck's political speech but that would invite the conclusion that censorship was appropriate.

Unsurprisingly, a war-weary nation — in the throes of a know-nothing hysteria over immigrant anarchists and socialists — welcomed the comparison between what was regarded as a seditious political pamphlet and a malicious shout of "Fire!" Ironically, the "Fire!" analogy is nearly all that survives from the Schenck case; the ruling itself is almost certainly not good law. Pamphlets of the kind that resulted in Schenck's imprisonment have been circulated with impunity during subsequent wars.

Over the past several years I have assembled a collection of instances — cases, speeches, arguments — in which proponents of censorship have maintained that the expression at issue is "just like" or "equivalent to" falsely shouting "Fire!" in a crowded theater and ought to be banned, "just as" shouting "Fire!" ought to be banned. The analogy is generally invoked, often with self-satisfaction, as an absolute argument stopper. It does, after all, claim the high authority of the great Justice Oliver Wendell Holmes. I have rarely heard it invoked in a convincing, or even particularly relevant, way. But that, too, can claim lineage from the great Holmes.

Not unlike Falwell, with his silly comparison between shouting "Fire!" and publishing an offensive parody, courts and commentators have frequently invoked "Fire!" as an analogy to expression that is not an automatic stimulus to panic. A state supreme court held that "Holmes' aphorism . . . applies with equal force to pornography" — in particular to the exhibition of the movie *Carmen Baby* in a drive-in theater in close proximity to highways and homes. Another court analogized "picketing . . . in support of a secondary boycott" to shouting "Fire!" because in both instances "speech and conduct are brigaded."

In the famous Skokie case — in which the Chicago suburb tried to censor a Nazi demonstration — one of the judges argued that allowing Nazis to march through a city where a large number of Holocaust survivors live "just might fall into the same category as one's 'right' to cry fire in a crowded theater." Most recently, a civil rights lawyer, in a *New York Times* op-ed piece, analogized John Rocker's bigoted statements about blacks, gays, and foreigners to shouting fire in a crowded theater.

Outside court the analogies become even more absurdly stretched. A spokesperson for the New Jersey Sports and Exposition Authority complained that newspaper reports to the effect that a large number of football players had contracted cancer after playing in the Meadowlands — a stadium atop a landfill — were the "journalistic equivalent of shouting fire in a crowded theater." An insect researcher acknowledged that his prediction that a certain amusement park might become roach infested "may be tantamount to shouting fire in a crowded theater." The philosopher Sidney Hook, in a letter to the *New York Times* bemoaning a Supreme Court decision that required a plaintiff in a defamation action to prove that the offending statement was actually false, argued that the First Amendment does not give the press carte blanche to accuse innocent persons "any more than the First Amendment protects the right of someone falsely to shout fire in a crowded theater."

Some close analogies to shouting "Fire!" or setting off an alarm are, of course, available: calling in a false bomb threat; dialing 911 and falsely describing an emergency; making a loud, gunlike sound in the presence of the president; setting off a voice-activated sprinkler system by falsely shouting "Fire!" In one case in which the "Fire!" analogy was directly to the point, a creative defendant tried to get around it. The case involved a man who calmly advised an airline clerk that he was "only here to hijack the plane." He was charged, in effect, with shouting "Fire!" in a crowded theater, and his rejected defense — as quoted by the court — was as follows: "If we built fire-proof theaters and let people know about this, then the shouting of 'Fire!' would not cause panic."

Here are some more-distant but still related analogies to shouting fire: a police slaying in which some members of an onlooking crowd urged a mentally ill vagrant who had taken an officer's gun to shoot the officer; the screaming of racial epithets during a tense confrontation.

Analogies are, by their nature, matters of degree. Some are closer to the core example than others. But any attempt to analogize political ideas in a pamphlet, ugly parody in a magazine, offensive movies in a theater, controversial newspaper articles, or any of the other expressions and actions cataloged above to the very different act of shouting "Fire!" in a crowded theater is either self-deceptive or self-serving.

The government does, of course, have some arguably legitimate bases for suppressing speech that bears no relationship to shouting "Fire!" It may ban the publication of nuclear-weapons codes, of information about troop movements, and of the identity of undercover agents. It may criminalize extortion threats and conspiratorial agreements. These expressions may lead directly to serious harm, but the mechanisms of causation are very different from that at work when an alarm is sounded. One may also argue — less persuasively, in my view — against protecting certain forms of public obscenity and defamatory statements. Here, too, the mechanisms of causation are very different. None of these exceptions to the First Amendment's exhortation that the government "shall make no law . . . abridging the freedom of speech, or of the press" is anything like falsely shouting "Fire!" in a crowded theater; they all must be justified on other grounds.

Abbie Hoffman once described an occasion when he was standing near a fire with a crowd of people and got in trouble for yelling "Theater, theater!" That, I think, is about as clever and productive a use as anyone has ever made of Holmes's flawed analogy. And it is about the right level of logical response Holmes's silly argument deserves. So let us hear no more nonsensical analogies to shouting fire in a crowded theater. Those who seek to censor speech will just have to come up with a somewhat more cogent illustration — one that bears at least some relationship to real speech.

# SEVENTEEN

# THE RIGHT TO BE WRONG

---

*One genre of speech and press not protected by the First Amendment is defamation — libel and slander. For a public figure to prevail in a defamation action, he or she must prove not only that the statement at issue is false but that it was made with malice — that is, with knowledge of its falsity or reckless disregard for its truth.*

*In the 1980s, two great defamation cases captured the headlines. One was brought by General William Westmoreland against CBS for allegedly misreporting important facts about the Vietnam War. The other was brought by Israeli general Ariel Sharon against* Time *magazine for allegedly misreporting facts about the Phalangist massacre of Palestinians in Lebanon. Renata Adler wrote an influential book about these cases, which I critiqued in this essay.*

---

RECKLESS DISREGARD, THE TITLE OF ADLER'S ACCOUNT OF THESE two great libel trials of the 1980s, derives from the legal standard for libel in a lawsuit involving a public figure. The full phrase, "reckless disregard for the truth," lies at the core of this influential book.

For a distinguished writer about the First Amendment, Renata Adler has an almost religious sense of "the Truth." A major thesis of her book is that *Time* magazine did not tell the truth about General Ariel Sharon's responsibility for the Phalangist massacre of Palestinian civilians in the Sabra and Shatila refugee camps, and that CBS did not tell the truth about General William Westmoreland's role in concealing enemy troop estimates in Vietnam. Another thesis of her book is that the First Amendment is somehow supposed to protect relatively small, highly moral, and dissenting voices (such as those in the civil rights movement), but not "unitary, powerful and monolithic [news organizations] like *Time* and CBS which are guilty of suppressing the very di-

versity that it was the purpose of the First Amendment . . . to protect."
We are hearing more and more of this kind of thinking by politically
correct critics of a more universalistic view of the First Amendment.

Adler advocates "different standards for small than for large publications" and argues that the First Amendment victories of the giant
press do not help to protect small publications. Her reasoning is that
"even if all large publications were to win their cases, small publications would be *in no way* protected [emphasis added], since rich libel
plaintiffs could still sue them and ruin them on legal costs alone."
What she neglects to tell the reader is that the protective legal precedents established by the large publications govern the cases brought
against the small publications. There is also developing law that punishes, by court costs and other financial sanctions, frivolous libel suits
brought in the face of dispositive precedents. Several recent cases show
a willingness to apply a more draconian standard for pursuing frivolous lawsuits for defamation. Thus the large publications, for better or
worse, are often the vanguard of protection for the First Amendment
rights of small publications as well as for individual citizens.

Adler is correct, of course, in reminding us how incredibly arrogant
and hypocritical the giant media can be in their self-righteous and self-
serving defense of their rights under the First Amendment. She does a
masterful job of documenting the sometimes shoddy reporting that
went into the *Time* and CBS accounts, and the unwillingness of *Time*
to acknowledge its serious mistakes. (CBS was far more willing to admit, at least internally, that its program was seriously flawed in its
methodology, if not its conclusions.) In a powerful coda, she devastates
CBS and to a lesser extent *Time*, as well as their lawyers, Cravath,
Swaine, and Moore, for trying to intimidate her publisher into "suppressing or at least delaying publication of the book." The spectacle of
these great defenders of the First Amendment attempting to use the
threat of libel suits against a book that criticizes their defense of libel
suits brought against them by those whom they criticized is enough to
bring joy to the heart of anyone who is skeptical about our ability to
determine the truth with finality or absoluteness.

An important assumption underlying our commitment to freedom
of expression is that truth is a *process*, not a *product*. I am confident that
Thomas Jefferson would have understood and enjoyed the old Jewish
folktale about the rabbi who concluded that the wife, the husband, and

the student were *all* right. Jefferson, who was somewhat more of a skeptic than the rabbi, probably would have told all of them they were wrong, but the point would have been similar and reflects an important premise underlying our First Amendment. The most basic right under that charter of liberty is "the right to be *wrong*," and, indeed, the need to err on the side of wrongly criticizing government and other powerful institutions rather than wrongly withholding such criticism.

Renata Adler, after persuasively demonstrating that both CBS and *Time* were probably wrong — at least in their methodologies and details, if not in the thrust of their stories — jumps to the conclusion that "neither the ninety minutes [of the CBS broadcast] nor the paragraph [in *Time*] should have been broadcast or published." She also believes that neither lawsuit should have been brought, or if brought "aggressively defended."

I respectfully dissent. The offending speech should have been broadcast and published, even at the risk of error. Obviously, if that risk could have been reduced — and the risk of error in fast-breaking, controversial stories of this kind can rarely be eliminated — it should have been reduced, as all responsible journalists would do. But the subjects of the stories were both high-ranking military leaders with enormous followings, power, and access to the media. Being attacked, even being wrongly attacked, comes with the job description, as Harry Truman so aptly reminded us with his famous kitchen metaphor. Generals Sharon and Westmoreland both chose to remain in particularly hot kitchens, giving orders that caused the deaths of numerous young soldiers and civilians. *If* they were wrongly accused of certain terrible actions (and I am prepared to assume they were), they had ample opportunity to present their accounts in the marketplace of ideas. And they did, repeatedly and angrily. Even persuasively! But when CBS and *Time* refused to retract their accounts, the generals sued, and the media defendants vigorously defended their constitutional right to broadcast and publish what they had believed to be true. Ms. Adler wishes they had rolled over and played dead, instead of hiring a law firm — both hired the same firm — that attacks its opponents like "a pack of Dobermans, who are clambering to be unleashed." But that too is part of our constitutional system of adversary justice.

Once a controversy turns into a libel case, it should be treated like a case capable of setting a terrible precedent for First Amendment freedoms. General Sharon's Doberman was Milton Gould, one of the most formidable litigators in the country. Not surprisingly, the *Time*-Sharon case ended in a draw. The jury found that *Time* had defamed Sharon by printing a false story but that the reporter had been negligent and careless rather than malicious or reckless. The trial judge's careful instructions encouraged that Solomonic resolution.

The CBS case resulted in an unconditional surrender by Westmoreland. Adler succeeds in convincing the reader that this surrender was the fault of Westmoreland's inept chief counsel, an inexperienced right-wing-cause lawyer, rather than a reflection of the weakness of his legal case or the truth of the CBS report. We are led to believe that had the lawyers in that case been a match, perhaps it, too, would have ended with an unequivocal result reflecting what Adler believes to be the truth — namely, that CBS, like *Time*, doctored the underlying facts to present a newsworthy scoop that the true facts would not have supported.

Adler ends her book by referring to a story she uses as a metaphor for the two cases. She tells of an earlier libel against General Sharon by an Israeli newspaper that had exposed a "scandal": that Sharon had erected an expensive fence around his home and had improperly charged the cost to the government. Sharon denied that there was a fence and asked the Israeli "press counsel" to check and determine whether there was indeed any fence. The press counsel issued a report denouncing Sharon as an evil brute but concluded, almost as an afterthought, that "there is no fence."

Renata Adler categorically informs us that in both the CBS-Westmoreland and *Time*-Sharon cases "there was no fence." In transferring this metaphor from a simple controversy over a single observable (indeed photographable) fact to a pair of the most complex epistemological disputes in recent history concerning moral responsibility, perceptual communication, and the theories of knowledge, Adler reveals her own naïveté about the truth.

I, for one, am glad the stories were run, the denials issued, the lawsuits defended vigorously, and the book written. Each of these exercises in free expression and advocacy contributed to the marketplace of ideas. The public now knows more about both sides of the Sharon-*Time* and Westmoreland-CBS controversies, more about the foibles and fallibilities of the press, more about how lawyers litigate libel cases, and even a bit more about how writers, like Renata Adler, can select and manipulate facts to support a strongly held point of view. I cannot claim to be glad that the libel suits were brought to court, because such suits, regardless of how they are resolved, sap the First Amendment of some of its vital ability to leave controversies to the marketplace of ideas where they belong. No court will ever determine the truth about Vietnam or Lebanon. That is not the judicial function. The most the courts can do — and they did it relatively well in these two cases — is to help keep the process of "truthing" untrammeled so that our citizens can make up their minds about controversies or, better still, keep their minds open.

---

*This 1980s dispute is as relevant today as it was then. Media giants have grown even more powerful than they were when Adler wrote. The war to control the information highways of the new millennium is well under way and is likely to result in even more narrow ownership of the means of mass communication. It is central to the mission of the First Amendment that critics like Adler keep watch over those to whom the exercise of our First Amendment has been largely entrusted. Freedom of speech and press are far too important to be left only to giant media conglomerates. For the marketplace of ideas to function properly, the public must know how to assess the various competitors in the elusive quest for truth. We must maintain the multiple processes for determining truth and keeping the media free of governmental control and accountable to its consumers.*

---

# EIGHTEEN

# DIRTY WORDS

---

*From the very beginning of our constitutional system, the First Amendment was not thought to cover obscene speech. Early on in our history, obscenity was deemed immoral and offensive. In recent years, a new claim has been made: namely, that a certain kind of sexist obscenity — called pornography — encourages rape, sexual harassment, and negative attitudes toward women. Thus the debate shifted from morality to empiricism. I have written articles on both aspects of this issue.*

*In 1977 the federal government prosecuted Al Goldstein, the publisher of a weekly newspaper called* Screw. *I used that case as an occasion to write about the "dirty words" exception to the First Amendment, emphasizing the moral issues. In a subsequent article (see next chapter), I focused on the empirical issues.*

---

Goldstein was hated and despised by everybody . . . every day and a thousand times a day, on platforms, on the telescreen, in newspapers . . . his theories were . . . ridiculed for the pitiful rubbish that they were — in spite of all this, his influence never seemed to grow less. . . . Goldstein['s] usual venomous attack [was] so exaggerated and perverse that a child should have been able to see through it, and yet just plausible enough to fill one with an alarmed feeling that other people, less levelheaded than oneself, might be taken in by it. . . . There were . . . widespread stories of a terrible book, a compendium of all the heresies, of which Goldstein was the author and which circulated clandestinely here and there. (George Orwell, *1984*)

Al Goldstein has the kind of mouth mothers used to wash out with soap. He uses filthy words, tells tasteless jokes, and does — or at least claims he does — disgusting things. But lots of people are like that.

What distinguishes Al Goldstein from other local degenerates is that he publishes a weekly newspaper — appropriately titled *Screw* — that prints his words, photographs his deeds, and reports on the dirty doings of the raunchy underground. As Goldstein admits — indeed proclaims: "What I'm selling . . . is tastelessness" — the photographs are the grossest; the language, the filthiest; and the humor, the sickest. Although *Screw* devotes much of its copy to the politics of sex, it brashly eschews any claim to "socially redeeming value." Goldstein is fond of saying: "A hard-on is its own redeeming value." *Screw*'s effect — if not its purpose — is to offend everybody in sight. Goldstein has strewn his verbal garbage over the entire spectrum of society: his targets have included everyone and everything from politicians ("the ultimate hookers") to the women's movement ("*Screw* doesn't think too highly of women's lib, or, in fact, women"). Nor does he immunize from his vitriol those who can help him: he has characterized the American Civil Liberties Union as "moronic . . . phony knee jerk liberals" and his own lawyer as naïve for believing that "this kinda shit is defensible." A recent cartoon plumbed the lowest depths of tastelessness by picturing the nine justices of the United States Supreme Court — the men who may ultimately decide Goldstein's fate — engaged in an array of perverse sexual acts with each other and with a bizarre assortment of animals, vegetables, and minerals.

It is not surprising that the Nixon-Mitchell Justice Department — which listed pornography, but not gun control, among the five most important law-enforcement priorities — should have set its sights on Goldstein and his smut empire. Since *Screw* is published in New York City and since the vast majority of its 100,000 subscribers and readers live in that city's metropolitan area, the Southern District of New York would have been the natural locus of the investigation, indictment, and trial. But the government was not taking any chances on the relatively cosmopolitan jury likely to be empanelled in the Big Apple. It is difficult to offend a New Yorker. By that city's standards of salaciousness, *Screw* stood somewhere near the middle of any "peter-meter" of raunch (the peter-meter is a Goldstein-concocted measure of the sexual explicitness of porno films). Several publications that are even more tasteless than *Screw* (the stomach boggles) are regularly seen on local stands. One can find any possible combination of sexes and species entangled in lustful embrace on the screens of Times Square movie houses. And the proliferation of massage parlors, health spas, and encounter studios — or whatever euphemism brothels are masquerading under these days — cater to all tastes, no matter how bizarre or anatomically inconceivable. There was a considerable risk that a jury daily exposed to this diet of degeneracy would return a ho-hum verdict of not guilty by reason of boredom. (As one New York federal judge recently commented: "In these times of . . . massage parlors with neon signs and street-corner pandering . . . , we suspect that many of our jurors selected within a fifty-mile radius of [New York City] are licentious or have friends who are.")

So the feds took out a map of Middle America and sought out a Bible-belt jurisdiction where Goldstein was likely to be viewed as the devil incarnate and *Screw* magazine as his *Gehenna Gazette*. What they wanted was a city populous enough to have a few *Screw* subscribers but parochial enough to guarantee an indictment and conviction. This calculation led them to Wichita, Kansas, a city of 350,000, of whom less than a dozen subscribed to *Screw* magazine. (There are no newsstand sales of *Screw* in that city.) None of these willing readers had ever complained to anyone, and so the government decided to create its own list of ersatz subscribers who would serve as "complaining" witnesses. During the very week of the Watergate break-in, several Wichita postal inspectors, apparently operating on instructions from Washington, filled out subscription applications for *Screw*. When the sealed envelopes arrived in Kansas, they were placed intact in another envelope and sent on to Washington. But despite the fact that the pristine atmosphere of Wichita was never actually contaminated by exposure to these infectious publications, the nefarious felony had been completed: obscene material had entered the territory of Kansas through the United States mail. The stage was set for the trial of the "Screw Two" — Al Goldstein and his partner, James Buckley.

As the prosecution proceeded, it became abundantly clear that the government had shrewdly chosen the site of its Bicentennial monkey trial. The grand jurors literally got down on their knees and prayerfully sought guidance from the Lord each day before hearing the evidence of *Screw*'s blasphemies. A thirteen-count indictment charging use of the mail to distribute obscene material was soon voted.

The first issue in this case was the legal propriety of having the trial in Kansas. The defense argued that the jurisdiction of the Kansas

Federal Court was contrived by the phony postal-inspector subscribers. They raised the specter of the federal government's dragging black militant publishers from Harlem to Mississippi and labor organizers from Michigan down to North Carolina in order to have them tried before maximally hostile jurors. Allowing a handful of contrived subscribers to determine the locus of a federal trial, they argued, gives the federal government the power to impose the most parochial standards of obscenity on magazines published for the most sophisticated audiences. But the trial was to be in Kansas, and all motions to transfer it to New York were denied. (It will be interesting to see how Chief Justice Warren Burger, who has frequently complained about New York City's imposing its sexual mores on Mississippi, will react to this ploy, under which Kansas can impose its mores on New York City.)

Once the four-week trial itself got under way, the government introduced a local literature professor as its "expert" witness. The expert — who conceded that modern literature was not his specialty — delivered a full-scale criticism of *Screw*: the editorials were unbalanced and abrasive; the movie reviews were shallow and poorly written; words were misspelled; grammar was sometimes incorrect; and arguments were not presented effectively. He acknowledged, on cross-examination, that most contemporary magazines and newspapers would flunk his exacting McGuffey standards. But he insisted that the public does not have an untrammeled right to choose what it wants to read: "I think there are some . . . books that shouldn't be published." Defense experts — who included Dr. Wardell Pomeroy, coauthor of the Kinsey reports and currently head of the Sex Education and Information Council of the United States — testified that *Screw* accurately represented sexual mores of our society and contained serious literary and political value.

But despite the legal and factual complexity of the case, it apparently took the jury — eight women and four men, most of whom had not gone beyond high school — several hours to review the evidence, but only seventeen minutes of deliberation to convict the defendants on every count. The issue, after all, was quite elementary: according to the prosecutor's closing argument, the case had nothing to do with the First Amendment — it was a simple battle between "decency" and "specialists in degeneracy." Goldstein and Buckley now face substantial prison terms unless the conviction is reversed on legal grounds.

The case will surely be appealed, eventually — if necessary — to the Supreme Court, where it would provide a compelling test of that Court's ability to apply the First Amendment to material that is both pornographic and political.

The Supreme Court recently devised a new test for determining whether a publication is legally obscene: the jury must decide (1) whether "the average person, applying contemporary community standards, would find that the work, taken as a whole, appeals to the prurient interest, . . . (2) whether the work depicts or describes, in a patently offensive way, sexual conduct, . . . and (3) whether the work, taken as a whole, lacks serious literary, artistic, political, or scientific value." The *Screw* conviction tests the good faith of the Supreme Court's assurance that if those standards are applied "the First Amendment values are adequately protected."

If there is one value of the First Amendment that is beyond dispute, it is the right of a newspaper to criticize the government. If the First Amendment means anything, it surely means that when a newspaper publishes attacks against government officials, these officials may not respond by prosecuting the newspaper. They may answer the criticisms, but they may not decide that the public shall not read the newspaper. There is certainly no marketplace of ideas when government officials can close down a shop selling ideas critical of those officials.

It seems clear that the prosecution against *Screw* and its publishers was motivated, at least in part, by the vicious diatribes against our established institutions and those who run them. There are now more than two dozen imitators of *Screw*'s format and many hundreds of other periodicals that publish equally raw pictures. But *Screw* has been singled out for federal prosecution because it sells pornography-cum-politics. Its politics are the politics of promiscuous sex. It advocates an approach to the human body — a lifestyle — totally at variance with those espoused by the established institutions of our society. Its politics, though disagreeable to most Americans, are no less authentic than the politics of vegetarianism, of gun ownership, or even of the euphemistically labeled "right to life" (many of whose advocates favor the death penalty).

*Screw*, moreover, is a political newspaper in the more traditional sense of that term: it supports and opposes political candidates; it editorializes on current issues; it investigates and exposes corruption.

Indeed, *Screw* performs one specific political function that no other medium attempts. It gathers information about the views and actions of politicians, judges, and other public figures in the area of sexual repression.

Just as the *Jewish Press* often asks the parochial question: Is it good or bad for the Jews? — and just as the *Pilot* frequently asks: Is it good or bad for the Catholic Church? — so, too, *Screw* magazine asks: Is it good or bad for the purveyors and consumers of raunch? Advocates of greater sexual freedom have just as much right to cast their vote with parochial concerns in mind as do other interest groups, and in order to cast their votes intelligently, they must know about the records and attitudes of politicians on the issues that concern them.

The language Goldstein uses in making his political points and in evaluating political candidates is always strong — often rancid. While other newspapers may characterize disfavored politicians as incompetent, unintelligent, or corrupt, Goldstein is apt to call them "assholes," "scumbags," or "hard-ons." In urging the defeat of a particularly hypocritical district attorney, Goldstein recalled Spiro Agnew's putrid prose by urging the voters to cleanse the "hemorrhoids of democracy . . . out of this nation's asshole." But strong language has typified a certain style of American journalism throughout our history. Namecalling, including some fairly vicious sexual allegations against King George III, was common among certain revolutionary elements in our population. The *Boston Gazette* called Governor Thomas Hutchinson "a rascal" snatched from the "dunghill." And a Tory writer retorted in kind by calling the *Gazette* "dunghill bred" and "Monday's Dung Barge." Another paper called on its readers to smear the houses of loyalists with "Hillsborough Paint" (a mixture of urine and feces that would warm the cockles of Al Goldstein's heart). The *New York Journal* likened Mother England to "an old abandoned prostitute crimsoned o'er with every abominable crime." This penchant for scatological epithets did not end with American independence: a leading postrevolutionary case involved a man who publicly expressed the wish "that a cannon had lodged in the president's posterior." Nor is Al Goldstein the first journalist to insult a justice of the Supreme Court. The *Aurora*, the nation's leading Republican paper, penned the following rhyme about Justice Samuel Chase: "Cursed of thy father, / scum of all that is base; / thy sight is odious and / thy name is [Chase]."

(Ironically — and relevantly — some of the worst abuse was reserved for postmasters accused of opening mail by melting the wax.)

Goldstein's prose — though considerably less elegant — is not different in kind from that of some of our revered forebears: yesterday's "dunghill" is today's slightly less refined "asshole," but the excretory referent is similar. Surely this kind of name-calling is political speech protected by the First Amendment.

It is probably true that if *Screw* limited itself to printing *only* unillustrated editorials and political information, even the Nixon administration might not have dared to prosecute Goldstein. (It is noteworthy, however, that one count of the indictment specifically charged him with publishing *reviews* of pornographic movies. The judge initially upheld that charge, but then, after an adverse editorial appeared in a local newspaper, reversed himself and dismissed it. Under the government's theory of that charge, I could probably be indicted for publishing this article.) The hook on which the government has attempted to hang the *Screw* prosecution is the undisputed fact that *Screw* magazine published — along with its editorials, consumer tips, and advertising — very dirty pictures. Some of the photographs are straight hard-core porn; others are scatological. Some are prurient; others, emetic. *Screw's* insistence on employing the media of scatology and pornography to dramatize its political message squarely raises the elusive question: Where does the pornography of politics end and the politics of pornography begin?

The interesting legal issue can be put in this way: Assuming that some of the pictures, *standing alone*, are criminally obscene, but that the editorials and most of the other material, *standing alone*, are constitutionally protected, what then is the constitutional status of the newspaper as a *whole*, combining — as it does — constitutionally protected political speech with constitutionally unprotected smut?

The Supreme Court has stated: "The First Amendment protects work which, *taken as a whole*, has serious literary, artistic, political, or scientific value, regardless of whether the government or a majority of the people approve of the ideas these works represent." But the Court has given no guidelines for determining how much weight must be given to the political and how much to the pornographic in a mixed publication.

A perusal of the indicted issues of *Screw* makes it clear that the vast majority of every issue consists of nonpornographic material. One such issue — the "strongest" one sexually — consists of the following: a cover drawing that is not even arguably obscene; an inside-page, hard-core close-up of a copulating couple; a one thousand–word editorial by Goldstein attacking everyone from the pope to the owner of the New York Yankees to Pan Am Airways to the president of the Teamster's Union to Vice President Rockefeller to New York City's finest; a five-page interview with a porno-film producer, accompanied by several nonpornographic photos; a pictorial feature — by a well-known photographer — of a couple urinating on each other; a three-page article on sex for older people entitled "Twat in the Twilight Years"; an editorial condemnation of "porno pirates" who sell bootlegged prints of sex films, accompanied by a boycott list of some fifty-seven theaters throughout the country where such prints are run; a two-page humorous potpourri of prose and pictures about the lighter side of sex, including one hard-core photograph; an item called "Smut from the Past," which reprints — in a humorous and nostalgic setting — one or two antique porno stills; a weekly column called "Shit List," wherein Goldstein castigates some unfortunate person or institution — this time the Chemical Bank — in scatological language; an autobiographical series by a stripper entitled "Diary of a Dirty Broad"; a photography collage of nonpornographic sexual sculpture; a column called "My Scene," which describes one reader's sexual adventures — this time a suburban housewife's floral fling with a plant salesman — illustrated by an explicit hard-core photo; a book column featuring reviews of several porno books as well as a review of Alison Lurie's best-seller *The War Between the Tates;* an absolutely tasteless editorial cartoon picturing President Gerald Ford attempting to insert his penis, which is marked "Nixon's Pardon," in the ear of John Q. Public, over the caption "Taking It in the Ear"; a column called "Dirty Diversions," which ranks porno films on the "peter-meter"; a five-page catalog of the sexual goings-on in New York, describing and ranking movies, burlesque houses, swingers' bars, and massage parlors; a weekly consumers' service called "Mail Order Madness," which cautions readers about mail-order houses that specialize in ripping off porno purchasers who are too embarrassed to complain. The rest of the paper is devoted to an assortment of advertisements for sexual products, services, and partners of every conceivable variety and price.

All in all, the forty-eight-page issue examined contained more than one hundred illustrations, not more than ten of which are even arguably hard-core. Most of the rest of the newspaper cannot be said — by any stretch of the imagination or contraction of the Constitution — to lack First Amendment protection. Yet a judge and jury concluded that this issue — "taken as a whole" — does not have sufficient value to warrant constitutional protection.

It would, of course, be possible to publish *Screw* magazine without the handful of dirty pictures. Only a few of the porno shots are really integrated into the editorial content of the magazine, and most of those could probably be softened a bit without losing their impact.

But the magazine is what it is, and it is not the job of the government or the courts to serve as supereditors. Moreover — and this is really the crux of the matter — the magazine would certainly lose a significant portion of its readership if it eliminated the hard-core pornography.

The essential question, therefore, boils down to this: Can explicit sex be used to increase the readership of a magazine that is, at least in significant part, political? Consider the following example: Assume that a small political magazine, whose specialty is exposing corruption in government, finds its readership dwindling to the point of bankruptcy; it adds a photo section, including hard-core pictures, and finds that this increases not only its circulation but also its political effectiveness in eliminating corruption. The government — which is being badly damaged by the magazine's increasingly widely read revelations — seeks to ban the photo section, knowing full well that this would reduce the political effectiveness of the magazine.

This scenario is not a contrived one: one of the most influential opposition magazines in Israel dramatically increased its circulation when it began to supplement its political rhetoric with pinups. It is a fact of life that sex sells magazines and that magazines that sell more have greater political influence. It cannot be doubted that magazines such as *Penthouse*, *Playboy*, *Esquire*, and *Cosmopolitan* exercise considerable political influence in this country. Nor can it be doubted that their circulation, and hence their influence, would be diminished significantly if they were not permitted to appeal "to the prurient interest" of their readership.

*Screw* simply takes that approach one step further: it hooks the readers on its tasteless raunch and then exposes them to its often equally taste-less politics. The issue that the courts will have to face in the *Screw* case — if they are candid — is whether, and to what degree, explicit sex may be integrated into a political publication in order to increase its salability and, inevitably, its political impact (as well, of course, as its profits). The implication of a decision against *Screw* for the American publication industry — and for the American reading public — could be significant.

It is widely assumed that the courts will find *some way* to reverse this outrageous and dangerous conviction. Perhaps that, coupled with Gold-stein's personal unpopularity, explains why the media has taken such slight interest in the *Screw* case. But lest anyone become too sanguine, it need only be recalled that Ralph Ginzburg did go to jail because he published *Eros* — which is indeed a work of art compared with much of today's fare — and that it was the liberal Warren Court that slammed his cell door shut.

Al Goldstein should not be imprisoned for using filthy words and pictures to sell his tasteless magazine to willing buyers. If he deserves to have his mouth washed out with soap, then surely the federal postal inspectors deserve to have their hands slapped. I was brought up to be-lieve that in America reading other people's mail is worse than telling dirty jokes.

# NINETEEN

# "WHY PORNOGRAPHY?"

*In recent years there have been few efforts to censor dirty words — scatology. But an uneasy coalition of right-wing fundamentalists and left-wing feminists have been the forefront of a movement to expand the government's power to censor pornographic books, films, videos, computer images, and magazines. They claim that pornography causes rape and other violence against women. In this previously unpublished essay, I consider these arguments.*

## WHAT IS PORNOGRAPHY?

Back in 1964 the late justice Potter Stewart acknowledged that he could probably never succeed in intelligibly defining the kind of "hard-core pornography" that was unprotected by the First Amendment. But, he quipped, "I know it when I see it." At that time the Supreme Court's definition of bannable hard-core material required that the work appeal to "prurient interest" of the "average person," applying "contemporary community standards," and that it have no "redeeming social importance." Several years later the definition was changed to make it easier to prosecute sexual material. Instead of requiring that the work be "utterly without redeeming social value" — a standard nearly impossible for prosecutors to meet — the new test permitted prosecution if the "patently offensive hard-core" material "taken as a whole, lacks serious literary, artistic, political or scientific value." Although the Supreme Court made it far easier to censor hard-core pornography in the 1970s, since that time there has been an outpouring of such material unparalleled in our history. It only began to abate in the 1990s — or more precisely, to move from the movie theater and peep-show screens to home videos and computers — as a result of reduced demand, rather than legal restriction. And the Supreme Court has mandated that the "reasonable" — rather than the "ordinary" — member of the community is the proper arbiter of the "seriousness" of the work. This led Justice Antonin Scalia to wonder whether the Court would soon have to rely on "the person of tolerably good taste," since reasonable people "have found literature in Dada and art in the replication of the soup can." Justice Scalia suggested, perhaps whimsically, that "we would be better advised to adopt as a legal maxim what has long been the wisdom of mankind: De gustibus non est disputandum. ('Just as there is no use arguing about taste, there is no use litigating about it.')"

But prosecutors around the country continue to litigate about taste and to prosecute pornography. Indeed, some have begun to prosecute with the zeal of avenging angels, as illustrated by a case in which then–attorney general Edwin Meese Jr. wrote a personal letter of commendation to the prosecutor who secured a *twenty-five-year* prison sentence — twice the average for murder, rape, and espionage — against a Baltimore adult-bookstore owner, with no prior record, who was induced by an FBI sting to mail into North Carolina six video cassettes depicting sex between humans and animals.[1]

Yet despite the resurrection of interest and intensity in prosecuting pornography — partly attributable to Attorney General Meese's Commission on Pornography, which purported to assess the scientific literature, hear witnesses, and arrive at policy conclusions — a contemporary Justice Stewart would not be any closer to an intelligible definition of pornography, "hard" or "soft." It is even doubtful that he would now know it if he saw it, because the "it" has undergone significant metamorphosis since Stewart penned his memorable bon mot. What used to distinguish hard-core pornography from other, "softer," stuff was the degree of sexual explicitness. The kind of hard-core porn that Justice Stewart claimed to know was characterized by explicit, graphic, visual portrayal of sexual intercourse — "penetration" or other "ultimate sex acts" (to quote the somewhat prissy language of the times). The more explicit and graphic the sex, the more pornographic the film or magazine.

In recent years, however, the word *pornography* has taken on a different meaning from the one used by the courts; it has been given a far more political emphasis by certain feminists — such as Professor

Catherine A. MacKinnon — who sees it as a "political practice" that is "central to the institutionalization of male dominance." What is objected to is not so much the *medium* of portrayal — whether it is close-up or distant, whether it is packaged as serious art or cheap smut, or whether it is explicit or implicit. It is the *message* of pornography: that "women are there to be violated and possessed, men to violate and possess them, either on screen or by camera or pen, on behalf of the viewer."[2] Thus the novels of Henry Miller and D. H. Lawrence are as dangerous and pornographic to MacKinnon as the video *Sex Kittens*.

The old debate about the morally corrupting and dehumanizing societal impact of pornography upon aesthetic sensibilities persists among intellectuals, as does the conflict between civil libertarians who would ban virtually nothing and paternalists who would censor to protect consumers from their own bad taste. But a new feminist dimension has now been added. The most concrete manifestation of the feminist critique of pornography — really the new perspective on the old pornography — has been the model "civil rights" statute drafted by Professor MacKinnon and author Andrea Dworkin, which would legally empower any woman to censor pornography because it is "an injury for all women."[3] That statute contains a definition that MacKinnon says captures what they "mean by pornography":

> Pornography is the graphic sexually explicit subordination of women, whether in pictures or in words, that also include one or more of the following: (i) women are presented dehumanized as sexual objects, things or commodities; or (ii) women are presented as sexual objects who enjoy pain or humiliation; or (iii) women are presented as sexual objects who experience sexual pleasure in being raped; or (iv) women are presented as sexual objects tied up or cut up or mutilated or bruised or physically hurt; or (v) women are presented in postures of sexual submission, servility or display; or (vi) women's body parts — including but not limited to vaginas, breasts, and buttocks — are exhibited, such that women are reduced to those parts; or (vii) women are presented as whores by nature; or (viii) women are presented being penetrated by objects or animals; or (ix) women are presented in scenarios of degradation, injury, torture, shown as filthy or inferior, bleeding, bruised, or hurt in a context that makes these conditions sexual.[4]

What this definition has in common with old-fashioned pornography is that it still must be "graphic" and "sexually explicit."[5] But the

new concept of pornography goes well beyond mere sexual explicitness — a term that is primarily descriptive and relatively neutral as to
the nature of its sexual content — and incorporates a normative theory
of sexual subordination. (It also eliminates some of what has conven-
tionally been regarded as pornography, such as explicit portrayals of
sex between men and between men and animals.) Under this new
feminist definition, the opprobrium of being labeled pornography is
applied to certain sexist portrayals, just as under fundamentalist definitions it is applied to antireligious, antifamily, and antiheterosexual portrayals.[6] Nor does the MacKinnon-Dworkin approach limit itself to
opprobrium; it authorizes women to seek court injunctions against offending material.

The Meese Commission acknowledged that "the range of materials
to which people are likely to affix the designation 'pornographic' is so
broad that it is tempting to note that pornography seems to mean in
practice any discussion or description of sex to which the person pe-
rusing it objects." As long as the issue was primarily semantic and the
consequence limited largely to private opprobrium, there was little
cause for public concern. But now that censorial feminists and fundamentalists have formed an uneasy alliance that has generated increased
prosecutorial and judicial attention, the stakes have changed.

## THE LABELING GAME

Why has it become so important for such divergent groups — feminists, fundamentalists, and plain old puritans[7] — to bestow the designation *pornography* on such a diverse array of material? Some feminists
claim that nonsexist erotic material — which MacKinnon loosely de-
fines as "sexually explicit material premised on equality," and which
she claims represents but a tiny fraction of commercially available
smut — should be excluded from the definition of pornography.[8] For
most fundamentalists and puritans, however, the equality of the explicit sex certainly would not make the material *less* pornographic or
offensive. Despite this basic disagreement about the central evil of
pornography, it seems important for all who would censor sexually explicit material of any nature to lay claim to the highly pejorative term
*pornography*. Recognizing the reality that most Americans do not want

to censor "mere" violence or sexism — these seem to be a staple of the novels, movies, and television shows that are widely distributed — but do want to censor explicit sex, some feminists have created an unholy alliance with some fundamentalists, puritans, and other opponents of sexuality for sexuality's sake.[9] Each group seeks to censor rather different media images. Feminists emphasize sexist violence and degradation, while fundamentalists concentrate on sexual explicitness. But they both agree to call the different evils by the same name, pornography. On such verbal ambiguities are political coalitions between strange bedfellows forged. Both feminist and fundamentalist censors can agree that "pornography" is the common enemy only so long as each group reserves for itself the ultimate power of inclusion and exclusion — of definition. As Lewis Carroll put it in a dialogue between Humpty Dumpty and Alice:

> "When I use a word," Humpty Dumpty said, in rather a scornful tone, "it means just what I choose it to mean — neither more nor less." "The question is," said Alice, "whether you can make words mean so *many* different things." "The question is," said Humpty Dumpty, "*which* is to be *master* — that's all."

In the debate over censorship of sexually explicit material, the powerful label *pornography* has indeed been master, because few in public life wish to come to the defense of so opprobrious a genre. And it has been served well by its handmaiden — deliberate ambiguity. Such ambiguity — calculated to keep fragile coalitions of convenience from falling apart — has made it all but impossible to discuss the subject rationally, either from a normative or an empirical perspective. It is difficult to have an intelligent discussion about a humpty-dumpty term that means "so many different things" and that carries so much emotional baggage.

## THE CHANGING DEBATE:
## FROM MORAL TO EMPIRICAL

In recent years, the pornography battleground has shifted from primarily moral claims to primarily empirical ones. Indeed, Catherine MacKinnon expressly rejects the premise that pornography presents "a moral issue." To her, pornography is a concrete "political practice" that produces specific harmful consequences to women: it "causes attitudes and behaviors of violence and discrimination that define the treatment and status of half the population"; it "coerces" and "silences" women; it is "a violent act against women."[10]

The central argument relied on by those who would censor pornography now seems to be the empirical assertion that pornography — however defined — provably causes measurable and nondebatable harms such as rape to identifiable victims. Inevitably, therefore, the champions of each side of the pornography-censorship battle have become social scientists. Professors Edward Donnerstein, Daniel Linz, and Steven Penrod, in their recent book *The Question of Pornography*, offer themselves as the scientific arbiters of the empirical dispute. They try to stake out a middle ground between those who claim that pornography should be censored because it is harmful and those who argue that it should not be censored because it is not harmful. On the basis of an exhaustive survey of social science research of all kinds — much of it their own[11] — they argue that some types of pornography (most particularly sexualized violence) are harmful, while others are not, but that government censorship is not the answer.

Putting aside for a moment their political arguments against censorship, Donnerstein, Linz, and Penrod's work as social scientists faces significant methodological barriers. Many of the experiments described in the book were conducted on undergraduate students who were exposed to "pornography" of various sorts and then tested for changes in attitudes and behavior. But how does a scientist determine whether one phenomenon, "pornography," which has no agreed-upon definition, causes another phenomenon, "harm," which is also subject to various meanings?[12] Valid experiments cannot be performed on metaphors with ever shifting meanings. Nor can the results of different experiments conducted in different settings be compared or contrasted when the material studied in some experiments is very different from that studied in other experiments, though both carry the common epithet *pornography*.[13] Even those experimenters who have attempted to break pornography down into subcategories — such as "sexually degrading," "violent," and "negative" — have employed quite subjective criteria of differentiation. For example, Donnerstein and his colleagues write about testing the effects of "material that . . .

are, *according to many*, demeaning and degrading to women," as illustrated by the film *Debbie Does Dallas* and "the 10–12 minute 'stag' or 'peepshow' films once widely available in pornographic book stores." Such vague concepts will simply not do for scientific rigor, since terms like *demeaning* and *degrading* are very much in the eye of the beholder and will be differently perceived by different experimenters and subjects.

## WHY PORNOGRAPHY?

At a more fundamental level, it is fair to ask *why* should an objective social scientist be *interested* in measuring the effects of so unscientific a phenomenon as "pornography"?[14] Or to use the title of the Donnerstein book: Why bother to ask "the question of pornography"? If the goal of the social science research is to discern the relationship, if any, between images in films, television, magazines, and books and violent actions or attitudes, then there are at least two rather different ways of putting the question: The way chosen by Donnerstein and his colleagues, MacKinnon, the Meese Commission, and religious fundamentalists is to ask whether, and to what degree, *pornography* increases sexual violence and negative attitudes against women. The other way would be to ask *which* types of expression have the greatest effect on such actions and attitudes. Would not a scientist, interested in learning the truth about the relationship between expression and actions and attitudes rather than in proving (or disproving) a political point (or an article of faith), prefer to put the question the second way?

Studies designed to answer the later question might well conclude that pornography — however defined — does contribute to these evils, but to a far lesser degree than other phenomena, such as TV or movie violence; news reporting about wars, crimes, and terrorism;[15] or even violent feminist literature (like Andrea Dworkin's novel *Ice and Fire*). The way a social scientist chooses to ask the question will probably depend on what the purpose of the experiment really is. If the purpose is to lay a foundation for the banning of pornography as such, then the focus will be on what evils *pornography* contributes to. If the focus is on *reducing violent actions and attitudes against women*, then the focus will be on what forms of expression most cause these actions and attitudes. For feminist and fundamentalist censors, the purpose seems clear: to prove that pornography — which is differently defined by each but inherently evil to both — causes specific and measurable harms. The Meese Commission's agenda was similarly unambiguous: to do something about pornography. It first selected pornography as the evil and then it set out to "prove" that it caused specific harms such as rape and sexist attitudes. Indeed, I asked a member of the commission, who had told me that he thought violent nonsexual films (such as R-rated slasher movies) caused more sexual violence than nonviolent sexual films (such as *Debbie Does Dallas*), why he had not said that in his report. He told me that he had been *directed* not to discuss anything that was not "pornography," since the commission's sole mandate was to focus on the *effects* of pornography, not the *causes* of sexual violence.

The difference is an important one, both for social science research methodology and for constitutional policy. If it were to turn out that pornography (however defined) contributed minimally to sexual violence but that nonpornographic violence contributed far more significantly, then it might follow — at least for some — that limiting the question to pornography, as did the Meese Commission and others, begs it. It would be as if an Orthodox Jew were trying to prove scientifically that the Old Testament was medically correct in prohibiting the eating of unkosher food. He might conduct an experiment designed to test the health of those who eat only kosher food and those who do not so restrict their diet. Even if he were to be able to show that those who eat kosher food are healthier than those who eat unkosher food, the experiment would prove little of relevance to those who were not already committed to the religious prohibition on a priori grounds. For the experiment to be useful outside the religious context, the experimenter would first have to deconstruct — break down — the concept of kosher and then turn the question on its head and ask which foods most contribute to health. It might turn out that pork (unkosher) is unhealthy, that shellfish (unkosher) is very healthy, and that chicken fat (kosher and eaten in quantity by more kosher than nonkosher people) is unhealthy. A person interested in improving his health — rather than in complying with the Old Testament on a priori religious grounds — might then adopt, not a kosher diet, but a shellfish diet that avoids pork and restricts the consumption of chicken fat.[16]

## DECONSTRUCTING PORNOGRAPHY

A rigorous approach to measuring the comparative impacts of pornography and other forms of expression on violent and sexist actions and attitudes would similarly have to deconstruct the heavily laden term *pornography* and break it down into component parts whose effects might be differentially tested. Let me try one such breakdown. The perceived evil characteristics of pornography include at least the following:

- The explicit portrayal of ultimate sex acts
- The graphic portrayal of violence
- The sexually degrading[17]

The perceived evil *effects* of pornography include at least the following:

- Contributing to violent actions against women
- Contributing to violent attitudes toward women
- Contributing to degrading or sexist attitudes toward women[18]

It would not be more difficult to conduct experiments designed to isolate and separately test these and other components than it is to test the composite term *pornography*. For example, it would be possible to create a series of films that hold everything else constant but simply vary the level of sexual explicitness, say on a scale of one to ten (one being distant nudity, two being close-up nudity, three being distant foreplay, eight being distant sexual intercourse, nine being close-up explicit sexual intercourse, and ten being clinical close-ups of sexual organs during intercourse). One could, of course, construct experiments that tested the effects of various aesthetic and other more-subtle characteristics of sexual material. By their very nature, the kinds of experiments conducted in this area must be relatively crude because of the need to hold constant all but the variable being tested.

It would be most interesting — and relevant to the current debate about the effect of pornography — to learn whether the degree of sexual explicitness alone had any measurable impact on any of the evils attributed to its consumption by some feminists and religious groups. It might turn out that explicitness does have some effect on sexual arousal but not on violent or sexist actions or attitudes.[19]

Another set of experiments might be designed to determine whether sexual explicitness, not alone but in combination with other components such as violence, had any measurable impact on any of the evils. If it turned out that hard-core sexual explicitness, either alone or in combination with other components, had no relationship to the evils, then at least some feminists might be inclined to change their definition of pornography so as to make sexual explicitness an irrelevant factor.[20] But once the hard-core sexual explicitness is taken out of pornography, the entire concept loses its core meaning — as well as much of its legal and constitutional basis for censorship. For radical feminists like Andrea Dworkin, who believe that all male-female sexual intercourse is inherently sexist and violent, no experimental findings would be relevant. This might be true, as well, for radical civil libertarians for whom no showing of harm would ever justify censorship. Equally important from a political perspective is the reality that if sexual explicitness were to be excised from the definition of pornography, the uncomfortable coalition between radical feminists and reactionary fundamentalists would fall apart, since sexual explicitness has been the wild card both sides have tried to use to build a winning poker hand.

## TAKING THE SEXUALLY EXPLICIT OUT OF PORNOGRAPHY

In light of the centrality of "sexual explicitness" to any definition of pornography, it is quite remarkable that none of the studies discussed in the Donnerstein book seems to support the proposition that the more sexually explicit — the more pornographic, as that word is commonly understood — the material is, the more negative are its impacts on attitudes and behavior. Thus, even if the "question of pornography" were the appropriate one, it is simply not being addressed properly.

Donnerstein and his colleagues do discuss studies that purport to test whether adding a *sexual component* to the violence component has any measurable effect on negative actions or attitudes. (It may.) But the sexual component need not be explicit or hard-core. Put another way, it is not *pornographic* images, as that term is commonly used, but rather *violent* images with a nonexplicit sexual component — such as appear in many R-rated slasher movies and television shows — that may contribute to negative actions and attitudes.

Even the Meese Commission — in a finding rarely cited — concluded that there is no evidence to support the view that any of the harms (such as rape or sexist attitudes) "vary with the extent of sexual explicitness, so long as the violence is presented in an undeniably sexual context." It acknowledges that "once a threshold is passed at which sex and violence are plainly linked, increasing the sexual explicitness of the material, or the bizarreness of the sexual activity, seems to bear little relationship to the extent of the consequences discussed here." Moreover, the so-called sexual threshold is quite low, including such benign visual images as "sexually suggestive nudity" and scenes of women taking showers or dressed in "nighties."[21]

If there is no evidence that the degree of sexual explicitness — indeed sexual *explicitness at all*, as distinguished from sexual *images* — is correlated with any of the evils considered by the Meese Commission and others, then it seems clear that the attempts to censor pornography, as such, cannot be justified by the empirical data. Nor would it seem useful to continue to focus research efforts on pornography — to ask "the question of pornography." Despite the subject and title of their book, Donnerstein, Linz, and Penrod seem eventually to acknowledge this:

> If this is true "that violence against women need not occur in a pornographic or sexually explicit context to have a negative effect on viewer attitudes and behavior" then to focus research efforts primarily on pornographic images of violence against women is somewhat misguided. By doing so, we ignore the substantial quantity of violence against women contained in R-rated movies. What is particularly troubling about these depictions is their tremendous availability. It is safe to assume that many more people have been exposed to violence against women in this form than have been exposed to violent pornography. Because sexually non-explicit forms of violence are more available to greater numbers of viewers, we need to ask: What are the effects of continued exposure to this material on our perceptions of violence and views about victims? Will viewers become callused toward violence, not only in the R-rated depictions themselves but also in more realistic circumstances?[22]

The implications of this conclusion — that we should not single out pornography for censorship or research — are far-reaching. Civil libertarians will see it as support for their opposition to all censorship. Others may see it as support for an even more pervasive regime of censorship, not limited to the sexually explicit.[23]

One point seems clear: *pornography* is a red herring. It is a word without relevant meaning that conceals the real issues in the continuing debate over the risks of freedom and the costs of censorship. In the name of rational discourse, we should declare a moratorium on its use. (Am I really arguing for censorship of "pornography"? I guess I am, in the sense of a self-imposed censorship on the use of the *word* itself!) In its place we should substitute descriptive terms that are capable of relatively precise and agreed-upon meanings. (For example, films like *Debbie Does Dallas* are sexually explicit, non-violent, and sexually degrading. Brian de Palma movies are often sexually violent and degrading but not explicit. And *Rambo* is violent but not sexual.) Maybe we even need numbers: ten levels of sexual explicitness; ten levels of violence; ten levels of degradation. Even these component terms lack rigorous scientific precision or uniform understanding, but at least they get closer to a common language that is designed to reduce, rather than expand, ambiguity.

By substituting these somewhat more understandable — and scientifically testable — components for the humpty-dumpty composite *pornography*, we can at least begin a more coherent and less politicized search for relationships between expression and negative actions and attitudes.

In the end, I doubt that social scientists, government commissions, polemical feminists, or fundamentalists will come up with truths so certain and eternal as to entitle them to close down the marketplace of opposing expressions and ideas.[24] Neither those who favor censorship of pornography nor those who oppose it are likely to be persuaded by empirical data. Those who favor censorship do so primarily because they are offended by the pornographic images — by the sexual explicitness, the sexism, or the other degrading elements. They seek confirmation and comfort for their a priori opposition in the empirical data. But the offensiveness alone is enough to justify a ban. Similarly, those who oppose censorship do so largely as an article of civil libertarian faith. If the empirical data support that article, so be it. If they do not, then the argument will be made in the face of the data.

The burden of persuasion should always be on those who would try to keep willing adults from satisfying their intellectual, emotional, artistic, or voyeuristic appetites by recourse to "offensive" materials. And candor and clarity require an acknowledgment that "the question of pornography" — as that term was understood by Justice Potter Stewart in 1964, and as it is commonly used today to connote sexual explicitness — is simply not the right question to ask, unless you are already sure you know the answer.

# TWENTY

# TELEVISION CENSORSHIP

*Although the television and motion picture industries, because they are non-governmental, are not directly subject to the First Amendment, they have enormous influence over the marketplace of ideas. I was asked several years ago to address a conference of television industry executives and lawyers on the free speech rights and responsibilities of their industry.*

I BEGIN WITH THE PREMISE THAT, DEEP DOWN, EVERYBODY wants to censor *something*. Human beings, no matter how committed to the principles of free speech, have a deep-seated distrust of the open marketplace of ideas, especially when they themselves — or the groups to which they belong — are "victims" of the excesses of free speech. How many times have we heard a Jewish friend say, "I believe in free speech for everybody, but Nazis marching through Skokie or Vanessa Redgrave playing a Holocaust survivor — that's different." Or a black friend saying, "Of course I believe in Martin Luther King's right to parade through Cicero, Illinois, because he was a man of peace — but the Klan, with their robes and burning crosses, or allowing schoolchildren to read *Little Black Sambo* or *Huck Finn* — that's different." Or a feminist friend supporting the right to advocate abortion but calling for the suppression of pornography, because it is sexist and encourages violence.

Sometimes I conduct a little experiment in my class. I ask for a show of hands on who is against censorship. Virtually the whole class raises its hands. Then I start listing the exceptions and asking who would support each. A few Jewish hands go up on the Nazis. A few black hands are raised against the Klan. Some women want to ban sexist porn. Some pacifists are willing to see *Soldier of Fortune* magazine suppressed. By the end of the class, it becomes clear that if the students — who are against censorship in principle — were each given the power to ban just one offensive genre, there would be little left of free speech. It is against this background that I offer some ideas.

There are but two pure models of the role of the state in relation to offensive speech. Under the first — whose paradigm was the former Soviet Union — the state must literally approve everything that is officially published (hence the term *samizadat* — illegally self-published without approval of the state). Everything that is published thus reflects affirmative government policy. Everything turned down for publication is against governmental policy. There are no neutral publications that are neither approved nor disapproved by the state but merely tolerated. There are no gray zones. No Soviet high official was ever heard to say to an author, "I disagree with what you are saying, but I will defend your right to say it."

The second pure model is one that no nation in history has ever achieved. But ours comes closest to it, at least at times. The model is one of complete content neutrality. The state neither approves nor disapproves of what is published, say, in the newspapers or magazines. Indeed, it does not even learn what is being published until after it has hit the streets (hence the importance of the prohibition against *prior* restraint). When an offensive item is published, the government can — and should — disclaim all responsibility for its content. The content, simply put, is none of the government's business: the government has neither approved it nor disapproved it.

Once the government gets into the business of disapproving of content on grounds of offensiveness, it has lost its claim to neutrality, and the trouble begins.

Assume that a group of militant feminists argues to a local government that a particular item of pornography — say, the film *Deep Throat* — is so offensive to women that it should be banned. Officials view the film, agree with the feminists, and ban it from their city. The next week, a group of blacks argues that the film *Birth of a Nation* is at least as offensive to blacks as *Deep Throat* is to women; a group of Jews will argue that the Nazi films are at least as offensive as *Birth of a Nation* and *Deep Throat;* a group of gays will make the same claim about the film *Cruising*.

If there is one thing that is clear about offensiveness, it is that there is no objective basis for comparison. If obscenity is in the eye of the beholder — or, as Justice William O. Douglas once quipped, "in the crotch of the beholder" — then offensiveness lies deep in the history and psyche of those who feel it. Can anyone — especially a government — make any comparative assessment of the offensiveness felt by a concentration camp survivor seeing a swastika, a descendant of a slave seeing a burning cross, a woman who has been raped seeing the horrible portrayal of sexual brutalization? If the government is to ban one, it must ban all. If it is to *refuse* to ban any, it must refuse to ban all.

Let me tell you a story from my own experience. I once went to Madrid representing Soviet dissidents at the Helsinki human rights meetings. During a meeting with Soviet officials, I complained about the recent publication of certain blatantly anti-Semitic material. The official responded — quite expectedly — by telling me that worse material was published in the United States. I agreed and took out copies of some horrible anti-Semitic material published here and showed them to him. I also showed him some of the copies of the material published in the Soviet Union. I asked him to look at both and tell me the difference. He understood immediately: the Soviet material bore a stamp signifying that it had been approved by Glavlit, the official censorship agency of the Soviet Union. The American material had been approved by no one except the National Socialist White People's party — whose stamp it bore. The Soviet material was awful; the American material was worse. But the Soviet material carried the imprimatur of its government — a government that will not allow the publication of material deemed offensive by *favored* groups but will encourage the publication of material deemed offensive to *disfavored* groups. Therein lies the difference — and a critical difference it is.

What does all this have to do with television? The television industry is not government, but it, too, must have a policy in relation to offensive material. And although there are considerable differences between government and the television industry, the latter can learn a great deal from the mistakes of governments.

The television industry has not followed the model of neutrality. It has disapproved of program content on grounds of offensiveness. It cannot claim — in the face of protests from the Moral Majority — that it never succumbs to pressure from offended groups. The best it can do is point to certain instances where it has resisted pressures. But it must then acknowledge that it has also succumbed and compromised on other occasions.

The television industry can point out that it is less monolithic than governments, that its program content is neither approved nor disapproved by a single centralized authority. Approval and disapproval decisions are made by producers, writers, sponsors, network executives, and even the Federal Communications Commission (FCC). Anticipatory censorship — excision made out of fear of censorship — is perhaps the most prevalent. Responsibility and accountability are so diffuse that they are difficult to pinpoint.

But nor can it be said, in fairness, that the TV industry has come close to the Soviet model of total approval or disapproval. There are gray areas where executives and at least some sponsors have said, "We disagree with your decision, but we will defend your right to stand by it."

How, then, in light of this mixed history, can and should the TV industry — and its component parts — respond to what promises to be the most massive and well-organized bombardment of pressure from the right that it has experienced since the McCarthy era?

TV can never become the model of neutrality: the government will not allow it to do so because of the power the FCC exercises by means of the technological pretext of allocating limited wavelengths. (A pretext because the government would surely not give up its power to license a medium as pervasive as TV even if there were — when there are — no limits to frequencies, cables, or other means available.) Nor will the sponsors, whether they be commercial sponsors or "charitable" sponsors on public television. The networks will not allow it. So even if the "artists" of the industry banded together to demand complete freedom for them and content neutrality by the "controllers," it would not come to be. The industry must learn to live in a twilight zone — a gray area — of censorship and make the best of it. Is it possible to live within that gray area and still maintain a considerable amount of freedom and integrity? I believe the answer is a qualified yes — if the right steps are taken *in advance*.

The two starting points — really poles — in any intelligent discussion of censorship based on offensiveness are, one, the *government* should *not* engage in content censorship based on offensiveness; and, two, private individuals and groups are absolutely entitled to express objections to speech that they find offensive. Indeed, the open marketplace of ideas presupposes vigorous response — and objection — to offensive speech. As William Safire once juxtaposed these two points, "Every American has the right to complain about the trash on TV — except Uncle Sam."

But these two poles do not provide answers to the really hard questions, such as: To what extent is it appropriate — put aside legal, for a moment — for a group that feels strongly about certain speech to express their objections through concerted economic pressures? Economic pressures surely cannot be ignored in any discussion of free speech. For if, to paraphrase George Bernard Shaw, assassination is the ultimate form of censorship, then bankruptcy is surely a penultimate form of censorship in a profit-motivated society. Most people answer the economic question differently, depending on which side of the dispute they happen to fall on. I know many feminists who were adamantly opposed to the Hollywood blacklist and also to the boycott threats generated by the Vanessa Redgrave controversy,[1] but who strongly favor boycotting general bookstores that include allegedly sexist material (such as *Penthouse*, *Playboy*, and *Hustler*) among their fare. Are there really any principled distinctions? Would they justify, as an exercise of free speech, an organized boycott by "pro-lifers" against a small-town bookstore that sold books advocating abortion or birth control? Would the black or Jew who boycotts a general bookstore selling Nazi and Klan material justify the boycott of a store selling evolutionary or anti–gun-control tracts? What would be left for the bookstore to sell if every group that objected to particular books boycotted the store? We used to be able to say that the store would be selling only books like *Mary Poppins*, but even that book has recently been subject to censorial efforts.

Is it possible to articulate general rules — rules of civility, rules of morality, rules of law, rules of constitutionality — that do not depend on whose ox is being gored or which group is being insulted?

What about organized boycotts of advertisers who sponsor TV programs deemed deeply offensive to certain groups? Can we devise neutral rules for when such boycotts are legitimate and when they're illegitimate? Again we can begin at the extremes. Surely it is more appropriate to boycott an advertiser who plays an active role in determining content than one who plays no role. If, for example, a sponsor were to say, "I'll advertise on this show only if there are more exposed breasts, or if it puts down gays, or if it casts a Klan member as Martin Luther King," then the propriety of an economic boycott becomes more obvious. But if the sponsor merely declines to remove his ad from an objectionable show, the propriety of a general product boycott becomes more questionable. A boycott against a sponsor because of the nature of that sponsor's own advertisements is easier to justify than a boycott of a sponsor because of the content of the program sponsored. A boycott of a specific program is more justifiable than a boycott of a station or a network.

These are the distinctions and refinements that we should be thinking about. Bill Rusher posed the question: "What's wrong with a product boycott based on program content?" The answer is, "Plenty!" — especially if the boycott is general and not specific. Our traditional rules distinguishing between primary and secondary boycotts reflect an important insight. We must persuade the American public that although most boycotts are constitutionally protected, some of them are morally *wrong*. There is, of course, no inconsistency between an expression of speech being *both* constitutionally protected *and* morally wrong. Hooting down a speaker, hurling racial epithets, and defaming a public figure are all examples of constitutionally protected but morally wrong speech. *It is morally wrong to exercise your freedom of speech — and freedom to purchase — to restrict the freedom of others to speak and learn what they choose.* Using the marketplace of ideas as a metaphor, it is morally wrong — and inconsistent with the premises underlying the First Amendment — to try to shut down a stall in the marketplace of ideas because that stall is selling ideas that are objectionable to you. Set up your own stall and sell better ideas. That is what the new electronic producers are doing by putting their own programs on TV. I applaud that.

Picking up on Bill Rusher's example that nudists have no right to parade down main street in the buff: nudists should not be allowed to mingle with clothed people who would be offended by nudity, but when there are enough beaches, some should be set aside as nude beaches where the clothed need not tread. I condemn those — both my friends and my foes — who would seek to establish a *single* national standard of morality. As George Bernard Shaw once put it: "Do not do unto others as you would they should do unto you. Their tastes may not be the same."

In the end, the challenge is yours! Only you — the producers, network executives, sponsors, advertising people — can address it. It is you who must devise a set of standards that are fair, that are neutral, and — most important — that will result in the proliferation of speech rather than its contraction. *Can* you devise advance rules concerning when you will and when you will not relent to pressure — without knowing whether the pressure will be coming from your friends or your foes? As a civil libertarian, I have the same goal, and I offer my help, my experience, and my counsel. But it is you who must make the hard choices.

# TWENTY-ONE

# MOTION PICTURE CENSORSHIP

---

*For many years I have been involved — as a lawyer — in cases challenging the motion picture rating system. In 1999 I wrote an essay about the system for the* Chronicle of Higher Education.

---

SINCE THE SHOOTINGS AT SCHOOLS IN LITTLETON, Colorado, and elsewhere, the government has focused on the media — particularly film, television, and computer games — as potentially troublesome influences on young minds. President Bill Clinton recently directed the United States Department of Justice to "study" whether the movie industry was violating its own voluntary ratings code — the study's implicit threat being that the code might become more than voluntary. The lightning-quick result: the National Association of Theater Owners promised to enforce the rating system more vigorously, by requiring proof of age for admission to R or NC-17 films.

Preliminary reports raise considerable doubt as to whether such enforcement will be possible, especially in multiplex theaters showing a number of films with various ratings (never mind trying to restrict what young people see on video). But even if it worked, would such enforcement have any discernible impact on teenage violence?

In our culture we glorify guns, machismo, the military, and aggressive sport not only in film but also in advertising, in music, on the news, and around the family dinner table. Even some religious leaders seem to preach the sanctity of the Second Amendment more rigorously than that of the Sixth Commandment. Take, for instance, the Reverend Willie Ramsey, a Kentucky preacher who pushed an amendment through the state's General Assembly that allows members of the clergy to carry concealed weapons in their sanctuaries. "This idea that the Lord would never have a gun around him," Ramsey told the *Lexington Herald-Leader.* "Well, they didn't have guns in those days, but his apostles had swords. Don't you suppose they were for self-defense?" In a similar vein, the Reverend Jerry Falwell wrote in a recent newsletter to pastors, "The left will not rest easy until they have disarmed every law-abiding citizen, leaving Americans with absolutely no means to protect themselves against the fierce acceleration of our culture of violence."

Teenagers are probably influenced more by such mainstream representations of, and responses to, violence than they are by the extreme depictions on the big screen that are the object of the president's wrath.

Advocates of the motion picture rating system claim that it is effective and voluntary. There are reasons to question both claims. For censorship to be effective, it must be pervasive, as it was in Hitler's Germany, Stalin's Soviet Union, and Mao's China. History shows that moderate censorship, such as that effected by the current rating system for movies, simply doesn't work.

The rating system promulgated by the motion picture industry has always been "voluntary" only in a sense. The self-imposed censorship arose from fear that the government would step in as the movies' moral gatekeeper if the industry didn't rein itself in. In 1922 censorial legislatures were starting to move toward imposing a regime of governmental control over what was quickly becoming a major source of mass entertainment. In response, the industry, under the leadership of Will Harrison Hays — chairman of the Republican National Committee and a former postmaster general — began its initial foray into self-censorship. The so-called Hays Office (which was formally called the Motion Picture Producers and Distributors of America), speaking on behalf of the movie moguls, told the legislatures, in effect, to "leave it to us."

Beginning in 1927, with a list of "don'ts" and "be carefuls" that served as guidelines for movie producers, and moving on to the comprehensive Production Code created in 1930, the Hays Office established a pervasive system of censorship, micromanaged by right-wing religious zealots with moralistic agendas.

Before a film could receive the Hays Office's imprimatur, it had to prove that it did not "lower the moral standards of those who see it," and that it did not throw the "sympathy of the audience to the side of crime, wrong-doing, evil or sin." The code covered everything from how to handle issues of crime and "vulgarity" to details about location ("the treatment of bedrooms must be governed by good taste and delicacy"), as well as subjective factors as vague as "National feelings" ("*the use of the Flag* shall be consistently respectful").

Of course, there could be no suggestion of sex, blasphemy, or marital infidelity. When the screenwriters of *Gone with the Wind* drafted Clark Gable's risqué line "Frankly, my dear, I don't give a damn," they also came up with two softer alternatives designed to placate censors, including, "I wish I could care what you do or where you go — but frankly, my dear, I just don't care." That they were permitted to go with the first option reflected the power of Selznick International Pictures more than it did changing mores.

But more than prohibitions defined the code. In its "reasons" section — formally enacted along with the code as the governing parameters for movie production — the Hays Office elaborated on the code's broader purposes. Film, because of its "mobility, popularity, accessibility, emotional appeal, vividness, [and] straightforward presentation of fact, . . . *reaches places* unpenetrated by other forms of art," and this has "special MORAL OBLIGATIONS." A dichotomy exists between "helpful" and "harmful" entertainment, the document explained, and the Hays Office clearly advocated, even insisted on, the former. "*Correct entertainment raises* the whole standard of a nation," while "*wrong entertainment lowers* the whole living conditions and moral ideas of a race." The Hays Office, in effect, enforced cinematographic correctness.

After World War II, censorship began to abate, and Hollywood began to push the envelope ever so slightly. Again, legislators responded by calling for official censorship. And again, the motion picture industry acted preemptively. This time, the Motion Picture Association of America (MPAA) and the National Association of Theater Owners came up with a voluntary ratings system, designed primarily to inform parents. In other words, the onus was to some degree transferred from filmmakers to film viewers. As Jack Valenti, since 1966 the president of the MPAA, put it in 1990: "The purpose of the rating system, its only purpose, then as now, was to offer cautionary warnings to parents to help them guide the movie-going of their young children."

There have been several problems with this approach from the very beginning. First, the ratings haven't given parents much information. An R rating could be given for "nudity with sensual scenes," "hard language," "tough violence," or any combination. Since legislative censors have always been more concerned with sex than with violence, the people who have determined the ratings have also, in my experience, been more likely to give an R to a film with substantial sexual conduct than to one that is quite violent. A parent more concerned with a child's seeing violence than with a child's seeing sex has not been able to determine from the rating whether a given film is suitable.

The system also has really been neither voluntary nor mainly informational. Many theaters have not shown X-rated films, so if a film did not qualify for an R rating, it was relegated to the small number of independent theaters willing to incur the wrath of community activists who did not want X-rated movie houses in their neighborhoods. Indeed, some communities have gone even further, placing restrictions in the leases of malls with theaters, since some of the malls have been financed with municipal bonds, tax breaks, and other governmental subsidies. The heavy thumb of government could be felt on the scales of public choice.

Those problems led to the addition of the NC-17 rating, which was designed for films that were deemed too sexual for the R rating but sufficiently artistic not to be tainted by an X rating. That symbol had come to be associated with "sexploitation" films, and X had become an advertising symbol for hard-core pornography. The motion picture rating board — consisting of eight to thirteen members who serve for periods of varying lengths — had come to realize that there was a genre of film sufficiently sexual to be unsuitable for children, even if their parents approved, but not deserving the damning X. The NC-17 rating — which excludes all children below the age of seventeen, regardless of parental wishes — was designed for that genre. NC-17 was, therefore, the first non-X rating that left parents no choice as to whether or not their children could see a given movie.

I urged the inclusion of an NC-17 category in the expectation that it would be treated by theaters and video stores more like an R than an X rating. When it became clear that the new rating was becoming an instrument of censorship, I fought against its imposition on films suited for teenagers.

One of the first films to challenge an NC-17 rating was *Clerks*, in 1994. I represented the film's coproducer Miramax Films on appeal before the MPAA's internal appeals board, and we prevailed. The next major challenge involved the film *Kids* (1995), a provocative look at the world of male teenagers who sexually exploit younger female teenagers. The target audience for this film was teenagers, along with their parents. It sent a powerful message about the dangers of promiscuity, particularly among teenage girls. If I had had teenage daughters or sons, I would have wanted to be able to take them to see the film. But the NC-17 rating took that decision away from parents and placed it in the hands of censors. We lost the appeal on a divided vote.

The Hays Office had it wrong as a matter of constitutional principle, but right as a matter of empirical fact: the only *effective* censorship is *complete* censorship, based on the content and moral message of a film. Ratings based on the presence or absence of specific words, acts, or images can easily be circumvented.

The problem is that our First Amendment prohibits pervasive governmental censorship. The solution is to answer bad speech with good speech, and to have the good speech prevail in the marketplace of ideas.

Persuading youngsters of the virtue of nonviolence and the vice of violence is more challenging than simply censoring violent images. But it is also more enduring, more likely to succeed, and more consistent with our Bill of Rights.

# TWENTY-TWO

# COMPUTER CENSORSHIP

---

*There is a close connection between the government's power to censor obscenity and its power to intrude into the privacy of its citizens, since obscenity is generally consumed in private. The advent of Internet porn has generated new variations on an old theme, which I explored in this 1999 article.*

---

THE RESIGNATION OF THE DEAN OF THE HARVARD DIVINITY School, Ronald F. Thiemann, because pornography was found on his university-owned computer, raises profound questions regarding privacy, values, and the role of universities. Because the decision to end Thiemann's distinguished career as dean is shrouded in secrecy, little is known about the case beyond that which has appeared in the press. We do know that Thiemann resigned from his deanship on November 13, 1998, citing health reasons, including depression. We also know that he has not been fired from his tenured position as professor. In addition, we are assured that the images did not involve children and were not "illegal" (whatever that may mean in the face of conflicting statutory and case law). Nor is there any dispute that the computer was technically owned by Harvard University but given to Dean Thiemann for his exclusive use both at home and in his office. Finally, the university did not initiate a search of the computer but, rather, responded to information provided by others who had seen the pornographic images, apparently after Thiemann had asked a university technician to transfer the files to a new drive.

The case is complicated by Professor Thiemann's role as founder of the Center for the Study of Values in Public Life. Some critics believe that the private viewing of pornography in one's own home is inconsistent with the values of the Divinity School. As Louis Smedes, Professor Emeritus of Christian Ethics at Fuller Theological Seminary in Pasadena, California, put it, "We and the clergy agree that pornography in society is on balance evil, a great evil." Some clergymen believe that oral sex, homosexuality, and abortion are also "great evils," but surely Harvard would never fire a dean for engaging in such conduct. Indeed, the official minister of Harvard University is openly gay, and no one — but a handful of homophobic alumni — has raised any challenge about his values. Simply put, it is none of the university's business whether its deans get their sexual jollies in the missionary position, by using pornography, or in any other manner not involving illegality or the exploitation of sexual partners.

What about the fact that Dean Thiemann used a university-owned computer to view pornography? Harvard's rules provide that university-owned computers should not be used outside the school's educational mission. But does anyone actually believe that Dean Thiemann would have been asked to resign if he had used his computer to store images of his private art or stamp collection? Harvard's ownership of the computer is simply a convenient legalistic hook on which to hang Harvard's decision to condemn the pornographic contents of Thiemann's computer. In an age when many universities, corporations, and government offices provide laptops to their employees, it is extremely dangerous to suggest that the technical ownership of these computers determines what can be stored on them for home use. If employers claim the right to control the content of computers given to their employees, they should explicitly warn all potential users that they are waiving privacy rights.

The implications go beyond computers, extending to e-mail and other modern technologies. Can it reasonably be claimed that a student who uses a university-owned telephone for "phone sex" or to have a steamy conversation with his girlfriend is subject to university intrusion and discipline? Are private e-mail messages that use the university server subject to review by the morals squad? As one alumnus of the Harvard Divinity School asked, "Because his home and computer are owned by Harvard, is his whole life owned by the Divinity School?"

Some of Dean Thiemann's defenders point to President Bill Clinton's sexual activities in the Oval Office as a precedent for not punishing private, consensual conduct in a place owned by the employer. It is

a far-fetched analogy, which does not serve the interests of Dean Thiemann. Harvard surely has the right to demand a higher standard of its
appointed deans than Congress can constitutionally of an elected president subject to removal only for "high crimes or misdemeanors." It
must have the power to ask for the resignation of a dean whose public
actions make it impossible for him to continue to do his job effectively.
But Harvard has no right to demand a dean's resignation for private
acts that violate no law or university value but that are deemed to be
"conduct unbecoming a dean." There may have been a time when
Harvard was so homogeneous an institution that everyone understood
what was meant by conduct unbecoming a dean, but in the thirty-five
years that I have been teaching at Harvard, I have witnessed an enormous and beneficial increase in the diversity of the university and of
the values it represents. It is no longer possible to give any meaningful
content to a phrase as broad and open-ended as "conduct unbecoming
a dean."

# TWENTY-THREE

# STUDENT CENSORSHIP

---

*University censorship has been imposed not only by administrations but by students as well. I critiqued this trend in two articles, which I have combined in this chapter.*

---

## SPEECH CODES

As students throughout the totalitarian world risk life and limb for freedom of expression, many American college students are demanding that Big Brother restrict their freedom of speech on campus. This demand for enhanced censorship is not emanating only from the usual quarter — the know-nothing fundamentalist right. It is coming from the radical — and, increasingly, not-so-radical — left as well.

Led by some minority students as well as women, gays, Jews, and other victims of campus persecution, these new student censors are demanding that university administrators enact stringent codes of campus behavior, including restrictions on offensive expression. And many administrators — who seem to value campus "peace" and "civility" over divisive dialogue — are complying. Universities ranging from Stanford to Michigan to Pennsylvania to Tufts, and many others, have adopted or considered significant restrictions on free speech.

The scenario is familiar and recurring: Some drunken fraternity goon paints an offensive slogan or symbol on a campus wall — maybe it is a swastika or a Ku Klux Klan acronym. If it wasn't spray-painted by a drunk, it may even have been the work of some off-campus townies, or maybe even a full-time hate monger. Do-gooder students — many of whom come from sheltered backgrounds — are outraged, since they have never seen anything like this before.

Student leaders convene endless soul-searching sessions, during which they exchange supportive hugs and pledge their commitment to do something about the deeper problems of intolerance, of which they all — or nearly all — acknowledge guilt. After long sanctimonious exchanges, they finally arrive at the simple-minded solution of banning the offensive material. They agree that there is really no need for divisive symbols of hate on a college campus. Such symbols are not, after all, *really* free speech, since they do not contribute to the marketplace of ideas.

Then comes the hard part: drafting a code or set of rules that bans the unnecessary and offensive expression but leaves unthreatened necessary speech that may contribute to the marketplace of ideas. Enthusiastic student censors are undaunted by the fact that no one in history has ever managed to accomplish this task. They are oblivious to the reality that offensiveness lies in the soul of the beholder and therefore cannot be defined objectively.

Nevertheless, student censors have come up with all manner of rules and regulations that ban "verbal behavior" that creates an "offensive academic, living, or work environment." These rules prohibit "written invasion or violation of any individual's rights through graffiti, obscene telephone calls, or other means." Some are so restrictive that they have already been struck down as unconstitutional by the courts.

Although the students' goals are to be admired, their methods should be condemned in the strongest of terms. Censors are censors, regardless of their motivation. As Supreme Court justice Louis Brandeis warned sixty years ago: "The greatest dangers to liberty lurk in insidious encroachment by men of zeal, well-meaning but without understanding." He could have been describing this new generation of student censors who have unwittingly set out to endanger our most cherished liberties. We must resist the urge to patronize them but rather take them seriously. We should fight them with all the strength we would muster against any enemies of liberty.

These students should be made aware of their own hypocrisy. Though they insist on being governed by the laws of the outside world when it comes to their personal lives, railing against visitor rules and curfews, they want their universities to adopt rules that restrict their

First Amendment rights of free speech in order to shield them from the ugly realities of prejudice.

The happy truth is that there has been a dramatic *decrease* in campus bigotry over the past several generations. Expressions of discrimination were endemic and institutionalized on most college campuses until fairly recently. Fraternities, sororities, secret societies, and eating clubs were racially and religiously segregated with the enthusiastic support and encouragement of university administrators. Sexist and gay jokes were a staple of classroom discussion. Bigotry was taught, both overtly and subtly, in the classroom and in the corridors. These conventions have been replaced by a welcome intolerance toward any form of bigotry.

Universities do, of course, continue to experience occasional eruptions of racism, sexism, homophobia, and anti-Semitism. But these incidents and the sentiments behind them lie at the periphery, not the core, of campus life. Still, hatred on any level should be fought, but not with the weapons of censorship. A university campus in a democratic society is no place to try to curb expression. Those institutions that do are failing in their responsibility to educate and prepare students for the real world. Campus censorship is both bad politics and bad education.


## POLITICAL CORRECTNESS


There is now a debate among pundits over whether the "political correctness" movement on college and university campuses constitutes a real threat to intellectual freedom or merely provides conservatives with a highly publicized opportunity to bash the left for the kind of intolerance of which the right has often been accused.

My own sense, as a civil libertarian whose views lean to the left, is that the "P.C." movement is dangerous and that it is also being exploited by hypocritical right-wingers.

In addition to being intellectually stifling, the P.C. movement is often internally inconsistent. Among its most basic tenets are the demand for greater "diversity" among students and faculty members and the need for "speech codes," so that racist, sexist, and homophobic ideas, attitudes, and language do not "offend" sensitive students.

I wonder if most of those who are pressing for diversity really want it. What many on the extreme left seem to want is simply more of their own: more students and faculty who think like they do, vote like they do, and speak like they do. The last thing they want is a truly diverse campus community with views that are broadly reflective of the multiplicity of attitudes in the big, bad world outside the ivory towers.

How many politically correct students are demanding — in the name of diversity — an increase in the number of evangelical Christians, National Rifle Association members, and right-to-life advocates? Where is the call for more anti-Communist refugees from the Soviet Union, more Afro-Americans who oppose race-specific quotas, and more women who are antifeminist?

Let's be honest: the demand for diversity is at least in part a cover for a political power grab by the left. Most of those who are recruited to provide politically correct diversity — Afro-Americans, women, gays — are thought to be supporters of the left. And historically, the left — like the right — has not been a bastion of diversity.

Now the left — certainly the extreme left that has been pushing hardest for political correctness — is behind the demands for speech codes. And if they were to get their way, these codes would not be limited to racist, sexist, or homophobic *epithets*. They would apply as well to politically incorrect *ideas* that are deemed offensive by those who would enforce the codes. Such ideas would include criticism of affirmative-action programs, opposition to rape shield laws, advocacy of the criminalization of homosexuality, and defense of pornography.

I have heard students argue that the expression of such ideas — both in and out of class, both by students and by professors — contributes to an atmosphere of bigotry, harassment, and intolerance, and that it makes it difficult for them to learn.

The same students who insist that they be treated as adults when it comes to their sexuality, drinking, and schoolwork beg to be treated like children when it comes to politics, speech, and controversy. They whine to Big Father and Mother — the president or provost of the university — to "protect" them from offensive speech, instead of themselves trying to combat it in the marketplace of ideas.

Does this movement for political correctness — this intolerance of verbal and intellectual diversity — really affect college and university students today? Or is it, as some argue, merely a passing fad, exaggerated by the political right and the media?

It has certainly given the political right — not known for its great tolerance of different ideas — a heyday. Many hypocrites of the right, who would gladly impose their own speech codes if *they* had the power to enforce *their* way, are selectively wrapping themselves in the same First Amendment they willingly trash when it serves their political interest to do so.

But hypocrisy aside — since there is more than enough on both sides — the media are not exaggerating the problem of political correctness. It is a serious issue on college and university campuses. As a teacher, I can feel a palpable reluctance on the part of many students — particularly those with views in neither extreme and those who are anxious for peer acceptance — to experiment with unorthodox ideas, to make playful comments on serious subjects, to challenge politically correct views, and to disagree with minority, feminist, or gay perspectives.

I feel this problem quite personally since I happen to agree — as a matter of substance — with most "politically correct" positions. But I am appalled at the intolerance of many who share my substantive views. And I worry about the impact of politically correct intolerance on the generation of leaders we are currently educating.

# TWENTY-FOUR

# THE FUTURE OF FREE SPEECH

*Modern technology — especially the Internet — creates important opportunities to expand freedom of speech globally. It also poses challenges to our traditional notions of freedom and censorship. I explore those issues in this chapter, as well as in the concluding section of the book.*

RECENT EVENTS DEMONSTRATE THE FRIGHTENING NEW USES to which technology can be put in the name of promoting as well as suppressing freedom. The fax, the cell phone, the shortwave radio, the computer, and the Internet have changed both the techniques and the stakes in the ongoing "spy versus spy" encounters between dissidents and governments, as well as between terrorists and law enforcement.

The student democracy movement in China established communications technology as an indispensable aid to revolutionary movements. We have long understood how powerful a tool it is in open, democratic societies like our own, but now we see its significance in closed regimes as well. In the bad old days when totalitarianism worked by controlling the flow of information, Big Brother could convey the "truth" to its citizens. This tactic no longer works.

In China, for example, the government-controlled press originally put out the story that no one except soldiers was killed in Tiananmen Square during that bloody weekend in early June 1989. But most Chinese soon learned that they had been fed falsehoods, since the tragic truth was quickly disseminated by shortwave radio. The facts were routed around the world to evade Chinese censorship: eyewitness accounts from Tiananmen Square were relayed to the United States and Great Britain and then broadcast back to China by the Voice of America and the British Broadcasting Corporation.

Students in America communicated with their counterparts in China by fax machine and computer modems. Leaflets were faxed and transmitted by modem between Beijing and Shanghai before the authorities could cut off the phone lines. Even after domestic phone lines were cut off, Chinese students in one city faxed information to the United States, which was then faxed back to another city in China. Cellular telephones were also used to relay messages on the run, and videotapes were made, sent out of the country, and then returned. And this was all quite primitive as compared with today's Internet technology.

The use of modern technology in the context of dissent is nothing new. For at least the past several decades, sophisticated equipment has been used by governments to repress dissent, free speech, and "subversive" organizations. Computer monitoring, electronic eavesdropping, and even satellite tracing have become the staple of government intelligence apparatuses. The FBI and other American intelligence-gathering networks have long kept tabs on subversives and political activists. The real news is that now this technology is being used to *further* freedom as well as repress it.

The government usually maintains the upper hand, since it controls the telephone wires and the airwaves, which are the nerve system of modern communications technology. A government determined to terminate all communications can do so — at least to a considerable degree — by cutting phone and satellite lines and denying all access to foreign journalists.

But actions such as these carry with them a high price. The Chinese government was unwilling to pay that price, because it realized that it would be cutting off the blood supply to its economic heart. The communication links that make censorship difficult are the same links that keep China operating. The students used the Chinese government's own network of business communications — direct-dial international phone lines, telex links, interhotel transmissions — to undermine the government's attempt to censor them. In the end, the government managed to turn technology against the students by using TV footage of the demonstrations to finger the leaders and later to show them signing confessions. It is a knife that cuts both ways.

Another such "knife" is the relative anonymity of modern communications. With considerable effort, most communications can be traced to their source, but it's not easy. This encourages both irresponsible use of communications by those who would distort the truth without accountability and courageous use by those who would convey truths unpopular with the powers that be. The difficulty of tracing communications also serves the interests of organized criminals, most particularly international terrorists, who have learned to use Internet connections in public libraries and other such places to communicate with each other. Now, law enforcement officials are seeking new powers — both legal and technological — to stay ahead of those who would use sophisticated communications to endanger our safety.

The new uses of sophisticated technology provide the best argument for free and open communication in the United States. Whoever controls communication links wields enormous power — power that can be used in the name of liberty or oppression. There is an ongoing struggle over who will control this technology — indeed, whether control will be centralized or decentralized. The resolution of this struggle may have considerable impact on the future of rights in the new age of instant communication.

❋

## PART III

# THE RIGHT TO BELIEVE
# AND DISBELIEVE — WITHOUT
# GOVERNMENT INTRUSION

THE FIRST AMENDMENT, IN ADDITION TO PRECLUDING MOST government censorship, also prohibits the making of any law respecting an establishment of religion or prohibiting its free exercise. The body of the Constitution also prohibits any "religious test" for office.

These rights and restrictions have sometimes appeared to be in conflict. When the Supreme Court has prohibited organized prayer in public schools, at graduations, and before football games, some have claimed that their right to free exercise has been curtailed. Others claim that the prohibition on teaching creationism as an alternative to evolution abridges the freedom of speech of religious fundamentalists. As I will try to show in these chapters, religious speech is quite different from other kinds of speech. We encourage argument — even disrespectful and rude argument — about politics, science, art, and literature. But honest disagreements about religion are out of bounds in most schools. Disrespectful criticism of particular religions is regarded as bigotry (although religious people are free to be disrespectful toward atheists and agnostics). Imagine an elementary school class in which Catholic, Protestant, Jewish, and Muslim students argued about which was the true faith. Or imagine how an atheist or agnostic student would be treated by his peers and teachers if he expressed belief that God did not exist or that God was not good or that religion is immoral.

Actually, it isn't necessary to resort to the imagination. President George W. Bush's inauguration was opened by a Protestant Evangelist minister officially dedicating the inauguration to Jesus Christ, whom he declared to be "our savior." Invoking "the Father, the Son, the Lord Jesus Christ," and "the Holy Spirit," Billy Graham's son, the man selected by President George W. Bush to bless his presidency, excluded the tens of millions of Americans who are Muslims, Jews, Buddhists, Shintoists, Unitarians, agnostics, and atheists from his blessing by his particularistic and parochial language.

The plain message conveyed by the Bush administration is that

George W. Bush's America is a Christian nation, and that non-Christians are welcome into the tent so long as they agree to accept their status as a tolerated minority rather than as fully equal citizens. In effect, Bush is saying: "This is our home, and in our home we pray to Jesus as our savior. If you want to be a guest in our home, you must accept the way we pray."

But the United States is neither a Christian nation nor the exclusive home of any particular religious group. Non-Christians are not guests. We are as much hosts as any Mayflower-descendant Protestant. It is our home as well as theirs. And in a home with so many owners, there can be no official sectarian prayer. That is what the First Amendment is all about, and the first act by the new administration was in defiance of our Constitution.

This was surely not the first time in our long history that Jesus has been invoked at an official governmental assembly. But we are a different and more religiously diverse nation than we were in years past. There are now many more Muslims, Jews, Buddhists, and others who do not accept Jesus as their savior. It is permissible in the United States to reject any particular theology. Indeed, that is part of our glorious diversity. What is not acceptable is for a presidential inauguration to exclude millions of citizens from its opening ceremony by dedicating it to a particular religious "savior."

Our first president, George Washington, wrote to the tiny Jewish community in Rhode Island that in this new nation, we will no longer speak of mere "toleration," because toleration implies that minorities enjoy their inherent rights "by the indulgence" of the majority. President Bush should read that letter and show it to the Reverend Franklin Graham, who told the media on the day before the inauguration that his prayer "will be for unity": instead, it was for the Trinity. Uniting for Jesus may be Graham's definition of unity, but it is as un-American as if a rabbi giving the official prayer had prayed for the arrival of the "true Messiah," thus insulting the millions of Christians who believe Jesus is the true Messiah.

Inaugurations are not the appropriate setting for theological proclamations of who is, and who is not, the true Messiah. Perhaps at Bob Jones University it is appropriate for an honorary degree recipient to declare Jesus to be the only king of the United States, but the steps of the Capitol should not be confused with the lectern of a denominational church.

The inauguration ended with another Protestant minister inviting all who agree that Jesus is "the Christ" to say "Amen." Senator Joseph Lieberman (D-Conn.), along with many others who do not believe that Jesus is the Messiah, was put in the position of either denying his own faith or remaining silent while others around him all said, "Amen." This is precisely the position in which young public school students are placed when "voluntary" prayer is conducted at school events. If they join in prayer that is inconsistent with their religious beliefs, they have been coerced into violating their conscience. If they leave or refuse to join, they stand out as different among their peers. No student should be put in that position by his or her public school at an assembly, just as no public official should be placed in that situation by the government at an inauguration.

We live in a country in which organized religion is falsely associated with personal morality. Many Americans honestly believe that only religious people can be moral, since religion is the source of morals. As I will try to show in these essays, there is no empirical or historical basis for this false association. But the fact remains that most Americans believe it, and therefore honest debate about religion is seen as out-of-bounds in many quarters. Once, in a debate with a religious fundamentalist about teaching the Bible in public schools, I proposed — for argument's sake — the following compromise: teach the Bible, but also teach Thomas Paine's *The Age of Reason* alongside the Bible. *The Age of Reason* is a mocking rebuttal to the Bible that, while extremely superficial, reflects the rhetorical flair of the great propagandist that Paine was. The fundamentalist was shocked at my proposal and rejected it immediately, out of fear that it might shake the faith of young people. The last thing religious fundamentalists want is an open and honest debate about faith. The only thing they want is one-sided religious propaganda preached from the pulpit of the teacher's desk and the principal's office.

In the following chapters, I will try to show how the wall of separation between church and state has worked well for organized religion, for the state, and for religious dissidents. It is not broken. We should not try to fix it by tearing it down.

# TWENTY-FIVE

# UPHOLDING THE WALL
# OF SEPARATION

---

*In 1990 I received the James Madison Religious Liberty Award from the Council for Democratic and Secular Humanism. I made these comments upon accepting the award.*

---

THE FIGHT FOR THE SEPARATION OF CHURCH AND STATE IS a struggle that never stays won; it is a struggle that will always continue. If you pause for just one moment, the separation — the wall — will crumble, because opposing pressures are there every moment.

We have never managed to persuade a majority of Americans, or a majority of people throughout the world, that religion has no place in government, and that government has no place in religion. We are constantly fighting a minority struggle. We sometimes fool ourselves into thinking we *may* become a majority. Never believe that. Because the moment we think we've won the battle, the opposition will come from directions that we can't anticipate, and they will tear down the wall. If that were to occur, the great experiment in separation of church and state would end.

No other country has even *tried* to build a wall of separation between church and state. The natural — it is felt by many — affiliation between government and religion has been so pervasive throughout history that when Madison, Jefferson, Hamilton, Paine, and others erected a wall of separation it was greeted with the greatest of skepticism. No one thought there could ever be government without religion, and, indeed, even after we won the initial preliminary battle and established the First Amendment, the enemies of separation did not give up. They didn't even pause. They almost immediately established a committee — in fact a series of committees — designed to amend the United States Constitution to include a declaration that we are a Christian nation. And indeed, some Christians today are still hoping that will happen. (Some Catholic friends say, "Wouldn't it be wonderful to go back to the days when people tried to declare us a Christian nation," without realizing that the "Christian nation" that was conceived of was a Protestant nation. Catholicism was not regarded as a part of *American* Christianity during our early history.)

Efforts to introduce a Christian doctrine into the United States Constitution continued for seventy or eighty years. But when the Civil War broke out — and particularly when the North started to lose some battles — preachers around the country began to talk about the war as "God's revenge" on the North and the United States in general for not having expressed our appreciation to him by enacting the "Christian nation" amendment to the Constitution. The Reverend George Jenkin of Lafayette College reminded his faithful in 1863: "For more than forty years a Fourth of July has seldom passed on which I have not preached and warned my countrymen of the defect in our Constitution and told them that if not supplied, God will pull down their temple and bury the nation in ruins."

Abraham Lincoln was approached and asked whether, since he declared a day of thanksgiving during the Civil War based on religious principles, *he* would support the "Christian nation" amendment to the Constitution. He came very close to doing so. During the terrible days of the Civil War he faced enormous pressure.

There were various proposals for the form the amendment would take. One talked in general terms about recognizing "Almighty God"; another about "Jesus the Messiah, the Savior and Lord of all of us"; and finally, the one that was indeed introduced to Congress virtually every year for the next eight years, began as follows:

> Recognizing Almighty God as the source of all authority and power in civil government, and acknowledging the Lord Jesus Christ as the governor among the nations, his revered will as the supreme law of the land, and in order to construct a Christian government . . .

Of course, there was some dissent to the proposed amendment. The Jews of Charleston, South Carolina, protested. There was a headline in the Charleston Jewish newspaper that read, "Are We Equals in This

Land?" In a famous historic letter George Washington had assured the country that there would be no more talk of toleration, that everyone was equal. Ultimately, the question of separation of church and state is a question of equality and status. It's a question of whether we have only one class of Americans in this country or different classes based on religious affiliation.

My family lives in Cambridge, Massachusetts. Many years ago when we were spending a year at Stanford and my son Elon was in the public schools of Palo Alto, he asked me: "In America do the people have to believe in God?"

I asked, "Elon, where does that question come from?"

He replied, "We were at the public school and we had an assembly, and the teacher wrote out the words of the Pledge of Allegiance. I couldn't believe it. I had been saying these words all this time, but I never realized it said 'under God.' I thought it said 'under guard.'"

New Englanders pronounce *guard* as *god*. Elon had never understood that he was being asked to pledge under "God"; and it was a very upsetting experience for him. His first question was, "Is the God in the Pledge of Allegiance the same as the Jewish God?"

I said, "Why does that make a difference to you?"

He said, "Well, I don't want to pray to somebody else's God."

I said, "But what if it is *our* God? Wouldn't it make you feel terrible that other people were praying to your God?"

He said, "Yeah, that's absolutely right. I'm not going to ever say that pledge again, because I don't want to be regarded as second best."

As a nine- or ten-year-old child, Elon understood that when you pledge to a deity, you have to ask questions about whose God it is; what about the other kids in the class; do we really have equality? He learned a very important lesson when he told the teacher that he didn't want to say the Pledge. She asked if he had discussed it with us, and when he said he had, she told him that he didn't have to stand for the Pledge or say the words. But then the peer pressure started. Elon was in the end regarded as different by his fellow students.

A year later he had the same experience — this time in Cambridge. One of the teachers looked him straight in the eye and said, "Are you an atheist? Don't you believe in God? Tell us why you don't believe in God."

I remember my son saying, "Well, why don't you ask the students in the class why they *do* believe in God?"

It became quite a dispute. And a few years later in Boston, a young Jewish woman named Susan Shapiro also refused to stand up for the Pledge of Allegiance for the same reason. Her life was threatened, and she had to be taken out of school for several weeks. We brought a lawsuit on her behalf. The teacher who had challenged Shapiro's stand had said to her, "Not standing up for the Pledge of Allegiance would be like me spitting on the Star of David."

Many people complained when we brought the lawsuit, saying that this teacher was the most sensitive, the nicest, and the warmest teacher in the whole school. Our response was, "That's the point! If the *nicest* teacher, the *best* teacher, the *warmest* teacher, the most *sensitive* teacher in Massachusetts, home of tolerance and heterogeneity, reacts this way, imagine what kind of pressure exists on other kids who want to opt out of this pledge."

During this crisis my son and I discussed what kind of country America is, whether or not it was religious. He pointed to the obvious signs, like the words *In God We Trust* on our coins. I tried to illustrate how complicated the issue was by relating a story from my father's experience. My father was an Orthodox Jew in New York and, therefore, could not keep his little store on the Lower East Side open on a Saturday. He was required by New York's closing laws (blue laws) to keep his store closed on Sunday, and he just couldn't afford to have his store closed two days a week, especially on the weekend, when there was a lot of business. So he would keep his store open on Sunday, and every so often he would get a ticket and would have to appear in front of a judge. One day he asked me to come with him. He always appeared before Judge Hyman Barshay. Judge Barshay would say, "All right, who's here for the Sunday closing law violations?" My father and two or three other businessmen from the Lower East Side would get up and would show their tickets. Then the judge would say, "All right, one at a time. The rest of you out of the room." He would call my father to the front of the courtroom and say, "So you were closed on Saturday, right?"

"Yes, I was closed on Saturday."

"Why were you closed on Saturday?"

"Because I am an observant Orthodox Jew."

"What was the Torah portion of the week?"

If my father got the answer right, the ticket would get torn up. And if my father got it *wrong*, he'd get a double fine.

It's a humorous story, but it makes a serious and important point: there is a *seductive quality* to mixing religion and state, particularly when more than one religion is given status. I believe there is now in place a more subtle process than the attempt in the nineteenth century to *directly* amend the Constitution. It's a two-step process, and one sees it all around us.

The first step is to say, "We prefer religion over nonreligion. A little bit of religion of a generic form can't really hurt." You hear that from even such great liberals as William O. Douglas in some of his opinions when he says, "We are a religious people whose institutions presuppose the existence of a Supreme Being." Or there was Ronald Reagan's "A little prayer won't hurt anybody." I debated Norman Podhoretz a couple of years ago on the issue of whether liberalism or conservatism is good or bad for the Jews. Podhoretz said, "Why are you liberals so concerned about prayer in the schools? I went to a public school in Brooklyn in the 1930s, and every single day I had to recite for five minutes in Latin parts of the Mass, and it didn't hurt me at all."

I responded, "But think what it meant to you as a kid in school. You *knew* your place in that school. You *knew* you were a second-class citizen. You *knew* you couldn't complain about it. You *knew* you didn't have standing to object."

We must have separation between church and state if we really believe in equality in America — and even equality is an experiment if you think of all the countries in the world today and how few espouse real equality. Look at what's happening in Eastern Europe, where the shackles of communism are being exchanged for the shackles of religion. The liberal Romanian students who were demonstrating in the streets are now demonstrating for church-sponsored schools and for laws against abortion. In Poland the government has introduced mandatory Catholic education into the public schools, clearly declaring Protestant, Jewish, and atheist Poles and others to be second-class citizens.

America is unique. Aside from the Native American population, we're all immigrants. The recency of our arrival on these shores is only a matter of degree, and as the generations pass, our ethnic origins become less important. In its first century of existence, when it was populated largely by white Anglo-Saxons, the United States was only a country with great aspirations, much like Canada, Australia, New Zealand, and others that had broken free from Britain. We became the greatest country in the world in our second century, *after* immigration, *after* desegregation began, *after* women became enfranchised. We became the great America *because* of our diversity, not *despite* our diversity.

Without a separation of church and state, it would be *impossible* for the first-class status of the United States to continue. Yet it gets challenged at every single turn, particularly during elections, when politicians not only wrap themselves in the flag but carry the cross as well. During the 1984 presidential campaign Walter Mondale found it necessary to remind Ronald Reagan that in the United States the president, unlike the queen of England, is "not the defender of faith" but the defender of the Constitution. At that point I had written a column that I sent to political candidates across the country setting out what I called "The Ten Comm*end*ments for Politicians." A comm*end*ment is something between a commandment and an amendment. They were:

1. Do not claim God as a member of your party or that God is on your side of an issue.
2. Do not publicly proclaim your own religious devotion, affiliation, and practices, or attack those of your opponents.
3. Do not denounce those who differ with you about the proper role of religion in public life as antireligious or intolerant of religion.
4. Do not surround your political campaign with religious trappings or symbols.
5. Honor and respect the diversity of this country, recalling that many Americans came to these shores to escape the tyranny of enforced religious uniformity and, more recently, enforced antireligious uniformity.
6. Do not seek the support of religious leaders who impose religious obligations on members of their faith to support or oppose particular candidates.
7. Do not accuse those who reject formal religion of immorality. Recall that some of our nation's greatest leaders did not accept formal or even informal religion.

8. Do not equate morality and religion. Although some great moral teachers were religious, some great moral sinners also acted in the name of religion.
9. When there are political as well as religious dimensions to an issue, focus on the political ones during the campaign.
10. Remember that every belief is in a minority somewhere, and act as if your belief were the least popular.

I wish that instead of the Ten Commandments, the first ten amendments to our Constitution would be put up in schools. Remember that even the most basic issues of separation are not universally accepted in this country. I remind you only of Judge W. Brevard Hand of Alabama, who ruled that each state may establish its own religion, just as it may pick its own bird, flower, song, and motto. Ed Meese, who was then attorney general, agreed with him. He took out his copy of the Constitution and showed it to a friend of mine who was then at the Justice Department and said, "*Show me* where it says that states cannot establish a religion. All it says is that *Congress* may not establish a religion." And, of course, historically, Hand and Meese were absolutely right — if you stop the Constitution at about the time of the Civil War. The First Amendment of the Constitution was not intended to restrict state establishment of religion, and as you know, states did establish religions. As late as the middle of the nineteenth century, Jews, Turks, infidels, and other non-Christians were precluded from holding office and swearing oaths as witnesses.

When Hand was asked, "What will people do who have no religion or who belong to a minority religion?" he said, "A member of a religious minority will simply have to develop a thicker skin if the state establishment offends him." When I saw that statement I wrote a column in which I gave him the "Ayatollah Khomeini Award" for attempting to divide the country along religious lines and described the implications of his view. In Massachusetts, for example, the struggle for official recognition would be between Catholics and Protestants. Where I grew up, in Brooklyn, the religious warfare would be among the Jews. In Utah, Mormonism would prevail; in California, the various cults and fringe religious groups might unite to present a common front. Even if a state settled on Protestantism, which denomination would be the official one? Fortunately the Supreme Court of the

United States reversed Judge Hand, characterizing his views as "remarkable," which is a judicial euphemism for "ridiculous." But we are still, even with the United States Supreme Court, seeing some very dangerous trends.

The trend of *broadening* religion in order to make it more acceptable has now gained momentum. You'll recall that a few years ago, the Supreme Court upheld the constitutionality of placing a crèche scene in a Christmas display, as long as a sufficient number of plastic reindeer and other accoutrements of secularity were included. In Pittsburgh, Pennsylvania, the city sponsored a Christmas tree, a crèche, and a Hanukkah menorah. Significantly, as the Court described it, the menorah was placed "in the shadow of the Christmas tree." The Court decided that if displays were allowed to include a Christmas tree, they should also allow a Hanukkah menorah. A lot of people in the Jewish community were disarmed by that decision, because it gave them status alongside Christians. But giving special status to religions is only the first step on the short road toward tearing down the wall of separation between church and state.

The second step is for the state, once it says religion is to be preferred over nonreligion, to *define* what religion means. You then have to define what is *true* religion and what is *real* religion. I defended Jim Bakker for a principled reason relating to that. In imposing his forty-five year sentence, United States District Judge Robert D. Potter of North Carolina said: "*We* [pointing to himself] who have a *true* religion" are offended by those who are charlatans and have a false religion.[1]

It's not the role of a judge in America to distinguish between true and false religions. Judge Potter is a very religious Catholic and belongs to a church that has had conflicts with the evangelical movement. The very idea of judges in this country, whether it be a Jewish judge like Hyman Barshay dealing with my father back in the 1940s, or a Catholic judge, or a Protestant judge, imposing their own religious values on a sentencing process is un-American. And it's intolerable to the continued separation of church and state.

There's another threat to separation that I want to bring to your attention, which I call "back-door establishment." It's part of the process we've been talking about. What happens is this: When a majority religion like mainstream Christianity seeks state help in establishing crèches at Christmas, the state says, "Christianity really is the majority religion in this country; therefore, when something happens in the name of Christianity, it's really secular, because so many Americans are Christians. Christmas is a secular holiday. And Thanksgiving, even with its religious origins, is a secular holiday. But if a smaller religion were to seek aid from the state, since the members are only a minority, then it would clearly be an establishment."

This is *precisely* the opposite of what the framers of our Constitution had in mind. The framers were not fearful of small, fringe, minority religions; they were fearful of the *majority* religion.

Chief Justice William Rehnquist has expressed this view. A few years ago a chaplain in the air force named Dr. Goldman, who was a psychologist, wore a yarmulke, which violated uniform rules. He was court-martialed. The Supreme Court did not uphold his claim of religious observance, because to do so would establish religion. Justice Rehnquist, who worried about the establishment of Orthodox Judaism in America, had no problems about the establishment of Christianity. He also participated in the crèche decision, saying that crèches could be permitted on public land.

Those are some of the problems that remain ahead of us. And they're not getting any easier. Fundamentalism, tragically, is pervasive throughout the world today. There is almost *no* part of the world that is not seeing an increase in fundamentalism — in know-nothingism; in I don't want to hear, I don't want to think, I don't want to know, tell me what I have to do, give me my marching orders, point me in the right direction and I'll go! We who reject that kind of approach in religion, in politics, in personal life, and in law are always going to have a very difficult struggle ahead of us. We are moving against the tide. Too many of us count on the possibility that the extremes within the evangelical movement have the seeds for self-destruction. We've been lucky until now that our enemies have included many fools and hypocrites. We can't continue to count on that. I predict the emergence of a far more intelligent, far more presentable fundamentalist movement throughout the world. We have to prepare for the day when we can't win the debate by laughing at our enemies, when we must out-reason them.

We must never assume that because we persuaded somebody yesterday, that person will remain persuaded today and tomorrow. Every day is a new day in the struggle for the separation of church and state. We must be willing to buck the tide of majority intolerance and bigotry and to struggle against religious bigotry because we have a vision. We know what losing this battle will do to America. We *know* that the greatness of this country depends on its being the most heterogeneous, the most diverse country in the history of the world. We understand the experimental nature of the American dream. So please, keep fighting.

# TWENTY-SIX

# THE RIGHT TO DISBELIEVE

*Most Americans recognize the right to believe in religions different from their own. But there is far less tolerance toward avowed atheists and disbelievers. In 1999 I wrote an article entitled "Taking Disbelief Out of the Closet."*

THE MOST INSIDIOUS GENRE OF CENSORIAL POLITICAL correctness in America today involves belief in God. Few people in public life are prepared to disclose that they are atheists, agnostics, skeptics, or humanists. For a politician, such a declaration would be death, as evidenced by a recent controversy in Canada when a young rising star in Parliament introduced a resolution seeking to remove a phrase from Canada's Charter of Rights and Freedoms that declared "the supremacy of God." He was immediately punished by parliamentary leaders and forced to apologize. Although there are many closet disbelievers in politics today, few have the courage to acknowledge their skepticism in the face of religious hegemony.

Even academics, whose tenure guarantees them the right to speak freely without consequence, rarely publicize their disbelief for fear of alienating students, alumni, and the administration. *Being* an atheist or agnostic in America is relatively cost-free, so long as you remain in the closet. Most public institutions have a "don't ask, don't tell" policy when it comes to disbelief.

The situation is very different throughout Europe, where atheism and agnosticism are openly acknowledged. Numerous heads of government have made no secret of their disbelief. Despite — perhaps because of — the fact that most European nations have established churches, there is more actual freedom of disbelief in Europe than there is in the United States, whose Constitution guarantees freedom of and from religion. Established churches have a way of encouraging freethinking among those who don't want to be told what they may believe or disbelieve.

The time has come for atheists, agnostics, skeptics, and humanists to come out of the closet and to openly confront the religious hegemony in America that has created a political correctness so powerful that even the most courageous are afraid to violate it openly. Unless such a challenge is mounted, the situation will simply grow more dangerous. Already the Democratic Party, which traditionally was more secular than the Republican, has begun to run on God's coattails. It started with Jimmy Carter. It got worse with Bill Clinton. And it got even worse with Al Gore, who is explicitly pandering to what he calls "faith-based organizations." Most Republicans don't even make a pretense of believing in separation of church and state. More and more American politicians are publicly advertising their religious beliefs — that they have been saved, that they have been reborn, and that they have accepted Jesus as their personal Savior. This puts additional pressure on other politicians to match and exceed their rivals in public devotion to God. Some lobbying groups rank candidates by the fervor of their religious commitments.

One reason that so many disbelievers are unwilling to acknowledge their views with intellectual honesty is that the religious establishment has managed to persuade large segments of the American public that there is some correlation between belief in a supernatural God and human ethics and morals. Disbelievers are deemed immoral. Consider the response of Canadian parliamentarian Randy White to the parliamentarian who tried to remove God from the charter: "What do we stand for in this country? What are the values? What are the morals? Every time you turn around, you see government slipping lower and lower into the gutters of this country." But history has shown that if there is any correlation between belief in God and personal morality — which I personally reject — it is as likely to be a negative as a positive one. Surely as much immorality has been committed in the name of religion as any other cause. The millions murdered by cynical, godless tyrants such as Hitler and Stalin are matched by those killed in the names of Jesus, Muhammad, and Jehovah. In any event, Stalin and Hitler do not represent the morality of disbelievers any more than Torquemada represents the views of believers. The most moral people in the world are those who act selflessly without promise of reward or threat of punishment in the hereafter. Pascal's wager — that it is better to bet on the existence of God even if he doesn't exist than to risk the punishment of disbelieving — is nothing more than a crude cost-benefit calculus having little to do with morality. I am aware of no empirical data showing that believers are less likely to commit crimes, cheat on their wives, or abuse their children than nonbelievers. Our prisons are full of people who profess religious beliefs, and the most beneficent human beings include many who are disbelievers.

I suspect that tens of millions of Americans are skeptics or nonbelievers but are afraid to speak out. We must make it safe for such people to express their views openly. Disbelief in God must become as legitimate as belief in God in every forum of American life. We must confront religious authoritarianism in the marketplace of ideas, with respect but with vigor.

Having called for more openness in the expression of views regarding the existence of God, let me follow my own admonition. I am a skeptic about everything, including God and atheism. I am not certain about issues of cosmology. Sometimes I believe that our universe is the result of random forces. Other times I believe that there must be some purpose or ordering force, though I do not begin to understand what or who it could be. I do not expect that these cosmic doubts will ever be resolved in my mind. I am more certain that the miraculous stories that form the basis of most religious beliefs are myths. Yet I respect the Bible and enjoy reading and teaching it. Indeed, I find it even more fascinating as a human creation than as a divine revelation. I consider myself a committed Jew, but I do not believe that being a Jew requires belief in the supernatural. When I attend synagogue, as I often do, or conduct Sabbath, Passover, or Hanukkah services at home, I recite prayers. I am comfortable with these apparent contradictions. I am part of a long tradition that links to my heritage through the words and melodies of prayer. Indeed, it is while praying that I experience my greatest doubts about God, and it is while looking at the stars that I make the leap of faith. But it is not faith in the empirical truths of religious stories or in the authority of hierarchical religious organizations. If there is a governing force, he (or she or it) is certainly not in touch with those who purport to be speaking on his behalf.

The important point is that everyone must have the right to question faith and to decide this eternal issue by his or her own lights, without being condemned for disagreeing with today's religious consensus. Remember that religious views change over the millennium. People were killed for believing in Jesus and then for not believing in Jesus, for accepting Catholicism and for rejecting Catholicism, and for many other religious disagreements.

Today, thankfully, Americans are not killed for their religious beliefs or disbeliefs. But they are condemned as immoral and unfit for public office if they publicly declare their skepticism. The world must be made safe and secure for disbelievers. America was founded on religious dissent and skepticism. We must not accept religious hegemony or preference for religion in public life. Atheists and agnostics are every bit as American, every bit as moral, and every bit as qualified to hold public office as people who believe in an intervening God. Disbelievers should not accept second-class status in a nation whose traditions and laws forbid tests of faith as a condition of citizenship or office holding.

# TWENTY-SEVEN

# WHEN THE WALL COMES TUMBLING DOWN

THE "WALL" HAS LONG BEEN A USEFUL AND POETIC METAPHOR. It separates neighbors as well as great nations. It protects and defends, but it also rejects and offends. The wall of separation between church and state, a metaphor popularized by Thomas Jefferson, is in danger of crumbling in the nation that first built it. There are multiple ironies in this danger. Unlike the broken wall that separated East and West Germany, the wall between church and state in America is not broken. Originally designed to protect the church against the secularizing intrusions of the state, our wall is working extremely well. Churches, synagogues, and mosques are thriving in this land of separation. Religious attendance is higher than in any Western democracy with an established church. Belief in God is widespread throughout the land. Yet the right to disbelieve or to be skeptical is accepted — at least in theory.

The successful status of American religion is to be contrasted with the sorry state of religion throughout most of Europe. When my family and I travel to Europe, we love to visit the old churches — not for prayer, but for artistic appreciation. Our favorite time to observe a church is on Sunday morning, when it is being used as intended. In recent years, we have seen fewer and fewer parishioners in churches throughout England, France, Italy, Germany, and Spain — except, of course, on special occasions. It is no coincidence, in my view, that organized religion is thriving in America and dying in much of Europe. The separation of church and state is good for religion. When church and state merge, the natural antagonism that citizens feel toward their government carries over to the church. Moreover, when the state tries to enforce religious practices, enmity is generated. Witness Israel, a country that I visit frequently. Because the mechanisms of the state are employed in support of Orthodox Judaism, a sharp division has developed between the Orthodox community and the vast majority of secular Jews. Many secular Jews feel strongly that their freedoms have been impinged, not only by Orthodox Judaism, but by the state as well. Today there is more anti-Orthodox feeling in Israel than in any other part of the world.

For these reasons, I believe that if the wall of separation were to crumble in America, the ultimate losers would be the churches, the synagogues, and the mosques. To be sure, organized religion would benefit *initially* from the support — financial, political, and ideological — of the state. Many religious leaders who are currently strapped for cash see the wall of separation as a barrier to filling their coffers. But in the long run, organized religion would suffer greatly from state involvement in their affairs. The state, by paying the organist, would call the hymn. This would be a tragedy for both religious and secular Americans. Religion, if it remains independent of the state, can serve as a useful check and balance on the excesses of government. For example, during the 1920s, eugenics became the rage among scientists, academics, and intellectuals. Thirty states enacted forcible sterilization laws, which resulted in fifty thousand people being surgically sterilized. In 1927 the United States Supreme Court upheld these laws in a decision by the great justice Oliver Wendell Holmes, who wrote: "It is better for all the world, if instead of waiting to execute offspring for crime or to let them starve for their imbecility, society can prevent those who are manifestly unfit from continuing their kind." The only dissenting opinion came from a religious Catholic. Churches fought hard against sterilization laws. In this instance, religion was right; government and science were wrong.

In countries where the state controls religion, it is far more difficult for churches to serve as checks upon the excesses of the state. Were the wall of separation to come crumbling down, disbelievers and skeptics would also suffer greatly — at least at the outset. I doubt we would have crusades, inquisitions, or pogroms — as in centuries past. But there would be discrimination. Indeed, even today, there is discrimination in practice despite its prohibition under the Constitution.[1] But in the long run, the number of openly skeptical Americans would increase. Church membership would drop.

Would this be good for America? Would this be good for secular humanists? Since none of us is a prophet, it is impossible to know with certainty what an America, without a wall of separation, would look like. It would almost certainly become a different place from the one we now inhabit, which is still the envy of the world. We are a prudent and cautious people. As such, we should not take the risks of breaking an edifice that has served us so well for so long.

## PART IV

＊

# THE RIGHTS OF SUSPECTS, DEFENDANTS, AND CONVICTED CRIMINALS

WE LIVE IN AN AGE IN WHICH POLITICAL LEADERS ARE fearful of saying anything that could be construed as being "soft on crime" or "procriminal." No modern American politician has ever lost an election for being too tough on crime. It has not always been this way. When Winston Churchill was the home secretary of Great Britain, he delivered the following comment to the House of Commons:

> The mood and temper of the public in regard to the treatment of crime and criminals is one of the most unfailing tests of the civilization of any country. A calm dispassionate recognition of the rights of the accused and even of the convicted criminal against the state; a constant heart-searching of all charged with the deed of punishment; tireless efforts towards the discovery of regenerative processes; unfailing faith that there is a treasure, if you can find it, in the heart of every man. These are the symbols which in the treatment of crime and criminals make and measure the stored-up strength of a nation and are sign and proof of the living virtue in it.

Dostoyevsky made a similar point when he once observed, "A society which looks upon such things [as the harsh punishment of its citizens] with an indifferent eye is already infected to the marrow." Even the United States Supreme Court, in 1962, agreed that "the methods we employ in the enforcement of our criminal law have aptly been called the measures by which the quality of our civilization may be judged." When evaluated against this standard, our civilization does not receive a particularly high grade. Though in theory our nation boasts of important constitutional safeguards for those accused of crime, in practice our system of criminal justice is neither fair nor particularly effective. In the chapters that follow, I will try to demonstrate some of those problems by focusing on the narrative of crime, the prevention of crime, the punishment of crime, and some defenses to crime such as insanity.

# TWENTY-EIGHT

# LIFE IS NOT A DRAMATIC NARRATIVE

*In the midst of the O. J. Simpson case, I was invited to participate in a symposium on narrative and law. I used the Simpson case, in which I was consulting, along with several other cases, to illustrate my thesis that life is not a Chekhovian narrative and that the law should not reflect the canons of traditional literature. I began by referring to another case, one I had fictionalized in my novel* The Advocate's Devil.

The case involved a businessman named Hamilton who had taken out a life insurance policy on his partner ten days before the partner was gunned down by a professional hit man. The DA was finding it easy to persuade the jury that the timing could not possibly be coincidental, and Abe [the defense attorney] had been raking his mind for an answer. Emma [Abe's seventeen-year-old daughter], finding that she simply couldn't get his attention, had decided to try to help him figure out a commonsense rebuttal to the DA's circumstantial case.

And she had.

"Daddy," she said, popping into his home office late one night, "the answer is Chekhov."

"Why Chekhov?" Abe asked, his head still buried in the books.

"Because Chekhov once told an aspiring dramatist that if you hang a gun on the wall in the first act, you had better use it by the third act. We read it in lit class."

"So what does that have to do with the Hamilton case . . . ?"

"Your jurors see Chekhov's theory on TV and in the movies every day. Don't you get it, Daddy? On TV, when they show a businessman or a wife buying life insurance on someone, every viewer knows there's going to be a murder, and they know who the murderer will be. It's a setup."

"You've got a point. Sure, on TV, when a character coughs or has a chest pain, you know he's dying. There's no such thing as a cold or indigestion. Everything has to be relevant to the drama."

"But in real life, Daddy, the world is full of irrelevant actions and coincidences. People take out insurance policies all the time, and then the person lives till Willard Scott can put him on the *Today* show."

"You've really got something there, Emma. I think I may use it."

And Abe had used it. He'd convinced the jury not to look at the Hamilton case as if it were a made-for-TV movie, but rather a slice of real life, full of irrelevant actions and coincidences. He'd asked the jurors how many of them had taken out life insurance on a loved one and what their neighbors would have thought if that loved one had died shortly thereafter.

After he'd won, several jurors had told him that his TV argument had turned them around.[1]


What Anton Chekhov actually told the writer S. S. Schovkin was, "If in the first chapter you say that a gun hung on the wall, in the second or third chapter it must without fail be discharged."[2] It should not be surprising that this canon of classic drama traces its origins back to biblical and other religious narratives. If we are part of a purposive universe — governed by God's law or by the cosmos — then the stories within that universe must have meaning.[3]

Many literary, biblical, and even constitutional scholars live by a rule of teleology that has little resonance in real life — namely, that every event, character, and word has a purpose. "To everything there is a season, and a time to every purpose under heaven," says Ecclesiastes (3:1). God does not engage in redundancy, say the Talmudists.[4] Freud, whose forebears came from that tradition, similarly believed that all words, even those dreamed or spoken in error, have meaning.[5] Some lawyers who view our Constitution in near-biblical terms — and who seek to discern the true meaning of those near-deities who wrote it — fall into the same teleo-theological trap: every word of that secularly sacred text must have a purpose, a meaning, and if we only had the wisdom of the framer's, we could discern it.[6]

But life does not imitate art. Life is not a purposive narrative that follows Chekhov's canon. Events are often simply meaningless, irrelevant to what comes next; events can be out of sequence, random, purely accidental, without purpose. If our universe and its inhabitants are governed by rules of chaos, randomness, and purposelessness, then many of the stories — if they can even be called stories — will often lack meaning. Human beings always try to impose order and meaning on random chaos, both to understand and to control the forces that determine their destiny. This desperate attempt to derive purpose from purposelessness will often distort reality, as, indeed, Chekhov's canon does.

In Chekhovian drama, chest pains are followed by heart attacks, coughs by consumption, life insurance policies by murders, telephone rings by dramatic messages. In real life, most chest pains are indigestion, coughs are colds, insurance policies are followed by years of premium payments, and telephone calls are from marketing services.

My colleague Stephen Jay Gould, in his magnificent narrative of the earth aptly entitled *Wonderful Life*, teaches us that much of life, on both the micro and the macro levels, is so random and without purpose that if we were to rewind the tape of life and replay it, it would come out differently every time.[7] *Homo sapiens* is not the preordained, logical, purposeful end of evolution. We are the accidental, random result of a series of historical contingencies that would never be replicated even if we could return to the time of the Burgess Shale and, like Michael Finnegan of the children's song, begin again. Most of what happens — from the dinosaur extinction to the Holocaust to the AIDS epidemic to random killings to brain tumors to the lottery — is not part of any plan. To believe otherwise is to accept a particularly nasty variant of the "naturalistic fallacy."[8]

To be sure, after the fact, we may be able to offer a plausible retrospective account, a story or a narrative of what happened. As Sartre put it: "When you tell about life . . . you seem to start at the beginning. . . . But in reality you have started at the end."[9] Narrative often starts at the end. But rarely can we employ such retrospective accounts to predict their reoccurrence. Nor is this lack of prophetic ability merely a function of our relative ignorance. Often it is simply in the nature of things.[10] Quantum physics corroborates on the micro level what paleontology teaches on the macro level. The most important rule in the game of life is that generally there are no knowable rules. Perhaps it is the often-unspoken recognition of this nihilistic reality that drives us so powerfully toward prescriptive human laws by which we can exercise some control over our mostly random destiny and toward purposive narrative by which we seek to impose an order on the largely disordered events of life.

This critical dichotomy between teleological rules of drama and interpretation, on the one hand, and the mostly random rules of real life, on the other, has profoundly important implications for our legal system. When we import the narrative form of storytelling into our legal system, we confuse fiction with fact and endanger the truth-finding function of the adjudicative process. Fact finders are familiar with the dramatic form — not only from Chekhov but also from pulp novels, mysteries, movies, and television shows.[11] A wonderful parody of the classic Chekhov canon appears in the film *Hot Shots!* (1991).

| | |
|---|---|
| DEAD MEAT: | Mary! Mary! (embrace) Have you come to watch me fly? |
| MARY: | There was a meltdown at the plant so they gave me the afternoon off. |
| DEAD MEAT: | Aw, terrific! (black cat runs across their path) |
| MARY: | Oh, good news! We just closed escrow in our little dream house. |
| DEAD MEAT: | Wonderful! When do we move in? |
| MARY: | Tuesday. I've got the kids stripping the asbestos off the pipes right now. |
| DEAD MEAT: | Aw, that's great. (walks under a ladder) Things just couldn't be better for us. I'm so blessed. |
| MARY: | Oh — your life insurance forms came for you to sign. (drops her mirror from her purse and it shatters) Oh, my mirror! |
| DEAD MEAT: | (pen doesn't work) Huh. |
| MARY: | I'll get another pen. |
| DEAD MEAT: | No need. I'll sign it when I get back. |
| MARY: | Well, you know best. |
| DEAD MEAT: | Honey, you know that global warming problem? I've discovered how we can reverse it. |
| MARY: | Tell me! |
| DEAD MEAT: | No, not now lovey bumpers. There'll be plenty of time for that later. And my investigation into the assassination of JFK . . . |
| MARY: | You found the evidence you were looking for?!? |
| DEAD MEAT: | Yes, I have proof. It's right here in my pocket. It's big, honey. It's really big. It goes all the way to the White House. |

MARY:        Do you want me to hold it for you?

DEAD MEAT:   It will be safe right here. I'm in a jet. What could go wrong?

MARY:        Oh, Dead Meat . . . We just couldn't be any more perfectly happy. (they blow kisses at each other)

Dead Meat's airplane then, of course, crashes.

Audiences expect a beginning, a middle, and an end to each story. Life, in drama, unfolds in acts or chapters or between commercials. There is an internal logic to the structure. Every narrative, unlike the pudding once criticized by Churchill, must have a theme. Even surprise endings must be foreshadowed, at least in retrospect.[12] False clues, deliberately planted by the author to throw the reader off, are frowned upon by critics. Even the deus ex machina of Greek literature has a purpose, though we may not be blessed with the insight to comprehend it fully.[13]

Among the most pervasive narratives in the human experience have been the stories of justice. In these stories virtue is rewarded, vice punished, and justice achieved. The Psalmist reports, "I was a child and then grew old, but I never saw a righteous person abandoned or his children begging bread." This is a narrative of justice. But it is a perversely false narrative. It is false because the history of humankind is replete with the abandonment of the righteous and their children. It is perverse because it implies that those who are abandoned must necessarily have been unrighteous.

As a matter of historical reality, there has been precious little justice in the history of the world. Most Nazis, even hands-on perpetrators of genocide, lived good lives after the war; many Holocaust survivors did not.[14] There is absolutely no empirical correlation between righteousness and reward or unrighteousness and punishment. Indeed, it is precisely because of that lack of correlation — the factual untruth of the narrative of justice — that human beings have been driven to create another narrative, one that cannot be proved or disproved. That is, of course, the narrative of heaven and hell, of punishment and reward in the world to come. By creating this narrative of faith, we can insist that virtue is rewarded and vice punished, if not here on earth, then somewhere else, where we can never apply the tests of empirical truth or falsity. Because the narrative of justice cannot be observed here on earth, we create an unobservable world where we can simply declare that the narrative of justice will come true.

The biblical story of Job is a wonderful example of the power of the justice narrative. God tests Job by killing his children (and taking his wealth) despite his — and their — righteousness. Job passes the test of faith, and he is given new children (and wealth). Only in such a primitive narrative of justice would replacement children make up for the death of other children, but even this primitive ending was apparently not in the original narrative. It was added later to satisfy the demands of the justice narrative.[15]

The concept of natural law, and its many variations, presuppose a narrative of justice and a teleological approach to drawing normative conclusions from natural phenomena. If there is a God whose laws ought to govern behavior, then the job of the natural lawyer is merely to discern these laws in divinely inspired texts, accounts, or the "nature" of human beings or God. Once these natural laws are discerned, the purposive narrative of justice may be implemented. But if there is no God, if there is no purpose to "nature," if there are only "laws" of science — such as the laws of energy and gravity — then human beings must invent, not discover, laws of morality and governance to regulate human conduct so that a narrative of justice can be enforced.[16]

All too often fact finders employ the canons of literature and interpretation in the search for truth, generally without any conscious awareness that they are doing so.[17]

A contemporaneous misuse of narrative, at least to this advocate, may have been at work in the O. J. Simpson case. The prosecution sought to persuade the jury that the canons of drama required it to conclude that O. J. Simpson's alleged history of spousal abuse inevitably led him to murder his wife. Why, after all, would the editor of the narrative — who is called a judge in our legal system — allow the jury to hear evidence of alleged abuse in the first chapter unless it resulted in murder by the third chapter? Surely these past incidents must be highly relevant to the question before the jurors: Did O. J. Simpson kill his wife? The prosecutor tried to strengthen this connection by working backward from the murder — employing Sartre's rule of narrative of the legal equivalent of the dramatic flashback — and arguing that in a large proportion of cases in which a man kills his present or former spouse, the killing is preceded by a narrative of abuse and control. The defense tried to get jurors to work forward from the alleged abuse by explaining that fewer than one-tenth of 1 percent of spousal abusers escalate to homicide and that no one can accurately predict which ones will actually commit murder, even by using such criteria as a pattern of controlling behavior.

In the words of our previous discussion, the prosecution tried to show that there is an internal logic, a sequential progression, to its narrative of abuse, control, and murder. The defense tried to show that in real life, as contrasted with fictional drama, the isolated acts of abuse appear to be relevant only because we now know that Nicole Brown Simpson was, in fact, murdered. But because we do not know by whom she was murdered and because this is real life filled with coincidences, randomness, and illogic, we cannot comfortably conclude that *this* alleged abuser became the one in more than one thousand whose acts culminated in murder.

Put another way, if we had a case — as we often do — where a defendant admitted that he killed his spouse, it might be logical to conclude that he probably abused her first, for a large proportion of the fifteen hundred or so annual spousal murderers were abusers first. But the logic of the narrative is far less compelling in a case where the question is: Did *this* alleged spousal abuser (one of several million each year) become one of those very rare spousal murderers? The issue is complex. It is probably true that a significant percentage of women who end up murdered by an unknown assailant were murdered by spouses or lovers who had previously abused them. But it is also probably true that a significant percentage of murdered women were murdered by spouses or lovers who did *not* abuse them. The question is the relative saliency of the *relationship* (spouse, lover) or of the *act* (battering). Again, the analogy to the dramatic narrative, with its literary license, is heuristically useful. In drama, if a character is shown having several scotches in the first act, you can safely assume that she will become an alcoholic by the third. And it is true that all alcoholics begin with several drinks. But only a small percentage of those who have two drinks become alcoholics. In fictional narrative, however, there would be no dramatic reason for showing the two drinks unless they were a prelude to a dramatic denouement. The same can be said of spousal abuse. If several instances of abuse are shown in the first act of a play, you can reliably predict that either the abuser will kill the abusee or vice versa by the third act. But in real life, such a lethal result is so rare as to be empirically insignificant (though morally significant, of course). That is why "bad man" evidence — a history of prior criminality — is always relevant in literature and rarely in criminal trials. And it is precisely because of its prevalence in literature that it is so prejudicial in court.

A related example of confusing narrative with real life in the Simpson case was the judge's ruling that the jurors should hear about the defendant's allegedly dreaming that he would kill Nicole. In literature, dreams come true. Indeed, in support of the argument, the prosecutor Marcia Clark cited a song entitled "A Dream Is a Wish Your Heart Makes," from the Walt Disney cartoon movie *Sleeping Beauty.* In real life, however, dreams do not come true. They are not even wishes. They are "primary-process" primitive images, which are ambiguous. As one court put it, this ambiguity "leaves the meaning of the dream in the realm of mere conjecture, surmise, and speculating, and one surmise may be as good as another. Nobody knows."[18] Yet despite the lack of any empirical relation between dreaming about killing and actual killing, there was the danger that some jurors might have applied Chekhov's canon — or Walt Disney's fantasy — and assumed that unless the dream was relevant, it would not have been presented. This would be especially dangerous in a case where the facts follow the narrative form: in the first act, the defendant dreams about killing his wife; in the second act, she is killed; and in the third act, the defendant is placed on trial for the killing. Regardless of the empirical reality that only an infinitesimal percentage of people who dream about killing do kill, some jurors might have ended the drama by convicting the dreamer of being a killer. A related misuse of narrative would be for a prosecutor to introduce evidence in a rape case that a defendant viewed pornography. In some feminist narratives, the viewing of pornography is followed by rape or, retrospectively, rapists admit that they were viewers of pornography. In the Dworkin-MacKinnon narrative, readers expect that the story of the viewer of pornography will end with his becoming a rapist. In real life, the story is far more likely to go something like this: "John started with *Playboy* as a child, then he moved up to *Penthouse,* and soon he was watching hard-core videos. Eventually, he became an accountant with a wife and three kids." Such boringly realistic narratives are never told, although they reflect the statistical reality that the vast majority of pornography viewers are and remain law-abiding citizens. Indeed, whenever I read agenda-driven narratives, I suspect selective editing. But such narratives are difficult for scholars to challenge without questioning the accuracy or integrity of the storyteller.[19]

Jurors, like most people, are not good at thinking statistically or probabilistically.[20] They are much more comfortable thinking literarily, teleologically, religiously, narratively. But such thinking is often misleading and inapt, at least when it comes to answering empirical questions in a world governed more by randomness than by canons of narrative drama.

An example of an area where the law has tried to remedy possible confusion between fantasy and reality relates to the rape shield law, which prevents the jury from hearing otherwise admissible evidence of the alleged victim's prior sexual behavior with other men. In the literature, when a young woman is shown in act one living a life of "promiscuity" (to use an anachronistic word from the world of literature), that life will become important to the plot: either she will continue her downward spiral toward a dissolute end, or she will be "saved." In act two if she has sex with an acquaintance that she claims was coerced and he claims was consensual, surely the reader will regard the history of promiscuity as relevant on the issue of consent. Why else would it have been presented in act one? But our legal editors have correctly concluded that unless special circumstances are present, the prejudicial impact of this history outweighs its probative value. For this (and other) reasons, the jury is not presented with this history. In life, unlike in art, a promiscuous woman does not always consent to sex.

To paraphrase Justice Oliver Wendell Holmes, the life of the law should not be teleologic or theologic (neither of which is *logic* at all); it should be human experience. And human experience cannot be cabined into the structure of traditional narrative. Let literature continue to borrow from law and life (though it would borrow more accurately if it looked less to Chekhov for its canons of structure and more to Proust and Mamet).[21] But let law develop its own rules of structure and editing — of evidence, relevance, and prejudice — by looking to the vagaries of real human experience. And let fact finders, especially jurors, be warned that life is not a Chekhovian narrative.

# TWENTY-NINE

# CRIME PREVENTION

---

*From the beginning of recorded history, prophets have attempted to foresee harmful occurrences, such as flood, famine, pestilence, earthquake, and volcanic eruption. Attempting to predict crime — to determine who is likely to become a criminal — has also captured the imagination of mankind for centuries. From the Bible's "stubborn and rebellious son," identifiable by his gluttony and drunkenness, to Cesare Lombroso's "born criminal and criminaloid," identifiable by the shape of his cranium, to Sheldon and Eleanor Glueck's three-year-old delinquent, identifiable by a composite score derived from familial relationships — "experts" have claimed the ability to spot the mark of the potential criminal before he or she has committed serious crimes. Though the results have not generally met with scientific approval, it is still widely believed — by many policemen, judges, psychiatrists, lawyers, and members of the general public — that there are ways of distinguishing real criminals from the rest of us. Most recently, it has been suggested that certain genetic markers may be associated with — and consequently predictive of — certain kinds of violent crimes. In 1969 I wrote the following essay about "preventive detention" of "dangerous" defendants for the* New York Review of Books.[1]

---

DURING THE 1968 PRESIDENTIAL CAMPAIGN, "CRIME IN the streets" emerged as a crucial political issue. All three major candidates vowed to make the nation's capital — where the crime rate is particularly high and painfully visible — a model of safety for our other urban centers. Now President Richard Nixon faces the task of transforming slogans into programs.

In his first major policy statement on crime, President Nixon proposed a law "whereby dangerous hard-core recidivists could be held in temporary pretrial detention when they have been charged with crime and when their continued pretrial release presents a continued danger to the community." By thus supporting "preventive detention" — albeit in cautiously vague terms — the president has provided substantial impetus to a movement that could have far-reaching significance not only in the District of Columbia but throughout the country.

The conditions giving rise to the call for preventive detention are not difficult to understand. A person suspected of committing a crime cannot stand trial on the day of his arrest; he must be given time to consult with his lawyer and prepare a defense. Although this should rarely take more than a few days, the delay between arrest and trial has been growing, until it is now almost as long as two years in some cities and a year in most other cities, including the District of Columbia. This is primarily the consequence of our unwillingness to pay for needed increases in judicial machinery.

At the same time, there has been a growing sensitivity to the plight of the indigent accused, who are unable to raise even modest bail; this is reflected in a 1966 bail reform law that authorizes federal judges to release most defendants without requiring money bail. The net result of bail reform and increased delays in court has been that more criminal defendants spend more time out on the street awaiting their trials than ever before. This has led to an increase — or at least the appearance of an increase — in the number of crimes committed by some of these defendants between arrest and trial. And so, in an effort to stem this tide of increasing crime, many political leaders, including senators as diverse in their political views as Roman Hruska and Joseph Tydings, have focused their attention on the defendant awaiting trial. The slogan "crime in the streets" has found its first political victim.

The resulting proposals for preventive detention vary: some are limited to the District of Columbia, while others apply to all federal courts; some would seem to authorize the confinement of a very large number of defendants, while others are narrower in their scope; some include methods for shortening the time interval between arrest and trial, while others seem satisfied to leave things pretty much as they are now.

But they all have one point in common: they permit the imprisonment of a defendant who has not been convicted, and who is presumed innocent of the crime with which he stands charged, on the basis of a prediction that he may commit a crime at some future time. These predictions would be made by judges on the basis of their appraisal of the suspect's dangerousness, after study of his prior record and the crime for which he is being tried. The proponents of preventive detention hope thereby to identify and isolate those defendants awaiting trial who account for the apparently high incidence of serious crime. The opponents of preventive detention, a heterogeneous group that includes not only Senator Sam Ervin of North Carolina but the American Civil Liberties Union, maintain that under our system of criminal justice, which is characterized by "the presumption of innocence," conviction for a past crime is the only legitimate basis for confinement; they are fearful that acceptance of this "novel" approach to crime prevention might be an opening wedge leading to widespread confinement of persons suspected, on the basis of untested predictions, of dangerous propensities.

Before the claims for and against pretrial preventive detention can be fairly evaluated, this misunderstood device must be placed in its historical and contemporary setting. Predicting who will commit crimes has long fascinated mankind. In the eighteenth century Cesare Lombroso, an Italian criminologist, thought that he could detect the criminal type by observing the configuration of bumps on the head: Sheldon and Eleanor Glueck, my colleagues at Harvard and pioneers in the prediction of juvenile delinquency, maintain that they can spot potential criminals at an early age by observing aspects of their family life; and some biologists now assert, on the basis of rather flimsy evidence, that they can identify potential criminals by examining the chromosomal structure of their cells.

One can sympathize with these efforts to predict and prevent crimes before they occur rather than to wait until the victim lies dead. Indeed, Lewis Carroll put in the Queen's mouth an argument for preventive detention that Alice found difficult to refute. The Queen says:

> "There's the King's Messenger. He's in prison now, being punished: and the trial doesn't even begin till next Wednesday; and of course the crime comes last of all."
> "Suppose he never commits the crime?" asked Alice.
> "That would be all the better, wouldn't it?" the Queen responded. . . .

> Alice felt there was no denying that. "Of course it would be all the better," she said: "But it wouldn't be all the better his being punished."
>
> "You're wrong . . . ," said the Queen. "Were you ever punished?"
>
> "Only for faults," said Alice.
>
> "And you were all the better for it, I know!" the Queen said triumphantly.
>
> "Yes, but then I had done the things I was punished for," said Alice: "That makes all the difference."
>
> "But if you hadn't done them," the Queen said, "that would have been better still: better, and better, and better!" Her voice went higher with each "better," till it got quite to a squeak. . . .
>
> Alice thought. "There's a mistake somewhere —"

And there is a mistake somewhere, but it is not where the opponents of preventive detention have sought to locate it.

The debate over pretrial preventive detention has proceeded on the assumption that confining people on the basis of predictions of future crime is unprecedented in this country (and throughout the civilized world). Opponents of the proposal are fond of quoting Justice Robert Jackson's dictum in a case where the government sought to deny bail to a number of Smith Act defendants:

> If I assume that defendants are disposed to commit every opportune disloyal act helpful to Communist countries, it is still difficult to reconcile with traditional American law the jailing of persons by the courts because of anticipated but as yet un-committed crimes. Imprisonment to protect society from predicted but unconsummated offenses is so unprecedented in this country and so fraught with danger of excess and injustice that I am loath to resort to it.[2]

But Justice Jackson's history is simply incorrect: "Imprisonment to protect society from predicted but unconsummated offenses" is quite common in this and every other civilized country. A justice of the Supreme Court of Burma came closer to the truth when he observed that "preventive justice which consists in restraining a man from committing a crime which he may commit but has not yet committed . . . is common to all systems of jurisprudence."[3]

No system of jurisprudence has ever required that its law enforcers always sit back and wait until the spear has been thrown, or even until the gun has been loaded. Societies have differed in their techniques of crime prevention, but for centuries people throughout the world have been imprisoned "to protect society from predicted but unconsummated offenses." That preventive justice was part of the English common-law tradition was a source of great pride to Blackstone: "And really it is an honor," he said, "and almost a singular one, to our English laws, that they furnish a title of this sort, since preventive justice is upon every principle of reason, of humanity, and of sound policy, preferable in all respects to punishing justice, the execution of which . . . is always attended with many harsh and disagreeable circumstances."[4]

The "preventive justice" to which Blackstone was specifically referring consisted of confining persons about whom there was "a probable suspicion that some crime is intended or likely to happen," unless they could find "pledges or securities for keeping peace, or for their good behavior." This "humanitarian" device led to the confinement of large numbers of "vagabonds" and "strangers."

During both world wars, Great Britain promulgated regulations explicitly authorizing the preventive detention of certain persons suspected of "hostile origin or association." During the Second World War the United States employed one of the grossest forms of preventive detention known to history: the mass transfer and internment of Americans of Japanese descent, allegedly on the basis of a prediction that otherwise some of them would sabotage our war effort on the West Coast and become victims of racial violence. The Supreme Court's approval of that device[5] laid the foundation for a statute, now on the books, that authorizes the detention, during a declared internal security emergency, of any person who "there is reasonable ground to believe . . . probably will engage in or probably will conspire with others to engage in acts of espionage or of sabotage."[6]

Nor is preventive detention limited to Blackstone's England or to wartime. Indeed, every American jurisdiction permits pretrial detention of at least one category of criminal suspects: those charged with capital offenses. And it should be recalled that at the time of the Eighth Amendment — which has been constructed to prohibit excessive bail in noncapital cases — many, if not most, felonies were capital; accordingly, many, if not most, accused felons were detained pending completion of their trials.

The most widespread form of preventive detention employed in the United States today is commitment of the mentally ill. More than half a million mentally ill people who have not been convicted of crime are imprisoned in state hospitals without adequate treatment and often with little hope of eventual release, on the basis of psychiatric predictions that unless confined they would do violence to themselves or to others.

Peace bonds — the Blackstonian technique of "preventive justice" — are still authorized in many parts of the United States. In a Pennsylvania case, a defendant was charged with assault and battery. He stood trial and was acquitted by a jury. Despite this, the judge required him to post a bond of one thousand dollars "to keep the peace for two years." In its opinion vacating the bond as inconsistent with the right to trial by jury, the state supreme court cited data indicating that during ten previous years "478 men, after acquittal of criminal charges, were compelled to serve an aggregate of over 600 years in . . . prison in default of bonds aggregating $613,200."[7]

"Juvenile statutes authorize confinement of young persons who have not yet committed criminal acts, but who are thought likely to become criminals. Indeed, in his separate opinion in the *Gault* case, Mr. Justice Harlan cited figures indicating that between 26 and 48 percent of the 600,000 children brought before juvenile courts 'are not in any sense guilty of criminal misconduct.'"[8] Some sex psychopath laws also authorize detention of persons who have never been convicted of crimes but are thought likely to engage in sexual misconduct. Many states permit the incarceration of so-called material witnesses — that is, persons not themselves charged with crime who may be important witnesses at another's trial, and who are thought likely to flee the jurisdiction unless confined. An alleged witness to the assassination of Dr. Martin Luther King was imprisoned under such a statute.

Another widespread American practice is the so-called preventive arrest, recently described in a report to the commissioners of the District of Columbia as follows:

A person trying front doors of stores, or peering into parked cars, in the early hours of the morning; a person "known" to the police as a pickpocket loitering at a crowded bus stop; a "known" Murphy game operator talking to a soldier or a sailor — such persons may be arrested . . . largely in order to eliminate at least temporarily the occasion for any possible criminal activity. The principle upon which such arrests are made appears to be: if the individual is detained until 10 or 11 A.M. the following day, at least he will have committed no crime that night."[9]

The courts are beginning to place limits on police discretion in some such situations. For example, the arrest of a person found wandering around toilets on the ground that there is cause to suspect that he is about to perform an act of homosexuality might not be sustained as a justifiable exercise of police discretion. But many legislatures have made it unnecessary for the police to justify such arrests by reference to as-yet uncommitted crimes. They make the "suspicious" act itself a crime justifying arrest. Thus a number of states now make it a crime "to loiter in or about public toilets" or "to wander about the streets at late or unusual hours without any visible or lawful business."[10]

A recent judicial decision has recognized that the "basic design" of vagrancy statutes is one of "preventive conviction imposed upon those who, because of their background and behavior, are more likely than the general public to commit crimes, and that the statute contemplates such convictions even though no overt criminal act has been committed or can be proved." The real issue in the enforcement of vagrancy statutes was viewed as "whether our system tolerates the concept of preventive conviction on suspicion." The United States Court of Appeals for the District of Columbia recently struck down such statutes as unconstitutional, observing that "statistical likelihood" of a particular person's or group's engaging in criminality "is not permissible as an all out substitute for proof of individual guilt."

But "statistical likelihood" — gross and impersonal as that sounds — is all we ever have, whether we are predicting the future or reconstructing the past. When we establish rules for convicting the guilty, we do not require certainty; we only require that guilt be proved "beyond a reasonable doubt." And that means that we are willing to tolerate the conviction of some innocent suspects in order to assure the confinement of a vastly larger number of guilty criminals. We insist that the statistical likelihood of guilt be very high: "Better ten guilty men go free than one innocent man be wrongly condemned." But we do not — nor could we — insist on certainty; to do so would result in immobility.

What difference is there between imprisoning a man for a past crime on the basis of "statistical likelihood" and detaining him to prevent future crimes on the same kind of less-than-certain information? The important difference may not be one of principle; it may be, as Justice Oliver Wendell Holmes said, that all legal issues are one of degree. The available evidence suggests that our system of determining past guilt results in the erroneous conviction of relatively few innocent people.[11] We really do seem to practice what we preach about preferring the acquittal of guilty men over the conviction of innocent men.

But the indications are that any system of predicting future crimes would result in a vastly larger number of erroneous confinements — that is, confinements of persons predicted to engage in violent crimes who would not, in fact, do so. Indeed, all the experience with predicting violent conduct suggests that in order to spot a significant proportion of future violent criminals, we would have to reverse the traditional maxim of the criminal law and adopt a philosophy that it is better to confine ten people who would not commit predicted crimes than to release one who would.

It should not be surprising to learn that predictions of the kind relied upon by the proponents of preventive detention are likely to be unreliable. Predictions of human conduct are difficult to make, for man is a complex entity and the world he inhabits is full of unexpected occurrences. Predictions of rare human events are even more difficult. And predictions of rare events occurring within a short span of time are the most difficult of all. Acts of violence by persons released while awaiting trial are relatively rare events (though more frequent among certain categories of suspects), and the relevant time span is short. Accordingly, the kind of predictions under consideration begin with heavy odds against their accuracy. A predictor is likely to be able to spot a large number of persons who would actually commit acts of violence only if he is also willing to imprison a very much larger number of defendants who would not, in fact, engage in violence if released.

This brings me to an obvious fact that is often overlooked in evaluating the accuracy of predictions. In order that the evaluation be fair, there must be information about both sides; we must know not only how many crimes that would have been committed by defendants out on bail were prevented but also how many defendants were erroneously imprisoned. Either of these alone tells you very little. It is no trick at all to spot a very high percentage of defendants who would commit acts of violence while awaiting trial: you simply predict that all or almost all will do so. (Of course, the number of erroneous confinements would be extraordinarily high, but most or all the crimes would have been prevented.) Conversely, it is easy to avoid erroneous confinement if that is your only aim: simply predict that few or none of the defendants will engage in violence pending trial. (In that case, you would prevent very few, if any, of the potential crimes, but the number of erroneous confinements would be minimal or nonexistent.)

The difficult task is to select a category that includes the largest number of defendants who would commit violent crimes and the smallest possible number who would not. If it were possible to select a category that included all those, and only those, who would commit such crimes, there would be little problem. But since this is impossible, a choice must be made. It must be decided how many defendants we should be willing to confine erroneously in order to prevent how many acts of violence. This will in turn depend on the nature of the violence to be prevented and the duration of the contemplated confinement: we should be willing to tolerate fewer erroneous confinements to prevent predicted purse snatching than predicted murder, and fewer again if the trial is a year off than if it can be completed within two weeks of the arrest.

Another reason predictions of the future are less reliable than reconstructions of the past concerns the process by which human beings make decisions. Participants in judicial decision making — lawyers, judges, even jurors — have some sense of what it means to decide whether a specifically charged act probably was or probably was not committed. The participants bring to their decisions some basis for sorting out the relevant from the irrelevant, the believable from the incredible, the significant from the trivial. And this basis — though often rough and intuitive — is far more than the judge is likely to bring to the process of predicting the future.

It is true that all judgments about human events, whether past or future, rest upon a superstructure of assumptions about how people behave; all decision making requires a theory. What I am suggesting is that participants in the judicial process are better equipped by their experience to construct and employ theories about what probably occurred in the past than theories about what is likely to occur in the future. Put another way, we are all historians, but few of us are scientists. Perhaps Lewis Carroll's Queen had a "memory" that worked equally well both ways: she remembered "things that happened the week after next" even better than things that happened yesterday. But Alice spoke for most of us when she said that her memory "only works one way. . . . I can't remember things before they happen."

The most serious danger inherent in any system of preventive detention is that it always seems to be working well, even when it is performing dismally; this is so because it is the nature of any system of preventive detention to display its meager successes in preventing crime while it hides its frequent errors. This has been demonstrated in other areas where detention rests on predictions of dangerousness. One such area — which I have studied in detail and about which I have written elsewhere[12] — is the confinement of the mentally ill on the basis of psychiatric predictions of injurious conduct. It has long been assumed that these psychiatric predictions are reasonably accurate, that patients who are diagnosed as dangerous would have engaged in seriously harmful conduct had they not been confined. The accuracy of these predictions has never been systematically tested, since patients predicted to be dangerous are confined and thus do not have the opportunity to demonstrate that they would not have committed the predicted act if they had been at liberty.

Accordingly, the psychiatrist almost never learns about his erroneous predictions of violence. But he almost always learns about his erroneous predictions of nonviolence — often from newspaper headlines announcing the crime. The fact that the errors of underestimating the possibilities of violence are more visible than errors of overestimating inclines the psychiatrist — whether consciously or unconsciously — to err on the side of confining rather than of releasing. His modus operandi becomes: When in doubt, don't let him out.

Recently the accuracy of psychiatric predictions has been called into considerable question. A decision of the United States Supreme Court in 1966, *Baxtrom v. Herald*,[13] resulted in freeing many mentally ill persons predicted to be dangerous. Grave fear was expressed for the safety of the community. But follow-up studies now indicate that the predictions of violence were grossly exaggerated and that very few of the patients have done what the psychiatrists predicted they would do if released. Similar studies in Baltimore support this conclusion of extreme overprediction.[14]

The same phenomenon is likely to plague efforts to predict violence pending trial if a preventive-detention statute is now enacted. Judges, like psychiatrists, will rarely learn about their erroneous predictions of violence, for these defendants, being confined, will not have an opportunity to demonstrate that they would *not* have committed the predicted crime. But every time a judge makes an erroneous prediction of *non*violence — every time he decides to release someone who then does commit a violent act — he learns about his "mistake" swiftly and dramatically.

Thus, if a statute is enacted authorizing pretrial preventive detention on the basis of judicial predictions of violence, we will never know how many defendants are being erroneously confined. And as more and more information is accumulated, most of it concerning defendants who were erroneously released, judges will keep expanding the category of defendants to be detained. There is evidence that this is already being done by some judges today. During its recent hearings, the Senate Subcommittee on Constitutional Rights considered a study of the decisions of two trial judges in the District of Columbia on pretrial release and detention: One judge routinely, if unlawfully, detained all suspects whom he regarded as "bad risks"; the other judge routinely released most suspects. Over the period of the study, the "tough" judge detained about half the defendants who came before him (144 out of 285), while the "lenient" judge detained only about one-fifth (46 out of 226). Of those released by the tough judge, twelve were charged with offenses — either felonies or misdemeanors — while awaiting trial; of those released by the lenient judge, sixteen were accused of such offenses.

In other words, in order to prevent about four more crimes (some of them misdemeanors), the tough judge had to confine almost a hundred more defendants. Moreover, of the 144 persons detained by the tough judge, 36 subsequently had their cases dismissed and another "large percentage of them" were acquitted. Most of the defendants in this latter group were therefore the victims of a compounded legal error: not only would they probably not have committed the predicted crimes but they were not even guilty — or so the process determined — of the past crime with which they stood charged.

Now, it may be that eventually criteria for confinement can be refined to the point where such errors are minimized. Perhaps the high rate of violent crime by certain categories of released defendants will produce a high degree of crime prevention without too many erroneous confinements. It is claimed, for example, that a very high percentage of defendants charged with armed robbery in the District of Columbia — some place the figure as high as 34 percent, others as low as 11 percent — commit new felonies while awaiting trial. But if a statute were to be enacted now authorizing the confinement of all persons awaiting trial who, on the basis of specified criteria, were predicted to commit violent crimes, then the development of such refined criteria would be seriously retarded.

It must never be forgotten that many years of experience administering an untested system will not always increase the accuracy of that system. Many years of experience are often only one year of experience repeated many times. The unknown mistake of the past becomes the foundation for a confident, but erroneous, prediction of the future. This was demonstrated many years ago, in a famous "experiment" in which a student threw darts repeatedly at a board to test the thesis that aim improves with experience — but the experimenter blindfolded the student and never told him when he hit or missed the target. Needless to say, his aim did not improve with "experience." Nor would the accuracy of judicial predictions necessarily improve simply as a result of judges spending more and more years meting out preventive detention without any accurate way to test their predictions.

The time is not yet ripe for resolving definitively by legislation the dilemma of pretrial preventive detention. We have just begun to understand what the problem is, but we do not yet have enough information to know what the optimal solutions are. We have not even tried other, less drastic, amelioratives, such as speedier trials, more supervision for released defendants, and perhaps even increased penalties for crimes committed while out on bail. If such solutions were tried, the problem of crimes committed by released defendants might become a very small one indeed. What must be avoided is a simple solution that freezes knowledge at its existing low state. And this is precisely what would occur if Congress now enacted a statute authorizing confinement of all defendants predicted to commit acts of violence while awaiting trial. What must be encouraged is an approach that is tentative, that continues to gather information, and that is in the nature of an experiment.

What I suggest is that any proposed criteria for confinement be tested to determine how accurate — or inaccurate — they are in predicting violence. This could be done in a number of ways. Judges might be asked to apply the criteria being tested — for example, those in the statute proposed by Senator Joseph Tydings[15] — and to predict on the basis of those criteria which defendants awaiting trial would engage in violent crimes. All of the defendants would then be released, even those who the judges think should be detained. Careful studies should then be conducted to determine how accurate the judges were in their predictions. There is, however, a serious problem with this kind of test. If the judges know that everyone will be released and their actions observed, they might be extremely cautious about predicting violence, more cautious than if they knew that the predicted criminals would be safely confined.

This suggests a variation that would increase the accuracy of the test — but at a substantial cost in human liberty. The judges would again decide who should be detained on the basis of the criteria being tested, but this time only some — say half — of those selected for detention would be randomly released and observed. This suggestion is not free of difficulties either, for the status of experimentation under the law is far from clear. But I am confident that a workable and constitutional approach can be devised.[16] Then we can see how many of these defendants would, in fact, fulfill the predictions.

What we learn about our ability to predict may be discouraging to those who advocate preventive detention. But it is far better to know the discouraging truth than to build a house — especially one with bars — on untested assumptions.

# THIRTY

# GETTING STUNG

---

*Another genre of crime prevention is the police "sting." The line between lawful sting and unlawful entrapment is the subject of this chapter.*

---

THE 1960S ARRIVED LATE IN SAINT ALBANS, VERMONT. IT had been an old railroad town until the early 1960s, when the Central Vermont Railway shut down the last of its repair yards. Though Union Carbide still assembles flashlights there, "it's been going downhill since they've closed the yards," remarked an aide in the mayor's office. Situated near the east shore of Lake Champlain and twenty-five miles north of the University of Vermont, the town of seventy-three hundred began to develop an unlikely business to replace railroading. It became a center of the drug trade for the surrounding area. It began slowly, with a few rural communes in the countryside of Franklin County, to which New York radicals brought their counterculture. Saint Albans's proximity to the Canadian border — coupled with its tiny and largely nonfunctioning police force — made that hundred-acre town an ideal place to conduct the small drug trade supporting the few local communes. But soon the word traveled south to New York, east to Boston, and even west to California: Saint Albans was a haven for druggies.

The drugs were mainly those of the white counterculture: marijuana, hashish, LSD, and speed. The young people who used them sported long hair and bedraggled clothing. They began to arrive by the busload, often with no place to stay and no work to do. Taylor Park and Main Street became their homes and their trading centers. The welfare office became a meeting place, as hundreds of transplanted city folk signed up to collect the limited resources of the rural dole. The entire face of the town was changing, and there was little the locals could do.

It was like the town of Hamlin in the fairy tale, except that instead of rats, Saint Albans had druggies. But the townsfolk were as concerned about the plague being spread by their unwanted guests as the townsfolk of Hamlin had been.

A pied piper was needed to rid Saint Albans of its druggies, and just as things reached the point of desperation in 1973, he arrived. His name was Paul Lawrence. He was in his late twenties and looked like many of the kids who had recently come to town. But he was a narc — an undercover policeman whose specialty was setting up drug deals and then arresting the dealers. Some people regard that as entrapment, but the town fathers of Saint Albans were not in a mood to worry about legal or ethical niceties. They wanted action.

As Mayor Melvin Kaye later recalled in a newspaper interview: "The laws seemed to be much more in favor of those accused, and the law enforcement officers had both hands tied behind their backs. The city council was alarmed. The taxpayers were demanding action."

And action they got. In a secret meeting, the city council voted to hire Paul Lawrence as an undercover narcotics agent. For eight thousand dollars he agreed to set up an ongoing drug scam. Within months, he promised, he would make Saint Albans as free of druggies as the Pied Piper had made Hamlin free of rats.

Lawrence set to work immediately. He blended into the drug subculture and began to ask where he could make a score. He spread the word that he was willing to pay top dollar for drugs — far more than the prevailing price in town. There were some nibbles and a few bites. Before long he made his move. Twenty-seven hippies were swept up in a series of drug raids and charged with the sale of heroin, cocaine, and LSD. It was more than the city council had anticipated. No one had even suspected that there was a heroin trade in town. But Lawrence produced the proof: the powder he had bought from the dealers and kept in his apartment was sent to the New York State Police laboratory in Albany, and the results came back high-grade heroin.

The defendants claimed they had been framed. All denied selling drugs to Lawrence, and some denied even meeting him. But the cry of "frame-up" is the typical response of the arrested drug dealer, and convictions were quickly secured on the basis of Lawrence's testimony and the evidence of the drugs he produced.

The half-life of a narc in a given community is extremely short: generally when an undercover agent surfaces to testify, his effectiveness is over. The word quickly spreads around town and nobody in the drug culture will have anything to do with him. But Lawrence managed to continue his scam for several more months, moving around to different groups, changing his cover, raising the price he was willing to pay. Eventually Lawrence's drug scams produced six hundred arrests and forty convictions. His job completed, Lawrence moved to a different town in another Vermont county to ply his trade. The town of Saint Albans was rid of its drug problem, its hippie problem, and its welfare problem.

But like the town of Hamlin, its real problem was just beginning: claims persisted that Lawrence had framed his arrestees — that he had made up cases, especially heroin cases. One woman swore she had been framed because she refused to sleep with him. The two defense attorneys in Saint Albans who had handled most of the drug cases became convinced that something was wrong: never had they heard so many claims of frame-up; never had there been so many arrests on heroin charges; never had a single narc, working alone, secured so many convictions. The lawyers arranged for several of their clients to take lie-detector tests. Asked whether they had ever sold drugs to Lawrence, they said no. The polygraph expert said they were telling the truth. The lawyers then brought a formal complaint before the state attorney general's office and requested a full investigation. The town of Saint Albans, they claimed, had substituted one form of railroading for another.

In the meantime, Lawrence was beginning to make cases at his new job. One of the policemen with whom he was assigned to work became suspicious. Patrick Leahy — then county prosecutor and now United States Senator from Vermont — also smelled a rat. Leahy decided that something had to be done to find out once and for all whether Lawrence was an honest cop who was getting a bad rap from angry drug dealers or a lying cop who was making up cases against innocent hippies. But how could they test him without his realizing he was being tested? Suddenly Leahy had an idea. It was as obvious as it was poetic: Leahy would set up his own scam, not unlike the ones used by

Lawrence. The bait would be dangled. If Lawrence didn't bite, he would prove his innocence. If he did bite, he would trap himself.

A new undercover agent was needed for this scam, one whose face wasn't known to Lawrence. They went all the way to Brooklyn, New York, and came up with Michael Schwartz — alias "the Rabbi." Schwartz, like Lawrence, was an undercover narc. He worked out of the Brooklyn district attorney's office. But in Vermont he was introduced around as a major-league drug dealer. His mug shot and ersatz record were smuggled into the police files of the city where Lawrence was working and Lawrence was assigned to try to make a case against the Rabbi.

The Rabbi, in the meantime, was wired for sound by prosecutor Leahy's office and placed under constant surveillance. He set up office on a park bench near city hall and waited.

Lawrence spotted him on the bench. He drove by several times in his car to be certain it was really the Rabbi. Having concluded it was, Lawrence went directly to the police station, where he filled out an arrest warrant and affidavit swearing that he had just made a heroin buy from the Rabbi. Lawrence had not even stopped to speak to Schwartz, as the tape and surveillance would prove, yet was claiming he had bought heroin from him.

The jig was up. Lawrence was arrested and convicted on charges growing out of the false buy. He was sentenced to a term of three to eight years in prison.

After an extended investigation, seventy-one of those people who had been convicted of drug crimes on the basis of Lawrence's testimony were granted full pardons by Vermont governor Thomas P. Salmon. It turned out, not unexpectedly, that some of Lawrence's cases had been good: they were supported by police evidence independent of Lawrence's testimony and drugs. Cries of entrapment by these defendants fell on deaf ears. But everyone whose conviction rested on Lawrence's uncorroborated word was freed.

Lawrence lost his job and went to prison. The phony entrapper had been caught in a real trap much like the ones he had used and pretended to use. It was poetic — but was it justice?

## THE QUESTION OF ENTRAPMENT

The remarkable case of Paul Lawrence raises troubling questions about the whole range of law-enforcement techniques that rely on "the scam" (also referred to as "the sting") — the government-agent-disguised-as-criminal sent out as bait to lure once and future criminals into committing crimes in the presence of the agent (or a recording device).

It was a scam that made it possible for the bad guy, Paul Lawrence, to do his dirty work. But it was also a scam that made it possible for the good guy, prosecutor Leahy, to trap and expose the bad guy. The Lawrence case presents, in a nutshell, most of the arguments for and against the scam as a technique of law enforcement. It demonstrates why prosecutors and police insist that it is an invaluable tool for catching criminals who would otherwise escape detection and continue to prey on the public. How else, they ask, could the secret crimes of a crooked cop, or a crooked politician, be detected? The Lawrence case also shows why many concerned citizens regard the law-enforcement scam as unlawful entrapment and want it stopped. They argue that the abuses uncovered in the Lawrence case, and in others like it, are inevitable once law enforcement authorities are permitted to act like crooks in an effort to lure suspects into committing catchable crimes.

The issue is as important as any being debated in the area of law enforcement, since the scam is quickly becoming a major prosecutional technique on both the national and local level. The FBI alone operates numerous scams. And nearly every major city — and many not-so-major ones — conducts them as well.

ABSCAM was, of course, the most famous and highly publicized federal scam. The Justice Department secretly videotaped congressmen and senators as they met with someone pretending to represent a wealthy Arab sheik seeking to buy asylum in the United States. Bribes were offered. Some of the public officials turned them down (including my former student, Senator Larry Pressler of South Dakota), but others willingly accepted them. The latter were indicted, convicted, and sentenced to prison.

The most controversial of the ABSCAM cases involved Senator Harrison Williams, a Democrat from New Jersey. Williams, who was not a target of the original scam, learned of the existence of the sheik and his money. The senator's personal lawyer initiated contact with the sheik's American representative — a con man named Melvin Weinberg who was working undercover for the government — and inquired about the possibility of a joint business venture. Several surreptitiously videotaped meetings were arranged among Williams, the sheik, Weinberg, and others.

I have seen some of the tapes, and they are quite remarkable. They show a somewhat aloof senator bragging about his considerable power and influence in Washington (and if that were a crime, our prisons would be full of public officials and private executives!). Williams seemed prepared to barter this power and influence for a $100 million loan from the sheik to finance a potentially profitable titanium mine in which the senator had a hidden interest. But the government agents were not satisfied with this; they wanted Williams to agree specifically that in exchange for financing by the sheik, he would use his office to obtain government contracts for the venture. Williams was plainly reluctant to commit himself. He would "try" — that was the most he originally would say. But the agents told him that trying would not be enough. In order to obtain the financing, he would have to promise to get the contracts. Government prosecutors had instructed the agents to get him to speak the words that would constitute a crime.

At one point, Weinberg coaches Williams about exactly what he should say to the sheik: "You gotta tell him how important you are, who you are, what you can do, and you tell him in no uncertain terms." Then he read Williams his lines: "Without me there is no deal. I'm the man. I'm the man who's gonna open the doors. I'm the man who's gonna do this and use my influence, and I guarantee this." He urged Williams to "mention names." Having given the senator a script that would seal his conviction, he assured him that it was "all bullshit."

After considerable hemming and hawing, Williams finally spoke the words the government wanted to hear. When asked whether he would be able to secure government contracts if the sheik agreed to finance the mining venture, Williams said, "No problem. . . . It will come to pass." And he mentioned a name: "I'll talk to the president of the United States about it, and, you know, in a personal way, and get him as enthusiastic and excited, because we know what our country needs."

Another videotaped interview illustrates the danger of the scripted scam. At one point, Williams — like the other congressmen and senator — was offered money in return for assisting the sheik with his immigration problems. Williams categorically rejected the offer, then began to explain why he was turning the money down. Before Williams could complete his explanation, another undercover agent burst into the room and told the sheik that there was an important phone call for him. The sheik excused himself and the conversation ended.

Williams contends that the government agents, monitoring the conversation from the adjoining room, deliberately cut off his explanation because they feared that he would say something on videotape that would help him when he was brought to trial in the titanium case — something that would support his defense that he intended to remain on the lawful side of the fuzzy line between criminal bribery and routine influence peddling. The government asserts that the interruption was part of the original script and did not prejudice the case for Williams. The judge and jury believed the government, and Williams was convicted of bribery and sentenced to three years in prison. His conviction was affirmed on appeal.

Other, less-publicized scams have been even more imaginative than ABSCAM. A few examples:

- In an operation called MIPORN — for Miami pornography — federal agents went into the porn business for several years and bought hundreds of films and other allegedly obscene material from suppliers. Eventually the FBI arrested fifty-five people in Miami, New York, Los Angeles, Cleveland, and half a dozen other cities.
- The New York City police went even further. Not only did they run a porn bookstore in Times Square for eight months, they actually commissioned and financed the production of an obscene movie. A policewoman helped to direct the on-camera sex acts of the participants to make sure they were sufficiently explicit to meet the legal definition of obscenity. (When the film's existence was leaked to the press, the police first denied it and then dropped the scam, as well as another one involving the operation — by the police department — of a house of prostitution.)

- The Los Angeles Police Department placed the following ad in a local paper: "Sexy hostesses needed for gambling junket. Entails foreign travel . . ." A phone number was given, and those calling were invited to a party and told: "It's to your advantage to be liked by the men." The men at the party were undercover police, and fifty-four women were arrested for trying too hard to be liked by the men.

- In Washington, D.C., the FBI set up a mammoth fencing operation in an abandoned warehouse. They spread the word that they were connected with a New Jersey organized-crime family and were willing to pay more than the going price for stolen items. They bought several million dollars' worth of hot goods from burglars and robbers and arrested more than a hundred people. In a related operation, the police sold the stolen goods, making it clear to the buyers that the cheap items were stolen. Among those arrested for buying stolen goods was an assistant United States attorney.

- The New York police sent an undercover policewoman as a patient to a dentist who was suspected of fondling the breasts of several of his anesthetized female patients. They recorded the dentist's actions on a hidden camera while he put the patient under. As soon as she was unconscious he began to fondle her, and was immediately arrested.

- The Los Angeles police sent out two policewomen to pose as streetwalkers. They arrested ninety-one "johns."

- In many cities the police regularly employ what has now come to be known as the "Nighthawk technique" (after the movie starring Sylvester Stallone). They send out policemen dressed up as women, old people, Hasidim, drunks — as members of any uniquely vulnerable group. The targets are invariably attacked, and the "victims" arrest them.

These examples of scams show why there is no simple answer to the question of whether scams should be permitted. There are good scams and bad scams. Many would approve — and quite reasonably — of the New York police departmental decision to send a policewoman into the dentist's office: there had been prior complaints; the victims were only partially conscious when the alleged assaults occurred and could not testify against their assailants; there was nothing particularly provocative about sending in a typical-looking patient and observing whether the doctor would do to her what others had claimed he had done to them. The dentist scam was, in many ways, like the scam that exposed Paul Lawrence as a corrupt and lying cop.

But many citizens would also disapprove of the police making a porn film, operating a brothel, or placing ads for sexy hostesses.

One important difference between the good scams and the bad scams is, of course, that hardly anyone would dispute the importance of prosecuting dentists or policemen who abuse their trust, while many dispute the importance — indeed the correctness — of arresting porn dealers, prostitutes, or johns.

Another difference is that in the dentist and Lawrence cases, the doctor and the policeman were suspected of prior misconduct; the scam gave them an opportunity to disprove or confirm reasonable suspicions. In the sex cases, on the other hand, the police actually stimulated the crimes by placing the ad, by paying for the film, and by sending out the prostitutes.

## THE ENTRAPMENT DEBATE

There are at least two different debates over the types of scams that are currently taking place. The first is in the courts: which kinds of scams, if any, constitute *unlawful* entrapment? The second, and potentially far more important, is the debate that is taking place among the public as a result of such highly publicized undercover operations as ABSCAM: regardless of what the courts may say, is it good public policy to allow prosecutors and police to stimulate crime in order to catch criminals?

The debate in the courts, though it sometimes employs confusing legal jargon, is rather simpleminded and ultimately not very enlightening. But since so much attention is paid to it, a brief summary is in order.

What is "entrapment" as a question of law? *Entrapment* is not a word mentioned in the Constitution or even in the statutes of most states or the federal government. It is not one of the colonial abuses over which we fought the revolution. As Anglo-American history goes, the entrapment defense is a fairly recent development. The Supreme

Court gave birth to it in 1932 and then said little about it again until the leading case of *Sherman v. United States* in 1958, where Chief Justice Earl Warren declared that the "function of law enforcement is the prevention of crime and the apprehension of criminals. Manifestly, that function does not include the manufacturing of crime." In that case, a government agent named Kalchinian met the defendant, Sherman, at a doctor's office where they were both seeking treatment for their narcotics addiction. Kalchinian asked Sherman if he knew of a good source of narcotics. Sherman tried to avoid the issue at first, but after several additional requests, he agreed to get Kalchinian some drugs. Kalchinian then informed the Federal Bureau of Narcotics that he had another seller for them. After observing Sherman selling narcotics on three occasions to Kalchinian, for money supplied by the government, the feds arrested Sherman and charged him with selling drugs; he was convicted and sentenced to ten years of imprisonment.

A unanimous Supreme Court reversed the conviction on the ground that the evidence established that Sherman had been unlawfully entrapped by the government agent.

"The case at bar illustrates an evil which the defense of entrapment is designed to overcome. The government informer entices someone attempting to avoid narcotics not only into carrying out an illegal sale but also into returning to the habit of use. . . . Thus, the Government plays on the weaknesses of an innocent party and beguiles him into committing crimes which he otherwise would not have attempted. Law enforcement does not require methods such as this."

There are two essential issues presented to the jury in cases in which the defendant raises a defense of entrapment: The first is whether a government agent *induced* the defendant into committing the crime. If the agent did induce the defendant, then the defendant cannot be convicted, unless — and this is a big unless — the government can prove that the defendant was "ready and willing" to commit the crime anyway and was simply waiting for the opportunity to present itself. If the government can prove the defendant was thus "predisposed" to committing that type of crime — which is the second issue — then it can convict him even if its agents "induced" him into committing it on that specific occasion.

Because of this "predisposition" exception, very few defendants prevail before a jury on an entrapment defense: it is known among criminal lawyers as a defense of last resort, to be used only when there is no other chance of acquittal. (Several of the ABSCAM defendants, for example, declined to raise the entrapment defense before the juries that tried them.) Because it is such a weak defense, many prosecutors are entirely willing to use inducement or scams as a law-enforcement technique, despite the Supreme Court's unequivocal condemnation of techniques that manufacture crime. Prosecutors are especially willing to use scams against unsavory characters — such as organized-crime leaders — since they are confident that any jury would find that such gangsters were "predisposed" to committing virtually any crime.

For example, in Robert Daley's factual book *Prince of the City*, on which the motion picture was based, a federal prosecutor named Edward Shaw proposed the following scam involving police officer Robert Leuci: "[We] call in the leaders of each of the city's five Mafia families. We tell them," Shaw said, "that they may be prosecuted for tax evasion. Then Bob [Leuci], here, reaches out to them through his organized-crime connections. He lets it be known that he has access to the IRS files. Then he meets with them, and they bribe him to get the files. Then we arrest them for bribery of a police officer."

Leuci — who had engaged in dozens of crimes against drug dealers — refused to participate in that kind of operation: "It's a total frame," he protested. "Tell a man he's being audited by the IRS, and he panics." He made the point that this kind of crime creation would make a criminal out of an accountant in Scarsdale, or Leuci's next-door neighbor, or Shaw's, for that matter.

Some judges and most scholars would eliminate the predisposition exception and establish objective criteria for entrapment uniformly applicable to all citizens. But the current majority view of the Supreme Court is that a predisposed defendant cannot invoke the entrapment defense. Several "swing" justices have left the door open to the possibility that police "over involvement in crime [might reach such] a demonstrable level of outrageousness" that even a predisposed defendant might be able to cry foul.

But the message to law-enforcement authorities is clear: at least until the courts begin to throw out some convictions on grounds of "outrageousness" — which they are not doing — the green light is on. Indeed, it seems that any speed will be tolerated in the highly competitive fast lane of scam operations by law-enforcement agencies.

It is unlikely that the courts will impose significant limits on the use of scams in the foreseeable future. Limits, if they are to be imposed, will have to come from legislation, from public and media pressure, from within the prosecutorial and police establishments.

An informed public, aware of the abuses inherent in most scam operations, is the most likely source of reform in the law of entrapment. But the public, for the most part, hears only two sides of the debate over scams: first, the law-enforcement side, presented in the form of press releases disclosing dramatic tales of successful intrigues resulting in the arrest of corrupt congressmen, pornographers, and other villains; and second, the defendant's side, presented in the form of shrill outcries by those who have been caught with their fingers in the cookie jar or their pants down around their knees. There is an important third side: the public perspective reflecting the voices of concerned citizens eager to catch corrupt criminals who prey on others but also concerned that unchecked and uncontrolled scams may create as much danger as the criminals.

The dangers of scams are multifold. First, there are the unanticipated consequences of unchecked scams.

Sir Walter Scott once wrote: "Oh, what a tangled web we weave, when first we practice to deceive!" The very object of these scams is, of course, to deceive. And the tangled — and sometimes deadly — webs woven by scams are legion. A few striking examples:

- Two teenagers learn that a local fence — in reality a police sting operation — is paying top dollar for stolen cars. In the process of stealing a car to sell to the fence, they kill the owner.
- An undercover policeman arranges a sale of drugs to some Hispanics. The "purchasers" are, in reality, a vigilante group attempting to get drugs out of their community. The vigilantes kill the policeman in the belief that he is a drug dealer.
- An undercover policeman pretending to be gay approaches an effeminate-looking man wearing mascara in a Greenwich Village bar. They go for a walk. Suggestive comments are exchanged. Suddenly the policeman pulls out his badge and announces that he is arresting the other man. The other man, an undercover cop as well, also pulls out his badge and says that he was about to arrest the first cop.

- The Chicago police assign an undercover cop to pose as a pimp. He infiltrates a ring of prostitution. Following the completion of the investigation, the undercover policeman continues on as a pimp, earning large sums of money.
- Police claiming to be organized-crime members interested in buying hot guns in Idaho stimulate a wave of burglaries and robberies of stores selling weapons.
- In several major cities, undercover police engaged in scams are shot and killed by uniformed police who mistake them for criminals. Minority undercover agents seem particularly vulnerable. Indeed, in New York alone, during a relatively brief time span, eight black policemen were shot — five fatally — by other policemen who thought they were criminals.

A second danger is that the proliferation of scam operations will deflect police concern away from predatory crime — crime involving involuntary victims — and onto consensual crime. It is no coincidence that the vast majority of successful scams have involved drugs, sex, and gambling transactions. There are generally no complainants in these kinds of "victimless" crimes. Some of the most successful and highly publicized scams — such as ABSCAM — have, of course, involved crimes where the public is the victim, even though there are no specific complainants. Other scams — such as the Nighthawk operations — are designed to prevent crimes of violence against real victims. But statistically, scams have had their greatest impact on victimless crimes, as evidenced by the fact that over the past fifteen years arrests for victimless crimes have doubled while the incidence of violent crime has skyrocketed.

Occasionally a scam operation involving victimless crime produces ironic, even humorous, results: the president of a Bible college who had just canceled a play involving nudity was arrested for soliciting a scam prostitute; several congressmen, notorious for their vendettas against sexual deviants, have been arrested for soliciting scam gays and prostitutes. Federal judge Harold Carswell, a rejected Nixon nominee to the United States Supreme Court, and General Edwin Walker, the right-wing fanatic who opposed integration in Mississippi, were each charged with making homosexual advances — the former in a men's room in a shopping mall, the latter in a city park — to undercover police officers.

But for every ironic instance where self-righteous hypocrites are exposed, there are numerous tragic situations where the victims are ordinary citizens who are hurting no one.

A recognized expert on scams, Professor Gary Marx of MIT, has concluded that scam operations "can be conducive to framing people and false testimony." The activities of Paul Lawrence illustrate this danger. But there is also the danger of the shakedown — of demand by corrupt policemen for payment for not arresting criminals caught in the scam. Police extortion is particularly prevalent in the drug and sex areas, where only the arresting officers know that the crime has been committed, and where the criminals generally have large amounts of cash in their possession. Bob Leuci, the subject of *Prince of the City*, has indicated how widespread the shakedown of drug dealers became among narcs conducting scam operations in New York. And shakedowns directed against prostitutes, pimps, and middle-class homosexuals caught in scam operations are also prevalent in some cities. (Extortions of the latter group are referred to as "fruitshakes.")

Even if all the external dangers associated with scams could somehow be prevented, there would still remain the fundamental questions inherent in all law-enforcement techniques based on governmental deception:

Do we want a society in which every citizen is always subject to being tempted by governmental ruses?

Do we want a society in which the honesty, the integrity — and perhaps, ultimately, the loyalty — of every citizen are open to testing by government agents?

Do we want a society in which deception by the government of its citizens becomes a way of life?

Kurt Vonnegut Jr., in his book *Mother Night*, writes that "we are what we pretend to be, so we must be careful about what we pretend to be." Robert Leuci is proof of how undercover narcotics policemen quickly become like their targets, as did the Chicago policeman who became a pimp. Other scams have also demonstrated the importance of Vonnegut's warning. Do we really want to become a scam society?

In the end, only two things seem clear: first, we cannot tolerate a society in which the government is empowered to conduct every manner of scam at will and without any regulation or accountability. That, in a nutshell, is the present situation. Second, it seems unlikely that we could realistically do without all scam operations. Some are obviously needed to catch predatory criminals, especially potential terrorists and assassins.

## A POSSIBLE SOLUTION

There is one possible safeguard that promises significant control over "bad" scams while allowing "good" scams to be used when appropriate. The object of the good scam is to give the predatory criminal the opportunity to do on camera what he has already been doing in private. Law-enforcement authorities should be required, therefore, as a precondition to conducting a scam, to obtain a warrant from a judge authorizing the operation. This scam warrant — like search warrants and wiretap warrants — would have to be based on probable cause for believing that the target of the proposed scam is involved in an ongoing criminal activity and that hard evidence of this activity cannot be obtained without a scam. If probable cause were shown, the judge could approve the scam and impose limits — of time, scope, and intrusiveness — on its implementation.

Being forced to obtain a scam warrant from a judge would not solve all the problems, any more than the requirement of a warrant for searches and wiretaps solves all problems associated with these sometimes necessary evils. But it would go a long way toward bringing the scam under the control of the law and imposing limits on its use.

The scam will always be with us, as it has been since the serpent tempted and tricked Eve into eating the forbidden fruit. But the scam as a technique of law enforcement is now out of control. Every prosecutor, undercover investigator, and policeman — every Paul Lawrence and Robert Leuci — is free to conduct any scam he sees fit to without fear of judicial rebuke. The Supreme Court, which gave birth to the entrapment defense, is in the process of committing infanticide on it. The courts have virtually abdicated all responsibility for controlling abuses of the scam.

The issues surrounding entrapment and scams are too important to be left to the Supreme Court: we all have a stake in imposing controls on a technique run amok. The government cannot be allowed to select targets at will, expose them to all manner of temptation, and then pounce on those who succumb. Legislation is needed to stop bad scams and control good scams: the proposal for a scam warrant holds some promise. But an informed and concerned public is the best protection of our liberty.

The net result of imposing controls on scam operations will be an increase in our collective freedom, but at the cost of permitting some scoundrels to remain free. Nonetheless, it will be well worth doing. As H. L. Mencken used to say: "The trouble about fighting for human freedom is that you have to spend much of your life defending sons of bitches: for oppressive laws are always aimed at them originally, and oppression must be stopped in the beginning if it is to be stopped at all."

# THIRTY-ONE

# PSYCHIATRY IN THE LEGAL PROCESS
## "A Knife That Cuts Both Ways"

*If a nation is to be judged by how it deals with its criminals, surely it must also be judged by how it treats its mentally ill. In 1968 I was invited to deliver a paper on that subject at the sesquicentennial of Harvard Law School.*

IN THE TRIAL SCENE FROM *THE BROTHERS KARAMAZOV*, Dostoyevsky, speaking through the lips of the defense attorney, issued a stern warning to the legal profession: "Profound as psychology is, it's a knife that cuts both ways. . . . You can prove anything by it. I am speaking of the abuse of psychology, gentlemen."

This essay will address another knife that cuts two ways: psychiatry in the legal process. Much has been written about one cutting edge: the contributions made by psychiatry. I will focus on the other side of the blade: the social costs incurred by the increasing involvement of the psychiatrist in the administration of justice. An important — if subtle — consequence of psychiatric involvement has been the gradual introduction of a medical model, in place of the laws' efforts to articulate legally relevant criteria. The cost of this substitution has been confusion of purpose, and in some instances, needless deprivation of liberty.

A brief look at the history of the insanity defense will serve to illustrate this process. The law had, for centuries, been groping for a rule that would express the deeply felt conviction that some people who commit condemnable acts are not themselves deserving of condemnation. In the seventeenth century, a person was held irresponsible if he "doth not know what he was doing, no more than an infant or a wild beast." There was an obvious relationship between this "wild beast" test and the rest of the criminal law: neither infant nor a wild beast was held responsible; so why, it was asked, should an adult who was functionally similar. In the much-vilified *McNaughten* case, the House of Lords also analogized irresponsibility to a deeply rooted principle of the criminal law. It held that a man who suffers from delusions must be considered in the same situation as to responsibility as if the facts with respect to which the delusion exists were real. This was a simple extension of the traditional mistake-of-fact defense to certain unreasonable mistakes.[1] The Lords' attempt to generalize this principle under the rubric "know the nature and the quality of the act" and know that it was "wrong" was surely not the clearest way of saying what they meant. But it *was* clear that they — like the framers of the "wild beast" test — were setting down a *legal* rule designed to further legal policies: they were not attempting to identify and exculpate a particular psychiatric category of persons — the mentally ill, the insane, or the psychotic. Indeed, the ruling explicitly recognized the rather limited role of the psychiatrist in administering the insanity defense. Nevertheless, much of the criticism of McNaughten has been premised on the erroneous assumption that the purpose of that test was to describe a psychiatric entity. Thus, Dr. Isaac Ray, an early psychiatric critic, called the McNaughten rule a "fallacious" test of criminal responsibility, arguing that "insanity is a disease, and, as in the case with all other diseases, the fact of its existence is never established by a single diagnostic symptom" — such as inability to distinguish right from wrong. But the Lords had not focused on inability to distinguish right from wrong because they thought it was a scientifically valid symptom of disease; they focused on it because that deemed it a just and useful legal criterion for distinguishing those who should be held responsible and punishable from those who should be held irresponsible and hospitalized. Now, this criterion may be criticized as unjust or unworkable, but to say it is "fallacious" is to misunderstand the nature of legal rules. Ray was attempting to substitute a medical model of responsibility for the legal one, and the law was not engaging in a fallacy by insisting on asking its own questions and establishing criteria relevant to its own purposes.

This attempt to impose a medical model on the legal process of distinguishing the responsible from the irresponsible continued through the nineteenth century and into the twentieth. It culminated in the case of *Durham v. United States*, decided in 1954. The argument for the Durham rule was simple — if one accepted Ray's erroneous premise. For if McNaughten was simply an attempt to identify those persons considered mentally ill by psychiatrists, then why bother to go through the indirection of listing symptoms? Why not make the test the existence of mental illness itself? The late justice Abe Fortas, counsel for Durham, argued that substitution of a new rule for McNaughten would permit psychiatrists to testify in "the terms of their own discipline, and not in the terminology of an irrelevant formula." Why the "right-wrong" formula was irrelevant for legal purposes the court was never told, except that it did not permit psychiatrists to testify in terms of their own discipline. The possibility that the terms of their own discipline are not particularly relevant to a perfectly rational legal rule was never considered. The court was simply urged to adopt the psychiatrists' medical model of "insanity" and abandon any effort of its own to articulate legally functional rules. The United States Court of Appeals for the District of Columbia accepted Fortas's arguments and adopted a rule framed in medical terms: "An accused is not responsible if his unlawful act was the product of a mental disease or defect." Although the author of Durham, Judge David Bazelon, has always regarded the case as merely an opening wedge in a continuing search for just and workable criteria of responsibility, many psychiatrists interpreted Durham as an invitation for them to decide who should not be held criminally responsible. Indeed, in one famous episode, the staff of a large mental hospital apparently took a vote to determine whether or not sociopath personality was to be regarded as a mental disease. The issue of criminal responsibility was finally where Isaac Ray thought it belonged: in the therapeutic hands of the psychiatrist.

This, then, is a capsule history of one encounter between law and psychiatry. It is not a complete history. There have been judicial adumbrations of disillusionment with the medical model. But it is a discouraging history of usurpation and abdication: of an expert's being summoned for a limited purpose, of his assuming his own indispensability and then persuading the law to ask the critical questions in terms that make him more comfortable and his testimony more relevant. The upshot has been to make the psychiatrist's testimony more relevant to the questions posed but to make the questions themselves less relevant to the purpose of the law.

This history has been repeated in other areas of the law, less well known than the insanity defense. Let me now turn to one in which psychiatric involvement has incurred even higher social costs — costs measured in years of needless and unjustified deprivation of liberty. I speak of the process known as civil commitment of the mentally ill, whereby almost one million people are today confined behind the locked doors of state mental hospitals, though never convicted of a crime.

Not in every society and not in every age were the insane confined by the state. The building of asylums on a wide scale did not begin until the seventeenth century. Such confinement — like the defense of insanity — was originally designed to further vaguely articulated legal goals. In the late eighteenth and the early nineteenth centuries these laws were part of the larger tapestry that included "suppression of rogues, vagabonds, common beggars and other idle, disorderly and lewd persons." The legislative purpose seems clear: to isolate those persons who — for whatever reason — were regarded as intolerably obnoxious to the community. Medical testimony had little to offer in making this judgment: the people knew whom they regarded as obnoxious. By the middle of the nineteenth century — again through the influence of Dr. Isaac Ray — madness was becoming widely regarded as a disease that should be treated by physicians with little, or no, interference by courts. The present situation comes close to reflecting that view: the criteria for confinement are so vague that courts sit — when they sit at all — merely to review decisions made by psychiatrists. Indeed, the typical criteria are so meaningless as even to preclude effective review. In Connecticut, for example, the court is supposed to commit any person whom a doctor reasonably finds "mentally ill and a fit subject for treatment in a hospital for mental illness, or that he ought to be confined." This circularity is typical of the criteria — or lack thereof — in about half of our states. Even in those jurisdictions with legal-sounding criteria — such as the District of Columbia, where the committed person must be mentally ill and likely to injure himself and others — the operative phrases are so vague that courts rarely upset psychiatric determinations.

The distorting effect of this medical model of confinement may be illustrated by comparing two cases from the District of Columbia. One involved Bong Yol Yang, an American of Korean origin who appeared at the White House gate asking to see the president about people who were following him and "revealing his subconscious thoughts." He also wondered whether his talents as an artist could be put to some use by the government. The gate officer had him committed to a mental hospital. Yang demanded a jury trial, at which a psychiatrist testified that he was mentally ill — a paranoid schizophrenic — and that although there was no "evidence of his ever attacking anyone so far," there was always a possibility that "if his frustrations . . . become great enough, he may potentially attack someone." On the basis of this diagnosis and prediction, the judge permitted a jury to commit Yang to a mental hospital until he is no longer mentally ill and likely to cause injury.

The other case involved a man named Dallas Williams, who at age thirty-nine had spent half his life in jail for seven convictions of assault with a deadly weapon and one conviction of manslaughter. Just before his scheduled release from jail, the government petitioned for his civil commitment. Two psychiatrists testified that although "at the present time [he] shows no evidence of active mental illness . . . he is potentially dangerous to others and if released is likely to repeat his patterns of criminal behavior and might commit homicide." The judge, in denying the government's petition and ordering Williams's release, observed that "the courts have no legal basis for ordering confinement on mere apprehension of future unlawful acts. They must wait until another crime is committed or the person is found insane." Within months of his release, Williams lived up to the prediction of the psychiatrists and shot two men to death in an unprovoked attack.

Are there any distinctions between the Williams and Yang cases that justify the release of the former and the incarceration of the latter? There was no evidence that Yang was more dangerous, more amenable to treatment, or less competent than Williams. But Yang was diagnosed mentally ill and thus within the medical model, whereas Williams was not so diagnosed. Although there was nothing about Yang's mental illness that made him a more appropriate subject for involuntary confinement than Williams, the law attributed conclusive significance to its existence *vel non*. The outcomes of these cases —

which make little sense when evaluated against any rational criteria for confinement — are typical under the present civil commitment process. And this will continue, so long as the law continues to ask the dispositive questions in medical rather than legally functional terms, because the medical model does not ask the proper questions, or asks them in meaningless, vague terms: Is the person mentally ill? Is he dangerous to himself or others? Is he in need of care or treatment?

Nor is it the only way to ask questions to which the civil commitment process is responsive. It will be instructive to restate the problem of civil commitment without employing medical terms to see whether the answers suggested differ from those now given.

There are, in every society, people who may cause trouble if not confined. The trouble may be serious (such as homicide), trivial (making offensive remarks), or somewhere in between (forging checks). The trouble may be directed at others, at the person himself, or at both. It may be very likely that he will cause trouble, or fairly likely, or fairly unlikely. In some instances this likelihood may be considerably reduced by a relatively short period of involuntary confinement; in others, a longer period may be required with no assurances of reduced risk; while in still others, the likelihood can never be significantly reduced. Some people will have fairly good insight into the risks they themselves pose and the costs entailed by an effort to reduce those risks; others will have poor insight into these factors.

When the issues are put this way, there begins to emerge a series of meaningful questions capable of traditional legal analyses:

What sorts of anticipated harm warrant involuntary confinement?

How likely must it be that the harm will occur? Must there be a significant component of harm to others, or may it be to self alone?

If harm to self is sufficient, must the person also be incapable, because he lacks insight, of weighing the risks to himself against the costs of confinement?

How long a period of involuntary confinement is justified to prevent which sorts of harm? Must the likelihood of the harm increase as its severity decreases?

These questions are complex, but this is as it should be, for the business of balancing the liberty of the individual against the risks a free society must tolerate is very complex. That is the business of the law, and these are the questions that need asking and answering before liberty is denied, but they are obscured when the issue is phrased in medical terms that frighten — or bore — lawyers away. Nor have I simply manufactured these questions. They are the very questions that are being implicitly answered every day by psychiatrists, but they are not being openly asked, and many psychiatrists do not realize that they are, in fact, answering them.

Let us consider two of these questions and compare how they are being dealt with — or not dealt with — under the present system with how they might be handled under functional, nonmedical criteria.

The initial and fundamental question that might be asked by any system authorizing incarceration is: Which harms are sufficiently serious to justify resorting to this rather severe sanction? This question is asked and answered in the criminal law by the substantive definitions of crime. Thus, homicide is a harm that justifies the sanction of imprisonment; miscegenation does not; and adultery is a close case about which reasonable people may, and do, disagree. It is difficult to conceive of a criminal process that does not make some effort at articulating these distinctions. Imagine, for example, a penal code that simply made it an imprisonable crime to cause injury to self or others, without defining injury. It is also difficult to conceive of a criminal process — at least in jurisdictions with an Anglo-American tradition — in which these distinctions were not drawn by the legislature or courts. It would seem beyond dispute that the question of which harms do, and which do not, justify incarceration is a legal — indeed a political — decision, to be made not by experts but by the constitutionally authorized agents of the people. Again, try to imagine a penal code that authorized incarceration for anyone who performed an act regarded as injurious by a designated expert, say a psychiatrist or penologist.

To be sure, there are differences between the criminal and the civil commitment processes: the criminal law is supposed to punish people for having committed harmful acts in the past, whereas civil commitment is supposed to prevent people from committing harmful acts in the future. While this difference may have important implications in some contexts, it would seem entirely irrelevant in deciding which acts are sufficiently harmful to justify incarceration, either as an after-the-fact punitive sanction or as a before-the-fact preventative sanction. The considerations that require clear definition of such harms in the criminal process would seem to be fully applicable to the civil commitment process.

Yet the situation that I said would be hard to imagine in the criminal law is precisely the one that prevails with civil commitment. The statutes authorize preventive incarceration of the mentally ill persons who are likely to injure themselves or others. Generally, *injure* is not further defined in the statutes or in the case law, and the critical decision — whether a predicted pattern of behavior is sufficiently injurious to warrant incarceration — is relegated to the psychiatrist's unarticulated judgments.

Some psychiatrists are perfectly willing to provide their own personal opinions — often falsely disguised as expert opinions — about which harms are sufficiently serious. One psychiatrist told a meeting of the American Psychiatric Association that "you" — the psychiatrist — "have to define for yourself the word danger, and then having decided that in your mind . . . look for it with every conceivable means."

My own conversations with psychiatrists reveal wide differences in opinion over what sorts of harm justify incarceration. As one would expect, some psychiatrists are political conservatives, while others are liberals; some place a greater premium on safety, others on liberty. Their opinions about which harms do, and which do not, justify confinement probably cover the range of opinions one would expect to encounter in any educated segment of the public. But they are opinions about matters that each of us is as qualified to make as they are. Thus, this most fundamental decision — which harms justify confinement — is almost never made by the legislature or the courts; often it is never explicitly made by anybody; and when it is explicitly made, it is by an unelected and unappointed expert operating outside the area of his expertise.

Consider, for example, the age-old philosophical dispute about the government's authority to incarcerate someone for his own good. The classic statement denying such authority was made by John Stuart Mill in *On Liberty*. He deemed it fundamental that

> the only purpose for which power can be rightfully exercised against
> any member of a civilized community, against his will, is to prevent
> harm to others. He cannot rightfully be compelled to do or forbear
> because it will be better for him to do so, because it will make him
> happier, because . . . to do so would be wise or even right.

The most eloquent presentation of the other view was made by the poet John Donne in a famous excerpt from his *Devotions upon Emergent Occasions:*

> No man is an island, entire of itself; every man is a piece of the continent, a part of the main; if a clod be washed away by the sea, Europe is the less . . . ; any man's death diminishes me, because I am involved in mankind; and therefore never send to know for whom the bell tolls; it tolls for thee.

These statements — eloquent as they are — are far too polarized for useful discourse. In our complex and interdependent society, there is hardly a harm to one man that does not radiate beyond the island of the person. But this observation does not, in itself, destroy the thrust of Mill's argument. Society may still have less justification for incarcerating a person to prevent a harm to himself that contains only a slight component of harm to others than if it contained a large component of such harm.

Compare, for example, a case that arose under the civil commitment process with a similar situation that produced no case at all. Mrs. Lake, a sixty-two-year-old woman, suffers from arteriosclerosis, which causes periods of confusion interspersed with periods of relative rationality. One day she was found wandering in downtown Washington looking confused but bothering no one, whereupon she was committed to a mental hospital. She petitioned for release and at her trial testified during a period of apparent rationality that she was aware of her problem, that she knew that her periods of confusion endangered her health and even her life, but that she had experienced the mental hospital and preferred to assume the risk of living — and perhaps dying — outside its walls. Her petition was denied, despite the continued litigation, and she was involuntarily confined in the closed ward of the mental hospital.

Compare Mrs. Lake's preference with the decision made by Supreme Court justice Robert Jackson, who, at the same age of sixty-two, suffered a severe heart attack while serving on the Supreme Court. As Solicitor General Simon Sobeloff recalled in his memorial tribute, Jackson's "doctor's gave him the choice between years of comparative inactivity and the risk of death at any time." Characteristically, he chose the second alternative and suffered a fatal heart attack shortly thereafter. No court interfered with his risky decision. A similar choice, though in a lighter vein, is described in a limerick entitled "The Lament of the Coronary Patient":

> My doctor has made a prognosis
> That intercourse threatens thrombosis
> But I'd rather expire
> Fulfilling desire
> Than abstain and develop neurosis.

Few courts, I suspect, would interfere with the coronary patient's decision. Why, then, do courts respond so differently to what appear to be essentially similar choices by Mrs. Lake, Justice Jackson, and the coronary patient? Because these similarities are obscured by the medical model imposed upon Mrs. Lake's case but not upon the other two. Most courts would distinguish the cases by simply saying that Mrs. Lake is mentally ill, while Jackson and the coronary patient are not, without pausing to ask whether there is something about her "mental illness" that makes her case functionally different from the others. To be sure, there are some mentally ill people whose decisions are different from those made by Justice Jackson and the coronary patient. Some mentally ill people have little insight into their condition, the risks it poses, and the possibility of change. Their capacity for choosing between the risks of liberty and the security of incarceration may be substantially impaired. And in some cases perhaps the state ought to act *in parens patriae* and make the decision for them. But not all persons so diagnosed are incapable of weighing risks and making important decisions. This has been recognized by some of the very psychiatrists who advocate the medical model most forcefully. Dr. Jack Ewalt, chairman of the Department of Psychiatry at Harvard, offered the following observation to a Senate subcommittee:

> The mentally sick patient may be disoriented, but he is not a fool. He has read the newspapers about overcrowded and understaffed hospitals. He is alert to the tough time he will have getting a job when he gets out, if he gets out. He knows that there lurks in the minds of his former friends the suspicion that he is a dangerous

fellow. He is sensitive that a mother may recoil in fright if he stops to give her child a pat on the head.

But Dr. Ewalt uses this observation not as an argument in favor of self-determination by the mentally ill but rather as showing the need for medical commitment without judicial interference.

The appropriateness and limitations of such benevolent compulsion are in the forefront of our concerns in the criminal law. Although there is much reason for concern about these issues in the civil commitment context, they are being ignored because the law has inadvertently relegated them to the unarticulated value judgments of the expert psychiatrist.

This is equally true of another important question that rarely gets asked in the civil commitment process: How likely should the predicted event have to be to justify preventative incarceration? Even if it is agreed, for example, that preventing a serious physical assault would justify incarceration, how likely should it have to be that the person would assault before incarceration is justified? If the likelihood is very high — say 90 percent — then a strong argument can be made for some incarceration. If the likelihood is very small — say 5 percent — then it would be hard to justify confinement. Here, unlike the process of defining harm, little guidance can be obtained from the criminal law, for there are only a few occasions where the criminal law is explicitly predictive, and no judicial or legislative guidelines have been developed for determining the degree of likelihood required.

But someone is deciding what degree of likelihood should be required in every case. Today the psychiatrist makes that important decision; he is asked whether a given harm is likely, and he generally answers yes or no. He may — in his own mind — be defining likely to mean anything from virtual certainty to slightly above chance. And his definition will not be a reflection of any expertise but of his own personal preference for safety or liberty.

Not only do psychiatrists determine the degree of likelihood that should be required for incarceration; they are also the ones who decide whether the degree of likelihood exists in any particular case.

Now this, you may be thinking, is surely an appropriate role for the expert psychiatrist. But just how expert are psychiatrists in making the sorts of predictions upon which incarceration is presently based? Considering the heavy — indeed exclusive — reliance the law places on psychiatric predictions, one would expect there to be numerous follow-up studies establishing their accuracy. Over the past year, with the help of two researchers, I conducted a thorough survey of all the published literature on the prediction of antisocial conduct. We read and summarized many hundreds of articles, monographs, and books. Surprisingly enough, we were able to discover fewer than a dozen studies that followed up psychiatric predictions of antisocial conduct. And even more surprisingly, these few studies strongly suggest that psychiatrists are rather inaccurate predictors — inaccurate in an absolute sense and even less accurate when compared with other professionals, such as psychologists, social workers, and correctional officials, and when compared with actuarial devices, such as prediction or experience tables. Even more significant for legal purposes, it seems that psychiatrists are particularly prone to one type of error — overprediction. In other words, they tend to predict antisocial conduct in many instances where it would not, in fact, occur. Indeed, our research suggests that for every correct psychiatric prediction of violence, there are numerous erroneous predictions. That is, among all inmates presently confined on the basis of psychiatric predictions of violence, there are only a few who would, and many more who would not, actually engage in such conduct if released.

One reason for this overprediction is that a psychiatrist almost never learns about his erroneous predictions of violence — for predicted assailants are generally incarcerated and have little opportunity to prove or disprove the predictions — but he always learns about his erroneous predictions of nonviolence, often from newspaper headlines announcing the crime. The higher visibility of erroneous predictions of nonviolence inclines him, whether consciously or unconsciously, to overpredict rather than underpredict violent behavior.

What, then, have been the effects of virtually turning over to the psychiatrists the civil commitment process? We have accepted a legal policy, never approved by an authorized decision maker, that permits significant overprediction — in effect, abiding by a rule that it is better to confine ten men who would not assault than to let free one man who would. We have defined danger to include all sorts of minor social disruptions. We have equated harm to self with harm to others without recognizing the debatable nature of that equation.

Now, it may well be that if we substituted functional legal criteria for the medical model, we would still accept many of the answers we accept today. Perhaps our society is willing to tolerate significant over-prediction. Perhaps we do want incarceration to prevent minor social harms. Perhaps we do want to protect people from themselves as much as from others. But we will never learn the answers to these questions unless they are exposed and openly debated. And such open debate is discouraged — indeed, made impossible — when the questions are disguised in medical jargon against which the lawyer, and the citizen, feel helpless.

The lesson of this experience — and our similar if less costly one with the insanity defense — is that no legal rule should ever be phrased in medical terms, that no legal decision should ever be turned over to the psychiatrist, that there is no such thing as a legal problem that cannot, and should not, be phrased in terms familiar to lawyers. And civil commitment of the mentally ill is a legal problem; whenever compulsion is used or freedom denied — whether by the state, the church, the union, the university, or the psychiatrist — the issue becomes a legal one, and the lawyers must be quick to immerse themselves in it. The words of Brandeis ring as true today as they did in 1927 and are as applicable to the psychiatrist as to the wiretapper:

> Experience should teach us to be most on our guard to protect liberty when the Government's purposes are beneficent. Men born to freedom are naturally alert to repel invasion of their liberty by evil-minded rulers. The greatest dangers to liberty lurk in insidious encroachment by men of zeal, well-meaning but without understanding.

## PART V

# THE RIGHT TO LIVE

"DEATH IS DIFFERENT," THE SUPREME COURT HAS SAID, when dealing with the unique sentence of capital punishment. The issue of whether to take life for life has plagued humankind from the beginning of recorded history. The first biblical reference to the death penalty occurs in the book of Genesis, when God prohibits the killing of the murderer Cain. Soon thereafter, God tells Noah that he who sheds human blood shall by humans have his blood be shed. The Ten Commandments prohibit murder, and the subsequent laws of the Bible authorize the death penalty for a variety of crimes, ranging from murder to being a stubborn child. But the procedural safeguards required before a person could be put to death were so stringent that the Talmud characterizes a court that sentenced even one person to death over a seventy-year period as a bloody court. By this standard American courts are bloody indeed. More than three thousand Americans now face execution on America's death rows. Only a portion of these will actually die at the hands of the state, since appellate reversal is far more common in capital cases than in cases involving imprisonment.

Recently, an array of conservative politicians, theologians, and commentators has joined with liberals in seeking a moratorium on the death penalty. This movement has grown out of the discovery that numerous innocent people have been wrongly sentenced to death. The advent of DNA testing has disclosed many instances of wrongful eyewitness identification. DNA is useful only in a limited number of cases. Many capital cases involve only eyewitnesses and circumstantial inferences. People have been put to death on the basis of one eyewitness, despite their plausible claims of innocence. But the execution of the innocent is not the only reason for concern about the death penalty. It has been imposed unfairly, especially against the poor and disenfranchised. Few on death row have received zealous representation from competent counsel. And racial injustice permeates the death-penalty process.

Since I was a high school student, I have strongly opposed the death penalty. I came of age as Julius and Ethel Rosenberg were being executed. A distant relative of mine was the chaplain who sought to comfort them at their death. In high school I debated against the death penalty. I still have my debate note cards on which I argued that "it is possible that mistakes have been made" and it is better that one hundred murderers go to prison "than one innocent man go mistakenly to the electric chair." In law school I wrote letters to the editor calling for its abolition. I even opposed the execution of Adolf Eichmann, the man responsible for the death of millions of Jews.

When I became a law clerk for Justice Arthur Goldberg on the United States Supreme Court, the justice asked me to write a memorandum arguing that the death penalty was cruel and unusual punishment prohibited by the Eighth Amendment to our Constitution. In the forthcoming chapters, I publish my 1963 memorandum for the first time and tell the story behind it. This is followed by an essay on how the courts measure the value of life. I conclude this part on the right to live with an article I wrote about mercy killing, which is another aspect of the right to live — and to die with dignity.

# THIRTY-TWO

# MEMORANDUM TO JUSTICE GOLDBERG ON THE CONSTITUTIONALITY OF THE DEATH PENALTY (1963)

THIS MEMORANDUM IS ADDRESSED TO THE QUESTION, IS THE death penalty "cruel and unusual punishment," within the meaning of the Eighth Amendment?

## CRUEL AND UNUSUAL PUNISHMENT

The proscription against cruel and unusual punishment first appeared in the English Bill of Rights of 1688,[1] was included in the Virginia Declaration of Rights of 1776, and was approved by Congress as part of the Eighth Amendment with little debate.

The first significant case to raise this issue was *Wilkerson v. Utah* (1878). The accused had been found guilty of "wilful, malicious and premeditated murder," and sentenced to "be publicly shot until . . . dead." He did not object to the death penalty as such but, rather, to the mode of execution, claiming that it was not authorized by the governing statutes. The Court held that it was, and that shooting — a traditional method of executing certain types of offenders — was not cruel and unusual. In arriving at the latter conclusion, the Court made the following statement:

> Difficulty would attend the effort to define with exactness the extent of the constitutional provision which provides that cruel and unusual punishments shall not be inflicted; but it is safe to affirm that punishments of torture . . . and all others in the same line of unnecessary cruelty, are forbidden by that amendment.[2]

Whereas *Wilkerson* involved a federal territory, the next significant case — *In re Kemmler* (1890) challenged the power of a state to take the life of a murderer by electrocution. It was not contended, as the Court noted, "it could not be, that the Eighth Amendment was intended to apply to the states." But it was urged that the due process clause prohibited the states from imposing cruel and unusual punishments. The Court held that reversal would be proper only if the state "had committed an error so gross as to amount in law to a denial . . . of due process," and that the state's conclusion — based as it was on "a voluminous mass of evidence" — that electrocution was a most humane mode of execution was not such an error. The Court quoted the above-cited paragraph from *Wilkerson* and added the following dictum:

> Punishments are cruel when they involve torture or a lingering death; but the punishment of death is not cruel, within the meaning of that word as used in the Constitution. It implies there is something inhuman and barbarous, something more than the mere extinguishment of life.[3]

Up to this time, therefore, the only alleged violations of the cruel and unusual punishment proscription involved not the extent of the punishment (i.e., death), but the mode of inflicting that assuredly valid punishment (i.e., shooting, electrocution). The next case, *O'Neil v. Vermont* (1892), raised the question of proportionality in the context of a long prison term and heavy fine, and saw the Court divided over the meaning and application of the Eighth Amendment for the first time. A jury found O'Neil guilty of 307 separate offenses of illegally selling intoxicating liquor, under a statute that made each sale a separate offense. He was sentenced to pay an aggregate fine of $6,140, and if that fine were not paid within a designated period of time, "he should be confined at hard labor, in the house of correction . . . for the term of 19,914 days." The Court declined to consider whether this punishment was cruel and unusual "because as a Federal question, it is not assigned as error, nor even suggested in the brief . . ."[4] and because, in any event, the Eighth Amendment does not apply to the states.

Justice Stephen Field dissented. He rejected the traditional reading of the Eighth Amendment, which would limit its application "to punishments which inflict torture," which "were at one time inflicted in England," and concluded that

> the inhibition is directed, not only against punishments of the character mentioned, but against all punishments which by their excessive length or severity are greatly disproportioned to the offense charged. The whole inhibition is against that which is excessive either in the bail required, or fine imposed, or punishment inflicted.[5]

The next case — which did not present the divisive question of the application of the Eighth Amendment to the states — saw the principles adumbrated in Justice Field's dissent adopted by the Court (by a vote of four to two, with three members not participating). In *Weems v. United States* (1910), an officer of "the United States Government of the Philippine Islands" was convicted of falsifying a public document, and sentenced to fifteen years of *"cadena temporal."* This ominous-sounding punishment was of Spanish origin and required the prisoner to "always carry a chain at the ankle, hanging from the wrists; [to] be employed at hard and painful labor, and [to] receive no assistance whatsoever from without the institution." In addition, the prisoner was to suffer "civil interdiction," which denied him the rights of "parental authority, guardianship of person or property, participation in the family counsel, marital authority, the administration of property, and the right to dispose of his own property by acts inter vivos."[6] He was also subject to "surveillance" during his entire lifetime.

The severity of the penalty was not challenged in the lower courts, but the Court decided to consider it under the "plain error" rule, stating that it has "less reluctance to disregard prior examples in criminal cases than in civil cases, and less reluctance to act under [the plain error rule] when rights are asserted which are of such high character as to find expression and sanction in the Constitution or Bill of Rights."

After a careful analysis of the historical experience, which formed the basis for the Eighth Amendment, the Court made the following observation:

> Legislation, both statutory and constitutional, is enacted, it is true, from an experience of evils, but its general language should not, therefore, be necessarily confined to the form that evil had theretofore taken. Time works changes, brings into existence new conditions and purposes. Therefore a principle to be vital must be capable

of wider application than the mischief, which gave it birth. This is peculiarly true of constitutions. They are not ephemeral enactments, designed to meet passing occasions. They are, to use the words of Chief Justice Marshall, "designed to approach immortality as nearly as human institutions can approach it." The future is their care and provision for events of good and bad tendencies of which no prophecy can be made. In the application of a constitution, therefore, our contemplation cannot be only of what has been but of what may be. Under any other rule a constitution would indeed be as easy of application as it would be deficient in efficacy and power. Its general principles would have little value and be converted by precedent into impotent and lifeless formulas. Rights declared in words might be lost in reality.

After analyzing the earlier authorities — including a 1689 case where the King's Bench struck down a 30,000 pound fine for assault as "excessive and exorbitant, against Magna Carta, the right of the subject and the law of the land" — the Court concluded that "the clause of the Constitution in the opinion of the learned commentators may be therefore progressive, and is not fastened to the obsolete but may acquire meaning as public opinion becomes enlightened by a humane justice."

In setting out the standards for applying the cruel and unusual punishment clause, the Court disclaimed the right "to assert a judgment against that of the legislature of the expediency of the laws or the right to oppose the judicial power to the legislative power to define crimes and fix their punishment . . . [because] for the proper exercise of such power there must be a comprehension of all that the legislature did or could take into account, that is, a consideration of the mischief and the remedy." The states have a "wide range of power . . . to adapt its penal laws to conditions as they may exist and punish the crimes of men according to their forms and frequency."

The Court then examined the penalty in question against the evil sought to be mitigated, and construed the "sentence in this case as cruel and unusual." In doing this, the Court observed that "the state thereby suffers nothing and loses no power. The purpose of punishment is fulfilled, crime is repressed by penalties of just, not tormenting, severity, its repetition is prevented, and hope is given for the reformation of the criminal." The Court concluded that since no legal sentence could be imposed under the governing law, "the judgment must be reversed, with directions to dismiss the proceedings."

Justice Edward White filed a dissenting opinion that was concurred in by Justice Oliver Wendell Holmes. The dissent accused the Court of considering the punishment in the abstract.

> I say only abstractly considered, because the first impression produced by the merely abstract view of the subject is met by the admonition that the duty of defining and punishing crime has never in any civilized country been exerted upon mere abstract considerations of the inherent nature of the crime punished, but has always involved the most practical consideration of the tendency at a particular time to commit certain crimes, of the difficulty of repressing the same, and of how far it is necessary to impose stern remedies to prevent the commission of such crimes. And, of course, as these considerations involve the necessity for a familiarity with local conditions in the Philippine Islands which I do not possess, such want of knowledge at once additionally admonishes me of the wrong to arise from forming a judgment upon insufficient data or without a knowledge of the subject-matter upon which the judgment is to be exerted.

The dissent concluded that the proscription was intended as a limitation only upon the infliction of "unnecessary bodily suffering through a resort to inhuman methods."[7]

Thus, the *Weems* case seems to be the turning point in the construction of the cruel and unusual punishment clause. To be sure, the earlier cases used words like *unnecessary* and *excessive*. But in those cases, the words were directed to the mode of effecting a punishment, the *extent* of which was not challenged. For example, on the assumption that death is a valid punishment for murder, the question was whether shooting produces unnecessary or excessive pain in causing death. The question posed and apparently answered in *Weems* was whether the extent of a given punishment was unnecessarily or excessively harsh, considering the admitted legislative power to "repress" crime, prevent its repetition, and reform the criminal.

In light of its antecedents, therefore, the *Weems* case can be read as announcing the following test: giving full weight to reasonable legislative findings, a punishment is cruel and unusual if a less severe one can as effectively achieve the permissible ends of punishment (i.e., deterrence, isolation, rehabilitation, or whatever the contemporary society considers the permissible ends of punishment). To this test must of course be added the traditional test: regardless of how effective they may be in achieving the permissible ends of punishment, certain punishments are always cruel and unusual if they offend the contemporary sense of decency (e.g., torture), or if the evil they produce is disproportionally higher than the harm they seek to prevent (e.g., the death penalty for economic crimes).

These two tests were apparently recognized by the opinions comprising the majority in *Trop v. Dulles*, when the Court in 1958 held unconstitutional a federal statute "punishing" desertion by expatriation. The chief justice, after reviewing the history of the Eighth Amendment and its application, concluded that "the Amendment must draw its meaning from the evolving standards of decency that mark the progress of a maturing society."[8] This seems to imply that no matter how effective certain penalties may be, they are unconstitutional if they offend such standards. Justice Brennan seems to have adopted the other test: "Clearly the severity of the penalty, in the case of a serious offense, is not enough to invalidate it where the nature of the penalty is rationally directed to achieve the legitimate ends of punishment."[9] In addition to rehabilitation, Justice Brennan included deterrence and insulation of the offender among the permissible purposes of punishment.

Justice William O. Douglas employed this test also, in his concurrence in *Robinson v. California* (1962), when he said: "A prosecution for addiction, with its resulting stigma and irreparable damage to the good name of the accused, cannot be justified as a means of protecting society, *where a civil commitment would do as well*"[10] (emphasis added).

## TESTS FOR CRUEL
## AND UNUSUAL PUNISHMENT

This section of the memorandum will attempt to apply the cruel and unusual punishment tests derived from the foregoing decisions.[11]

Thus, the death penalty is unconstitutional

1. if, regardless of its effectiveness in preventing, for example, murder, it is condemned as inherently barbaric or uncivilized

by "the evolving standards of decency" now prevalent in our society;

2. if, assuming that deterrence, isolation, and rehabilitation[12] are the presently accepted goals of punishment, it can be convincingly shown that a punishment less severe than death can as effectively achieve these goals; and

3. if, assuming a consensus that life is more valuable than anything else, the death penalty is imposed for an act that does not endanger life.

The most that can be said about the present standard of decency as related to the imposition of the death penalty for at least certain types of murder is that it does not lean clearly in either direction.

There have been some public opinion polls conducted on this subject (for what they are worth), and the results seem inconclusive.[13] The religious leaders of the country seem to favor abolition, but they are by no means unanimous. The same may be said about the commentators: the vast majority of writers favor abolition, some professional prosecutors (and others of that ilk) have written against abolition, and a very few thoughtful and respected writers have opposed abolition (at least total abolition). Moreover, although the worldwide trend favors abolition, there are still many civilized countries that employ capital punishment.

Against this background, I would agree with Justice Frankfurter (concurring in *Francis v. Resweber*) that one is not denied due process when the state "treats him by a mode about which opinion is fairly divided." If this is true, then the chief justice is correct in his observation in *Trop v. Dulles* that the present standards of decency are not yet sufficiently high to condemn capital punishment (for at least certain crimes) on moral grounds alone.

The next question is whether capital punishment has any uniquely deterrent effect on prospective murderers. It is generally agreed among thoughtful commentators (particularly those of a utilitarian leaning) that if it could be shown that the death penalty really does prevent murders, then capital punishment for murder is justified. For in that case, the state would not be "taking" a life; it would merely be choosing to save one life at the cost of others. As Jerome Michael and Herbert Wechsler have put it:

We need not pause to reconsider the universal judgment that there is no social interest in preserving the lives of aggressors at the cost of their victims. Given the choice that must be made, the only defensible policy is one that will operate as a sanction against unlawful aggression.[14]

Or, as stated more recently:

The only conceivable moral ground which a state can have that will justify it in taking a citizen's life ... is simply that one man's life is necessary and indispensable for the protection and preservation of many other citizens' lives.[15]

Thus, if capital punishment really does deter certain types of murder to a significantly greater degree than any other punishment would, then there would arguably be no real objection to its imposition for those types of crimes. Capital punishment would not then be "excessive" in terms of at least one of the permissible goals of punishment — deterrence.

But does capital punishment really deter any murders? Much research has recently been conducted on this question, and many such claims have been predicated upon the results of this research. The most that can be said, however, is that "there is no clear evidence in any of the figures . . . that the abolition of capital punishment has led to an increase in the homicide rate, or that its reintroduction has led to a fall."[16] But as Professor H.L.A. Hart has warned, this conclusion (and the statistics upon which it is based) should be taken to mean only that "there is no evidence from the statistics that the death penalty is a superior deterrent to imprisonment"; it should not be taken to mean (as some have argued) that "there is evidence that the death penalty is not a superior deterrent to imprisonment."[17] Professors Francis Allen[18] and Richard Donnelly[19] have joined in this caveat. The meaningful question — at least at this point in the development of our methods of studying the relationship between punishments and crimes — is not whether capital punishment really deters crime (for we cannot know the answer to this question), it is "Where [does] the onus of proof [lie] in this matter of the death penalty?"[20] For if the state must prove that capital punishment has a unique deterrent impact, then it has failed. But if the advocates of abolition must prove that capital punishment lacks a unique deterrent impact, then they have failed.

This question assumes particular significance against the standard ordinarily applied by this Court in passing on the reasonableness of legislative findings based on conflicting evidence. The state is always presumed to act rationally, absent a persuasive showing to the contrary. This seems to suggest that unless it can be affirmatively shown that capital punishment does not uniquely deter murder, then at least certain types of murder may be constitutionally punished by the death penalty.

It may be argued, however, that the standard generally applied in passing on legislative findings is not applicable when human life is in the balance, and that to take life, the state must affirmatively show an overriding necessity. The Court has held on many occasions (admittedly in different contexts) that doubts should always be resolved against the application of the death sentence. See, for example, *Andres v. United States.*[21]

Putting aside the question whether the death penalty for murder is unconstitutional as a general principle, we may still ask whether, under the tests previously mentioned, the death penalty may be inflicted in a particular case or category of cases where it could not serve as a unique deterrent.

Consider, for example, the case of *White v. Washington*, presently before this Court on a petition for certiorari. In that case, the highest court of the state sanctioned the imposition of the death penalty on a murderer about whom the psychiatric evidence was unanimous that he could not possibly have been deterred by the threat of any penalty, no matter how severe, and about whom the court found that "there was substantial evidence from which the jury could have found that appellant could not control his own behavior."[22] It seems clear that for this type of murderer, capital punishment is not a unique deterrent; thus, under the test previously mentioned, the imposition of the death penalty on such a murderer would violate the constitutional proscription on cruel and unusual punishments.

Consider also, the case of *Snider v. Cunningham*, now before this Court on a petition for a writ of certiorari (collaterally attacking his conviction and sentence on different but related issues). The district court, after a hearing on federal habeas corpus, found that the accused "has an irresistible sex urge which he is, at times, unable to control." And the Court of Appeals held that "he has little or no control of his sex urges in the presence of a female under his control in a secluded place."[23] Thus, it seems clear that although the accused may have had some control over the situations in which he might find himself, once he was alone with a female, the fear of capital punishment could not prevent an attempt to satisfy his "sex urge."

The foregoing case also raises the broader issue, whether capital punishment may ever be constitutionally imposed for a sexual crime that does not endanger life. A persuasive argument can be made — much more persuasive than can be made in relation to murder considered as a category — that the threat of capital punishment is not a unique deterrent to sexual crimes, considered as a category. Again, there is no convincing statistical data. But the psychiatric and psychological observations about the motivation of sexual offenses seem persuasive of the conclusion that if these crimes can be deterred at all, they can be deterred as well by the threat of a long prison sentence as by the threat of death.

Moreover, even assuming that sexual crimes not endangering life are uniquely deterred by the threat of death, there still remains the question posed by the last of the tests previously described: May human life constitutionally be taken by the state to protect a value other than human life? Certainly, if the value sought to be preserved were economic, the taking of human life would be unconstitutional regardless of the efficacy of the deterrent. Here, however, the value sought to be preserved is probably considered nearly as important as life by a substantial portion of the populace. Nonetheless, I would think that there is a general consensus that the value is still less than life. And when this consensus is coupled with the questionable efficacy of capital punishment as a unique deterrent to sexual crimes, a persuasive argument can be made that death may not constitutionally be imposed for sexual crimes that do not endanger human life.[24]

Thus, my tentative conclusions on the matter of capital punishment and the Eighth Amendment are as follows:

The Supreme Court should not at this time hold that the death penalty always violates the Constitution. It should hold that the death penalty for rape (and other sexual crimes) does violate the Constitution. It should hold that the death penalty is unconstitutional when imposed upon certain types of murderers (i.e., those for whom capital punishment is not a unique deterrent). It should hold that the death penalty is unconstitutional when imposed for certain types of murders (e.g., noncommercial passion killings about which it is fairly certain that capital punishment does not uniquely deter). It should carefully scrutinize the few (and becoming fewer) capital cases that come before it, in an effort to define categories of cases where the death penalty is unconstitutional.

In this way, as Professor Alexander Bickel suggests, "a process might [be] set in motion to whose culmination in an ultimate broader judgment [— the moral inadmissibility of capital punishment itself —] at once widely acceptable and morally elevating, we might [look] in the calculable future."[25]

---

*In 1969–70, Justice Arthur Goldberg and I coauthored a law review article entitled "Declaring the Death Penalty Unconstitutional," which appeared in* Harvard Law Review *83, no. 8 (1970), 1773–1819.*

# THIRTY-THREE

## HOW IT ALL BEGAN
### *The Death Penalty in the Court*

THE FIRST SUBSTANTIVE CONVERSATION I EVER HAD WITH Justice William Brennan was about the death penalty. I had just arrived at the Supreme Court as a clerk to Justice Arthur J. Goldberg in the late summer of 1963. My initial assignment was to write a memorandum on the possible unconstitutionality of the death penalty. I set to work but found no suggestion in the case law that any court had ever considered the death penalty to be of questionable constitutionality. Just five years earlier, Chief Justice Earl Warren had written in *Trop v. Dulles* (1958) that "whatever the arguments may be against capital punishment, both on moral grounds and in terms of accomplishing the purposes of punishment — and they are forceful — the death penalty has been employed throughout our history, and, in a day when it is still widely accepted it cannot be said to violate the constitutional concept of cruelty."

I duly reported this to Justice Goldberg, suggesting that if even the liberal chief justice believed that the death penalty was constitutional, what chance did he have of getting a serious hearing for his view that the cruel and unusual punishment clause should now be construed to prohibit the imposition of capital punishment? Justice Goldberg asked me to talk to Justice Brennan and see what his views were. Unless Justice Brennan agreed to join, the entire project would be scuttled, since Justice Goldberg, the Court's rookie, did not want to "be out there alone," against the chief justice and the rest of the Court.

I had previously met Justice Brennan several times over the preceding few years, since his son, Bill, was my classmate and moot-court partner at Yale Law School. I had also had lunch several times with the justice and his friend Judge David Bazelon, for whom I had clerked the previous year. But none of our discussions had been substantive, and I nervously anticipated the task of discussing an important issue with one of my judicial heroes.

I brought a rough draft of the memorandum I was working on to the meeting, but Justice Brennan did not want to look at it then. He asked me to describe the results of my research to him, promising to read the memorandum later. I stated the nascent constitutional case against the death penalty as best I could. I told him that *Weems v. United States* could be read as recognizing the following tests for whether punishment was "cruel and unusual": (1) giving full weight to reasonable legislative findings, a punishment is cruel and unusual if a less severe one can as effectively achieve the permissible ends of punishment (that is, deterrence, isolation, rehabilitation, or whatever the contemporary society considers the permissible objectives of punishment); (2) regardless of its effectiveness in achieving the permissible ends of punishment, a punishment is cruel and unusual if it offends the contemporary sense of decency (for example, torture); (3) regardless of its effectiveness in achieving the permissible ends of punishment, a punishment is cruel and unusual if the evil it produces is disproportionally higher than the harm it seeks to prevent (for example, the death penalty for economic crimes).

In addition to these abstract formulations, I also told Justice Brennan that our research had disclosed a widespread pattern of unequal application of the death penalty on racial grounds. I cited national prison statistics showing that between 1937 and 1951, 233 blacks were executed for rape in the United States, while only 26 whites were executed for that crime.

Justice Brennan encouraged me to continue my research, without making any promise that he would join any action by Justice Goldberg. Several weeks later, Justice Goldberg told me that Justice Brennan had agreed to join a short dissent from the denial of certiorari in *Rudolph v. Alabama* (1963) — a case involving imposition of the death penalty on a black man who was convicted of raping a white woman. Justice William O. Douglas signed on as well. The dissenters invited the bar to address the following questions, which they deemed "relevant and worthy of argument and consideration":

1. In light of the trend both in the country and throughout the world against punishing rape by death, does the imposition of the death penalty by those States which retain it for rape violate "evolving standards of decency that mark the progress of [our] maturing society," or "standards of decency more or less universally accepted"?

2. Is the taking of human life to protect a value other than human life consistent with the constitutional proscription against "punishments which by their excessive . . . severity are greatly disproportional to the offenses charged"?

3. Can the permissible aims of punishment (e.g., deterrence, isolation, rehabilitation) be achieved as effectively by punishing rape less severely than by death (e.g., by life imprisonment); if so, does the imposition of the death penalty for rape constitute "unnecessary cruelty"?

As soon as the dissent was published, there was an immediate reaction. Conservative journalists had a field day lambasting the very notion that a court could strike down as unconstitutional a long-standing punishment that is explicitly referred to in the Constitution. One extreme criticism appeared in the *New Hampshire Union Ledger* under the banner headline "U.S. Supreme Court Trio Encourages Rape":

> In a decision handed down last week three U.S. Supreme Court justices, Goldberg, Brennan, Douglas, raised the question of whether it was proper to condemn a man to death for the crime of rape if there has been no endangering of the life of the victim. This incredible opinion, of course, can serve only to encourage would-be rapists. These fiends, freed from the fear of the death penalty for their foul deed, . . . will be inclined to take a chance.
>
> Thus, not content with forbidding our schoolchildren to pray in school, not content with banishing Bible reading from our schools, and not content letting every type of filthy book be published, at least three members of the Supreme Court are now out to encourage rape.

Several state courts went out of their way to announce their rejection of the principal inherent in the dissenting opinion. This is what the Georgia Supreme Court said:

With all due respect to the dissenting Justices we would question the judicial right of any American judge to construe the American Constitution contrary to its apparent meaning, the American history of the clause, and its construction by American courts, simply because the numerous nations and States have abandoned capital punishment for rape. First we believe the history of no nation will show the high values of woman's virtue and purity that America has shown. We would regret to see the day when this freedom loving country would lower our respect for womanhood or lessen her legal protection for no better reason than that many or even all other countries have done so. She is entitled to every legal protection of her body, her decency, her purity and good name.

There was scholarly criticism as well. In the *Harvard Law Review*, Professor Herbert Packer of Stanford wrote:

In an interesting development, some members of the Supreme Court appear disposed to employ [recent constructions of the "cruel and unusual punishments" clause] to regulate the appropriate relation between crime and punishment. Three justices recently noted in their dissent from a denial of certiorari in terms that invite speculation about the role of constitutional adjudication in solving the age-old problem of whether and how the punishment may be made to fit the crime. . . . [However,] sympathy with the legislative goal of limiting or abolishing the death penalty should not be allowed to obscure the difficulties of taking a judicial step toward that goal on the theory outlined by Justice Goldberg in [*Rudolph v. Alabama*]. . . . If one may venture a guess, what Justice Goldberg may really be troubled about is not the death penalty for rape but the death penalty. The problem may not be one of proportionality but of mode of punishment, the problem that concerned the framers of the eighth amendment and to which its provisions still seem most relevant. The Supreme Court is obviously not about to declare that the death penalty *simpliciter* is so cruel and unusual as to be constitutionally intolerable. Other social forces will have to work us closer than we are now to the point at which a judicial *coup de grace* becomes more than mere fiat. Meanwhile, there may well be legitimate devices for judicial control of the administration of the death penalty. The burden of this Comment is simply that the device proposed by Justice Goldberg is not one of them.

These were the short-term reactions. Far more important, however, was the long-term reaction of the bar, especially the American Civil

Liberties Union and the NAACP, which combined forces to establish a death-penalty litigation project designed to take up the challenge of the dissenting opinion in *Rudolph*. The history of this project has been recounted brilliantly by Professor Michael Meltsner in his book *Cruel and Unusual*, and I could not possibly improve upon it here. But the results achieved were dramatic. Meltsner and the other members of the Legal Defense Fund, a group that included a number of talented and committed lawyers, litigated hundreds of cases on behalf of defendants sentenced to death and, in many of these cases, succeeded in holding the executioner at bay until the Supreme Court was ready to consider the constitutionality of the death penalty. The strategy was simple in outline: The Supreme Court should not be allowed the luxury of deciding the issue of capital punishment as an abstraction; instead, it must be confronted with the concrete responsibility of determining the immediate fates of many hundreds of condemned persons at the same time. In this way, the Court could not evade the issue, or lightly refuse to decide it if the Court's refusal would result in the specter of mass executions of hundreds of convicts. However, the Court could decline to decide the ultimate issue — the constitutionality of capital punishment — if in doing so it could find some other way of keeping alive those on death row. And the litigants always provided the Court with this other way — a narrower issue, usually in the form of an irregularity in the procedure by which the death penalty was imposed or administered. Thus in the late 1960s the Supreme Court decided a number of cases involving the administration of the death penalty; in each of these cases the Court declined to consider the ultimate issue, but it always ruled in favor of the doomed, thereby sparing their lives — at least for the moment. With the passage of each year, the number of those on death row increased and the stakes grew higher and higher.

Then in 1971 the Court took its first turn toward the noose: In *McGautha v. California*, it held that a condemned person's constitutional rights were not violated "by permitting the jury to impose the death penalty without any governing standards" or by permitting the imposition of the death penalty in "the same proceeding and verdict as determined the issue of guilt." At that point it looked like the string might have been played out: there were no more "narrow" procedural grounds. The Court would have to confront the ultimate issue. But it was not the same Court that had been sitting when the strategy was originally devised; there were four new Nixon appointees, and it was clear that at least some of them believed the death penalty to be constitutional. The umpires — if not the rules — had been changed after the strategy of the game had been worked out and irretrievably put into action. Now there was no pulling back.

The drama intensified. The Court let it be known that finally it was ready to decide the ultimate issue. Knowledgeable lawyers — counting noses on the Court — were predicting that the death penalty would be sustained. Some thought that it might be struck down for rape but sustained for murder. Some predicted that the Court would once again find — or contrive — a reason for avoiding the ultimate issue. A few, of optimistic bent, kept the faith and expressed the belief that the Court — even this Court — would simply not send hundreds to their death.

And then a major and unanticipated break. The California Supreme Court — perhaps the most influential state court in the nation — ruled that *its* constitution (which had substantially similar wordings as the federal Constitution) forbade the death penalty. Then, on the last day of the United States Supreme Court's 1971 term, the decision was rendered: the death penalty, as administered in this country, was unconstitutional.

When the Court decided *Furman v. Georgia* in 1972, there were six hundred condemned prisoners awaiting execution on America's death rows. The Court ruled, in a five-to-four decision, that the death penalty, as implemented in the United States, was unconstitutional because of the randomness of its application. Never in the history of the courts had a single decision resulted in the saving of so many lives. Never in the history of the American judiciary had so many laws — both state and federal — been struck down with one judicial pronouncement. And never before had so important a social change been accomplished by the courts in so short a period of time.

In *Furman*, each of the five justices voting for reversal of the death sentence wrote separately, including Justice Brennan, who for the first time articulated his view that the imposition of the death penalty, under all circumstances, was per se unconstitutional. According to one commentator, Justice Brennan reached this conclusion using a mixture of "precedent, legal reasoning, moral imperatives, and overall — hope — that the power of the Court could improve a society that appeared ambivalent about death as a punishment." Justice Brennan begins his attack on the death penalty in *Furman* by discussing the history surrounding the adoption of the Eighth Amendment, and by concluding that it is impossible to determine "exactly what the Framers thought 'cruel and unusual punishments' were." Given this ambiguity, Justice Brennan deemed it the Court's responsibility to interpret and apply this portion of the Eighth Amendment:

> The very purpose of a Bill of Rights was to withdraw certain subjects from the vicissitudes of political controversy, to place them beyond the reach of majorities and officials and to establish them as legal principles to be applied by the courts.

Were the Court to abdicate this responsibility, by blindly accepting the unreviewability of the power of the legislative branch to prescribe punishments for crimes, Justice Brennan warned that the "Cruel and Unusual Punishments Clause would become, in short, 'little more than good advice.'"

Having decided that the courts must interpret the open-ended language of the clause, Justice Brennan reasoned that it "must draw its meaning from the evolving standards of decency that mark the progress of a maturing society." He then elaborated on this idea.

> At bottom, then, the Cruel and Unusual Punishments Clause prohibits the infliction of uncivilized and inhuman punishments. The State, even as it punishes, must treat its members with respect for their intrinsic worth as human beings. A punishment is "cruel and unusual," therefore, if it does not comport with human dignity.

In an effort to provide more specific content to the meaning of the phrase "does not comport with human dignity," Justice Brennan offered the following test:

> The test, then, will ordinarily be a cumulative one: If a punishment is unusually severe, if there is a strong probability that it is inflicted arbitrarily, if it is substantially rejected by contemporary society, and if there is no reason to believe that it serves any penal purpose more effectively than some less severe punishment, then the continued infliction of the punishment violates the command of the Clause that the State may not inflict inhuman and uncivilized punishments upon those convicted of crimes.

Justice Brennan proceeded to analyze the death penalty under this paradigm, after which he concluded:

> In sum, the punishment of death is inconsistent with all four principles: Death is an unusually severe and degrading punishment; there is a strong probability that it is inflicted arbitrarily; its rejection by contemporary society is virtually total; and there is no reason to believe that it serves any penal purpose more effectively than the less severe punishment of imprisonment. The function of these principles is to enable a court to determine whether a punishment comports with human dignity. Death, quite simply, does not.

Justice Brennan declared that the death penalty is surely the most severe degrading punishment that society can inflict upon an individual, as evidenced by the following facts: there is a national debate over the death penalty, where there is no such debate over other forms of punishment; the death penalty has been continually restricted by the states, and some have even abolished it; death is reserved for only the most heinous crimes; cases in which the death penalty is available are treated differently by lawyers, judges, and state legislatures; the death penalty is unique in its finality and enormity; and finally, the death penalty, unlike all other punishments, ensures that the executed person "has lost the right to have rights."

On the second principle, the issue of arbitrariness, Justice Brennan began his argument with the observation that the death penalty is actually imposed very infrequently in modern society, with the number decreasing every year since 1930, even though the population of the United States and the number of capital crimes committed by its citizens have been growing steadily. Based on the fact that in a country of more than 200 million people, fewer than fifty people per year were being executed, Justice Brennan argued that we should draw strong inference of arbitrariness in the application of the death penalty. In response to the argument that these statistics can be explained by the fact that only the most "extreme" cases receive the death penalty, Justice Brennan observed that there is no logical distinction based in fact that separates those individuals who are condemned to die from those who are sentenced to life imprisonment. Justice Brennan also observed that the Court's prior decision in *McGautha v. California*, which rejected a defendant's claim that due process had been violated, since the jury that condemned him was permitted to make that decision wholly unguided by standards governing the choice, serves to undercut the argument that the criminal justice system can systematically and non-arbitrarily separate the most "extreme" cases from others.

Justice Brennan then turned to the third principle, whether a punishment has been rejected by contemporary society, and concluded that the death penalty had been almost totally rejected, both in the United States and in other countries. As circumstantial evidence of this conclusion, Justice Brennan noted that our society has gradually moved toward less inhumane methods of execution, from firing squads and hanging to lethal gas and "more humane" electrocutions, and that public executions, once thought to enhance deterrence, have been completely done away with. In addition, the class of crimes for which the death penalty is actually being imposed is constantly shrinking; at the time Justice Brennan wrote his dissenting opinion in *Furman*, nine states had abolished the death penalty altogether; many others had not employed the punishment in many years; and the highest court of one state, California, had already declared that punishment unconstitutional under that state's counterpart of the Eighth Amendment.

The final principle that Brennan used to disqualify the death penalty from the range of possible punishments authorized by the Eighth Amendment was the notion that a punishment may not be excessive in view of the purposes for which it was inflicted. The primary argument that Justice Brennan was required to answer is that execution deters murder and certain other heinous crimes better than life imprisonment. Justice Brennan first denied that the death penalty provides specific deterrence any better than life imprisonment; techniques of isolation, as well as focusing on the effective administration of the state's parole laws, can eliminate or minimize the danger of future crimes while the individual is confined. With respect to claims of increased general deterrence, Justice Brennan denied the possibility that there exists a significant number of persons in society who would commit a capital crime knowing that the punishment is long-term, perhaps even life, imprisonment but who would not commit the crime knowing that the punishment is death. In addition, although Justice Brennan admitted that the statistical evidence available in 1972 was inconclusive with respect to the deterrent value of the death penalty as opposed to life imprisonment, he buttressed his argument by observing that to a person contemplating a murder or rape, the risk of being executed, taking into account the method under which the death penalty was currently administered, was remote and improbable, whereas the risk of long-term imprisonment was near and great. Given these incentives, Justice Brennan concluded that there was simply no reason to believe, or any hard, statistical evidence to support, the claim that the death penalty provides greater deterrence, either general or specific, than does life imprisonment.

Aside from deterrence, Justice Brennan also rejected the suggestion that the death penalty serves the retributive goal of punishment any better than life imprisonment. First of all, Justice Brennan denied that a sentence of death, since it is inflicted so rarely in the United States relative to the number of capital crimes committed, serves either to prevent private enforcement of the laws, to inculcate a respect for the laws in our citizens, or to satisfy some sense of just desert for these criminals better than life imprisonment; in fact, he took the position that executing so few people actually undermines each of these values that compose the retributive goal of punishment. Justice Brennan summed up his position in the following passage:

> When this country was founded, memories of the Stuart horrors were fresh, and severe corporal punishments were common. Death was not then a unique punishment. The practice of punishing criminals by death, moreover, was widespread and by and large acceptable to society. Indeed, without developed prison systems, there was frequently no workable alternative. Since that time successive restrictions, imposed against the background of continuing moral controversy, have drastically curtailed the use of this punishment. Today death is a uniquely severe punishment. When examined by the principles applicable under the Cruel and Unusual Punishments Clause, death stands condemned as fatally offensive to human dignity. The punishment of death is therefore "cruel and unusual," and the States may no longer inflict it as a punishment for crimes. Rather than kill an arbitrary handful of criminals each year, the States will confine them to prison. "The State thereby suffers nothing and loses no power. The purpose of punishment is fulfilled, crime is repressed by penalties of just, not tormenting, severity, its repetition is prevented, and hope is given for the reformation of the criminal."

The moratorium on the imposition of the death penalty that had been achieved in *Furman* turned out to be short-lived. In 1976 a majority in *Gregg v. Georgia* reinstated the death penalty for murder on the ground that adequate procedural safeguards had been adopted that made the imposition of the death penalty no longer in violation of the Eighth Amendment. In a dissenting opinion coauthored by Justice Thurgood Marshall, Justice Brennan attacked the majority's holding.

The fatal constitutional infirmity in the punishment of death, they observed, is that it treats "members of the human race as non-humans, as objects to be toyed with and discarded. [It is] thus inconsistent with the fundamental premise of the Clause that even the vilest criminal remains a human being possessed of common human dignity." As such it is a penalty that "subjects the individual to a fate forbidden by the principle of civilized treatment guaranteed by the Clause." Justice of this kind is obviously no less shocking than the crime itself, and the new "official" murder, far from offering redress for the offense committed against society, adds instead a second defilement to the first.

In the cases following *Gregg v. Georgia*, Justice Brennan continued to adhere to his position that the death penalty is per se unconstitutional, offering additional arguments and statistical evidence to support this claim. For example, in his dissenting opinion in *McClesky v. Kemp* (1987), Justice Brennan refuted the Court's claim that Georgia and other states have enacted appropriate safeguards to ensure fair determinations in the special context of capital punishment by citing a study that suggests that taking into account some 230 nonracial factors that might legitimately influence a sentence, the jury more likely than not would have spared McClesky's life had his victim been black instead of white. In addition, Justice Brennan cited statistics indicating that in Georgia, the rate of capital sentencing in a white-victim case is 120 percent greater than the rate in a black-victim case. These statistics provide support for Justice Brennan's arguments about the probability of arbitrary imposition of the death penalty that he first promulgated in *Furman;* however, rather than confirming his claim that the death penalty is *arbitrarily* imposed — that is, not imposed in only "extreme" cases — these statistics indicate that the death penalty is being systematically imposed against the killers of white victims more than the killers of blacks.

In the following passage from *McClesky*, Justice Brennan used these statistics to draw an analogy about the imposition of the death penalty to the burden of proof:

In determining the guilt of a defendant, a State must prove its case beyond a reasonable doubt. That is, we refuse to convict if the chance of error is simply less likely than not. Surely, we should not be willing to take a person's life if the chance that his death sentence was irrationally imposed is more likely than not. In light of the gravity of the interest at stake, petitioner's statistics on their face are a powerful demonstration of the type of risk that our Eighth Amendment jurisprudence has consistently condemned.

In addition to the statistical evidence, Justice Brennan also noted that prosecutors in Georgia have limitless discretion to seek the death penalty and that Georgia provides no list of aggravating and mitigating factors, or any standard for balancing them against one another, in making the sentencing determination. Both of these facts, Justice Brennan asserted, raise the specter of arbitrary enforcement of the death penalty and suggest reasons why the statistical evidence should be regarded as valid. In the concluding paragraph of his dissent in *McClesky*, Justice Brennan made the following haunting statement:

It is tempting to pretend that minorities on death row share a fate in no way connected to our own, that our treatment of them sounds no echoes beyond the chambers in which they die. Such an illusion is ultimately corrosive, for the reverberations of injustice are not so easily confined. "The destinies of two races in this country are indissolubly linked together," and the way in which we choose those who will die reveals the depth of moral commitment among the living.

Only time will tell whether Justice Brennan's views — and those of Justice Goldberg — on the constitutionality of the death penalty will ultimately prevail, as have the views of other great dissenters in the past. They surely will continue to prick the conscience of a nation that today seems bent on increasing the number of executions. Whatever the outcome of this great debate, Justice Brennan should be credited with having helped to save the lives of more Americans who have been condemned to die than any other judge in our history.

# THIRTY-FOUR

# THE VALUE OF A LIFE —
# AND A DEATH

*One of the most disturbing aspects of the death penalty is its unequal application. The killer of a white person is far more likely to receive the death penalty than the killer of a black person. This sort of sentencing disparity — based on the perceived "value" of the victim — is pervasive in our criminal justice system. I wrote about this in 1989.*

OUR CONSTITUTION FORBIDS ANY STATE FROM DENYING its citizens "the equal protection of the law." But a Texas judge recently denied gay citizens precisely the protection to which they were entitled. In sentencing the murderer of two gay men to a "lenient" punishment — by Texas standards — of thirty years, Judge Jack Hampton offered the following explanation: "I put prostitutes and gays at about the same level and I'd be hard put to give somebody life for killing a prostitute." Thus in one fell swoop, Judge Hampton denied both gays and prostitutes the equal protection of his law.

That kind of attitude is widespread throughout the criminal justice system. The degree of justice one receives depends on how much one is valued by the judge, jury, police, and even defense attorney. "Valuable" citizens are better protected by our laws. The police respond more quickly to burglary calls from expensive neighborhoods than to calls from the projects. When a prominent citizen is murdered or mugged, the prosecutorial energy devoted to the case is far greater than if an ordinary or "marginal" person is attacked.

Nowhere is the disparity greater than in criminal sentencing. If an African-American man murders a white man, he is ten times more likely to receive the death penalty in some states than if a white man murders an African American. This inequity is due in part to the race of the murderer, but according to studies, the race of the murdered person plays an even greater role in life-or-death sentencing decisions. In cases involving the killing of Asian Americans and Hispanic Americans, a similar pattern of "leniency" for their white murderers has been displayed. Nor is this unequal protection of the law in capital sentencing limited to race alone. It reflects a far more general problem of inequality throughout our legal — and indeed our political — system.

The more valued the murder victim is by the particular judge or jury, the harsher will be the sentence meted out to his or her murderer. Race is one way by which our racist society measures worth. All things being equal, a predominantly white jury will value white life more than African-American or other racial-minority life. Many heterosexual judges and jurors will value heterosexual life more highly than homosexual life.

Judge Jack Hampton's devaluation of the lives of gays and prostitutes is not merely an isolated outburst by an obnoxious bigot in black robes. He simply made the mistake of publicly articulating — and defending — what many other judges and juries believe and do in the privacy of their secret deliberations.

The facts giving rise to Judge Hampton's sentence lend some support to the claims by gay rights advocates that under "Hampton's Law," there would be "open season" on gays. Apparently the eighteen-year-old murderer and a group of his friends set out to murder — or at the very least harass — homosexuals. They pretended they were themselves gay and went to an area of Dallas frequented by gay men. The murderer was armed. When two young gay men drove up and invited them into their car, the murderer and a friend got in. The foursome drove to a secluded area, whereupon the murderer drew his pistol and shot the two gay men in cold blood. One died on the spot; the other died a few days later. It was the equivalent of the kind of racial lynchings so prevalent in the South during the early part of the century.

But instead of treating it as a lynching, the judge put the victims on trial, declaring that they would not have been killed "if they hadn't been cruising the streets picking up teenage boys." He rejected the prosecution's recommendation of a life sentence as too harsh and instead sentenced the murderer to a term that will make him eligible for parole in seven years. He then explained his bias against the victims to a local newspaper: "I don't care much for queers cruising the streets. I've got a teenage boy." He showed far more sympathy for the cold-blooded killer because he attended college and was reared in a good home with a father who is a police officer.

Perhaps the sentence itself was appropriate, considering the fact that the defendant was a first offender. But the reason offered by Judge Hampton had more to do with lack of sympathy for the victims than with compassion for the perpetrator. (Indeed, Judge Hampton is not known for his compassion toward convicted criminals in general.)

The message sent by Judge Hampton and others of his ilk is loud and clear: there is a different law for those victims the judge cares for than for those he doesn't "care for." The implications of this double standard of unequal protection are frightening; it means that gay Americans — and others in disfavor in certain parts of the country — cannot rely on the full and equal protection of the law. It means that *their* lives are worth something less than — and that their deaths are not as great a loss as — *ours* would be. Once this nation begins to accept the concept of second-class citizenship for gays or anyone else, our constitutional guarantee of equal protection is greatly endangered for every American. We are a nation of minorities, and for every minority there is a judge or juror sitting in wait to spew forth the kind of bigotry expressed by Judge Hampton against gays.

Although Judge Hampton's actions are being investigated, the executive director of the Texas Commission on Judicial Conduct has found no violation of any rules. As far as Judge Hampton's own reaction: "Just spell my name right. If it makes anyone mad, they'll forget it by 1990" — the year he faces reelection. I have more faith in the good people of Dallas.

———————————

*Judge Hampton was reelected.*

———————————

# THIRTY-FIVE

# THE RIGHT TO CHOOSE HOW AND WHEN TO END ONE'S LIFE

---

*"Right to life" is asserted by those who would criminalize assisted suicide and abortion. Some "right-to-lifers" who favor the death penalty talk about "the right of innocent life." In 1989 I wrote about the right to choose death over life in the context of an intriguing case of assisted suicide.*

---

IT WAS COMPARABLE TO "A SERIALIZED GANG MURDER," according to the director of the International Anti-Euthanasia Task Force. Not to be outdone, conservative commentator and former White House aide Patrick Buchanan likened it to acts committed by the Nazis under Adolf Hitler.

What horrible deed warranted these comparisons? Mass murder? A gangland hit? A terrorist attack? No. At issue was the assisted suicide of a forty-three-year-old woman who, dying of a fast-spreading and painful form of cancer, decided to pick the time and circumstances of her death rather than leave it to the vagaries of her illness.

The story is the kind of nightmare every family fears. A routine medical checkup, a suspicious finding, further tests — and then the dreaded news: cancer. Every possible treatment and therapy is tried, but the cancer has spread throughout the body, even to her brain. It is hopeless, and death will not be painless and dignified. It will involve convulsions, vomiting blood, and indescribable pain.

Most families confronting the inevitability of a painful death simply let nature take its inexorable course. But a growing number of victims of incurable diseases are deciding to take control over their own dying. Patricia Rosier was one such cancer victim, whose decision to end her life with her husband's assistance was compared to serialized gang murder and Nazi atrocities.

Although the media characterized her death as a "mercy killing," it is more aptly described as a "mercy suicide," because *she* made the decision to end her life, not her family or doctors. We don't even have a technical term for this growing phenomenon — a term akin to the rather cumbersome *euthanasia*, which is defined as "the act . . . of painlessly putting to death persons suffering from incurable conditions or diseases." In the absence of a pronounceable Greek term — *heosthanasia* will never catch on — I will stick to *mercy suicide*.

A mercy suicide, when committed by an adult of sound mind, is not a crime. In some religions it may be a sin to play God by hastening death even by minutes or hours. Under some philosophies, it may be morally wrong to deny oneself a few extra days of painful life. But regardless of philosophy or religion, no civilized society today would regard a terminal patient who attempted suicide as a criminal.

Mercy killing — the taking of the life of another person who is suffering and usually no longer sentient — is qualitatively different from mercy suicide in the eyes of the law. Indeed, it is fair to say that the eyes of the law are blind to the very notion of mercy killing. The letter of the law simply does not recognize mercy as a defense to murder: it regards all deliberate killing as murder, whether done in the name of love or hate. Although in practice most prosecutors close their eyes to such cases, vindictive or opportunistic ones occasionally will try to make a test case out of a mercy killing that has come to their attention.

The line between mercy suicide and mercy killing is not always crystal clear. Sometimes it is simply a function of timing or happenstance. When what was originally intended as an unassisted mercy suicide cannot be completed without the help of others, it becomes, in the eyes of a prosecutor, a criminal mercy killing.

That is essentially the Rosiers' story. What began as a clear case of mercy suicide by Patricia Rosier ended up with the trial of her husband, Peter, for first-degree murder, conspiracy to murder, and attempted murder.

The basic facts were not in dispute, but the legal consequences of those facts gave rise to one of the most contentious and emotional cases in Florida legal history.

Peter and Patricia met when they were thirteen and married at twenty-one, during his first year of medical school in New York. Peter became a doctor specializing in pathology and was eventually chairman of the pathology department at the local hospital in Fort Myers, Florida.

The two had been married for more than twenty years when Patricia was diagnosed as having cancer. They were a handsome couple — she a beautiful blonde, he with rugged good looks and boundless energy. They drove his-and-hers Rolls Royces, traveled to South America to hunt butterflies, and played a mean game of tennis. They lived in an expensive home on well-manicured grounds in an exclusive neighborhood of Fort Myers. Their living room was decorated with what the local newspaper described as "semi-nude photographs of Pat taken by a professional photographer." They had two teenagers.

Like other couples living in the fast lane of a slow town, the Rosiers' lives were not without controversy. Their somewhat ostentatious lifestyle generated resentment and gossip among some neighbors and colleagues. When Peter once strayed from his otherwise faithful devotion to Patricia — he had a brief affair with a hospital secretary several years before Patricia's illness — there was talk of divorce. But Peter ended the liaison and the couple lived happily — until that terrible spring day in 1985 when a chest X ray, part of a routine medical checkup, disclosed a suspicious shadow on Patricia's lung. Three days later a biopsy was performed at her husband's hospital. He was the pathologist in charge, and as soon as he looked at the slide, he knew that it was lung cancer. He decided to give up his practice to devote himself to caring for his wife and children.

The couple tried everything — surgery, chemotherapy, radiation. Nothing worked. Within months, four brain tumors were discovered, and there were no more treatment options. Patricia's doctors told her that if she terminated all treatment, she would die within hours, days, or — at most — weeks.

The pain was beginning to be unbearable. The vomiting of blood and pus was persistent. But Patricia remained emotionally strong and mentally rational. She even appeared on television to lend strength to other cancer patients undergoing debilitating therapies. She discussed her situation with friends and continued to be a loving mother and wife.

Then she made the fateful decision to pick the time and circumstances of her death, not wanting to leave it to the unpredictable clock of the cancer. When she told her husband of her decision, Peter said that he would end his life with her. They had lived their entire lives together and would face death together. When the children learned of this, they pleaded with their father not to take his life. Losing both mother and father would be too much for them. Peter relented. No one tried to talk Patricia out of her decision to commit suicide, for two reasons: first, she had made up her mind; second, it wasn't really suicide, since her act would only hasten her imminent and painful demise.

Patricia selected the day and time of her death and planned a formal farewell dinner for her family.

Among those in attendance at the dinner, in addition to her husband and children, were her stepfather and her two half brothers. Patricia had been alienated from her stepfather for many years, but past tensions between the two were forgotten, at least for the moment.

There was wine and there were toasts. Patricia wore an elegant dress and had her nails polished. Despite her pain, she wanted to look beautiful for her last evening, wanted to leave her family with glowing memories. After dinner they watched a video of the movie *Harold and Maude*, about an elderly woman who commits suicide to prevent herself from "growing old." When it was over, Peter Rosier and his wife retired to the bedroom, drank some more wine, and made love. After bidding farewell to family members, Patricia Rosier took twenty pills that she had selected for her suicide. One relative recalled that she downed them like "jelly beans," so anxious was she to end her suffering. She quickly fell into a coma. She expected never to awake — to drift into a quiet and dignified death.

But something went wrong. The coma began to lighten. She had obviously taken too few pills to induce death. Would she awaken or remain comatose? Would there be brain damage? Pain? Emotional turmoil? No one could know. All Peter knew was that his wife did not want to awaken. She had determined to die. What was his obligation to his comatose wife? Would he be breaking his final promise to her if he did not assist her in achieving her goal: a painless and dignified death? He could not ask her advice. The decision was his to make, but it was her decision — she had already made it and acted on it, albeit incompletely.

"I administered something to her to terminate her life," Peter Rosier recalls. That something was morphine, a painkiller that is lethal in sufficient dosage. But the morphine was insufficient, and Patricia continued to breathe. While Peter was outside the house, pacing and crying, Patricia's stepfather decided to end her life by suffocating her. He placed his hands over her nose and mouth. In his own words, "She was alive before I took my hands and put them over her face. She was dead when I removed my hands."

Peter didn't learn at the time what had happened inside the bedroom. Her stepfather and brothers simply informed him that Patricia was dead.

For about a year, the circumstances surrounding Patricia's death remained a family secret. Then Peter decided to write a book about his late wife's courage. After completing a first draft, Peter gave an interview to a local television reporter in which he related what he believed were the circumstances of his wife's death, still unaware that her stepfather had administered the coup de grâce.

As soon as the interview was aired, the local prosecutor began an investigation. As part of the information-gathering process, the authorities wanted to interview Patricia's stepfather. Through his lawyer, he demanded total immunity from prosecution for himself and his sons as a condition of being interviewed. That should have tipped off the authorities that he had something to hide. But instead of asking for a "proffer" — a truthful outline of the facts — before deciding whether to grant immunity, the prosecutor acceded.

With blanket immunity, the stepfather disclosed for the first time that he had actually caused Patricia's death by suffocation. The prosecutors were dumbfounded. They had committed a blunder feared by every law-enforcement official: they gave the wrong person immunity. But they could not back out of their deal. The only possible target was Peter Rosier, and the prosecution's star witness, Patricia's stepfather, had no love for his late stepdaughter's husband.

Despite the certainty that Peter had not actually killed his wife, and despite the certainty that she wanted to take her own life, the prosecutor treated the loving husband as if he were indeed the triggerman in a serialized gang murder. Peter Rosier was indicted on charges of first-degree murder and conspiracy to murder. The prosecution's theory was that the stepfather's ultimate act was merely the final stage in a family conspiracy of which Peter Rosier was the architect and chief participant.

Suddenly Peter Rosier found himself in jail, facing a possible death sentence in a state that has one of the highest execution rates in the country. He called me from prison on the day of his arrest and asked me to help him. I worked with his local lawyer to get him out on bail and to formulate the legal strategy used in his trial. In the event of his conviction, I was to be his appellate lawyer.

It was a groundbreaking case. Whatever verdict the jury or court would reach in this case would *become* the precedent for cases of this kind.

The defense was relatively straightforward. This was a mercy suicide, not a mercy killing. It was the will of Mrs. Rosier, not that of Dr. Rosier, that led to her death. Neither did her husband wish her to die nor did he kill her. The cancer caused her death, in the sense that but for that terminal illness she would still be alive. She herself determined the time of her death. And the ultimate means of her death was selected and implemented by her stepfather without consultation with Dr. Rosier. If this was a mercy killing, it was carried out by Mrs. Rosier's stepfather, not her husband.

Notwithstanding this defense, the jury could easily have convicted Dr. Rosier of attempted murder on the basis of existing law. True, he did not initiate the dying process — that was done by Mrs. Rosier, who swallowed the pills by herself. True, he did not administer the coup de grâce — that was done by Mrs. Rosier's stepfather. But Dr. Rosier did acknowledge to a reporter, on videotape, that after his wife's initial coma began to lighten, he "administered something to her to terminate her life." This could be enough, under the strict letter of the law, to constitute an attempt to commit murder.

The jury had to be convinced, therefore, not to follow the strict letter of the law but, rather, to rule in the spirit of the law — to serve as the conscience of the community. The jurors had to be made to wonder what they would have done under such excruciating circumstances. And they had to be made to conclude that criminal law should not sit in judgment over loving family members who had to make a tragic choice between keeping a promise to a comatose loved one or abandoning her in a moment of crisis.

The trial was punctuated by heated exchanges and emotional outbursts. Peter Rosier cried when the evidence of his wife's suffering was introduced. His local trial lawyer, Stanley Rosenblatt of Miami, did an excellent job persuading the jury that the murder and attempted-murder statutes were put on the books not for loving husbands like Peter Rosier but for brutal killers like Charles Manson and Ted Bundy. He tried the case with emotion and empathy, inviting the jurors to put themselves in the unenviable situation Peter Rosier faced on that terrible night. The prosecutor, on the defensive for having given Patricia's stepfather immunity before he knew the facts, played the role of avenging angel. He demanded that the jurors simply apply the law to the facts and not distinguish among murders on the basis of motive.

The jury understood — even if the prosecutors and others did not — the differences between love and hate, between self-willed death and death imposed by others. After weeks of trial, it took the jury — at least two of whom had themselves executed living wills instructing doctors to pull the plug if they were terminally ill — only a few hours to acquit Peter Rosier of all criminal liability. It is clear that the prosecution lost all credibility by asking the jury to treat Dr. Rosier as if he were the functional equivalent of a gangland killer. Had the prosecution charged Dr. Rosier with assisting the suicide of another — which is a crime under Florida law — it might have had a better shot at a conviction. But by *overcharging* him with first-degree murder, it made it difficult for the jury to take its case as anything but a misguided vendetta.

Although jury verdicts have no formal precedent-setting effect, highly publicized jury acquittals such as this one have an impact on other juries throughout the country. Jurors often remember what other jurors did in similar cases, and this may give them the courage to do likewise. More important, politically motivated prosecutors follow jury verdicts the way arbitrageurs follow takeover rumors. One highly publicized acquittal may constitute a trend to a prosecutor anxious to avoid the embarrassment of a highly visible loss. An acquittal of the kind delivered in the Rosier case thus becomes a kind of self-fulfilling prophecy: the strong chance of an acquittal frightens prosecutors away from pursuing comparable cases.

The impact of the Rosier acquittal is even likely to transcend cases involving terminal cancer patients. There already have been reports of AIDS patients being helped with their suicides.

Inevitably, there will be more prosecutions, despite the Rosier acquittal. And in some of these cases, there will probably be greater doubt about whether the dead person truly wanted to be put out of his or her misery. It is possible, as opponents of mercy killing have argued, for there to be abuses. Sometimes family members and doctors are more anxious for the loved one's demise than is the loved one.

The potential for abuse will become even more troubling in light of medical advances. As sick people live out "technological lives" in which bodily functions are maintained by machines while the quality of life is sapped, there will be more and more terminal patients seeking to control their own dying. As Dan Callahan, an ethicist at the Hastings Center, a bioethical think tank, recently put it, "It is an increasing terror of medical progress. . . . People feel the only way they can regain self-control is to have available the possibility of suicide." As long as these patients retain the mental capacity to choose and leave unambiguous evidence of that choice, as Patricia Rosier did, there will be few problems beyond the occasional vindictive prosecutor.

But where the patient is insufficiently rational to make the choice, the law will have to devise rules to assure that the decision to terminate life is made out of love, not out of convenience or other less-noble motives.

As academics and ethicists publicly debate the theoretical pros and cons of legalizing mercy killing and mercy suicide, the reality is that a great many friends and relatives assist in suicides, and a great many doctors practice euthanasia. It is impossible to know the extent of such acts, since they are accomplished around the privacy of the deathbed. But in preparing for the defense of the Rosier case, I learned that they are far more widespread than might be suspected.

The prevalence of this practice leads some academics to call for its legalization and regulation, while others see it as an argument in favor of more-vigorous enforcement of existing laws prohibiting all mercy killing. Medical ethicist Arthur Caplan recently warned a standing-room-only audience of the American Public Health Association that giving doctors "a license to kill would seriously undermine the trust between patient and doctor." Sick people have enough to worry about without always having "in the back of their head" the fear that their doctor may be planning to end their suffering without asking them. This fear was exacerbated recently when an anonymous doctor wrote an article in a prominent medical journal boasting of how he decided to pull the plug on a patient he regarded as terminal.

There is no immediate likelihood that we will see the enactment of new laws legalizing or regulating the dying process in circumstances such as those the Rosiers faced. In the meantime, anyone who assists in a mercy suicide or participates in a mercy killing risks prosecution, conviction, and imprisonment. Peter Rosier's acquittal somewhat reduces those risks, but it does not eliminate them. The risks increase when there is no evidence that the dead person actively sought to end his or her life and are also probably more serious for doctors than for family members. And they also are surely greatest when the act is publicized, rather than handled discreetly.

The risks are lowest when there is taped or documentary evidence that it was the terminal patient's decision to end his or her life and that the decision was rational and unambiguous. A living will, executed well in advance of the actual decision, won't be nearly as helpful as a contemporaneous and unambiguous expression of intentions.

Mercy killing and mercy suicide are so fraught with emotion that our legal system will never be able to treat them in an entirely logical manner. They will continue to be practiced in the netherworld of dying without express legitimation by our legal system. There are inherent tensions between the need to assure that the precious gift of life is not taken too casually and the desirability of keeping government a decent distance from an individual's deathbed. In the Rosier case, the Florida prosecutors demonstrated that they could not distinguish between an act of love and an act of murder. Fortunately for Peter Rosier — and for others confronting similar tragedies — the jury understood that a loving husband who helps his pained wife die in dignity is not a criminal. But other juries could rule differently. An act of love that causes the death of another is still an act of civil disobedience fraught with danger of prosecution. It takes courage to confront death. It takes courage to challenge the law. Peter Rosier and his late wife were courageous people.

## PART VI

✻

# THE RIGHT TO A ZEALOUS AND ETHICAL LAWYER

THE ROLE OF THE ZEALOUS ADVOCATE HAS BEEN MISUN-derstood throughout history. "How can you represent someone like that?" is a question that has been asked of lawyers since the beginning of the legal profession. It is a question I am asked by many people, including even my mother. History's first recorded lawyer is the patriarch Abraham in the Book of Genesis, who argues on behalf of the sinners of Sodom. Like most lawyers who represent guilty clients, he lost his case. But in doing so, he established the important principle that authority must always be challenged and that every person facing the wrath of authority must be represented by a zealous advocate.

Lawyers are not particularly popular with the public, except in countries experiencing tyranny. Tyrants have long understood the cry of Dick the Butcher in Shakespeare's *Henry VI*, part 2, "The first thing we do, let's kill all the lawyers." That's precisely what Hitler, Stalin, Pol Pot, and Mao Tse-tung did to those lawyers whom they could not convert to their cause. In the essays that follow, I explore a number of issues relating to zealous and ethical representation.

# THIRTY-SIX

# UNEQUAL JUSTICE

*Following the disclosures that led to President Richard Nixon's resignation, the legal profession began to look at itself in the mirror. Professor Jerold Auerbach wrote a scathing critique of the organized bar,[1] which the* New York Times *asked me to review.*

"HOW IN GOD'S NAME COULD SO MANY LAWYERS GET involved in something like this?" asked John Dean about Watergate. In Jerold Auerbach's remarkable book *Unequal Justice*, about America's elite lawyers and their quest for power and profit, Auerbach — a Wellesley history professor and a former Fellow in Law and History at Harvard Law School — goes a long way toward explaining why lawyers have played such central roles in perpetuating so many injustices, ranging from racial and religious discrimination to McCarthyism to the denial of legal representation to the poor. This is not to deny that some lawyers have also played significant roles in helping to secure justice and equality, but that is a familiar story celebrated in Law Day speeches, at bar association banquets, and in the authorized histories of the bench and bar.

*Unequal Justice* is an unauthorized history of the legal "four hundred," compiled by an outsider and employing as its primary source the words of the lawyers themselves, spoken with pride in prior generations but anachronistically embarrassing to the modern ear. It reveals the hitherto unexplored dark side of the moon, which turns out to be much larger and uglier than the bright side that has been exposed to public view. Auerbach's basic theme is that for every Abraham Lincoln and Clarence Darrow produced by the bar, there have been several John Mitchells — and it is very likely that the Mitchells have been far more active in the American Bar Association than the Lincolns or Darrows.

Auerbach examines the development of the modern law firm during this century, but his major emphasis is on the social and religious bigotry of the elite bar, a bigotry that excluded all but a handful of blacks from the American Bar Association (ABA) and all but a few "white" Jews from prestigious Wall Street firms until quite recently. His point "is not that lawyers have been more prejudiced than other Americans. It is, instead, that bias in the legal profession has had particularly serious consequences in a society that depends so heavily upon the legal profession to implement the privilege of equal justice under law."

Auerbach relates how in 1912 the American Bar Association admitted three lawyers who, unbeknownst to the membership committee, were black. The executive committee immediately passed a resolution rescinding the admission under "the settled practice of the Association . . . to elect only white men as members." The membership saw the issue as "a question of keeping pure the Anglo-Saxon race." But a lawyerlike compromise was reached whereby the three duly elected black lawyers were permitted to retain their membership provided that all future applicants were required to identify themselves by race. Thirty years later the situation had not changed much: in 1939, when distinguished federal judge William Hastie, a black Harvard Law School graduate, was proposed for membership in the ABA, "a prominent civil liberties lawyer in the Association questioned the wisdom of pressing for his admission at that time."

The bar's attempt to limit the number of Jewish lawyers — especially those with Eastern European backgrounds — was somewhat more subtle. Leaders of the bar, including future chief justices Harlan Stone and William Taft, made no bones about their dislike of Jewish and other immigrant lawyers who, in Stone's words, "exhibit racial tendencies toward study by memorization" and "a mind almost Oriental in its fidelity to the minutiae of the subject without regard to any controlling rule or reason." Others complained at the influx of Eastern European immigrants "with little inherited sense of fairness, justice and honor as we understand them." Auerbach quotes Henry S. Drinker — who was chairman of the ABA Ethics Committee for many years and whose treatise on legal ethics is still among the most widely relied upon by bar associations — on the ethics of "Russian Jew boys who came up out of the gutter [and] were merely following the methods their fathers had been using in selling shoe strings and other merchandise."

The attempt to equate Jewish "racial" traits with unethical behavior reached its nadir when President Woodrow Wilson nominated Louis Brandeis to the Supreme Court. The leaders of the American Bar Association lined up solidly against the nomination. Six former association presidents, at the instigation of incumbent President Elihu Root, declared that Brandeis was "not a fit person to sit on the Court." Auerbach tells how former president and future chief justice Taft dipped his "pen in vitriol [dispatching] letter after letter of calumny to friends and family, berating Brandeis for his ethics, politics and his religion." Numerous local bar associations and individual elite lawyers alleged that Brandeis had a "defective standard of professional ethics." Brandeis's eventual confirmation only strengthened the resolve of the Anglo-Saxon legal establishment to preserve its hegemony. As James Beck, former solicitor general of the United States, wrote in 1922: "If the old American stock can be organized, we can still avert the threatened decay of constitutionalism in this country."

Not surprisingly, the tack taken by the elite lawyers was to increase the power of the American Bar Association to impose their own conception of legal ethics on all lawyers, practicing and prospective. This was far better designed to achieve the intended goal than an increase in educational requirement, which, as one bar association lawyer observed, might "keep our own possibly out." Accordingly, "character" committees sprang up throughout the country, charged with the function of screening prospective lawyers. It is not surprising that these committees, manned by the likes of Root, Drinker, and other lawyers with a distinct prejudice against immigrants, would disqualify a large percentage of "Russian Jew boys," blacks, and other ethnic undesirables.

Auerbach describes in detail the systematic and successful efforts of one state, Pennsylvania, to "cleanse" its bar; the number of Jewish applicants declined more than 20 percent after the establishment of screening mechanisms, and not a single black was admitted to practice between 1933 and 1943.

Those who made it past the character committees still had formidable obstacles to overcome. They had to align their professional, and all too often their personal and political, conduct with the ethical precepts that Drinker and others ordained to be *the* ethics of *the* bar. It is not surprising that lawyers who declared Brandeis's ethics to be "defective" and who adopted the ethics of men like Drinker and Root would turn out canons that did not make it an unethical practice for a law firm to discriminate on grounds of race, religion, or sex but did make it an unethical practice for an unknown lawyer to attempt to attract clients away from established firms by advertising or price-cutting. The contingent fee, the only mechanism whereby poor accident victims could sue large corporations, was frowned upon and closely regulated by an elite bar more concerned with protecting its corporate clients than with assuring just compensation for indigent victims.

Auerbach, the historian, is at his best in reconstructing the past bigotries of the bar. However, his analysis of the contemporary legal scene is flawed by his failure to recognize real changes that have, in fact, occurred during the past decade. Bar associations are far less monolithic than they once were. While they still represent some of the most reactionary elements of the legal profession, a younger and more diverse group of lawyers — including minority-group members and women — are beginning to have some voice in formulating policies. The District of Columbia Bar and the Association of the Bar of the City of New York — to mention two of the established legal associations most responsive to change — have taken considerable steps in the direction of promoting minority rights, consumer interests, and constitutional liberties.

In his zeal, Auerbach sometimes seems unwilling to give credit where credit is at least partially due: he views every liberalizing action taken by the established bar as designed to preserve its powers under "the stress of severe social turmoil"; and he interprets every refusal to embrace liberal trends as evidence of resurgent racism. But despite this weakness, *Unequal Justice* stands as a powerful and well-documented indictment of the elite bar's failure to live up to the trust that has been bestowed upon it by our system of justice.

Watergate revealed to the public that corruption and venality exist at every level of the legal profession; that they are not limited to Jewish, Italian, Irish, or black "street" lawyers, as the established bar would have had us believe; that they touch lawyers in the elite firms, lawyers in the Justice Department, and lawyers in the White House.

The American Bar Association's characteristic response to Watergate has been to require law schools to offer compulsory courses in legal ethics. Unfortunately, many such courses will begin and end with the official ethics of the American Bar Association. But if history has taught us anything, it is that the American Bar Association should no more have exclusive responsibility for the formulation of legal ethics than the American Medical Association should have for medical ethics. *Unequal Justice* reminds us that — at bottom — the American Bar Association is a lobby group for a particularly influential segment of an enormously powerful profession, that its primary goal is to maximize the prerogatives and profits of its members and their clients. The ABA is neither a government agency nor the authorized representative of the legal profession. It is a voluntary organization that has historically excluded large segments of the best and most honorable lawyers. Even today — although it no longer discriminates on grounds of race, religion, or sex — a considerable number of lawyers, including some of the very best, have chosen not to be counted among its membership.

Auerbach's review of the failings of the elite bar during this century suggests that reform will not come by having law schools preach the ethics of the American Bar Association but, rather, by restructuring the legal profession so that its ethics no longer remain the nearly exclusive preserve of a lobby group whose history is replete with bigotry, injustice, and the expansion of professional prerogatives at the expense of the citizenry. Legal ethics committees should include lawyers who are not members of the ABA as well as nonlawyers — perhaps philosophers and consumers of the law — who can view legal ethics from a *broader* perspective than that of the entrepreneurs of the law. I, for one, propose to have my legal-ethics students read *Unequal Justice* before they read the ABA's Code of Professional Responsibility.

# THIRTY-SEVEN

# WHY ARE THERE SO MANY JEWISH LAWYERS?

*How quickly things change. In the 1920s Jewish lawyers were an endangered species because of discrimination. By the beginning of the twenty-first century, we were again endangered, but this time because of our success. The golden age of Jewish lawyers was coming to an end. I was asked to write about this phenomenon in 1997.*

WHY ARE THERE SO MANY JEWISH LAWYERS? WHY NOT? Do you have a problem with that? Jews are quarrelsome people. Even God called us stiff-necked. We argue with everybody. And why shouldn't we, considering our heritage? In Genesis 17, God selects Abraham to become the father of his people, and by Genesis 18 Abraham is already arguing with God over God's plan to destroy the evil city of Sodom. "Far be it from you . . . to kill the righteous with the wicked," Abraham challenges God, displaying characteristic Jewish chutzpah. In defending the few innocents among the many sinners of Sodom, the father of the Jewish people became the first lawyer in recorded history. Our Torah commands us to pursue justice ("Justice, justice shall thou pursue"). Our Talmud is the first preserved record of legal arguments — with dissenting and concurring opinions. We fought against persecution, discrimination, and victimization for millennia. Our rabbis have served as advocates, judges, and lawmakers, resolving disputes among quarreling Jews for centuries. Even our jokes reflect our contentiousness, as in the one about the Jew who was finally rescued from a desert island after ten years of solitude. The rescuers notice that he had built two synagogues. When they ask why, he replies, "That one I pray in; the other one I don't get along with."

In light of this long tradition of contentiousness, it is not surprising that today's Jews — who make up 2 percent of the population of the United States and a fraction of a percent worldwide — have become a dominant force in the legal profession, both in this country and throughout Europe, South America, Canada, Australia, South Africa, and everywhere else Jews live.

There are no reliable statistics on precisely how many Jewish lawyers practice in the United States, though some observers say the figure might exceed 20 percent of the total. Indeed, there is even a dispute — not surprisingly, among Jewish law professors — over exactly who qualifies as a Jewish lawyer. In a provocative essay in the *Cardozo Law Review* entitled "Identifying the Jewish Lawyer," Professor Sanford Levinson of the University of Texas Law School points out the difficulty of defining who is a Jewish lawyer when we can't even agree on who is a Jew or who is a lawyer. Is "Jonathan Goldberg" — whose father is Jewish but whose mother is not and who never attends religious services but who considers himself Jewish — a Jew? Is the same "Jonathan Goldberg" — who graduated from law school, passed the bar, but now works as an investment banker — even a lawyer? Levinson proposes an inclusive definition of *Jewish lawyer,* while other Jewish law professors propose more specific, religiously based, definitions. I am pleased to have been explicitly included in all of the proposed definitions (though some Jews have recently sought to exclude me as a result of my participation on the O. J. Simpson defense team, which they regard as very "un-Jewish").

In one respect, of course, anyone named Dershowitz or Goldberg who graduated from law school is a Jewish lawyer. Back in the first quarter of this century, when Jews began to attend law school in significant numbers, the established bar knew who was a Jew and tried desperately to keep them from becoming lawyers. The elite of the bar — ranging from Chief Justice William H. Taft and Columbia Law School dean Harlan H. Stone to American Bar Association president Elihu Root to the dean of the legal ethics bar, Henry S. Drinker — might have had difficulty defining a Jewish lawyer, but they certainly knew one when they saw one.

For purposes of preserving the apartheid approach to the practice of law, which existed until the 1960s, it didn't much matter whether our fictional "Jonathan Goldberg" had a non-Jewish mother or went to synagogue. He was a "Jew boy" as far as the elite law firms were concerned.

Even as late as the early 1960s, when I graduated from Yale Law School, apartheid was alive and well in many big city law firms. During my second year at Yale, I was first in my class, editor in chief of the law journal, and on my way to a Supreme Court clerkship. I applied to more than twenty-five law firms for a summer job, but I was turned down by every one of the WASP firms and ended up working in a Jewish firm.

By the mid-1960s the barriers against Jewish lawyers crumbled, and by the 1980s Jews had become members of most of the major law firms that had previously been restricted. Jews had moved from pariahs to partners in one generation.

Today there are no barriers to Jewish lawyers. Without trying to count the numbers with any precision, it is fair to say that there are more Jews, in proportion to their numbers in the general population, in positions of power in the legal profession than any other group. The same is true of judges, law professors, and deans of law schools.

In light of the history of Jewish victimization it is not surprising that Jewish lawyers have long been among the leaders in the civil rights movement, in the quest for international human rights, in the women's movement, in gay rights, in environmental protection, and in the provision of legal aid to indigents. But Jews are also active in conservative legal causes, such as the Federalist Society. Even the chief counsel for Pat Robertson's American Center for Law and Justice was born Jewish, though he now practices Christianity. Every list of the most influential lawyers in the United States is dominated by Jewish names. It is difficult to imagine today's legal profession without Jews. We have become the legal establishment while also remaining its dissidents. But as quickly as Jewish lawyers moved from second- to first-class status in the legal profession, we may vanish altogether from the American legal scene. This is because American Jews as a whole — at least those kinds of American Jews who become lawyers — are beginning a decline that may bring a virtual end to the Jewish presence in the country by the middle of the coming century.

The statistics are daunting. Jews were 4 percent of the United States population in 1937. We are 2 percent today, and we are shrinking rapidly. Although most non-Jews believe that Jews constitute 20 percent of the American population — because of our high visibility in the media, the professions, and business — we are, in fact, a tiny and dwindling minority. We have lower birthrates, higher intermarriage rates, and a higher level of assimilation than ever before. Jewish lawyers are in the vanguard of these trends, since they are among the most acculturated, best educated, wealthiest, most successful, and least religious of Jews — precisely those kinds of Jew who are most quickly dwindling in numbers. To be sure, there are Orthodox Jews — some quite distinguished — in the legal profession. But the vast majority of Jewish lawyers are not particularly observant, and almost none are Hasidic Jews, whose birthrate is above average and whose intermarriage and assimilation rates are negligible.

A chart prepared by Antony Gordon and Richard Horowitz reproduced in my book *The Vanishing American Jew* projects four generations into the future and, employing current rates of childbearing and intermarriage, demonstrates that two hundred secular Jews (a category into which many Jewish lawyers fit) will produce only ten future Jews, while two hundred Hasidic Jews (a category into which hardly any Jewish lawyers fit, since Hasidim do not generally attend college) will produce more than five thousand future Jews. If these projections are anywhere close to accurate, there will be plenty of Hasidic Jews but hardly any Jewish lawyers by the time we celebrate our tercentennial in 2076.

There will, of course, be many lawyers who will be Jewish by heritage. But most of them will not be Jews by religion or by membership in the Jewish community. This is likely because current demographic data show that the vast majority of children and grandchildren of mixed marriages are not raised exclusively as Jews and do not identify themselves as Jewish in conventional ways. Nor is there much that can be done to reverse these trends, since the primary cause of the reduction in the number of Jews is the great success Jews are currently experiencing.

When I was a youngster, nobody wanted to marry a Jew. Today everyone wants to marry a Jew — except, apparently, other Jews. When I was a young lawyer, Jewish lawyers practiced law primarily with other Jewish lawyers. Today the practice of law is far more integrated, as are schools, neighborhoods, summer camps, and other places where people meet and marry. When Jews were persecuted, discriminated against, and marginalized, they tended to circle the wagons and stick together. Today Jews live in what I call "the postpersecution era of Jewish history." We do not feel the need for religious or ethnic cohesiveness as much as we did when we were ostracized. Today's Jewish lawyers live among non-Jews, go to school with non-Jews, work with non-Jews, and not surprisingly, often marry non-Jews and raise their children and grandchildren as non-Jews. Jews have been welcomed into the most prominent of American families, including the Roosevelts, the Kennedys, the Cuomos, and the Rockefellers. The primary cause of our assimilation today is not hate, as it was in prior generations, but, rather, love. And it is difficult and futile to fight against love.

The bottom line, therefore, is that the number and percentage of Jewish lawyers practicing, teaching, and judging by the second half of the next century will be considerably lower than the number and percentage now. This phenomenon raises the intriguing question of whether the nature of law practice in America will change along with this dramatic demographic change.

There can be little doubt that the influx of Jews into the legal mainstream over the past thirty years has changed the nature of law practice. Competition increased, the practice became less conservative, and the integration of other excluded groups — women, Hispanics, people who are openly gay — moved more quickly once Jews entered the profession. In one sense the bigoted former solicitor general James Beck was right: When "old American stocks" dominated the legal profession, the practice of law was different from when Jews began to enter in large numbers.

Some critics argue that law has become more of a "business" and less of a "learned profession" since the days of legal apartheid. And, indeed, it was Steven Brill — a Jewish lawyer — who brought the business aspect of law practice to the surface with the 1979 debut of his publication *The American Lawyer*. I believe these changes have been largely for the better, because they have made things more honest. After all, the practice of law is a business as well as a profession. In any event, there can be little doubt that the Jewish influence on the practice of law in this country over the past several decades has been considerable, in part by making it more inclusive.

It does not follow, of course, that the diminution in the number and percentage of Jewish lawyers during the next century will have comparable impact. That will depend on several complex factors.

First, is there a uniquely Jewish way of being a lawyer? In his essay "Identifying the Jewish Lawyer," Sanford Levinson makes an intriguing analogy between law and baseball. He asks whether Sandy Koufax was a "Jewish ballplayer." It is true, of course, that the great Brooklyn (and, to my everlasting regret, Los Angeles) Dodger refused to pitch on Yom Kippur, even during the World Series. This made him a Jewish hero. (I can certainly attest to that, since he and his parents lived a block away from me during his early baseball career.) Levinson says: "It is crucial to recognize the limited nature of Koufax's status as a Jewish pitcher. That identity comes from his refusal to pitch on Yom Kippur. Yet what about those days he did pitch? Could anyone looking at his behavior as a pitcher — the choice of pitches, his particular pitching 'style' — argue that this had anything to do with his being Jewish? . . . All we can say with confidence is that Koufax's Jewishness, on occasion, would dictate when he would engage in his role as a professional baseball player, just as Jewish physicists might not perform experiments on Yom Kippur, but not how that role would be performed. One would not expect an analyst to describe the physicist as performing experiments 'like a Jew' or to say that Koufax 'pitched like a Jew.'"

But being a lawyer is different from being a pitcher or even a physicist. For me, my Jewish heritage greatly influences my life. I think Jewishly. I teach and practice law Jewishly. I conduct my professional and personal life Jewishly. My family life is Jewish and my politics are Jewishly inspired. Even my agnosticism is Jewish, since the God whose existence I wonder about is the Jewish God.

When I confront a personal or professional problem, I consult Jewish sources as well as contemporary American sources. I do not feel compelled to obey the Jewish answers, but I consult the Jewish sources because I value their wisdom. They provide a worldview that reflects an ancient tradition of which I am a part. My Jewish views help me challenge conventional wisdom, just as modern learning enables me to challenge traditional Jewish views. To ignore the wisdom of our sages is both arrogant and ignorant. It would be like deciding a complex constitutional issue without bothering to find out what the framers of our Constitution had in mind.

Just as there is no one way of being a Jew, there is no one way of practicing law Jewishly. But just as there is a common core of being a Jew, there is a common core of being a Jewish lawyer. The bigots of the bar thought they knew what it meant to be a Jewish lawyer back in the 1920s. They associated Jewish lawyers with greed, aggressiveness, and shoddy ethics. In fact, Jewish lawyers have been involved disproportionately in pro bono representation, cause-oriented litigation, government service, human rights and civil rights work, constitutional protection, and other public-interest activities. Among the concepts that have characterized many Jewish lawyers have been "Thou shall not stand idly by," "Repair the world," "compassion for the downtrodden," and the difficult search for justice. The *New York Times Magazine* recently had an article about John Rosenberg, a Jewish immigrant from Nazi Germany, who made his life in the most un-Jewish of places — rural Kentucky — trying to bring justice to the poor. Among his associates were three other lawyers with Jewish-sounding names (David Rubinstein, Dan Goldberg, and Ira Newman). Although the title of the piece, "What Is a Nice Jewish Lawyer Like John Rosenberg Doing in Appalachia?" tried to make this seem unusual, it is not. Because whenever the downtrodden need legal representation, you will often find a Jewish lawyer refusing to stand idly by, repairing the world, showing compassion, and seeking justice.

This does not mean, of course, that non-Jews cannot arrive at the same point by consulting Christian sources, or that Jews make better lawyers than non-Jews. It does suggest that we are all the products of our experiences, personal and historical, and that these experiences may inform the manner in which we practice our profession and live our lives. I know that I chose to become a criminal defense lawyer at least in part because I am Jewish. I was taught from the earliest age that Jews must always remember that they were persecuted, and that we must stand up for those who now face persecution. "Thou shall not stand idly by the blood of thy neighbor" was more than a slogan. "Repair the world" was an imperative. I recall vividly a class in Talmud in which I learned that a Jewish Sanhedrin (religious court) that had imposed the death penalty by a unanimous vote could not carry out the sentence, since unanimity meant that the accused did not have a zealous advocate presenting his arguments within the tribunal. Even the people of Sodom had Abraham as their advocate. I always wanted to be a Jewish lawyer, and though many Jews disapprove of some of my clients, I believe I am a lawyer in the Jewish tradition. I also believe that many other Jewish lawyers are influenced by their Jewish heritage in the way they practice law, teach law, or judge. So the dwindling of Jewish lawyers during the next century may well have a profound impact on the general practice of law in America, and on the social conscience of the law in particular.

But it is also possible that the Jewish influence on the law has become so pervasive that it will continue even in the absence of large numbers of Jewish lawyers. For example, if Jews were to vanish from the face of the earth — as we almost did during the Holocaust — the influences of the Jewish Bible would continue, because much of the non-Jewish world has incorporated the Jewish Bible into their own religions and worldviews. Would the same be true of the influence of Jewish lawyers? I believe it might, for several interesting reasons. First and foremost, the influence of Jewish lawyers — and of the Jewish tradition of law — has become an important part of the American legal system. The privilege against self-incrimination, the idea that it is better that ten guilty go free than one innocent be confined, the concept of equal protection for all, and the idea of proportionality between a crime and its punishment all have roots in Jewish law. Even without the continuing presence of Jewish lawyers to nurture this influence, it is likely to continue.

Moreover, there will still be many lawyers — indeed, even more than there are today — who reflect a partial Jewish heritage. There is every reason to believe that lawyers of partial Jewish heritage will continue to practice law in a somewhat Jewish manner, even as they go to synagogues less often or identify less with an exclusively Jewish heritage. The great paradox of Jewish life is that most of the positive values we identify with Jews — compassion, creativity, contributions to the world at large, charity, a quest for education — seem more characteristic of secular than ultra-Orthodox Jews. There are exceptions, of course, but it seems the closer one lives to the religious core of Judaism, the further one is likely to be from the Jewish values so many of us cherish.

However, it is possible that even if the number and percentage of Jews were to increase in the next century — an extremely unlikely prospect in light of the current demographics — their unique influence would still diminish. This would be so if their past influence were exclusively a result of their history of persecution and poverty and the progressive values that stem from such a background. Tomorrow's Jewish lawyers, who are children and grandchildren of the high, mighty, and wealthy, might act like other children and grandchildren of the high, mighty, and wealthy. Experience does not suggest that this will happen, though. As one sociologist put it, "Jews live like Episcopalians but vote like Puerto Ricans." The recent referendum on Proposition 209 in California confirms this. Although Jews have never been the direct beneficiary of affirmative action — indeed, many have been disadvantaged by it — a significant majority of Jewish Californians voted to preserve race-based affirmative-action programs.

The Talmud teaches that since the destruction of the Second Temple in Jerusalem (about seventy years after the birth of Jesus), prophecy has been limited to fools. It is impossible to assess accurately the impact that the diminishing Jewish population will have on American life in general, or on the law in particular. The bagel will endure, along with the many colorful words — from *schlepp* to *schmuck* to *yenta* to *chutzpah* — we have contributed to the American lexicon. Jewish jokes will continue, even in the absence of many Jewish comedians to tell them. I hope that the Jewish legacy in law will persist as well — a legacy that has had so great an impact in so short a period of time. But there are no guarantees. An America without Jews will be a less exciting, innovative, progressive, compassionate place. (Just as an America without blacks, Hispanics, gays, women, Asians, Greeks, Irish, Italians, and — hard as it is to imagine — WASPs, would be a less interesting place.)

The Jewish contribution has never been a matter of quantity. But even so, if our numbers and percentage are so reduced that we fall below the 1 percent mark, which is likely to occur fairly early in the coming century, our influence will necessarily become marginalized.

It may be difficult to remember the days during the first part of this century when there were more Jewish athletes and gangsters than lawyers and journalists. Now, instead of playing on basketball teams, we own them; instead of boxing in rings, we own the casinos in which the matches are held; and instead of belonging to Murder Incorporated, we represent those accused of murder and mayhem. As Ecclesiastes says, "To everything there is a season." Perhaps we will soon witness the end of the brief Jewish season in the American courtroom and law firm. We will have left our mark. We will continue to leave a mark, but we will be different and the mark we leave will be different. That has always been the nature of Jewish life, wherever we have lived. But just as an America with far fewer Jews will be a less creative and compassionate place, an American legal profession with far fewer Jewish lawyers will be a less creative and compassionate profession.

# THIRTY-EIGHT

# O. J. SIMPSON

*My involvement in the O. J. Simpson Case — I was a constitutional consult-ant to the trial team and would have argued the appeal had Simpson been convicted — unleashed a wave of primitive McCarthyism unlike anything I had ever experienced. Remarkably, many of those who criticized me for being willing to represent an "obviously guilty man" — as they put it — came from the left. Some of the most vicious attacks were from Jews. For example, Michael Lerner, the leftist editor of* Tikkun *magazine, wrote that my "hands" were "still dripping from the blood of the victims whose assassins he protected." Dean Laurie Levinson of the Loyola Law School — who should know better — suggested that I was an unrighteous person for defending un-righteous clients. Professor Peter Gabel of New College of California said it was unethical for lawyers to defend their client zealously "when they know or strongly suspect or even believe that their clients are lying or have been guilty of acts of cruelty or brutality." Other critics, as we will see in the article that follows (which was written for* The Jerusalem Report *in 1995), were far less polite.*

AN OLD JEWISH JOKE TELLS OF THE YESHIVAH STUDENT FROM Minsk who enrolled in the University of Saint Petersburg at the end of the nineteenth century. Each time his professor gave an assignment — be it about Kant, the economy, or anything else — the student man-aged to write about how the assigned subject affected Jews. Finally, in exasperation, the professor called him in and demanded that he write about pachyderms. The determined student duly submitted an essay entitled "The Elephant and the Jewish Question."

Though there is nothing humorous about the O. J. Simpson case, I was put in mind of this story by the mail that I've received since the verdict — mail that can fairly be characterized as being about the O. J. Simpson case and the Jewish question. My anti-Semitic hate mail is well known — I wrote about it in my memoir *Chutzpah*. I display it outside my Harvard office so that my students can see for themselves that anti-Semitism is still alive and well in some quarters. Until the Simpson case, virtually all of my hate mail was from non-Jews. Since the verdict, the majority has come from Jews. It is every bit as vicious and as bigoted as the hate mail from non-Jews. In this case, the bigotry involves attitudes toward blacks and toward Jews perceived as being on "their" side. Initially, I hoped that some of the writers who identified themselves as Jews were imposters. But I have checked and, tragically, they are authentic.

The Jewish hate mail has several recurring themes. The first is typical of all my hate mail: How can *you* represent someone who *I* think is guilty. A few representative examples:

Dear lying Jew (remember, I'm Jewish): Congratulations — a murdering butcher is on the street. If the nigger is so innocent, then he should have no problem speaking. May you catch cancer.

That charming note was from a practicing dentist and was written on his prescription pad. I called him and he confirmed his authorship. Another of this genre:

How could you help get a "Jew-killer" off? The homicidal "nigger" (an epithet I've shunned all of my life, but shall use from now on . . .) did it, and you know it.

Yet a third:

I hope I can still be alive when I hear someday that you have terminal cancer or even better, that you are a victim of a vicious crime which would be so appropriate for "dreck" like you.

I am used to this kind of hate mail. I have gotten precisely the same kind of criticism from anti-Semites and anti-Zionists for representing Jonathan Pollard, Rabbi Meir Kahane, members of the Jewish Defense League, Rabbi Bernard Bergman, and other Jews. I received similar mail about Claus von Bülow, Mike Tyson, Michael Milken, and Leona Helmsley. The only difference is that, in effect, these letters from Jews on the O. J. case charged me with disloyalty for siding with a black defendant rather than a Jewish victim. This genre of criticism simply refuses to understand the role of defense counsel in our adversary system of justice. In my novel *The Advocate's Devil*, I responded to such arguments by letting a young lawyer recount a Talmudic story in a conversation with an older colleague:

> "Shimon, the son of Shetah, had presided over a case in which a guilty murderer was let off because there was only one witness. The Bible expressly requires at least two witnesses in capital cases. The acquitted murderer then goes out and kills again, and the judge sees him with 'the sword in his hand, the blood dripping, and the dead man still twitching.' [The judge says he] is surely not responsible because he followed the Biblical rule, requiring two witnesses."
>
> "Well, that seems right, doesn't it?" asks the older lawyer.
>
> "Maybe for a judge, certainly not for a lawyer," the young lawyer said.
>
> "To the contrary. It seems to me more justified for a lawyer than for a judge."
>
> "Why so?"
>
> "Well," the older lawyer explained, "both have to obey the law. A lawyer's primary responsibility is to his client, while a judge's is to society in general. If a judge does the right thing by occasionally letting a guilty person go free — perhaps even to murder again — it would seem to follow that an advocate can't be blamed for doing the same thing."

My responsibility as a criminal defense lawyer is not to judge the guilt or innocence of my client. Generally, I don't know. My job is to advocate zealously, within the rules. That is what I did in the Simpson case, and I am proud of my work.

The second theme in the hate mail is particularly disturbing, coming as it does from Jewish letter writers. It articulates a stereotype about Jews that usually comes from bigoted non-Jews: that all Jews care about is money. The word *greed* appeared over and over again, but this time from the mouths of Jews. Some examples:

> I cannot even fathom how you can have the beitzim [balls] to even think of walking into a shul, to defend your disgusting greed for money.

As a Holocaust survivor, I am ashamed you are a Jew. You never met a $ you did not like. You fulfill the stereotype of a Jew and I declare you: not Jewish.

You showed your greediness — your chutzpah — when you went to California to plead for another greedy — not a black man — but a nigger who like all black men use drugs and all cheat on their wives. Be a Jew. Go to the defense of Jews.

The buck über alle$$. You may become anathema to us Jews, but what the hell, justice must always play second fiddle to $$$$$$.

Your role in the O. J. Simpson case showed a clearer picture of a lawyer who will sell his own mother — if the price is right. . . . I am a Holocaust survivor and very often I think about the Judenrate in my native Lodz ghetto or for that matter in other ghettos. . . . You remind me of them, but your price is in dollars and cents.

Perhaps Harvard should change its noble insignia to read VERITA$.

This form of hate mail was particularly inappropriate in the Simpson case, since the fees to all the lawyers were quite modest and the time commitment considerable. By joining the defense team, we had to give up lucrative opportunities to become paid commentators on the case. Moreover, because of Simpson's unpopularity — particularly in the Jewish community — I had several paid speaking engagements canceled. In any event, lawyers are supposed to be paid for their time, especially by relatively wealthy clients. There is no shame in being compensated for one's professional work. Yet the stereotype of doing everything "for the money" was a dominant theme within the Jewish letters. It led me to wonder whether some Jews have not incorporated this anti-Semitic stereotype into their own thinking.

The third — and most disturbing — theme revolved around the actions of my cocounsel Johnnie Cochran in "comparing" Detective Mark Fuhrman to Adolf Hitler, in surrounding himself with Nation of Islam bodyguards after receiving death threats in the courtroom, and in "playing the race card." Here are some examples:

How can you and the other Jewish attorneys be associated with an anti-Semitic [*sic*] like Johnnie Cochran? Who is a pal of Farrakhan, the most anti-Semitic person in the United States, who also happens to be Cochran's personal body guard?

You have let down your fellow Jews who have loved, honored, supported and admired you, until you aligned yourself now with a racist attorney who has engaged a racist, anti-Semitic Nation of Islam group to defend him.

You made me proud when you wrote *Chutzpah* and paraded your Jewishness so boldly, but you now embrace a blatant murderer and his champions and even justify that chief champion's invocation of Hitler to justify his utterly unabashed demagogic appeal in the defense of a client. How can you so turn your back on 6 million of our brothers and sisters?

Due to your recent participation in the trivialization of the Holocaust, I am no longer interested in your discussions of Jewish ethos and ethics.

I find it impossible to believe that the same man who wrote *Chutzpah* linked arms with and acted so deferentially to a man who was guarded by members of the Nation of Islam and who is supporting those self-avowed anti-Semites in the march in D.C.

It is remarkable how many of the letter writers completely misinterpret the message of *Chutzpah* as a tribal plea for parochial Jewish rights rather than for universal human rights from which Jews must not be excluded. More to the point here, the Jewish outrage at a black man making reference to Hitler seemed a bit overdone, especially since many Jews seem to make far more outrageous Hitler comparisons with far less criticism. David Ben-Gurion compared Menachem Begin to Hitler. Several Israeli politicians and American rabbis had compared Yitzhak Rabin to Hitler. The former director of the Anti-Defamation League called Farrakhan a "Black Hitler." Others who have recently been compared to Hitler include Vladimir Zhirinovsky, Yasir Arafat, Ariel Sharon, Saddam Hussein, and talk show host Gordon Liddy. One rabbi who criticized Cochran had himself compared Rabin to Hitler.

Non-Jewish whites also frequently invoke Hitler comparisons without incurring Jewish wrath. The *New York Times* of October 23, 1995, featured a story entitled "Using Nazi Images to Hit Political Opponents."

It listed numerous instances of politicians accusing their opponents of Hitler-like behavior. There was no mention of any criticism by Jewish leaders. But the criticism against Cochran was loud, sustained, and broadly based, including a highly publicized broadside from the executive director of the Anti-Defamation League.

Yet the fact is that Johnnie Cochran did not compare Mark Fuhrman to Hitler. He compared their views. This is what he said:

> There was another man not too long ago in the world who had those same views, who wanted to burn people, who had racist views and ultimately had power over people in his country. People didn't care. People said he is just crazy. He is just a half-baked painter. They didn't do anything about it. This man, this scourge became one of the worst people in the history of this world. Adolf Hitler, because people didn't care or didn't try to stop him . . . And so Fuhrman, Fuhrman wants to take all black people now and burn them or bomb them. That is genocidal racism.

In fact, Cochran differentiated between Hitler and Fuhrman, pointing out that Hitler "ultimately had power" and was able to carry out his racism.

Cochran's statement — according to the *Los Angeles Times* — was inspired by a conversation that Cochran had with a Jewish lawyer named Charles Lindner:

> "When Johnnie and I started talking about Fuhrman, I brought up my mother's experiences in Munich . . . ," Lindner, the former president of the Criminal Courts Bar Association, said. . . . "Her entire family was killed in the gas chambers by a house painter who was crazy and no one took him seriously until it was too late."

Lindner recounted his family history to Cochran in an effort, he said, "to get Johnnie into the frame of mind to talk about Mark Fuhrman as the personification of evil." The newspaper quoted Lindner as continuing:

> "I was the stimulus for Johnnie's comments. And for those who say that Hitler is proprietary to the Jews, he isn't. What we were trying to convey . . . is that we shouldn't allow men like this — either Hitler or Fuhrman — to have control over people's lives."

Cochran was absolutely on target in warning his listeners that when people don't care about racism and don't try to stop it, it can get out of control. I have heard similar statements made by prominent Jews on many occasions. Imagine if Fuhrman had said about Jews what he said about blacks — if he had said "The only good Jew is a dead Jew" or that "Jews should be rounded up and burned" and "turned into fertilizer." Would anyone object if a Jewish lawyer had said that these were the "same views" expressed by Hitler? I doubt it. Nor would Jews object were a fellow Jew to express concern that if we ignored such views, they could escalate into actions. No one should object when an African American expresses concern that by ignoring genocidal talk against blacks by a police officer, we may be inviting genocidal action against others as well.

The universal message of the Holocaust was perhaps best captured by the German Protestant minister Martin Niemoller, who said:

> When Hitler attacked the Jews I was not a Jew, therefore, I was not concerned. And when Hitler attacked the Catholics, I was not a Catholic, and therefore, I was not concerned. And when Hitler attacked the unions and the industrialists, I was not a member of the unions and I was not concerned. Then, Hitler attacked me and the Protestant church — and there was nobody left to be concerned.

We must applaud, not condemn, African Americans who take this lesson seriously and understand that when "they" are threatened by bigotry "we" too are threatened. We must also support black leaders who characterize Hitler as one of the worst villains in history, especially at a time when too many blacks and whites are minimizing Hitler's villainy. To hold an African American like Johnnie Cochran to a more exacting standard than we demand of fellow Jews is to flirt with racism. It is also self-defeating to turn against a black man like Cochran, who is a strong supporter of Israel, has visited the Holocaust memorial at Yad Vashem, and has always been a friend of the Jewish people. We have made that mistake before, in too quickly attacking black friends with whom we should be building bridges.

Interestingly, some of the same Jewish letters that criticize Cochran's reference to Hitler make their own comparisons to the Holocaust:

No wonder they are reheating the ovens again. You embrace the true Nazi of WABC radio, Lynn Samuels. . . . Jewish lawyers are only too happy to defend the new Master Race, the Black Master Race.

The other criticism directed at Cochran was that he used Nation of Islam guards to protect himself from death threats. Although Cochran has assured me that he used these bodyguards only as an emergency stopgap and that he intended no message, I believe it was a mistake — and I told him that. He agreed and assured me that he would no longer use them. Nor has O. J. Simpson employed Nation of Islam bodyguards. And neither Simpson nor Cochran attended the Farrakhan-sponsored march on Washington. In fact, Cochran specifically condemned Farrakhan's message of hate. By recognizing the difference between a friend with whom I had a disagreement (Johnnie Cochran) and an enemy with whom I could not reason (Louis Farrakhan), I was able to have some influence on the friend.

Finally, as to the "race card": the term itself — as Henry L. Gates Jr., a friend of the Jews, tells us — is "a barrier to interracial comprehension" that "infuriates many blacks." Race was irretrievably introduced into the trial when Marcia Clark embraced Mark Fuhrman *after* being told of his racism, sexism, and neo-Nazism. She knew that he had painted a swastika on the locker of a policeman who was dating a Jewish woman and that he celebrated Hitler's birthday. She had to know that Fuhrman was lying when he denied using the "N" word. So did dozens of other prosecutors, policemen, and friends of Fuhrman, who all sat silently by and allowed the lie to go uncorrected until the tapes were discovered. The so-called race card was dealt by the prosecution and *trumped* by the defense, as the defense was obliged to do.

As the respected judge Leon Higginbotham put it:

> If the defendant had been Jewish and the police officer had a long history of expressed anti-Semitism and having planted evidence against innocent persons who were Jewish, I can't believe that anyone would have been saying that defense counsel was playing the anti-Semitism card.

Would anyone feel that the Jewish defendant had been adequately defended if the bias of that anti-Semitic witness had not been exposed?

Yes, race was an issue in the Simpson case — in several respects. A critical witness for the prosecution was a racist and anti-Semite. More important, black jurors may have been more open, initially, to the possibility of police perjury and evidence tampering. In the end, all the jurors — including those who were not black — were persuaded that, in the words of the world's leading forensic expert, Dr. Henry Lee, "something was wrong" with the prosecution's case and that it could not be trusted beyond a reasonable doubt.

In addition to the Jewish hate mail, I also received some thoughtful letters from Jews who were extremely critical of my role, as a Jew, in defending O. J. Simpson. One, from an old friend, quoted Maimonides and various Talmudic sources in condemnation of freeing the guilty. I responded with equally authoritative Jewish sources on the importance of fairness and evidentiary rules, reminding him that it was much harder to convict the guilty under Jewish law than it was under American law. Others, ranging from college professors to law students, expressed what they termed to be genuine Jewish pain over a miscarriage of justice.

Many rabbis, too, delivered sermons on the injustice of the verdict from a Jewish perspective. I have been told that the vitriol of some rabbis matched the letters I have received. Even some usually thoughtful Jewish columnists — such as Frank Rich and William Safire — joined the cacophony. Rich said that Cochran had "trivialized" Hitler's crimes. Did he read the same quote as I did? And Safire compared the joy some blacks expressed at the verdict to "Palestinians cheering from the rooftops at incoming Iraqi scud missiles." Talk about trivializing!

I understand the pain. I even understand the vehemence of the feelings. What I do not understand is the Jewishness of the pain, vehemence, and even hate that I have read and heard. This is surely not the first case in which Jews have felt that there has been a miscarriage of justice. Such miscarriages are widely reported in the media, including erroneous acquittals, convictions, and even death sentences. Yet these are rarely the subject of the kind of rabbinic rage or lay letters I have observed following this verdict. Why is this case different? What is the "Jewish question" here? This is not the John Demjanjuk case, where the defendant was accused of the mass murder of Jews *because* they were Jews. I was in Israel during that trial and shortly after the reversal of the conviction. I saw and understood the Jewish rage there, though I agreed with the Supreme Court's reversal. There was a reasonable doubt that Demjanjuk was Ivan the Terrible of Treblinka, though there is no doubt that he was another terrible Ivan of Sobibor. The fact that this butcher of Jewish men, women, and children went free was an understandable source of Jewish pain and outrage.

The Simpson case, on the other hand, raises an American question, not a Jewish question. Yes, Ron Goldman was Jewish, but even those who believe that Simpson killed him do not believe he targeted him because of his Jewishness. The ethnicity of the victims does not fully explain the extraordinary Jewish reaction to the verdict. Why, then, the special Jewish pain, outrage, and hate?

I hope it is not because of what I suspect it may be. I hope that the Simpson case has not, in some way, become a surrogate for Jewish outrage at African Americans. I hope that the specifically *Jewish* rage at the verdict is not an unconscious deflection onto one black defendant of more generalized Jewish rage against African Americans.

Some of the Jews who wrote to me made an explicit connection between the Simpson verdict and the Farrakhan-sponsored march on Washington. Others referred to the anti-Semitism of "blacks." I have long believed that the Jewish history of victimization and persecution inoculated us against the universal disease of racism — at least somewhat more than other groups. And perhaps it has. Maybe that is why it has taken what many regard as a gross miscarriage of justice in a case involving a Jewish victim and a black defendant to provide an outlet for feelings pent up by a commendable need to suppress the unacceptable.

One should not draw broad, general conclusions from the reactions to a single verdict or a few hundred angry letters from individual Jews or a handful of overreactions by columnists or even outrage expressed by several dozen rabbis.

The vast majority of Jews — whatever their feelings about the Simpson verdict — will continue to support civil rights and racial equality.

But I must admit that I am concerned. In more than a quarter century of involvement with the American Jewish community, I have never felt quite this level of Jewish hostility. We did not see this kind of Jewish outrage at the acquittal, by a white Simi Valley jury, of the police officers caught on videotape beating up Rodney King, or at the acquittal of Bernard Goetz on the grounds of self-defense, though he admitted that he continued shooting after the danger had passed. I doubt that we would see this intensity of Jewish reaction if there were acquittals in the Oklahoma bombing trial or the Menendez retrial.

Something disturbing may be at work here. We must look at ourselves and acknowledge what it may be and why some of us may feel it. No Jew should permit his or her *individual* anger at the Simpson verdict to become transformed into *Jewish* anger at Simpson's black lawyer, the black jurors, or blacks in general. Anger at the Simpson verdict is legitimate for those who disagree with it. Anger at "blacks" is not. I fear that some Jews may be using the Simpson verdict as a way of legitimating other, less acceptable, feelings. By directing their rage against the verdict toward the black lawyer, the black defendant, the black jurors — and the Jewish lawyers who "sided" with the "enemy" — some Jews may be able to channel unacceptable feelings into an acceptable outlet.

Doing so will neither make those unacceptable feelings disappear nor contribute constructively to Jewish-black relations. I have been a vocal critic of anti-Semitism among certain elements of the African-American community. I will continue my criticism so long as such bigotry persists. But the reactions I have read, heard, and seen by some Jews to the Simpson verdict demonstrate painfully to me that we Jews still have much work to do on Jewish-black relations — and that not all of it is external.

# THIRTY-NINE

# IS LEGAL ETHICS ASKING THE RIGHT QUESTIONS?

*In 1996 I was invited to deliver the following paper at a conference on legal ethics at Hofstra Law School.*

I AM HERE TO COMPLAIN ABOUT THE AGENDA OF LEGAL ETHICS. Thirty years ago Professor Monroe Freedman set the agenda for the debate over legal ethics in the United States in criminal cases by posing three provocative questions. You're probably all familiar with them, but I'll repeat them. One: Is it proper to cross-examine for the purpose of discrediting the reliability or credibility of an adverse witness whom you know to be telling the truth? Two: Is it proper to put a witness, including the defendant, on the stand when you know he will commit perjury? And three: Is it proper to give your client legal advice when you have reason to believe that the knowledge you give him will tempt him to commit perjury?

These questions have been debated endlessly and productively in ethics classes, bar associations, judicial opinions, and lawyers' bull sessions. Unfortunately, the focus of these debates has been almost exclusively on defense lawyers, rarely on prosecutors, while I believe the far more important focus should be on prosecutors. Yet there has been little debate about whether prosecutors who know when they put a witness on the stand that the witness is likely to be committing perjury, particularly a police witness — whether or not it is proper for that prosecutor to engage in that kind of conduct. In fact, as anyone who has practiced criminal law will know — and that excludes virtually all the current sitting United States Supreme Court justices — this problem arises far more frequently with prosecutors than it does with the defense attorneys. This is so for a very obvious reason: defense attorneys rarely put on an affirmative case, while prosecutors always put on an affirmative case.

The first and third questions arise more frequently with defense attorneys, but they do arise with a significant degree of frequency with prosecutors as well, yet there is little discussion of them either, except again in the context of the role of the defense attorney. This misfocus of attention sends precisely the wrong message and has contributed to the current crisis of confidence in our criminal justice system, and especially in the role of criminal defense counsel.

Let me start with the second and most provocative and most debated of the questions: witness perjury. A man who used to be the police commissioner of San Jose and before that was the police commissioner of Kansas City, and before that was a beat cop in New York, made the following statement in the *Los Angeles Times* of February 11, 1996: "As someone who spent 35 years wearing a police uniform, I've come to believe that hundreds of thousands of law enforcement officers commit felony perjury every year in testifying about drug arrests." He's limiting himself only to drug arrests. Police commissioner William Bratton of New York, formerly of Boston, at a conference in Harvard in 1995, said he has come to believe that "testilying," which is the term used by New York police to describe what some of them do in search and seizure cases, is a particularly serious problem and must not be ignored. The Mollen Commission, the Knapp Commission, every commission that has studied the problem of police perjury, has in my view seriously understated the problem and yet has come to the conclusion that police perjury is rampant. Judge Irving Younger, when he sat as a criminal judge in New York, described the circumstances of "dropsy" testimony that came to his court on an almost daily basis, in which the police officer sees a drug suspect, approaches him, and miraculously the drugs are dropped on the floor, thereby invoking two exceptions to the exclusionary rule at the very same time. This led Judge Younger to quip that there must be some impact that drugs have on the ability of the finger to hold the drugs or some other physical property. Judge Alex Kazinski of the Ninth Circuit recently said that every judge knows that police perjury in these kinds of cases is rampant.

Is it possible that hundreds of thousands of transparent cases of police perjury are occurring every year in the courts of this country without prosecutors and judges knowing about it, and even encouraging it? I don't think so. And I think that has to become a serious focus of our attention as legal ethics teachers. I want to illustrate these issues by reference to the Simpson case. Let me suggest what I believe was in the minds of the police officers and in the minds of the prosecutors in that case, because I think it's fairly typical. I think that Marcia Clark and Chris Darden and Judge Lance Ito all sincerely believed that O. J. Simpson committed these double murders. That was their subjective state of mind. They believed it. That was their truth, their ultimate truth. They also believed that Detective Mark Fuhrman was now, at this point in time, a good cop.

Now let me tell you how I think they define a good cop. A good cop is defined as a policeman who would not plant evidence, though he might stretch the truth of a search and seizure to fit an exception to the exclusionary rule, a rule that in the view of cops disserves ultimate truth. Clark and Darden knew, however, that Fuhrman had in fact used the "N" word previously. It was very obvious, because when he made a claim for a disability in 1983, he included an interview with a psychiatrist. In the interview with the psychiatrist, he used the "N" word. He said those "N's" and Mexicans should be in jail. "I don't know why I have to treat them the way I have to treat them." And he talked about how outraged he was at "N's" and Mexicans, and he used it in a very conversational way. They also knew that he was a racist, a liar, and potentially an evidence planter. How did they know that?

Another district attorney named Lucien Coleman, a woman with eighteen years of experience in the DA's office, went over to Marcia Clark and warned her to be really careful about Fuhrman, since she had been hearing bad things about him. Marcia Clark responded, "Oh, you've been listening to the defense." And she said, in effect, "No, no, I've been listening to my police officers. My police officers are telling me that this guy is an evidence planter, this guy is a racist, this guy is a liar, this is a guy who put a swastika on the locker of a police officer who had recently married a Jewish woman." And story after story. And Marcia Clark threw her out of the office, saying, "Stop interfering with my case. Everybody's trying to get a piece of this big case. I don't want to hear from you anymore, and I'm going to put Fuhrman on the witness stand." And she asked herself, since she believed that Fuhrman didn't plant the evidence and was now not a racist (this was her subjective state of belief), Why, why should these old problems interfere with her being able to achieve the ultimate truth, the truth she maintained confidence in — namely, that the defendant was guilty.

They also knew, and Judge Ito knew this as well (let's not mince any words about it), that the police account of the search was a cover story. Everyone suspected Simpson on the morning of the murders. In my book *Reasonable Doubts*, I describe my reaction when I first saw the television news of the two victims, one of them being Simpson's former wife, and heard an account of Simpson's previous arrest for spousal abuse. I turned to my wife and said, of course O. J. is the obvious suspect. The husband is always the first suspect.

So everybody suspected O. J. Simpson, with the exception of five people: the five police officers who swore under oath that they didn't suspect Simpson. As Detective Philip Vannatter put it, "I no more regarded O. J. Simpson as a suspect than I did you, Mr. Shapiro." Now, there is no way anybody can believe that story. And yet two judges and many prosecutors claimed to believe it. The two judges are much, much more guilty in this respect because the judges had to make credibility determinations, whereas you might argue that prosecutors don't have to make credibility determinations. Those two judges held their noses, closed their ears, and shut their eyes, and said that they believed this evidence. There is no way they could have believed that evidence. They pretended to believe that evidence. Why? In the interest of truth. Why did they participate in a lie in the interest of truth? They participated in a lie because they knew that if they allowed that intermediate truth to be registered, namely that this was a false cover story, evidence of Mr. Simpson's guilt would be excluded, and that would thwart the search for ultimate truth.

Now, Professor Richard Hodes of Indiana, who's here today, will of course ask the question, What do you mean "know"? And he has challenged the defense bar and said that when the Supreme Court in *Nix v. Whiteside* and the rules of ethics say "know," they don't mean know only in the sense of "Did the client confess to you?" They mean commonsense "know." Certainly by Professor Hodes's standards, Marcia Clark and Chris Darden knew that that story was a phony cover story. They've heard it dozens and dozens of times. It's number seven in the Letterman top ten list of favorite cover stories that the police tell. The Mollen Commission, in fact, has a list, and it quotes a police supervisor giving a police officer a choice of which of the cover stories is most likely to succeed. And I don't even want to trivialize the intelligence of this audience by suggesting for a minute that you can make an argument that under that standard of knowledge, the prosecutors didn't know. Of course they knew. We're going to have an interesting debate — and Professor Hodes and I have had that debate — as to whether the same standard of "know" should apply to defense attornies as should apply to prosecutors. I believe it should not.

Defense attorneys do have a conflict — that is, they have zealous representation of their client, they are confronted with a situation under which if they don't put a witness on the stand, they can be held as ineffectively assisting their client, because as the Second Circuit recently held in the *DeLuca* case, the defendant has a constitutional right to take the stand. And if a lawyer doesn't put the defendant on the stand, the lawyer can be held to a standard of ineffective assistance of counsel. Even under the so-called breathing-on-the-mirror standard in the *Strickland* case, the Second Circuit recently reversed a conviction because the lawyer did not put a defendant on the witness stand — notwithstanding there being some questions about why that decision was made and whether it was ethically based. So the defense attorney has a real conflict. He learned incriminating information in confidence from a client, and he has an obligation to satisfy the constitutional right of the client to take the witness stand.

There are no conflicts of that kind with a prosecutor. A prosecutor is not in a lawyer-client relationship with a police witness. The police witness has no right to take the stand. The levels of zealous advocacy for a prosecutor are different from the levels of zealous advocacy for a defense attorney, and I think it should be clear that the standard of knowledge — whatever it may be, whether it be the Hodes standard or some other standard for the defense attorney — is surely at the very least the Hodes standard for a prosecutor. And I'd like to hear from anybody an argument that that standard was not met in this case, either as to Fuhrman's use of the "N" word or as to Vannatter's testimony concerning whether he regarded O. J. Simpson as a suspect.

Now, you might try to wiggle out of that by invoking an argument that I made in my novel *Advocate's Devil*, and that is to point to the following issue, which is in fact rarely discussed in the literature and which is quite common. You know, when Monroe Freedman asked the question, Should a defense counsel be able to put a possibly perjuring witness on the stand? he was addressing one part of that dilemma. But the far more frequent occurrence is going to be a situation where you put your client on the stand and you don't elicit a lie from him on direct, but you know that on cross a lie will be elicited naturally by the cross-examination. And I challenge you to find in all the vast discussion of legal ethics an answer to that question. It's just not there. Are you as a defense attorney or as a prosecutor obliged to stand up and correct your witness's perjured testimony, when it's elicited on cross-examination? You would think there would be some discussion of that. I don't expect that discussion to occur in the Supreme Court, because when you allocate the decision to nine people, none of whom has any experience to speak of in real administration of criminal justice, really understanding the dynamics of lawyer-client relationships from their own experience, it's very hard to expect that they will anticipate these problems instead of discussing them in an abstract context or in the context of a particular case that comes before them.

So these are questions that I think have to be debated. And I think they have to be debated far more extensively in the context of the role of the prosecutor and in the context of the role of the judge. The time has come to shift the focus away from its almost exclusive past focus on the defense attorney.

Let me illustrate the problem of cross-examination by brief reference to the Simpson case. In the Simpson case, a woman named Kathleen Bell, who hated O. J. Simpson, who thought he was probably guilty, who wanted him to be convicted, called the prosecution and the defense (first the prosecution and they didn't return the call, and then the defense), and said, "You know, this guy Fuhrman, he may have been telling the truth about the glove. I don't know. But I have to tell you I once had an encounter with him in a bar, and he used the 'N' word repeatedly, and he told me that he would arrest any black man he saw with a white woman and make up a cover story, and he would like to round up all African Americans (he didn't use that word) and burn them all to death. It was the most horrible thing anybody ever said to me. I'll never forget it."

Let me tell you what Marcia Clark set out to do to this Good Samaritan, decent woman. She set out to absolutely destroy that woman's life. She put investigators on her, she encouraged private investigators to be put on her. She sent messages to this woman over and over again, If you testify, we will find everything out about your sex life, about your background, about your work life. If you testify in this case, you will be destroyed and demolished. And she would have done it, and she knew that Kathleen Bell was telling the truth. How did she know that Kathleen Bell was telling the truth? Because it was consistent with everything else that other people, police officers and others, were saying, and because she knew Kathleen Bell had no motive to testify falsely in this case. Fortunately, we came upon those tapes, and as the result of those tapes — and here's something that I think the media haven't understood: What was important was not the fact that Judge Ito allowed us two snippits from the tape, showing that in fact Fuhrman had used the "N" word. (I was in favor of not even using those two snippits, because they made it sound like they were two snippits that could have been used by anybody, a comedian or something, they were in such an innocent context. And also, he could easily have said, "Gee, I don't remember that.") The importance of the tape is that with the tape, Marcia Clark knew she couldn't cross-examine Kathleen Bell, because if she tried to prove that Kathleen Bell was lying about remembering a statement about burning the African Americans, we had something on tape that said the exact same thing, and we then would have been able to use that piece of tape to prove she was telling the truth. So the impact of the tape was not on what the jury heard but on what the jury didn't hear. It precluded Marcia Clark from doing what she fully intended to do, that is, destroy a decent woman who she knew was telling the truth. Why? In the interest of truth. Marcia Clark honestly and genuinely believed that if Kathleen Bell testified, the jury would misfocus its attention on whether Fuhrman was telling the truth, a small minor truth, about whether he had used the "N" word, and that would obscure a larger truth, namely, that he didn't plant the glove and that Simpson was in fact guilty in her view.

So this problem of prosecutorial abuse occurs, I think, quite frequently and quite dramatically, and yet I saw no attention by legal ethicists, by the media, to this question. Because we have become so wedded to the issue of defense attorneys' ethics in the context of a world where prosecutorial misconduct in these kinds of cases is not only rampant but approved by the judiciary and is felt to be right. Why? Because they're on the side of the angels and we are on the side of the devils. Because the vast majority of criminal defendants are in fact guilty. Because ultimate truth resides in most cases with the prosecution, they are far less sensitive to issues of intermediate truth, and we as ethicists are far less sensitive to these issues of intermediate truth.

A statement was recently made by Police Commissioner William Bratton of New York. When a prosecutor is really determined to win, the trial prep procedure may skirt along the edges of coercing or leading the police witness. In this way, some impressionable young cops learn to tailor their testimony to the requirements of the law. This is a very serious and recurring problem. It's not that prosecutors tell the police witnesses to lie. It's that prosecutors give lectures at police academies, brief police witnesses, outline for them the parameters of the exceptions to the exclusionary rule, and then turn a blind eye to the amazing coincidence that virtually every search happens to fit into one of the exceptions to the exclusionary rule. Now, these days there are so many exceptions to the rule that it's not hard to fit into one. Prosecutors must have an obligation not only to make sure that their witnesses testify consistent with the way they want them to testify but also that they testify truthfully.

The time has come to shift the focus back to prosecutors. The time has come for the courts to understand that they are a serious part of the problem. If there are hundreds of thousands of cases every year of transparent perjury, and only handfuls of cases where the judges disbelieve that transparent perjury, there is an ethics problem involving judges. Judges at every level of every court. Judges who are the ones who say they believe it. The appellate judges who say, We believe the judges who said they believe it. And the Supreme Court justices who say, We believe the appellate judges who said that they believe the district judges who believe it. The time has come to cut that Gordian knot and for some judges to show the courage of their convictions and to start doing in public what they are perfectly prepared to do in private — to start doing in specific what they are prepared to do in the abstract. Judges will tell you that police perjury is rampant, but try to find an opinion in which this is actually stated and used as a basis to justify the exclusion of evidence.

So, I think we have to begin to look more realistically at the criminal justice system. It has been wonderful to have academics debate this issue, to have judges in the abstract debate this issue, to have ethicists debate this issue, but we have to begin to look statistically and empirically at what the problem is and start to focus attention more on where the problem is most serious, and I think it is most serious with judges and with prosecutors — without diminishing the seriousness and importance of continuing to maintain pressure on defense attorneys to act in the highest ethical manner possible. I'm not here suggesting any diminishing of the ethics of defense attorneys. What I am suggesting is an elevation in the ethics of prosecutors.

Let me just end with a quote from the Bible which says, "Justice, justice shalt thou pursue." The commentators ask the question, Why is *justice* mentioned twice? And one of the most beautiful commentaries to the Bible says that the reason that *justice* is mentioned twice is that it was intended to refer to the two kinds of justice: the means of justice and the ends of justice. And today we focus far too much on the ends of justice. And I believe that the message of the Bible and the message of legal ethics must be that one cannot trust the ends of justice unless the means of justice, the intermediate truth, are also considered.

❋

# THE RIGHT TO AN HONEST JUDGE

I AM FORTUNATE TO HAVE SERVED AS A LAW CLERK TO TWO extraordinary judges, both of whom exemplified wisdom and compassion. The first was Chief Judge David Bazelon of the United States Court of Appeals for the District of Columbia. The second was Justice Arthur Goldberg of the United States Supreme Court. Perhaps that is why I have always held judges to so high a standard. Throughout my professional career, I have been willing to criticize judges — sometimes quite vociferously. I have even brought charges against judges when I believed they were warranted. In the chapters that follow, I write about the institution of the judiciary as well as some of the individuals who have served in it. I write about the way we pick judges, the way we judge judges, and the way we remove judges.

# FORTY

# DON'T PICK JUDGES
# THE WAY WE DO!

---

*In 1998 the British magazine* Punch *asked me to compare the American and British systems for selecting judges. I used the article as an opportunity to write about judges, their powers, and the people selected to ascend the bench.*

---

AS THE BRITISH BENCH, BAR, AND PUBLIC CONTINUE TO debate the way judges are selected, I urge you, *please* do not look to my country for guidance. Britain and the United States are today separated not only by a common language but also by a common legal tradition. Yours is far too elitist. Ours is far too populist. There must surely be a happy medium somewhere between your white, male aristocracy of Oxbridge-educated former barristers and our politically correct amalgam of mediocre lawyers who happen to know a senator or a governor and happen to be of the race, gender, ethnicity, or political persuasion required to achieve the desired balance of the day.

Our judges are, of course, far more powerful and influential than are yours. Ours can strike down laws duly enacted by Congress, can enjoin the president from taking actions supported by a majority of our citizens, and can even require the state and federal governments to spend our tax dollars in ways of which we disapprove. Ours is the most powerful — some would say, meddlesome — judiciary in the world. Part of the reason is that we have a written constitution and the Bill of Rights. But so does Canada. Yet its courts are not nearly as influential as ours. We have a tradition of judicial activism that dates back to the time when Alexis de Tocqueville reported on the new republic and marveled at how every issue of significance eventually ended up in the American courts.

This extraordinary judicial power is necessarily a double-edged sword. Because the American courts have so much power over the political branches of our government — and over the daily lives of our citizens — it really matters to our citizens who sits on our courts. This explains, for example, the remarkable confirmation battles we have been through over the nominations of judges such as Robert Bork, and the equally remarkable — if more disturbing — removal of judges such as Justice Rose Bird from her position as chief justice of California. The former was blocked because he was too conservative; the latter was unseated because she was too liberal. It also explains why our Republican Senate is currently delaying the confirmation of dozens of Clinton nominees to the federal courts. Our judges are not perceived as nameless and faceless legal oracles who simply pronounce the law from under their homogenizing wigs. We know the names of our judges and we know their politics and predilections. And we darn well should — considering the reality that they may have as much influence over our daily lives as our elected executive and legislative branches.

Which brings me to the state court judges in our country, who are — in many states — *elected* to the judiciary. Yes, they actually run for office: they campaign, they raise money (mostly from lawyers who will appear before them), and they brag about how tough they will be on crime. The election of judges was part of the populism that swept our nation following its separation from Great Britain. We also elect most of our state prosecutors — a great stepping stone to higher office, as evidenced by the fact that President Bill Clinton, dozens of congressmen, and many governors were elected prosecutors before they went on to bigger and better things. In one state, Florida, they even vote for their public defenders. (Just imagine the campaign: candidate A boasts of his graduation from Harvard Law School and of his success rate in freeing accused murderers, robbers, and rapists, while candidate B proclaims his lack of qualifications and promises to lose most of his cases, thereby keeping the street safe from his clients — guess who would win.)

In sum, our system of picking judges is the worst in the Western world. In light of this sad reality, it is quite remarkable how many good judges have emerged from this wacky selection process. Some of the greatest were picked by accident — the late, great justice William Brennan is a good example. He was picked because he was an urban,

Irish-Catholic Democrat and President Dwight Eisenhower needed the votes of that particular constituency. (The conservative president who "accidentally" selected Brennan later regarded that decision as the "worst mistake" of his presidency.) Some great judges were elected by defrauding the voters — promising a lock-'em-up-and-throw-away-the-key approach and then breaking that promise by becoming balanced jurists with a commitment to constitutional principles. But occasional accidental excellence is not a persuasive argument for perpetuating a system that is inherently flawed. Our inherent flaw is our unwillingness to recognize that the judicial branch can serve as a check and balance on the political branches only if it is removed from partisan politics and shorn of its hyper-populist input.

Does this mean that we should move toward adopting your hyper-elitist system? No way! Your system produces, on average, far more learned and professionally respected judges — but at far too high a cost. The cost of your flawed system is its perpetuation of sexist and racist stereotypes and assumptions. The small clique of elitists who select your wigged Platonic guardians seem to believe — quite honestly — that there is a white, male gene for intellect, integrity, and professionalism. How else to explain the current situation, in which of the ninety-three most highly paid judges only seven are women and all are white? No wonder that David Pannick, Q.C., described your system as resembling a "pre-1965 Conservative leadership contest or a Papal conclave, rather than the choice of lawmakers in a modern democracy." Others have described it more simply as an "old boys' network." Boys will pick boys, and boys from Oxford will pick boys from Oxford.

Recently a change was made under which the position of high court judge will be "advertised" and potential candidates can "apply" rather than wait to be "tapped," as in some ancient fraternity ritual. But this "reform" seems cosmetic, intended to head off demands for more fundamental changes, such as the proposal for a judicial appointment commission that would include lay participants. Nonlawyers participating in the selection of judges frightens the established bar as much as nonpriests selecting the pope would scare the Catholic clergy. And there is good reason for the concern: nonlawyers are more apt to subordinate professional qualifications to populist criteria. Judges should be selected on the basis of merit and professional qualifications, not on how well they pander to popular taste. Accordingly, I do not favor lay participation in the judicial selection process. That is not an argument against a judicial appointment commission; it is only an argument for limiting the membership of such a commission to members of the legal profession. But these lawyers can reflect the broadest array of professionals and not be limited to the old boys' club that currently whispers its approval of fellow Oxbridge barristers. The commission should include highly regarded academics, solicitors, and other members of the legal profession who are today excluded from the judicial selection process. It should also include younger lawyers, a change that would inevitably increase the number of women and ethnic minorities. This new blood would produce the names of qualified judicial candidates who are today unknown to the elitists who currently pick judges. It would diversify the judiciary without compromising its quality.

Indeed, there is movement in some parts of the United States toward judicial selection commissions, but in our country these commissions are designed to ameliorate the populist and political influences on the judiciary rather than the elitist influences. In Massachusetts, for example, the governor appoints from a list prepared by such a commission; thus constraints are imposed on his ability to use the judiciary for patronage.

The virtue of a well-designed judicial selection commission is precisely that it is capable of ameliorating the extremes of both too much populism and too much elitism. Perhaps if both of our countries were to adopt such a system, we could narrow the separation between us and settle on that happy medium that does not sacrifice quality for diversity.

# FORTY-ONE

# THE ULTIMATE FRATERNITY

*In 1980 the* Saturday Review *invited me to review the first in-depth book ever written about the inner workings of our Supreme Court. My review of* The Brethren: Inside the Supreme Court, *by Bob Woodward and Scott Armstrong (New York: Simon and Schuster, 1980), focuses on how the personalities and politics of the individual justices impact the high court's role in our system of governance.*

THOUGH IT APPEARS TO BE LITTLE MORE THAN A GOSSIPY collection of anecdotes about seven years of recent Supreme Court history, *The Brethren* raises profound questions about the justification for judicial review in our society. It is, after all, an anomaly that in a democracy, the final arbiter of national policy is often a group of nine judges appointed for life and responsible to no electorate. No other country vests as much power in its judiciary as we do in ours. Our Supreme Court — unlike those of other nations — can overrule decisions of Congress, state legislatures, governors, and even presidents. In recent years it has decided cases involving the most far-reaching and controversial of national policies: desegregation, abortion, busing, capital punishment, even the obligation of a president to disclose secret White House tapes.

By what right and power do these nine justices decide such monumental issues of national policy, often against the will of an overwhelming majority of Americans? They have no constituency, they appropriate no money, they command no army or police force. Alexander Hamilton characterized the American judiciary as "the least dangerous branch." Today, however, it is in many respects the strongest branch.

The late professor Alexander Bickel — perhaps the most influential theoretician of the American Supreme Court — articulated a justification for judicial review that focuses on the institutional differences between the judicial branch of government (the courts) and the political branches (the legislative and executive). The courts, he believed, are better equipped to be the "pronouncer" and "guardian" of our "enduring values." Courts, he said, have

> certain capacities for dealing with matters of principle that legislatures and executives do not possess. Judges have, or should have, the leisure, the training, and the insulation to follow the ways of the scholar in pursuing the ends of government. This is crucial in sorting out the enduring values of a society. . . . It calls for a habit of mind, and for undeviating institutional customs.

For some years, Bickel's justification has reigned as the accepted wisdom on the subject. Even those who now attack it, such as my colleague John Ely, rely on a view of the Supreme Court that places it above the petty give-and-take of partisan politics. For if the justices were to behave as other politicians behave, what conceivable reason could there be in our democracy for assigning such awesome power to these nine unelected and life-tenured persons?

The portrait Bob Woodward and Scott Armstrong paint of our nation's highest tribunal is one that can lend no comfort to any of the currently accepted justifications for judicial review. Warren Burger emerges as a vicious and conniving chief justice. He lies to his colleagues, he repeatedly casts "phony" votes at conferences in order to maximize his leverage, he pressures the Court to refrain from reversing a particular conviction because to do so would be "embarrassing both to him as chief and to the Nixon administration," he decides cases to "even" scores with old rivals, he distorts the facts and the law to reach political results, he votes against his principles in order to "correct" his public image, he attempts to sneak a rule change past his brethren in order to affect the outcome of a particular commercial case of importance to the Nixon administration, and he appears to have no principles about or understanding of the Constitution. His judicial philosophy is summarized in his own words: "We are the Supreme Court and we can do what we want."

According to Woodward and Armstrong, Burger is regarded by his colleagues as stupid and incompetent. After reading one Burger opinion, Justice Lewis Powell reportedly declared that "if an associate in my law firm had done this, I'd fire him"; and Justice Potter Stewart repeatedly told his clerks that Burger's initial draft of the Nixon-tapes opinion "would have got a grade of D in law school." Burger's personal views are presented as sexist ("I will never hire a woman clerk") and racist ("Blacks . . . make talented gardeners. . . . They have such a great sense of color"). His leadership qualities are nonexistent. According to Woodward and Armstrong, Justice Stewart has compared the Court under Burger's leadership to the old ocean liners run by two captains: "One for show, to take the women to dinner. The other to pilot the ship safely. The chief is the show captain. All we need now is a real captain." Woodward and Armstrong tell us that during the deliberations over the Nixon-tapes case "the justices found themselves entering the clerks' long-standing debate: Was the chief evil or stupid?"

The associate justices are portrayed in somewhat more balanced terms, but in the end most of them emerge as petty bureaucrats who horse-trade votes, jockey for good assignments, bicker with each other like spoiled brats, change sides in order to avoid additional work, vote so as not to antagonize their friends, and occasionally decide monumental cases on the basis of personal peeves and prejudices. The newest justice — John Stevens — is said to have complained that his "colleagues make pragmatic rather than principled decisions — shading the facts, twisting the law, warping logic."

These unflattering portraits are obviously overdrawn. Sources — especially unnamed sources — are more likely to remember and report the bizarre, the sensational, the self-flattering. If Woodward and Armstrong are to be entirely believed, the Supreme Court sometimes looks more like a Marx Brothers caricature ("The Marx Brethren") than a court of law. But regardless of how much is discounted as the hyperbole of cynical young law clerks, it is clear that the Burger Court bears little resemblance to the Bickel or Ely models of a nonpolitical institution committed to principled decision making or "enduring values."

Insiders have long known this. Former clerks, law professors, and frequent Supreme Court practitioners have been aware of the lack of congruence between the Supreme Court's image and its reality. There has been, in effect, a conspiracy of silence designed to keep the American public in the dark about the internal dynamics of the high court.

It has been feared — both by the justices and by those in the know — that any washing of the Court's dirty laundry in public will demean the perceived majesty of that institution and thereby diminish its legitimacy and influence.

The justices themselves have been the worst offenders. They have insisted on secrecy for secrecy's sake and have not been selective about what is properly the business of the public and what may appropriately be kept from it. They have, in certain cases, refused to disclose some of the most important rules that governed their actions; at least one time they covered up unethical conduct by a member of their own bar; and they have declined to make public the processes by which they decide cases.

Woodward and Armstrong recount several episodes in which the justices joined together to prevent the public from learning of their political machinations. The abortion cases, which were argued in the fall of 1971, provide the most telling example. The initial vote of the justices favored the striking down of at least portions of some restrictive abortion laws on constitutional grounds. Chief Justice Burger was in dissent. The unwritten rule of the Supreme Court has been that when the chief justice is in the majority on any given case, it is he who selects the justice who will write the opinion; but when the chief is in the minority, that prerogative falls to the senior justice within the majority. In the abortion cases, the senior majority justice was the late William O. Douglas. But *Burger* assigned the case to his "Minnesota twin," Harry Blackmun. Douglas was outraged. Woodward and Armstrong write, "Never, in Douglas's 33 years on the Court, had any chief justice tried to assign from the minority in such fashion." Blackmun, the newest justice, "was by far the slowest writer on the Court." Douglas believed that Burger had assigned the controversial opinion to Blackmun in order to do the political bidding of Richard Nixon's White House:

> Douglas ascribed to Burger the most blatant political motives. Nixon favored restrictive abortion laws. Faced with the possibility that the Court might strike abortion laws down in a presidential-election year, the chief wanted to stall the opinion.

Subsequent events confirmed Douglas's worst fears. Blackmun took an inordinate amount of time producing the opinion. Finally, in May of 1972 — near the end of the Court's term — Blackmun's opinion striking down most state laws against abortion was circulated among the brethren. Burger immediately realized that it would be a major embarrassment to the Nixon administration, and he set out to prevent its publication before the election. He lobbied mercilessly. An apparent bargain was eventually struck between the chief justice and Blackmun: the chief would change his vote in the Curt Flood case (which raised the question of whether baseball was subject to the antitrust laws) in exchange for Blackmun's agreement to withdraw his abortion opinion until after the election.

Douglas was furious with this blatant political wheeling and dealing. He decided to blow the whistle on the chief justice and drafted a dissenting memorandum that he threatened to publish if the announcement of the abortion decision was postponed. The memorandum — which the authors have somehow uncovered — included the following:

> When . . . the minority seeks to control the assignment, there is a destructive force at work in the Court. When a chief justice tries to bend the Court to his will by manipulating assignments, the integrity of the institution is imperiled. . . .
>
> The plea that the cases be reargued is merely strategy by a minority somehow to suppress the majority view with the hope that exigencies of time will change the results. That might be achieved of course by death or conceivably retirement. . . .
>
> But that kind of strategy dilutes the integrity of the Court and makes the decisions here depend on the manipulative skills of a chief justice.
>
> The *Abortion Cases* are symptomatic. This is an election year. Both political parties have made abortion an issue. What the parties say or do is none of our business. We sit here not to make the path of any candidate easier or more difficult. We decide questions only on their constitutional merits. To prolong these *Abortion Cases* into the next election would in the eyes of many be a political gesture unworthy of the Court.

The circulation of that draft dissent created havoc among the brethren. Even Douglas's closest allies on the court — Justices William Brennan and Thurgood Marshall — were, say the authors, appalled:

> No one in the history of the Court has published such a dissent. The chief might be a scoundrel, but making public the Court's inner machinations was a form of treason. . . . They pleaded with Douglas

to reconsider. His dissent would undermine the Court's credibility, the principle source of its power. Its strength derived from the public belief that the Court was trustworthy, a nonpolitical deliberative body. Did he intend to undermine all that? . . . What good would it do to drag their internal problems into public view?

Eventually Douglas gave in to the entreaties of his colleagues and the abortion decision was put off until after the reelection of Richard Nixon. In fact, in a final political maneuver, Burger again postponed the decision until two days after Nixon's inauguration, and the public never learned of Burger's machinations until, of course, Woodward and Armstrong disclosed the story.

It is to the credit of Woodward and Armstrong that they were willing — and able — to shatter this conspiracy of silence. It is certainly in the highest tradition of investigative journalism to expose the realities of institutions that affect our lives as greatly as the Supreme Court does. Nor can the justices rightly complain about the revelation of their shenanigans to the public. If they are indeed doing what Woodward and Armstrong say they are doing — and the authors make a compelling case — the public is entitled to know about it. If the result is a loss of respect for the Supreme Court, it is the justices who are to blame, not the messengers. A Supreme Court whose most important ruling required President Richard Nixon to disclose his tapes should hardly complain about disclosures of its "tapes."

The real issue is not whether the publication of *The Brethren* will weaken or strengthen the Supreme Court as an institution. Truth has its own claims, especially in a democratic society. If an institution cannot survive disclosures about its internal dynamics, then serious questions are raised about the legitimacy of that institution — or at least of its current membership.

*The Brethren* is not a book of legal scholarship. But the data — anecdotal as they are — pose a difficult challenge to legal scholars who would justify judicial review on the basis of the special qualities of the judiciary to remain above partisan politics and popular passions.

The challenge can be met, but not without significant changes in the process by which appointments are made to the Supreme Court — especially to the chief justiceship. *The Brethren* teaches us that no court can be better than the men and women who sit on it.

# FORTY-TWO

# THE SOURCE OF JUSTICE
# IN THE MIND OF A JUSTICE[1]

---

*Three of the most influential justices of the twentieth century were Felix Frankfurter, William O. Douglas, and Hugo Black, who served together from the late 1930s through the 1960s. This trio of justices all led fascinating lives both off and on the Supreme Court. Not surprisingly, they became the subject of judicial biographies. This chapter and the following two present my reviews of several of these books, written for the* New York Times Book Review. *In the reviews I explored the interaction between the personalities and philosophies of our high court justices.*

---

THE ART OF JUDICIAL BIOGRAPHY IS FINALLY COMING INTO its own in America. For generations, books about judges — especially Supreme Court justices — tended to be uncritical adorations of the Great Robed Men. For the most part, the judiciary was not subjected to the kind of scathing exposés and attacks reserved for presidents and other politicians. Judges were, after all, supposed to be above the fray. They were oracles of the law. Their job was to discern and apply the existing jurisprudence, not to impose their own views of policy or politics.

Why then, it might have been asked, do we need to know anything about the personalities of these impersonal secular priests?

American legal realism — which began to be influential in the 1920s and continues to dominate jurisprudential thinking to this day — put the lie to this simplistic mythology. Judges were people, we were told, whose opinions reflected their individual passions, their group biases, their economic self-interest, and their political preferences. The legal realists made their points in rather general terms, without reference to particular judges. It is surprising that critical judicial biography was not a more important part of their arsenal; relating the life experiences of judges to their work as jurists would seem a natural outgrowth of legal realism. But the legal realists, after all, were themselves lawyers — many of them distinguished, respected, and established. As such, they were insiders, members of the club. (Several of the most influential legal realists — including Thurman Arnold, Jerome Frank, and William O. Douglas — also became judges and justices.) They had a stake in preserving some of the mystique of the courts, or at least of their incumbents.

It has taken outsiders — journalists, political scientists, nonestablishment lawyers — to introduce the fine art of muckraking into judicial biography. First came *The Brethren* by Bob Woodward and Scott Armstrong. Like most first efforts, it was flawed: it was overstated, it relied too much on gossip, it presented a somewhat skewed portrait of an institution at work. But it was a crucial and valuable counterweight to the adorations of the past.

Now there has appeared a brilliant and sure-to-be-controversial judicial psychobiography that strikes a balance between the extremes of uncritical adoration and unselective condemnation. H. N. Hirsch's *The Enigma of Felix Frankfurter* is an admiring but deeply critical study of one of the most interesting, complex, and controversial personalities ever to grace the Supreme Court bench.

While *The Brethren* peered into the closed chambers and conferences of the Marble Temple, *The Enigma of Felix Frankfurter* attempts to penetrate the very psyche of the man characterized by Mr. Hirsch as perhaps the most influential jurist of the twentieth century. The task is ambitious; the results are satisfying but far from complete or definitive. Mr. Hirsch has selected the perfect subject for this initial foray into judicial analysis. Frankfurter (1882–1965), perhaps more than any other justice, wore his unconscious on the sleeve of his robe. He often invoked his own background and experiences in his judicial and other writings. In the divisive and emotional 1943 case involving the power of a public school to compel a Jehovah's Witness to salute the American flag (of which more later), Frankfurter opened his opinion on an unusual autobiographical note: one who belongs to the most vilified and persecuted minority in history is not likely to be insensible to the freedoms guaranteed by our Constitution.

Mr. Hirsch begins his study by introducing his readers to the psychodynamic theories of such analysts as Erik Erikson and Karen Horney. Emphasizing the importance of "self-image," Mr. Hirsch postulates that when a self-image is created and employed for "purposes of compensation," the individual will feel a constant need to prove himself, to overreact to criticism, to direct self-hatred outward and to conceal self-doubts.

Although Mr. Hirsch disavows any attempt to reduce Frankfurter's jurisprudence "to the content of his psyche," he does argue that the justice's neuroses and private insecurities "led him to harden his stands, to behave in a certain way toward his colleagues, to emphasize certain strands in his philosophy and to exclude others when they were adopted by his enemies, to ignore and rationalize certain contradictions in his legal theory." The goal of Mr. Hirsch's innovative study is to "explain certain characteristics of Frankfurter's behavior that are difficult to account for in a purely 'ideological' explanation." The method employed toward this ambitious end is a systematic in-depth study of the justice's personality. The conclusion, offered in the opening pages, is that Frankfurter — a distinguished professor and an adviser to presidents as well as a justice of the Supreme Court — can best be understood "psychologically as representing a textbook case of a neurotic personality."

Mr. Hirsch acknowledges the paucity of data upon which to construct his grand psychological theories. If there is one accepted tenet of psychodynamic theories, it is the centrality of early childhood and familial experiences. But the information covering Frankfurter's youth is certainly "meager." Few hard facts are known about his father; Mr. Hirsch is forced to speculate that "Frankfurter's family structure fits squarely within a fairly typical immigrant pattern."

Mr. Hirsch's whirlwind tour of Frankfurter's hectic life begins in earnest at New York City College, where the young Frankfurter (who was twelve years old when his family emigrated from Vienna) immersed himself in American culture. We are then taken to Harvard Law School, the bastion of meritocracy, where the only thing that mattered was "excellence in your profession," and where — according to Frankfurter — "your father or your face" was irrelevant. Self-conscious about his short stature and his immigrant background, Frankfurter decided to parlay his intellectual brilliance into what Mr.

Hirsch calls "a certain degree of social acceptance from Brahmin, Yankee culture."

While at Harvard, Frankfurter met Louis Brandeis, the first of "a remarkable trio of elder mentors" (or substitute father figures, as the analysts would say). Soon thereafter he came under the influence of Oliver Wendell Holmes Jr. and Henry L. Stimson. These three men were to remain dominant influences in his life (though his personality differed markedly from each of theirs).

The Horatio Alger story continues as we follow Frankfurter through the corridors of power in Washington, where he served in the Bureau of Insular Affairs and later in the War and Labor Departments, to his return in 1914 to the Harvard Law School as a controversial law professor, his friendship with Franklin D. Roosevelt, his influence on the New Deal, his eventual appointment to the United States Supreme Court in 1939, and his twenty-three-year tenure as an associate justice.

Throughout this remarkable career, Frankfurter manifested the qualities that Mr. Hirsch characterizes as neurotic: He was a hopeless sycophant, constantly fawning on and flattering those in power, even when privately critical of their actions. (Frankfurter once wrote — "presumably with a straight face," as Mr. Hirsch dryly observes — that he "would without doubt reserve [capital punishment] for the fawners and flatterers of those in power.") He was excessively rigid in his views and took criticism as personal attack. He was extremely manipulative, playing people against one other and often keeping his real agenda hidden. He was — even to the end — trying to prove himself and conceal his self-doubts.

There is, of course, another side to Felix Frankfurter, and Mr. Hirsch does well by it. Frankfurter was always brilliant and charming, often caring and kind, and occasionally courageous. He was a remarkable man on a Court that had tolerated far too many quite ordinary men. He would be a fascinating subject for a psychobiography even if he had not reached such dizzying heights and such power and prestige.

It is in the nature of psychobiography, however, for the author to ascribe too much significance to particular events about which considerable data happen to be available. For example, Mr. Hirsch exaggerates the importance of the two Jehovah's Witnesses flag-salute cases in which the Supreme Court reversed itself between 1940 and 1943. In the first case — *Minersville School District v. Gobitis* — Frankfurter wrote the Court's eight-to-one opinion sustaining the power of a state to compel a student to violate his deeply felt religious beliefs by saluting the flag. Preferring the values of patriotism and authority — especially while a war was engulfing the world — over those of individualism and liberty, Frankfurter wrote a paean to the American flag as "the symbol of our national unity (evoking) that unifying sentiment without which there can ultimately be no liberties, civil or religious." Justices Hugo Black and William O. Douglas, also recently appointed to the Court, joined in Frankfurter's opinion and praised it as a magnificent example of judicial statesmanship.

But the media did not agree; more than a hundred newspapers condemned the decision, and only a handful approved it. Within months, Justices Black and Douglas reconsidered their views and shortly thereafter publicly stated that they had changed their minds and "now believed that it was wrongly decided." Then in *West Virginia State Board of Education v. Barnette*, three years later, the Court formally reversed itself and held that a state could not compel a Jehovah's Witness to salute the American flag. This reversal drew from Frankfurter the stinging dissent in which he invoked his own minority background as evidence of his sensitivity toward religious freedom. He also accused his colleagues of paying too much attention to the press.

Mr. Hirsch sees these cases as a turning point in Frankfurter's career and especially in his stormy relationship to his colleagues:

> Psychologically, the period marked off by Barnette . . . produced in Frankfurter a sense of being under siege. Unexpectedly, he found himself in a position of opposition; his leadership had been rejected. He would react in a manner that had become a familiar part of this psychological make-up.

Mr. Hirsch asserts that the remainder of Frankfurter's tenure on the Supreme Court — nearly twenty more years — was in a very real sense the inevitable result of his behavior in these early cases:

> Both in his relationships with his brethren and in the development of his judicial doctrines Frankfurter was left to play out the scenario he had written for himself. New Justices came and went, new issues preoccupied the Court, but Frankfurter could neither change his political style nor dig himself out from under the hardened ideological commitments he had made.

The mold into which Mr. Hirsch casts Frankfurter seems a bit too rigid and deterministic. But it is surely true that after his first few years on the bench, Frankfurter became increasingly contentious, divisive, and defensive. He seemed to lose the qualities of playful experimentation and bold creativity that had characterized his earlier years in Washington and Cambridge. Frankfurter will be revered as a great justice capable of rationalizing the past, but he will not be remembered as an innovative justice who broke ground in dealing with new and unanticipated problems.

In the end, Mr. Hirsch does not succeed entirely in resolving the enigma of Felix Frankfurter. The author's attempt to answer the "most puzzling" question of all — "Why did a man known before his appointment to the Supreme Court as a civil libertarian . . . become . . . our most famous and persistent spokesman for austere judicial self-restraint?" — is not really satisfactory. The key to that mystery lies more in legal philosophy than in psychoanalysis, though we are perhaps aided in understanding the philosophy by knowing more about the philosopher.

Notwithstanding its imperfections, Mr. Hirsch's study is an important addition to the literature of judicial biography. Courts and their incumbents must be studied, criticized, and — if necessary — exposed. They are among the most powerful and least accountable institutions and individuals in any democratic country. The tools of the journalist, the historian, the economist, the political scientist, and the psychologist must be employed in this enterprise. Lawyers, especially insiders, should be encouraged to speak up. Television cameras, which the Supreme Court has now ruled may be brought into at least some courtrooms — though not, of course, the Supreme Court itself — should be made part of the effort to oversee the judiciary. None of these, working alone, will uncover the complete story. But each will disclose an important part. *The Enigma of Felix Frankfurter* is an invaluable contribution to the essential enterprise of making our citizens aware of the inner workings of their most important court.

# FORTY-THREE

# INSIDE THE SANCTUM SANCTORUM[1]

THE AUTOBIOGRAPHY OF THE LATE WILLIAM O. DOUGLAS, one of the most remarkable jurists in Anglo-American history, raises profound questions about the role of the Supreme Court in the American system of government. The simultaneous publication of James Simon's somewhat critical, though admiring, account of Justice Douglas's life and judicial career underscores these questions: How, in a democratic society, can nine unelected and politically nonresponsible men overrule the policy choices of state legislatures, Congress, popular referenda, and presidents? Why should judges have the last word — apart from the unwieldy and unlikely extreme of a constitutional amendment — on such emotionally laden issues as abortion, busing, pornography, and even national security? Such questions lie close to the surface of all intelligent discussion of judicial review in our country. Like smoldering volcanos, they erupt periodically — usually when the Supreme Court is under attack for having rendered a particularly unpopular or controversial decision.

The current burst of questions has not been provoked by any judicial decision, political attack, or even general dissatisfaction with the Supreme Court. Indeed, the Court is currently in a period of relative calm under the uninspired leadership of Chief Justice Warren Burger. (It is perhaps the calm before the storm that may follow the anticipated resignation of several justices during the next presidential term.)

In *The Court Years: 1939–1975* — the second of William O. Douglas's two-volume autobiography — the controversial justice takes us inside the marble halls of the Supreme Court and into the sanctum sanctorum of the justices' conference. He introduces us to the personalities beneath the impersonal robes and behind the imposing bench. While extremely critical of many of the thirty justices with whom he served, Douglas finds some kind words to say about nearly every one of his brethren. (Even Justice James McReynolds, who called blacks "niggers" and who regarded President Franklin D. Roosevelt as "insane," emerges as "a very delightful companion.") But the basic message is clear: the Supreme Court consists of nine very human men (remarkably, there has not yet been a woman justice in the Court's 191-year history)[2] who are generally mediocre lawyers, often former politicians, sometimes inspiring personalities, hardly ever overtly corrupt, and almost always selected for the Court on the basis of political considerations. Douglas put it this way: "Most Presidents name Justices who, they think, will vote the way they would vote." And since few presidents have been known for their sensitivity to civil liberties, "our only hope as a people [has been] that a President would make a mistake." And "mistakes" have, in fact, given us Earl Warren, William Brennan, and perhaps, John Paul Stevens.

In this memoir, Justice Douglas does not provide us with a systematic account of his thirty-five iconoclastic years on the world's most powerful court. These are ragged-edged fragments and hasty over-the-shoulder glimpses. The manuscript was written in his later years and edited by his publisher. Neither his own nor his colleagues' philosophies emerge in coherent fashion. But the book is still a gold mine of valuable information and perceptions. It is valuable primarily for what it tells us about the human qualities and foibles of the individuals who passed into and out of the nine high-backed chairs during Douglas's unprecedented long tenure on the Court.

To Douglas, judicial attitudes can be understood only against the backdrop of each judge's personal experiences. Justice Felix Frankfurter's philosophy of judicial restraint derived, according to Douglas, from his enormous desire to be accepted by "the Establishment" because of his deep "feeling of inadequacy." Despite Frankfurter's protestations that his decisions were based on an abstract judicial philosophy, he was — according to Douglas — a victim of his own overpowering emotions: "Frankfurter's skein of life was woven with a design that was duplicitous, for no one poured his emotions more completely into decisions, while professing just the opposite."

The opinions of Justice Hugo Black, who professed to be following a literal interpretation of the Constitution, were also a product of his emotions and experiences. Many have wondered why Black, who espoused an absolutist view of free speech, was never sympathetic to picketing (which, after all, is little more than speech on a stick). Douglas provides a personal analysis: when Black was nominated for the Court and it was discovered that he had been a member of the Ku Klux Klan, his own house was picketed en masse, "an experience that . . . colored his decisions in all subsequent cases involving picketing."

Douglas argues persuasively that most justices decide momentous cases on the basis of their own predilections, personal loyalties, and political preferences. Near the beginning of Douglas's career on the Court, Chief Justice Charles Evans Hughes whispered the "shattering" truth to the novice justice: "Justice Douglas, you must remember one thing. At the constitutional level where we work, ninety percent of any decision is emotional. The rational part of us supplies the reason for supporting our predilections." This is probably an overgeneralization: There have been justices throughout history who have eschewed personal and emotional preferences and have applied somewhat neutral principles. Oliver Wendell Holmes, Benjamin Cardozo, John Harlan, and — on occasion — Felix Frankfurter exemplified this approach. One is hard pressed, however, to think of any current justices who do not regularly vote their personal politics in controversial cases. This is as true of the Nixon appointees, who purport to be advocates of "judicial restraint," as of those justices who are regarded as activists.

It is perfectly reasonable, in a democracy, for voters to cast their ballots on the basis of their emotions. But justices of the Supreme Court are given the enormous power to overrule popular, democratically arrived-at decisions largely on the assumption that they decide cases on the basis of principle rather than expediency; that they are capable of raising themselves above the passions and politics of the day; that their backgrounds and training, combined with the institutional processes of the Court, have endowed them with a unique capacity to discern the enduring values of our society.

The more the public learns about the inner workings of the Supreme Court — through publication of internal Court papers, judicial biographies and autobiographies, exposés like *The Brethren*, and word of mouth — the harder it becomes to justify the special power of this elite institution in our governmental scheme. And the justices know this. That is why they — and their protectors in the elite bar — have cooperated to construct unjustifiably thick walls of judicial secrecy around the workings and deliberations of this powerful branch of government. But the walls are crumbling. Ironically, the Supreme Court itself was the Joshua whose trumpet blast leveled the most impenetrable wall of all: the one protecting the secrecy of presidential conversations in the Oval Office. It should come as no surprise that the next wall to fall would be the one surrounding the justices' conference room. There are, of course, no tapes of these weekly conferences during which the justices alone — without law clerks or other staff — debate the issues and cast their votes. All we have are the cryptic notes and self-serving recollections of an occasional justice and the gossipy snipings of some law clerks.

But in the right hands, these isolated strands can be woven into a fascinating, if incomplete, tapestry. James Simon has done just that in *Independent Journey*, his excellent biography of Justice Douglas. Employing the private papers of other justices, interviews with Douglas's former brethren and law clerks, and additional private and public Court records, Mr. Simon has presented us with a far more probing yet balanced picture of Justice Douglas and his colleagues than appears in any recent work. Reading Douglas's autobiography and Mr. Simon's biography together is sometimes like viewing the classic Japanese movie *Rashomon*, in which a single event is perceived entirely differently by various participants and observers.

The two very different accounts of the Rosenberg case provide a striking example of how a critical biography can serve as a check on the candor of autobiography. The public facts are undisputed. On the eve of the Rosenbergs' scheduled electrocution in 1953, Justice Douglas issued an order staying the execution and then immediately left town, since the Supreme Court term was over. When word of the stay reached the public, all hell broke loose. The Justice Department petitioned Chief Justice Frederick Vinson to convene an extraordinary Special Term of the Supreme Court to vacate Douglas's stay. Vinson convened the Special Term, the stay was vacated, and Ethel and Julius Rosenberg were executed the next day.

In his autobiography, Douglas boasts of his heroism and concern for human life in issuing the stay in the face of massive public opposition. He tells of receiving a telegram from his hometown of Yakima, Washington, threatening a "lynching party" for him if he were to grant the stay, and of becoming "a leper" whom people — including his dear friend Lyndon Johnson — avoided as a result of his granting it. But Mr. Simon's sources present Douglas in a somewhat less heroic light. It turns out that Douglas had voted against Supreme Court review of the Rosenberg case on five separate occasions prior to his dramatic public issuance of the stay. Moreover, according to Justice Felix Frankfurter's notes, Douglas's vote to deny review to the Rosenbergs was "uttered with startling vehemence."

On several of those prior occasions, Douglas's vote against the Rosenbergs was pivotal: had he cast it in favor of hearing argument, the Rosenbergs' petition for review would have been granted, and their lives might well have been saved. But it appears from Mr. Simon's account that Douglas was more interested in having things done "on his terms alone" than in seeing justice done to the Rosenbergs. His highly publicized last-minute decision to grant the stay was seen by his colleagues — the only ones who knew the whole story of his prior actions — as grandstanding. Justice Robert Jackson characterized Douglas's performance in the Rosenberg case as "the dirtiest, most shameful, most cynical performance that I have ever heard of in matters pertaining to law."

Jackson was wrong: his own performance in the Rosenberg case was worse. According to Mr. Simon, "Justice Jackson arranged a meeting with Chief Justice Vinson and Attorney General Herbert Brownell to discuss their strategy if, as anticipated, Douglas stayed the Rosenbergs' execution." At this secret meeting — according to FBI documents — Jackson, Vinson, and Brownell planned the entire scenario in which the Justice Department would petition for, and Vinson would grant, the Special Term of the Court to overrule Douglas's stay. The Canons of Ethics — then as now — forbade any judge or justice from secretly discussing legal tactics in a criminal case with the prosecutor in the absence of the defense attorney.

The issue raised by the Douglas and Simon accounts of the Rosenberg case is not which justice comes out looking worse. (At one crucial point, after forcing Douglas to back down, Jackson clucked to Frankfurter: "That S.O.B.'s bluff was called.") The important question is this: What, if anything, distinguishes the nature of judicial decision making in highly controversial and political cases from legislative or executive decision making? Unless there are discernible differences, it is difficult to justify turning over to unelected judges the power to make ultimate decisions about controversial questions of policy.

By his life's work, Douglas provides one possible answer to this conundrum. Few people in the history of our country have been as single-mindedly dedicated to the human rights of the individual in relation to government. His credo was that the Bill of Rights was designed "to take the government off the backs of the people." With a few notable exceptions, he did not allow considerations of efficiency, popularity, or political loyalty to sway him. He championed the rights of every person to speak his or her mind — no matter how foul or obscene the message. He refused to bend to the pressures of McCarthyism, crime hysteria, big business, religious fanaticism, or Richard Nixon. He survived four efforts to impeach him. He even resisted the seductive allure of reverse racial quotas, an expedient advocated by most of his longtime civil rights allies both on and off the Court. Acknowledging that he once made the mistake of sustaining a classification based on race in the World War II Japanese-exclusion cases, he concluded that racial quotas — no matter how benign and well intentioned — were "a wholly un-American practice, quite inconsistent with equal protection."

It is difficult to conceive of an elected public official sustaining that kind of commitment to principle throughout so long a career. A government of legislators and executives dominated by considerations of efficiency and electability can afford some iconoclasts and gadflies in positions of power, or at least in positions to check and limit power. William O. Douglas was the personification of this important role.

There will never be an entirely satisfactory justification for the power of judges to overrule popular decisions. As long as judges are human beings — with passions, prejudices, and politics — their rulings will not always conform to a model of principled decision making. But some judges will be able to act in a somewhat more principled fashion over a longer period of time than most elected officeholders generally do. So at least some judges can act as imperfect checks on the excesses of the other branches. It must always be remembered, however, that the allocation of such power to an unelected and life-tenured judiciary is not without its costs: judges can be — and many are — petty tyrants with little public check on their own excesses.

During Justice Douglas's tenure on the Court, I was sometimes asked by students: "What would happen to the country if we had nine Douglases on the Supreme Court?" I always answered with a question of my own: "What would happen if we had no Douglases on the Supreme Court?" We have no William O. Douglas on the Court today, and despite his sometimes questionable judicial behavior and his always quixotic nature, we are the poorer for it.

## FORTY-FOUR

# THE JUDGE JUDGED[1]

FIVE YEARS AFTER HIS DEATH AT THE AGE EIGHTY-FIVE, Hugo Lafayette Black, who stood near the center of our national life for nearly half a century, remains an enigma. Gerald Dunne's ambitious biography, *Hugo Black and the Judicial Revolution*, seeks to unravel the mystery of the Klan-supported Alabama senator who became one of the most influential Supreme Court justices in history.

Dunne asks how a man, once an honored citizen of the "Invisible Empire" (the Ku Klux Klan), then the unscrupulous chairman of a witch-hunting Senate committee, could emerge as the judicial apostle of racial equality and civil liberties. And why, in the waning years of his illustrious career, he seemed to revert to some of the less compassionate residues of his past.

Dunne's search for the real Hugo Black takes us behind some generally unbreachable barriers: into the "Kloreros" (secret meetings) of the KKK, the clandestine machinations of the Senate caucus rooms, the closed conferences and private correspondence of the least public of all government institutions, the Supreme Court.

Here we see the forty-year-old Hugo Black, victorious in his first campaign for the Senate, being honored by the Birmingham Klan, without whose vigorous support he could not have been elected. Amazingly, a transcript of the entire event, reflecting the paradox of Black's participation, has been preserved. It reveals the Senator-elect sitting silently through various antiblack, anti-Jewish, and anti-Catholic diatribes (including the parading across the stage of nine Catholic orphans to the boast that "before we get through with them they will be Protestants"). The results of the recent election are then described: "You have given us a man named Black who wears white to occupy a seat in the Senate." But Black's cryptic remarks look more to the future than the past: "The thing I like about this organization is not the burning of crosses. . . . I see a bigger vision, . . . the principles of human liberty."

We are then taken to the Senate committee room, where we see Chairman Black abusing the subpoena power for political ends, trampling on the rights of corporate witnesses, and berating them for invoking their constitutional privileges.

Next we move to the office of the secretary of the Senate, where the second-term senator, having been nominated to the Supreme Court by a shrewd President Franklin D. Roosevelt, who knew that even anti–New Deal senators would vote to confirm one of their own, is listening to the confirmation debate. The charge had been made that the prospective justice had once been a member of the Klan. It was manifest that if this charge could be proved, the nomination would be killed. But the nominee, in full knowledge that the public and some senators were being misinformed on a crucial fact, remained silent. Without evidence, the nomination was confirmed.

Within a month, the deception was exposed by an enterprising reporter who uncovered the transcript of the secret Birmingham Klorero. Caught flagrante delicto, Justice Black took to the airwaves to convince the American public that he should retain his seat on the Supreme Court. "I did join the Klan. I later resigned. I have never rejoined," was his simple statement. He did not attempt to justify the cover-up. The American public was apparently satisfied, and the new justice commenced his service on the high court.

Dunne devotes most of the book to a painstaking analysis of that service, particularly to the evolution of Justice Black's unique judicial philosophy — a philosophy that defies characterization by such conventional labels as liberal versus conservative, judicial activist versus judicial passivist. His was a philosophy born of his Baptist upbringing: the relevant text, whether of the Bible or of the Constitution, must be construed literally, without the need for human interpretation, whether by priest or judge. Justice Black was fond of saying that when the framers of the Constitution said "Congress shall make no law . . . abridging the freedom of speech," they meant *no law*; they did not mean *some* laws subject to the approval of judges.

Black did not fear judicial power as such: he was prepared to — and indeed did — strike down as unconstitutional all manner of federal and state legislation. What he did fear was judicial *discretion:* he did not want judges to be able to exercise personal judgment in constitutional adjudication.

His biblical literalism also led to some results that were restrictive of liberty. He concluded, for example, that since the Bill of Rights contained no express guarantee of privacy, the government was empowered to wiretap private conversations or to prohibit the use of birth control in the privacy of the marital bedroom.

Black's last years on the Court coincided with a growing militancy by civil rights and antiwar groups, a spiraling crime rate, and an unprecedented effort by civil liberties organizations to stretch the Bill of Rights to its farthest limits. His opinions, during the final several terms, began to reflect his apparent distress over these developments. He wrote about the right of restaurant owners "to refuse service to Negroes." He insisted that it was "high time to challenge the assumption . . . that the groups who . . . have been mistreated have a constitutional right to use the public's streets . . . to protest whatever, and whenever they want." He inveighed against releasing, on legal technicalities, professional criminals "to prey upon society with impunity." Something had changed. Although Dunne does not tell us what it was, he does give us sufficient data from which to draw our own conclusions.

The Dunne biography of Hugo Black is indispensable to an understanding of his judicial philosophy. For the justice's philosophy grew out of the man's life. It is a philosophy that at bottom is premised on a deep distrust of the ability of judges to remain aloof from personal ambitions, biases, and passions. Black understood that power corrupts.

He himself — whether out of ambition, bias, or peer pressure — had joined a despicable racist organization; he himself, in a quest for national recognition, had violated the constitutional rights of others. He did not, even as tenured justice, trust himself or others like him to set internal limits capable of preventing him from succumbing to the temptations of power.

The tragedy of Hugo Black's life is that in the end even he could not be held in check completely by his own tightly constructed philosophical shackle. Some of the nasty passions and biases of his youth seem to have slipped through in his old age. But it would be unfair to judge the contributions of Justice Black by either his earliest or his latest years in public life. His mature middle period, spanning nearly thirty years, will be remembered as among the most creative and illustrious in American judicial history.

# FORTY-FIVE

# APPRECIATING LIBERTY[1]

*Professor Alexander Bickel of Yale Law School was among the most significant influences on my legal thinking. I took a seminar with him that turned into a dialogue between our diametrically conflicting views of liberalism and conservatism. We soon became great friends and continued our dialogue, especially during the summer of 1965, which we both spent at Stanford Law School. Alex died in 1975 at the height of his career. He had just published a volume entitled* The Morality of Consent, *which summarized his theory of legal rights. The* New York Times Book Review *asked me to review it. I used it as an occasion both to eulogize my mentor and to continue our dialogue on the best way to achieve liberty.*

ALEXANDER BICKEL'S SHORT BUT PROVOCATIVE VOLUME, completed just one week before his death, is a fitting testimony to the author's extraordinary, though tragically brief, career as a constitutional scholar, lawyer, and teacher. In just a hundred and fifty literate pages, we are treated to vintage Bickel insight into every major political issue of the decade, from the civil rights movement to the Warren Court, through the frenetic university upheavals, and — inevitably — to Watergate.

But this is no jumble of themes: it is a tapestry woven by a master of subtle color and texture. Bickel does not merely restate history: he relates events and movements one to the other in ways that are both challenging and disturbing. He sees the Nixon presidency and Watergate as the "utterly inevitable" consequence of the undisciplined liberalism and "result-orientation" of the Warren Court. A strange relationship, probably wrong, and surely overstated. But Bickel makes out a plausible case: the Imperial Presidency, he argues, "is a leaf from the Warren Court book," since they both justify the aggregation of power as a necessary means for doing "more effectively what other institutions, particularly Congress, do not do very rapidly or very well." The Warren Court, he argues, was engaged in a quest for "moral imperative"; it was willing — indeed it "took the greatest pride in" — "cutting through legal technicalities, . . . piercing through procedure to substance." If the Warren clique could proudly boast of finding shortcuts around legal niceties to achieve its conception of the "right" and the "good," why should the Nixon gang — which had a broader popular mandate than the Warren Court — comply with such legal obstacles as the search warrant and the right to bail in its march to the right and good society based on the gospel according to Mitchell, Mardian, and Haldeman?

Bickel's account of modern legal history comes fully adorned with both villain and hero. The villain is moralistic liberalism with its various champions, from the social contractarian Jean-Jacques Rousseau to the constitutional absolutist Justice Hugo Black. The hero is "Whig-Conservatism" with its champions Edmund Burke and his judicial successors Oliver Wendell Holmes and Felix Frankfurter.

The "Liberal contractarian model," Bickel explains, rests on the vision of inalienable rights which predate society and are derived "from a natural, if imagined, contract"; it is "moral, principled, legalistic, ultimately authoritarian." The "Whig model," on the other hand, rests on "a natural skepticism" that recognizes "human nature as it is seen to be." It is "flexible, pragmatic, slow-moving, highly political": its goal is "an imperfect justice, for there is no other kind." Not surprisingly, Bickel declares the Burkean tradition "my own model," and proceeds to argue how it has been the excesses of liberalism that have produced the most enduring wounds to our body politic.

His examples tend to the polemical, and they are not always convincing. Bickel points out that Chief Justice Roger Taney, author of the *Dred Scott* decision, which held that the descendant of an African slave could not be an American citizen, "was a liberal" to whose philosophy "the concept of contract was central." From this ad hominem he seeks to persuade us that liberalism, with its emphasis on the original contract, contributed to the reification of racism in our pre–Civil War constitutional history. But he fails to show how Taney's racism can any more be attributed to his liberalism than can Burke's anti-Semitism be attributed to his conservatism. The sad truth is that the evils of the human condition transcend labels such as liberal and Whig. No political group has a monopoly on vice or virtue.

But even Bickel's overdrawn examples succeed in making an important point. The *Dred Scott* decision does demonstrate the dangers of emphasizing the rights of "citizenship" rather than "personhood." And it is arguable — though not at all obvious — that the Warren Court acted regressively when, more than a century later, it unwittingly echoed Taney's litany about the centrality of citizenship to the rights conferred by our Constitution.

"Citizenship," wrote Warren in several important decisions, is "that status, which alone assures the full enjoyment of the precious rights conferred by our Constitution." If that is so, argues Bickel, then the noncitizen — the alien, the visitor, the expatriate — can be denied these rights with impunity.

Surely it is preferable, as Bickel suggests, for a government to operate "under a constitution to which the concept of citizenship matters very little, that prescribes decencies and wise modalities of government quite without regard to the concept of citizenship."

Bickel's argument against preferential university admissions based on race is convincing as well, at least to this reader.[2] But, interestingly, it rests on the very moralisms and natural rights for which he so roundly criticizes the liberals. Is this really Bickel speaking: "To reject an applicant . . . who has met established, realistic . . . qualifications in favor of a less-qualified candidate [just because the less qualified candidate is black] is morally wrong and in the aggregate disastrous." "If the Constitution prohibits exclusion of blacks . . . on racial grounds, it cannot permit the exclusion of whites on similar grounds." Here we have pure, doctrinaire constitutional moralism! Precisely the kind we might expect from Justices Hugo Black or William O. Douglas.[3]

Where is Burke's flexible, pragmatic recognition of situational and imperfect justice? From whence does the principle of meritocracy — a principle to which I join Bickel in subscribing — derive, if not from classical liberal premises? Would not a true Whig argue that the realities of past social injustice require some temporary compromise with the principle of meritocracy, at least until a significant number of blacks are introduced into the mainstream of American higher education? What Bickel fails to tell us is why certain kinds of controversies demand an absolutist, moralistic approach, while other kinds of controversies call for a pragmatic, compromising solution.

At bottom, Bickel's jurisprudence — of which this volume is the most coherent and general treatment — is a prescription for normalcy, for crisis avoidance. His vision of the good society is not a static one where correct principles prevail and govern, it is a dynamic society of "untidy accommodations" between competing principles, of "fundamental tensions that are bound to exist." The role of the judiciary is "to ease rather than finally resolve" tensions, to "invent compromises and accommodations before declaring firm and unambiguous principles."

His vision presupposes "moderation" by the competing forces; it can work — as Bickel acknowledges — "only when there is forbearance and continuance on both sides." It cannot survive "the politics of moral attack." And therein lies the crucial difference between Bickel and the classic civil libertarian: Bickel's prescription for cure is to avoid the disease; he has constructed a magnificent hospital for preventive medicine but failed to include an emergency ward.

Having lived through the Nazi Holocaust, Bickel shared Learned Hand's conviction that when liberty dies in the hearts of the people "no constitution, no law, no courts can save it [or] even do much to help it." Cataclysmic crises kill liberty and must therefore be avoided at all costs. There is little sense in constructing a system whose purpose it is to conserve liberty during periods of "extremis," since that task is doomed to failure.

The civil libertarian, on the other hand, designs his constitutional system for maximum survivability. He is willing to forego significant benefits during periods of normalcy in order to improve the chances, even slightly, of keeping the spark of liberty ignited during times of stress.

In the end both Bickel and the civil libertarian seek the same goal: the preservation of liberty in a world where the vast majority of people have no appreciation of it, except when it is taken away. The history of mankind's responses to crises does not point unambiguously to one approach or the other; neither is villainous nor heroic. It all depends on the values of those in power. I, for one, would not hesitate to embrace the Bickel approach if I could be assured that those who governed would be as humane and compassionate as Alexander Bickel. But if history teaches one verity, it is, as our Supreme Court once cautioned, that no nation has the "right to expect that it will always have wise and humane rulers."

# FORTY-SIX

# JUDICIAL REVIEW

---

*One of my classmates in Professor Alexander Bickel's seminar was John Hart Ely, who soon became one of the nation's leading constitutional theorists. We have remained friends, colleagues, and collaborators. When he retired from the deanship of Stanford Law School in 1987, I was asked to write an appreciation, in which I discussed his — and my — legal perspectives on judicial review and constitutional interpretation.*

---

JOHN HART ELY, WHOM I HAVE KNOWN AND WORKED WITH for more than a quarter of a century, is an original. His views on the Constitution are not "like" those of any other scholar. He is neither a Holmesian nor a Frankfurterian. He is not "of" the Bickel school or the Dworkin school. He holds no membership cards in the critical legal studies or law and economics clubs. He fits into no preexisting molds or pigeonholes. He is not even a disciple of his hero, Earl Warren. His vision of the Constitution derives not from an unearthing of the past but, rather, from an understanding of the present and a vision of the future. Like all creators, he has stood on the shoulders of giants to expand his visions. But they are his visions.

John's opinions have always been unique, from his memorable battles with our professors at Yale to his current criticisms of judges and justices. His great book *Democracy and Distrust: A Theory of Judicial Review* sets out a theory of judicial construction that is coherent, compassionate, and faithful to the text and history of the document he brings to life. Unlike the many post hoc and ever shifting "theories" of constitutional interpretation now in fashion, or the "theories" that are trotted out to rationalize crass political results already arrived at, Ely's is a genuine theory: it does not always bring him where he would wish to go as a citizen or legislator, but it brings his Constitution into its proper role as facilitator of democracy. His Supreme Court is neither rubber stamp nor superlegislature. It is a working part of our system of checks and balances with a special role to perform. The bicentennial of our Constitution is an appropriate occasion for all Americans to thank John Hart Ely for his gift to us.

## DEMOCRACY AND DISTRUST

John Ely's theory of judicial review, as set out in *Democracy and Distrust*, provides a coherent, persuasive alternative to what the author describes as the "false dichotomy" that pervades modern constitutional theory and debate. Pursuant to this widely accepted dichotomy, constitutional interpretation must either be limited to the norms stated or clearly implied in the written provisions or legislative history of the text ("interpretivism" or "originalism"), or else content can be given to these provisions only by looking beyond the four corners of the document, by identifying and enforcing values that are considered "important" or "fundamental" ("noninterpretivism" or "values-identification"). While Ely carefully analyzes, and indeed borrows from, these competing visions of constitutional interpretation and adjudication, he rejects both in favor of a unique, third approach — a "participation-oriented, representation-reinforcing"[1] theory of judicial review, which protects minority interests from majoritarian prejudices and barriers to the political process, while remaining consistent with the underlying democratic assumptions of our system of government.

Ely is quick to admit the allure of the interpretivist theory.[2] Interpretivism, he notes, comports with our accepted conceptions of the manner in which laws should be applied — a court, in interpreting a given statute, will generally "limit itself to a determination of the purposes and prohibitions expressed by or implicit in its language."[3] More fundamentally, interpretivism — at least compared with noninterpretivism — is reconcilable with a democratic theory of government. By confining the scope of judicial review to enforcing only those constitutional norms found in the explicit provisions or legislative history of the text (original intent), "clause-bound interpretivists" claim to be protecting the will of the majority from the "values" and "principles" of a nonelected few.

In rejecting this vision of the Constitution, Ely observes that the most powerful argument against clause-bound interpretivism lies in the document itself — that the Constitution, "the interpretivist's Bible," contains several provisions "whose invitation to look beyond their four corners — whose invitation, if you will, to become at least to that extent a noninterpretivist — cannot be construed away."[4] The content of these open-textured provisions — such as the Eighth and Ninth Amendments and the due process, privileges, and immunities and equal protection clauses of the Fourteenth Amendment — cannot, as Ely deftly describes, be derived from "anything within [the Constitution's] four corners or the known intentions of its framers,"[5] but rather requires the interpreter to look to sources and materials beyond that of the document's ambiguous text and limited legislative history.

Ely, however, is similarly skeptical of interpretivism's widely accepted competing school of thought — that the Supreme Court "should give content to the Constitution's open-ended provisions by identifying and enforcing upon the political branches those values that are, by one formula or another, truly important or fundamental."[6] Ely discusses, and rejects, various methods of "discovering fundamental values" — sources ranging from the judge's own values, to tradition, to natural law. Ely demonstrates, as did Alexander Bickel before him, the ultimate futility of such an enterprise, acknowledging the inability to objectively and democratically choose one external source of fundamental values over another.

The brilliance and importance of John Ely's work lie in his development of a principled alternative to this dichotomy — dispelling the sanctity of the assumption that interpretivism and noninterpretivism are the only two options available for judicial review. Ely erects, in essence, an "anti-trust," as opposed to a "regulatory," approach to constitutional interpretation — a theory premised upon the assumption that courts should intervene in the political market, not when they disagree with the results of government conduct, but when they determine that the market is systematically malfunctioning. At the core of Ely's theory of judicial review is his view that courts play an indispensable role in preserving the integrity of the political process. Influenced greatly by the recently maligned *Carolene Products* footnote,[7] and more generally by the history of the Warren Court, John Ely develops a theory of judicial review that exhibits a healthy distrust in the concept of a majority — the ins — policing the political process. Ely observes that malfunction

> occurs when the process is undeserving of trust, when (1) the ins are choking off the channels of political change to ensure that they will stay in and the outs will stay out, or (2) though no one is actually denied a voice or a vote, representatives beholden to an effective majority are systematically disadvantaging some minority out of simple hostility or a prejudiced refusal to recognize commonalities of interest, and thereby denying the minority the protection afforded other groups by a representative system.[8]

The Supreme Court, under Ely's vision, can close the open-ended provisions of the Constitution by preserving the political process. The proper function of the judiciary, under John Ely's theory of judicial review, is to protect the integrity of the process by (1) clearing the channels of political change of obstacles erected by the majority, and (2) facilitating the representation of minorities in the face of prejudice in the political marketplace. By assigning to the courts the role of opening channels of democracy, and protecting those minority groups that, as a result of "malfunctioning" in the political process, are incapable of protecting themselves, Ely confines issues of constitutional interpretation to questions of participation rather than to the "substantive merits" of the political choices under attack.[9]

## APPLICATION

There is a wonderful legend recounted in the Talmud[10] — the traditional Jewish version of the *United States Supreme Court Reports*, a compilation of judicial disputes among rabbinic judges — that casts an interesting light on the contemporary American debate over the original intent of our constitutional framers. The great Rabbi Eliezer was engaged in an acrimonious dispute with the other sages about an arcane point of law. Eliezer was certain that his interpretation of the Torah was the correct one and he "brought forward every imaginable argument, but they did not accept them." Finally, in desperation, he invoked the original intent of the author of the Torah, God himself. Eliezer implored, "If the halachah [the authoritative meaning of the law] agrees with me, let it be proved from Heaven!" — whereupon a heavenly voice cried out to the others: "Why do ye dispute with R[abbi] Eliezer, seeing that . . . the halachah agrees with him!" (Pretty authoritative evidence of the original intent!) But another of the rabbis rose up and rebuked God for interfering in this very human dispute. "Thou hast long since written in the Torah" and "we pay no attention to a Heavenly Voice." The message was clear: God's children were telling their Father, "It is our job, as the rabbis, to give meaning to the Torah that you gave us. You gave us a document to interpret, and a methodology for interpreting it. Now leave us to do our job." God agreed, laughing with joy, "My . . . [children] have defeated Me in argument."[11]

No single person — divine or otherwise — drafted the American Constitution, its Bill of Rights, or its post–Civil War amendments (which together comprise our current Constitution). Indeed, the Constitution is full of mistakes, poor choice of language, and other manifestations of the obvious haste in which it was written. Our contemporary rabbis in robes cannot call for a heavenly — or even an earthly — voice to confirm the correctness of their constructions of such terms as *due process*, *equal protection*, *freedom of speech*, or *cruel and unusual punishment*. But I wonder if Jefferson, Madison, Hamilton — and our other farsighted framers — would not respond to a contemporary Eliezer's call for authoritative interpretation by declining to interfere and by saying: "It is a constitution you must expound. We wrote its phrases long ago in a different era. Pay no attention to those who would invoke voices of certainty from the grave or the heavens."

But to ignore completely the intent of the framers would be as simpleminded and meaningless as pretending to know with certainty the precise and singular meaning of language that was probably selected, at least in part, for its open-endedness and its capacity for redefinition over time.

The paradox of the American system of judicial review — with its concomitant debate over original intent — is that you can't live comfortably with it or without it.

An America without judicial review of legislative, administrative, executive, and other governmental actions impinging on individual rights would be unthinkable. Although most nations, even democratic ones with traditions of liberty, survive without judicial review (at least judicial review as we have come to know it), the power of our courts to declare unconstitutional the actions of the other branches has become an indispensable aspect of our sovereignty. American sovereignty, unlike most other Western democracies, does not reside in one branch of government, or even in the majority of the people. Our sovereignty is a process, reflected in such concepts as checks and balances, separation of powers, and judicial review.

But taken to an extreme, the power of judicial review can be transformed into an undemocratic veto by an appointed and unaccountable aristocracy in robes. A judiciary whose interpretations of such broad concepts as "due process" and "equal protection of the laws" are unrooted in some broad historical purpose can quickly become a superlegislature in robes, simply voting to overrule inferior legislatures and executives.

On the other hand, a judiciary confined by the narrow visions of a past generation — a generation whose leaders were limited to white Protestant males — is a judiciary incapable of adapting to new dangers that were unforeseen by the framers, or a judiciary made insensitive to these dangers by its parochial background. Parenthetically, it is no mere coincidence that so many (John Hart Ely is a striking exception) of those who so loudly proclaim slavish obeisance to the narrow intent of the framers are so like them in background.

There is no perfect solution to the paradox of judicial review and the mystery of original intent. No one — no scholar, justice, lawyer, or layman — has discerned or devised the correct rationale, limiting principle, or methodology for judicial review. Every commendable attempt to do so has generated equally commendable responses.

Perhaps the most persuasive thus far has been the process-oriented approach offered by Dean John Hart Ely. This approach sees the courts — especially the Supreme Court — as opening up channels of democracy that have been closed off by artificial blockages, such as malapportionment, racial discrimination, and curtailment of voting and free speech rights. It too raises as many close questions as it answers, but it provides a coherent framework for analysis that does not require a simpleminded choice between rigid adherence to an unknowable original intent or an unconstrained power to legislate, or at least veto without accountability. Dean Ely would, I think, be the first to admit that his justification for judicial review was not necessarily the original intent of the framers, in the sense of a carefully worked-through rationale. He has not "discovered" the true meaning of the Federalist Papers (*The Federalist*), the compromises in Philadelphia, or even *Marbury v. Madison*.[12] He has "invented" a set of limiting principles that achieves a workable balance among competing claims of democratic theory.

One of the great paradoxes of constitutional law scholarship is that it can never seem to make up its collective mind about what it is doing — about its epistemology. Is it discovering, desiring, synthesizing, discerning, constructing, inventing, creating, advocating, or fabricating? The law in general is somewhat like religion in that you win awards more for discovering the meanings of others than for creating new realities. In law, as in religion, you score points by being able to point to others in the past who agree with you. Originality — ideas without citations — is at best suspect, at worst heresy.

There are few constitutional scholars or practitioners — by which I mean to include judges — who do not begin with desired outcomes and then deduce approaches that lead to or justify their outcomes. To be sure, committing oneself to a systematic approach necessarily entails some compromise with some outcomes, in the sense of occasionally not deriving a particular desired outcome from the approach. Some constitutionalists confronted with such conflict abandon the particular outcome. Others insist on the outcome and continually modify the approach so that it produces virtually every desired outcome.

The easiest ("most simpleminded" would be a more apt phrase) constitutional approach to justify is the one that purports to be based on original intent: The Constitution is supreme law, and hence undemocratic, in the sense that it is not subject to change by simple, current majority vote, either direct or representative; supreme law entails content, rather than merely process (a somewhat dubious and question-begging conclusion). It follows, therefore, that the best evidence of the content of the supreme law is what those who wrote it, debated it, and voted on it had in mind. Anything else requires the substitution of one group's current interpretation for another's.

The very act of constructing a new theory of judicial review is regarded as suspect by many, because it necessarily requires creativity beyond what the framers expressly contemplated. Yet the very legiti-mation of the power of judicial review was an act of creation, albeit done by one close to — though not at — the original creation of the Constitution. *Marbury v. Madison* was not simply the inevitable corol-lary of the enactment of the Constitution. It was a judicial amendment. If *Marbury* has become part of our Constitution, then our Constitu-tion now contains a methodology for evolving theories of judicial re-view, such as those proposed by Ely.

Another theory, not dissimilar to Ely's, is based on the relatively simple notion that the Constitution extends its protection to certain people who do not have the power to protect themselves through the political processes. If disenfranchised and powerless minorities do in-deed have rights that cannot be effectively vindicated through elec-tions, lobbying, the media, or other popular avenues, then it is not unreasonable to see the courts as having a special mandate to enforce those rights against the powerful and the majority.

## MISAPPLICATION

Surely among the least defensible approaches to judicial review is the one currently being practiced by the Rehnquist Court. This Court, along with its predecessor, has ceased any pretense at being a court of last resort for citizens' rights, except to the extent that a new and disin-genuous vocabulary of rights has been developed to misdescribe power as rights, such as in "victims' rights" and in the "right" to be free from pornography. The high court has become a court of last resort for gov-ernmental power. As Professor Alexander Bickel taught John Ely and me twenty-five years ago, you can tell more about the Supreme Court by looking at which cases it chooses to decide than by looking at how it decides them. Week after week, this Court decides to hear the petitions of aggrieved governments — national, state, and local. These govern-ments petition the high court for relief from lower court decisions — generally federal, but increasingly state court decisions as well — that construed the Constitution (or other governing law) in favor of citizens' rights. The current Supreme Court apparently sees itself as the guardian of governmental power rather than of citizens' rights.

Perhaps the most perverse manifestation of this change in role has been the eagerness, indeed aggressiveness, the Court has shown in granting review of state criminal cases. For example, the Supreme Court of Kentucky recently ruled that "in addition to the right of confrontation provided by the Sixth Amendment to the United States Constitution, the Eleventh Section of the Bill of Rights of the Kentucky Constitution guarantees the accused in a criminal prosecution the right to be heard by himself and counsel and to meet the witnesses (against him) face to face."[13] The Kentucky court went on to cite several Kentucky state cases, but not a single federal case, in support of a defendant's right to confront witnesses at a pretrial hearing.[14] It clearly rested its decision on an adequate state ground, thus precluding jurisdiction by the Supreme Court. Yet the Supreme Court — at the request of the state prosecutor — granted review of this case in order to vindicate the power of state prosecutors rather than the rights of defendants.[15] All of this occurred in the false name of judicial restraint and states' rights! Other examples abound of this Court reaching out, down, and around to guard against individual rights and to vindicate collective power.

The upshot of the current Supreme Court's approach to judicial review is to drive citizens away. It has now become a technique of experienced litigators concerned for individual rights to seek to structure litigation so as to keep the case as far away from the Supreme Court as possible. Like the rabbi blessing the czar in *Fiddler on the Roof*, many civil liberties lawyers pray to keep the Supreme Court "far away from us." That is a sad commentary indeed on the current state of our highest court.

For judicial review to make any sense in a multibranch democracy, the judiciary should not simply be yet another branch representing the same majoritarian constituency as the legislative and the executive branches and reflecting the identical values of power, efficiency, and immediate gratification.

This is especially so in light of our modern history. Because the Supreme Court has taken its mandate more from the Bill of Rights and the post–Civil War amendments (our document of rights) than from the body of our Constitution (our document of power), the other branches of government have grown used to abdicating responsibility for individual rights to the courts. Now that the Supreme Court has also abdicated that role — at least in a positive manner — we are experiencing a crisis of mutual abdication. The popular branches mistakenly believe the Supreme Court will vindicate individual rights, while the Supreme Court purports to be leaving such vindication to the popular branches. The upshot is a phenomenon similar to the one described in *The Execution of Private Slovik*,[16] about the only American soldier actually executed for desertion during World War II. This obscure young man experienced the firing squad because everyone in the process — from the members of the original court-martial through the reviewing courts and up to the president — all mistakenly assumed that someone else along the line had made the considered decision that Slovik really deserved to be singled out for execution. The tragic truth was that no one made that decision; it got made by inertia and omission, and Slovik simply slipped through the cracks of the bureaucracy and fell to his death.

Compare that nondecision to the one recently made concerning preventive detention of arrested persons who are presumed innocent but believed to be dangerous. When the various proposals for preventive detention were being considered by Congress and by several administrations, it was difficult to get any popularly elected officials to focus on the individual liberty issues. Their constituents do not include large numbers of potential detainees, but they do include people who identify with the potential victims of those who would be detained. "If the preventive detention is incompatible with civil liberties," the politicians assured us, "the courts will strike it down." And sure enough, a court did. The United States Court of Appeals for the Second Circuit held provisions of the law unconstitutional.[17] But the Supreme Court rushed to the rescue of governmental power and ruled that Congress clearly did not intend pretrial detention to be "punishment" but instead conceived of it "as a potential solution to a pressing societal problem" (as if somehow "punishment" can never be a "solution" to a societal problem).[18] The Court concluded that Congress had appropriately balanced the "individual's strong interest in liberty" against society's compelling "interest in crime prevention," and that it would not interfere in the legislative process.[19] But the Court was wrong. Congress had made no serious effort at striking such a balance. Most members of Congress who voted for the law — and the vote was overwhelming — considered only the crime-prevention portion of the balance, leaving individual liberty concerns to the courts. And that is all too typical of legislative and executive actions that require a balance between majority power and the rights of nonconstituents. The result is an imbalance and an abdication: a skewing of checks and balances.

The preventive detention decision also illustrates the cynical sophistry employed by the courts in selectively invoking and ignoring original intent when it serves their political agenda. There is no evidence that the framers contemplated pretrial detention based on dangerousness, any more than they intended nonunanimous juries or warrantless searches of the kind now routinely encouraged by the Court. The manner by which this Court has selectively invoked original intent is as unconvincing as its claim to be exercising judicial restraint while it reaches out to decide cases and issues not properly before it with as much aggressiveness as any court in history.

It is sometimes argued that judicial abdication of responsibility for individual rights may prove a positive development, since it will put pressure on the members of the popular branches to take more seriously their responsibility to comply with the Constitution. This argument envisions legislatures refusing to enact legislation that in their view violates the Bill of Rights, and it envisions executives vetoing such legislation on constitutional grounds. While increased legislative and executive attention to the Constitution would be commendable, it is unlikely ever to be a substitute for judicial review. The structure and accountability of the branches make the courts far more institutionally suited to reflect values that are not immediately popular with the electoral majority. If those who do not control the elected branches — noncitizens, the homeless, the malapportioned, prisoners, the mentally ill, minorities unable to form political coalitions, religious and nonreligious dissidents, the illiterate or those literate in languages other than English, and others — do indeed have constitutional rights, it blinks reality to expect them to be able to vindicate those rights by resorting to majoritarian political processes. Their rights will be vindicated by the courts or by no one.

For the Supreme Court to become the implacable constitutional foe of these disenfranchised people — as many believe it is quickly becoming — is to turn any reasonable conception of judicial review on its head.

The powerful, if shifting, majorities that control the popular branches do not need yet a third branch to vindicate their interests. To see the role of the courts as redundant rubber stamps is to insult the intelligence of those who crafted our system of checks and balances, separation of powers, and judicial review.

The primary question that should be asked by the Supreme Court before it decides whether to take a case, and if so, how to decide it, is: Will our decision in this case vindicate important constitutional values that cannot or will not be vindicated by other branches? This should not be the only question; nor will the answer to this question necessarily dictate the outcome of every case. But it is a reminder about priorities, about institutional roles, and about our national commitment to individual and minority rights in an age of increasingly selfish exercise of majority power. John Hart Ely's theory of democracy and distrust provides a vision of justice that requires the best, rather than the worst, of us all. It is indeed a vision of justice from a lofty and democratic perch.

# FORTY-SEVEN

# THE CONFIRMATION PROCESS
*The Senate Need Not Allow the President
a Partisan Victory*

---

*In the fall of 1971, the Supreme Court had two vacancies, resulting from the retirements of Justices Hugo Black and John Harlan. Having already appointed a new chief justice and one associate justice, President Richard Nixon had the opportunity to reshape the high court. His first two attempts to fill these associate justice positions — Judges Clement Haynsworth and G. Harrold Carswell — failed. Much controversy ensued. The New York Times asked me to write a series of articles about this process for the "Week in Review" section. In two of the articles, encompassed by this chapter, I tried to explain the meaning of "judicial philosophies" in the context of Supreme Court nominations and the process of senatorial confirmation.*

---

IN 1932, ANOTHER REPUBLICAN PRESIDENT WAS FACED with the responsibility of filling a great Supreme Court "chair," the one occupied by Oliver Wendell Holmes. When President Herbert Hoover showed his list of prospective candidates to Senator William E. Borah of Idaho — who was known to favor a Western Republican — Senator Borah pointed to the bottom name and said, "Your list is all right, but you handed it to me upside down."

The bottom name was that of Benjamin Cardozo, a Democrat from New York and a Jew — but also the nation's most respected state judge and a paragon of judicial virtue. President Hoover responded that there were already two New Yorkers and one Jew on the court, but Senator Borah declared: "Cardozo belongs as much to Idaho as to

New York [and] anyone who raises the question of race is unfit to advise you concerning so important a matter." The rest, of course, is history: The Cardozo nomination was unanimously — indeed, instantaneously — approved, and President Hoover was credited with having "performed the finest act of his career as President."

If the list of six potential nominees that that administration submitted to the American Bar Association last week is any barometer,[1] there will be no "Cardozos" nominated to fill the current vacancies on the Supreme Court. It seems clear that President Nixon's primary considerations were regional, political, and sexual. Whether the two candidates eventually nominated will face confirmation battles of the kind that defeated two previous Nixon nominees is not yet known. But a central question raised by the Haynsworth and Carswell episodes has effectively been posed once again: What is the Senate's appropriate role in passing upon those proposed as nominees to the nation's highest tribunal?

Views about what a senator may and may not properly take into account vary. Charles Black, professor of constitutional law at Yale and a leading scholar of the Supreme Court, takes what is perhaps the most expansive view of the Senate's role: "There is just no reason at all for a Senator's not voting, in regard to confirmation of a Supreme Court nominee, on the basis of a full and unrestricted view, unencumbered by any presumption of the nominee's fitness for the office." Others take an extremely restrictive view of the Senate's proper role: according to them, a powerful presumption operates in favor of the president's choice, a presumption that may be overcome only in firm instances of demonstrated incompetence or corruption.

Standing between these poles is a continuum of views about the considerations — political, judicial, philosophical, and regional — that may properly be weighed by the Senate in exercising its constitutional duties to join with the president in appointing justices of the Supreme Court.

The words of the Constitution and the history of its adoption seem to support a position closer to the expansive view advocated by Professor Black than to the restrictive view that has held sway in the Senate during most of the twentieth century. Article 2 of the Constitution says that the president "shall nominate and by and with the advice and

consent of the Senate, shall appoint . . . judges of the Supreme Court."
The original proposal — which received considerable support at the
Constitutional Convention — was for the Senate alone to appoint justices. Ultimately, a compromise was unanimously reached whereby the
appointing function was divided between the president and the Senate.
The Federalist Papers make it clear that the Senate is supposed to take
its "advice"-giving function seriously, in order to prevent the president
from making undistinguished appointments — not merely incompetent or corrupt ones: "He would be both ashamed and afraid to bring
forward candidates who had no other merit than that of coming from
the same state . . . or being in some way or other personally allied to
him, or of possessing the necessary insignificance and pliancy to ren-
der them the obsequious instruments of his pleasure."

In this respect, there is an important distinction between the Senate's role in confirming a nominee for the Supreme Court and one for
a cabinet, or other executive, position. The president should be given
great latitude in picking his cabinet — the people who will be working
with him and for him. Being "personally allied" to the president may
well be a distinct qualification for a cabinet post. But Supreme Court
justices are not supposed to be the president's men; they are supposed
to work neither with him nor for him. They should be as independent
of him as they are of the Senate.

Moreover, the judicial history of our first century as a nation is
replete with instances of Senate refusal to confirm Supreme Court
nominees who were neither incompetent nor corrupt. As an early
commentator put it: "A party nomination may be justly met by party
opposition." Stated more generally, if a president nominates a justice
on the basis of factors other than judicial excellence — factors such as
party, region, or political views — then, the argument goes, the Senate
is entitled to prefer its own party, region, or political views to those of
the president. The Federalist Papers support the conclusion that the
Senate need not sit back and allow a president to reap partisan political advantage from an appointment to the Supreme Court: "It would
be an excellent check upon the spirit of favoritism in the President, and
would tend greatly to prevent the appointment of unfit characters . . .
from a view to popularity." Thus, if a president is entitled to try to implement a "Southern strategy," then the Senate is held to be equally
entitled to try to frustrate it.

Under this view, then, it is the president who decides the rules of the game: If he submits a nomination that is regionally motivated, the Senate may properly reject it on regional grounds; if he submits a nomination to achieve certain political objectives, then the Senate may properly reject it if it does not share these objectives. But if the president submits the name of a man or woman of real distinction or potential judicial greatness, then it would be improper for the Senate to attempt to convert the nomination into a political issue.

The truly perplexing issue arises in the context of a nominee who lacks sympathy with the values reflected in the Bill of Rights — who believes in "order" more than "justice," "security" more than "liberty," and "efficiency" more than "equality." Clement Haynsworth and G. Harrold Carswell were both denied confirmation — at least in part — because of their reputed views on racial issues (as were a number of nominees during the pre- and post–Civil War eras). And a compelling case can be made for a senator's voting against an otherwise qualified nominee with a record demonstrating callousness about — or opposition to — civil rights or civil liberties.

The executive and legislative branches are adequate protectors of order, security, and efficiency. But there must be a coequal branch that is committed to the far more subtle — and far less popular — values of justice, liberty, and equality. That branch is the Supreme Court, and if its members — or a majority of them — were simply to mirror the values of the popular branches, then the uniqueness of the Court would be at an end. Under our constitutional system of government, it is as much the responsibility of the Senate as of the president to make certain that this does not happen.

## JUDICIAL PHILOSOPHY

In announcing the nominations of Lewis Powell and William Rehnquist as associate justices of the Supreme Court, President Richard Nixon declared that he had based his selection on two criteria: (1) their "excellence" as lawyers and (2) their "judicial philosophy." There can be little doubt about what the president meant by the first criterion, or about the fact that his nominees met it. Both Mr. Powell and Mr. Rehnquist are well-educated and successful lawyers who seem intellectually equipped to compete on what Mr. Nixon characterized as "the fastest track in the nation."

What the president meant by "judicial philosophy" is far less clear. "Now I paraphrase the word 'judicial,'" he said, and "by judicial philosophy I do not mean agreeing with the President on every issue." A justice, he continued, "should not twist or bend the Constitution in order to perpetuate his political and social views."

After assuring his audience that the nominees shared his judicial philosophy and that they were conservatives ("but only in a judicial not in a political sense"), the president went on to give an example of what a conservative judicial philosophy means to him: "As a judicial conservative I believe that some Court decisions have gone too far in the past in weakening the peace forces as against the criminal forces in our society. The peace forces must not be denied the legal tools they need to protect the innocent from criminal elements."

Two critically important phrases occur and recur in the president's words: *judicial philosophy* and *judicial conservative*. Though their meaning may appear, to a layman, abundantly clear, Mr. Nixon's usage seems to fly in the face of traditional legal understandings of just what those words connote.

Thus, the president's law-and-order attitude is not a "judicial philosophy." It is just the sort of "personal political and social view" that the president emphasized should not be perpetuated by a Supreme Court justice.

A judicial philosophy deals with the roles of the Court as an institution. It is responsive to questions such as: What precedential weight should be given to prior decisions? What power should the Court exercise over the other branches of the federal government and over the states? What tools of judicial construction should it employ in giving meaning to a constitutional or statutory provision? A judicial philosophy — if it is truly judicial rather than "political" or "social" — does not speak in terms of giving the peace forces "tools" to "protect the innocent from criminal elements."

A "conservative" judicial philosophy is one that respects precedent and avoids deciding cases on constitutional grounds whenever a narrower ground for a decision is available. Most important, a judge with a conservative judicial philosophy abjures employing the courts to effectuate his own political or social program — he is a decider of cases rather than an advocate of causes.

Justice Oliver Wendell Holmes described such a judge as one who has "no thought but that of which he is bound," and who has learned "to solve a problem according to the rules by transcending [his or her] own convictions and to leave room for much that he would hold dear to be done away with." In short, he or she is a judge who focuses concern on process rather than results, and who lets the political chips fall where they may.

This is why it is so difficult to predict how a true judicial conservative will decide a given issue. For him, so much depends on how the issue is framed: on what the statute says, on the prior cases, on whether it arose in a federal or state context. Justice Louis Brandeis was a judicial conservative, though a political liberal. Justice Holmes was a judicial and political conservative. But the judicial opinions of these giants tell us little about their individual political (or economic or social) views; for that we must go to their extrajudicial writings. Indeed, many people are surprised to learn how differently these men felt about the social and political issues of their day, since their judicial opinions were so similar.

Justice James C. McReynolds, the inveterate opponent of New Deal legislation, represents the other side of the coin. A political conservative and a judicial activist, he reached out to strike down statutes that were inconsistent with his political and economic views.

Mr. Nixon's two previous appointments to the Supreme Court — Chief Justice Warren Burger and Justice Harry Blackmun — were also described as having a conservative judicial philosophy. Yet they have seemed to show no reluctance to overrule prior decisions or to "perpetuate [their] own political and social views," especially on issues of criminal justice and civil liberties.

In the *Harris* case,[2] for example, Chief Justice Burger wrote an opinion holding that a defendant who takes the witness stand on his own behalf can be confronted with an illegally obtained confession. This opinion significantly undercut the Court's prior decision in the *Miranda* case. Many observers commented that he had decided a critical constitutional issue that could well have been avoided considering the record of that case. In the *James* case[3] — holding that welfare searches could be conducted without a warrant — Justice Blackmun overruled a long line of prior decisions, though the government had sought a decision on far narrower grounds. Thus, in this sense, the two previous Nixon appointees came closer to reflecting the judicial activism of Justice McReynolds (coupled with his political conservatism) than the judicial conservatism of Justice Holmes or Brandeis.

It is too early, of course, to speculate about the judicial philosophies of President Nixon's most recent nominees. Since neither of them has ever served in the judiciary before or has written about judicial issues, virtually nothing is known about their views on precedent, judicial restraint, and the other factors that go into making a true judicial philosophy. Mr. Rehnquist did make a speech last year suggesting that the Court should overrule decisions like *Miranda*, without feeling bound by "stare decisis" (former decisions) — a position that cannot be characterized as judicially conservative.[4] Somewhat more is known about their attitudes toward law and order: They favor wiretapping, increased police power to investigate, and far greater protection for the victims of crime. (Mr. Rehnquist once wrote an article charging his fellow Supreme Court law clerks with "extreme solicitude for the claims of Communists and other criminal defendants, expansion of Federal power at the expense of state power, [and] great sympathy toward any government regulation of business.") More may be learned about their true judicial philosophies when the Senate Judiciary Committee considers their nominations in the weeks ahead.

———————————

*Powell emerged as a judicial moderate with strong conservative leanings, whereas Rehnquist was a judicial activist who had little hesitancy in implementing his extremely conservative political philosophy. After being promoted to chief justice, he became somewhat more respectful of precedent and other institutional constraints, though not in the case of* Bush v. Gore, *in which he voted to stop the Florida hand count of votes cast in the 2000 presidential election, despite the precedents to the contrary.*

———————————

# FORTY-EIGHT

# THE QUALITY OF JUSTICE

*Most Americans have some rudimentary knowledge of the United States Supreme Court but little familiarity with the lower courts, which administer justice in retail fashion. The following foreword to a study of Boston's lower criminal courts discusses some of the problems found by authors Stephen Bing and S. Stephen Rosenfeld.[1]*

AMONG THE MOST IMPORTANT, BUT LEAST STUDIED, PHENOMENA in the administration of justice today is the arbitrary judge. The judge who refuses to follow the law. The judge who displays (or who feels without displaying) favoritism toward the prosecution. The judge who always resolves factual disputes in favor of the police, though he knows they frequently lie. The judge who lacks elementary manners in dealing with certain kinds of defendants and attorneys. The judge who knowingly distorts the record. The judge who has two sets of jury instructions — one for defendants he thinks are guilty, the other for those who may be innocent. The judge who threatens — either openly or covertly — to throw the book at the defendant unless he waives his right to trial or appeal. The judge who regularly, but improperly, meets with the prosecutor outside the presence of the defense attorney. The judge who — pure and simple — is on the take!

Such judges really do sit in numerous courts today, although you wouldn't know it by looking at criminal law casebooks or law review articles. (A striking exception is Herman Schwartz's fine article "Judges as Tyrants" in the March 1971 issue of the *Criminal Law Bulletin*.) We, as law professors, simply have not come up with teaching techniques or research methodologies capable of surfing this hidden agenda of criminal law reform. The Socratic method of teaching and the analytic technique of legal scholarship now prevalent in most American law books are certainly not suitable vehicles for flushing out these kinds of issues. Indeed, these methods — with their focus on appellate decisions — do much to keep such matters below the surface. The gap between criminal law scholarship and the nitty gritty is still of Grand Canyon dimensions. The critical challenge of the coming decade is to narrow this gap. The job will not be an easy one.

The 1960s saw a considerable amount of desirable reform in the area of criminal justice. Most of the changes were brought about by decisions of the appellate courts, especially the Supreme Court. What we saw in the 1960s was not, for the most part, a revolution of new "rights"; it was a revolution of new "remedies." It had long been recognized, for example, that it was illegal for state police to engage in "unreasonable" searches. *Mapp v. Ohio* created a remedy — the exclusionary rule — to enforce this right. It had long been recognized that it was illegal to extract an involuntary confession. *Escobedo v. Illinois* and *Miranda v. Arizona* attempted to give meaning to that right by requiring a set of warnings and access to counsel during the interrogation process.

The court established these and other new remedies in the only way courts are able to — by reversing convictions in cases where the record revealed clear violations. But we are now beginning to hear that the new remedies are not working, that the conduct of the police has not changed fundamentally in response to these decisions. Moreover, the age of new decisions is — at least for a time — well behind us. If the past few months are any barometer, we will begin to see a considerable undercutting of the Warren Court's criminal justice decisions (inartfully disguised as principled refusals to go any further).

This is a proper occasion, in my view, for the exercise of a kind of litigation "restraint" by civil liberties groups. The courts, and especially the Supreme Court, should not now be pressed to extend the principles articulated in the 1960s. It is better to have no decision — or a favorable "old" decision — than to have a limiting decision or a decision explicitly refusing to go further.

Where, then, should the energies of criminal law reform-minded people be directed over the next (one hopes, few) years? In precisely the direction taken by the authors of "The Quality of Justice." What is needed now is an all-out attack on obvious injustices at the lower levels of criminal law enforcement, on practices so clearly wrong that once exposed and documented, they could not be ignored by even the most law-and-order-minded critics of the Warren Court.

The groundbreaking study of the Boston lower criminal courts is, therefore, one of the most important criminal law documents to be published in recent years. It deserves the widest public circulation and readership. It tells it like it is, but in a detailed and scholarly way. I am not competent to comment on the details of the report, but as a whole it certainly rings true. It is precisely what my friends and former students have been telling me for years: "The judge's personal power and personal prejudice overshadow established rules of law in the district courts."

Here we see a judge announcing, "We don't follow those Supreme Court decisions here." There we see a judge exclaiming, "The day I throw out a [search] warrant that uncovers 100 decks of heroin is the day they'll throw a net over my head." Another judge resolves a disputed factual case with the following Solomon-like judgment: "Well, I don't know who to believe. Just to be safe I'll find you guilty." While still another pronounces sentence in these terms: "If [he doesn't pay the money back] I'll sentence him to six months on the Island [Deer Island]. If he wants to appeal, I'll make it a year." Then there is the judge telling the man with forty cents in his pocket to "hire a forty-cent lawyer."

These anecdotes, and others like them, demonstrate that some judges are simply not obeying the law. They are — put most charitably — engaging in civil disobedience. I am certain that many of them are well intentioned. They simply do not agree with the limitations imposed by the Constitution as interpreted by the Supreme Court, and so they disobey these limitations in the service of, what is in their view, a "higher morality" — convicting the guilty without regard to due process.

How, you may ask, can judges get away with this kind of conduct? Part of the answer — but only part of it — lies in Boston's anachronistic trial de novo system, under which a defendant dissatisfied with the verdict in the lower court may obtain a new trial in the Superior Court. If a defendant seeks this trial de novo, the slate is wiped clean and the errors committed by the lower court judges are ignored. Effectively insulated from appellate review, these lower court judges continue to mete out a brand of justice that bears little relationship to what the Supreme Court has mandated. This is not to suggest that appellate review — as it presently operates — would focus on the attitude and demeanor of the trial judge. The absence of review simply magnifies a problem prevalent in many of our lower courts.

The lower court trial is not, of course, a free run-through. It costs something to seek a trial de novo: if a defendant is reconvicted in the higher court, he will probably receive a higher sentence. Nevertheless, there are some responsible defense attorneys who disagree with Bing and Rosenfeld's report's conclusion to eliminate trial de novo. Instead, they propose that the lower courts become courts of record and that no increase of sentence be permitted.

The main virtue of this report is not in its recommendations or its anecdotes. It is in its attempt to gather statistical evidence to support its conclusion that "certain lower criminal courts in Greater Boston seriously abuse principles of fairness and due process." For example, it had long been sensed that defendants who insist on being represented by counsel fare worse than those who "waive" that right. The authors of this report have now accumulated convincing statistical evidence that this is indeed the case.

More of this kind of statistical inquiry is needed. It is easy to deny the reality of abuses when they are stated in anecdotal form. It is far more difficult to dispute a carefully constructed and well-researched study.

In the last analysis, we must improve the quality of our judges, especially at the lowest levels. Justice is far too important to be left to the defeated politicians and loyal party workers who so often are "retired" to the judiciary. We simply cannot afford to continue the practices that have put our lower courts in the sad state they currently occupy. Happily, there is now some evidence of concern, and even slight reform, in the Boston lower courts.

The tragedy of our lower courts is not only that they are often unfair; it is that they are also ineffective in controlling serious crime. A system that focuses on such considerations as whether a defendant takes a plea or whether he demands counsel is not only too harsh on some defendants, it is also too lenient on others.

Just as no defendant should receive a higher sentence than he deserves for asserting his rights, so, too, no defendant should receive a lower sentence than he deserves for "waiving" his rights. Sentences should reflect culpability, dangerousness, and the need for deterrence; not the going price of a bargained plea.

Reform in this area will not be easy to accomplish. The lower courts will resist objective studies of their operation. And the authors of such reports will be attacked for having reached conclusions of the kind reached in this report. It will take people of courage to stand up to this kind of pressure. But it must be done.

※

## PART VIII

# CAN RIGHTS BE SUSPENDED FOR EMERGENCIES?

ON SEPTEMBER 11, 2001, A COORDINATED TERRORIST ATTACK WAS directed against the United States by foreign terrorists. Immediately thereafter demands arose within our country to curtail certain basic liberties and new laws were enacted in the name of terrorism prevention and national security. Emergencies have often been used by governments to justify the suspension of individual rights. Throughout our history, presidents — including Lincoln and Truman — have invoked national security to suspend constitutional protections. In many other democratic countries, rights have also been suspended during wartime, insurrection, and other internal and external threats. In 1970 I conducted a series of studies involving the suspension of rights in the United States, Canada, Great Britain, and Israel. I also served as a consultant to the Canadian government on civil liberties when it invoked the War Measures Act in 1970. In 1971 I published some of my conclusions in a series of articles. The following year I published an article on wiretaps and national security. Then in 1989 I traveled to Israel to study the use of "physical pressure" — nonlethal torture — on suspected terrorists during times of emergency and wrote several articles about that. Finally, in September 2001, I wrote about the terrorist attack on the World Trade Center. These studies and articles form the basis of part VIII.

# FORTY-NINE

# COULD IT HAPPEN HERE?
## *Civil Liberties in a National Emergency*

*A version of this essay appeared in* The Nation, *March 15, 1971.*

AT FOUR O'CLOCK ON THE MORNING OF OCTOBER 16, 1970, Prime Minister Pierre Trudeau proclaimed the existence of a "state of apprehended insurrection" throughout Canada. Pointing to the kidnapping of a Canadian cabinet minister and a British consul by members of Le Front de Libération du Québec (FLQ), he invoked the War Measures Act, thereby authorizing extraordinary powers of arrest, search, and detention. Before dawn, the police — who had been strategically deployed in anticipation of the announcement — began their roundup of French Canadians suspected of association with the FLQ. Though most of the 450 arrested were never charged with any crime, many were detained incommunicado for considerable periods of time. The Canadian Bill of Rights — which prohibits such detention — was rendered inapplicable by the emergency decree.

In the middle of the night of December 4, 1970, Irish prime minister John Lynch announced that a grave emergency existed in his country. Citing information that Éire Shaor (a splinter group of the Irish Republican Army) was conspiring to kidnap "prominent" ministers, he declared that "unless this threat is removed," he would, without further notice, empower the police to "intern any citizen without trial." The government issued instructions "that places of detention be prepared immediately" and that the Council of Europe be notified that "these proposals will involve derogations from certain provisions of the European Convention on Human Rights."

Ten days later — in the wake of kidnapping and demonstrations in support of six Basques on trial for murder — Generalissimo Francisco Franco granted emergency powers to the Spanish police, authorizing them to detain persons for up to six months without a hearing. Franco's proclamation of emergency powers automatically suspended that nation's Bill of Rights.

Within just a few months, therefore, we have seen three Western countries suspend, or threaten to suspend, fundamental constitutional protections in response to political kidnappings and other disruptions of a kind not unknown to our own shores. This raises the obvious question: Can it happen here? Could an American president take to the airwaves some night and announce that this nation is confronted with an emergency situation requiring suspension of the American Bill of Rights?

"It could not happen here under any circumstances" was the categorical answer given to me in an interview with then deputy attorney general Richard Kleindienst, the man to whom President Nixon has delegated the task of planning for a domestic emergency.

> We wouldn't suspend the Bill of Rights even if the whole cabinet, the chief justice, and the Speaker of the House were kidnapped. In the first place, we wouldn't have to, because our existing laws — together with our surveillance and intelligence apparatus, which is the best in the world — are sufficient to cope with any situation. And in the second place, we wouldn't be allowed to; as I understand the law, the courts would have to be closed — unable to operate — before we could invoke martial law.

I pressed him on his last point: What if there were a concerted attack on the courts — judicial kidnappings of the kind attempted in San Rafael, California; bombing of courtrooms, harassment of jurors? Would that constitute an effective closing of the courts and justify a presidential declaration of martial law? Mr. Kleindienst had obviously given some thought to this possibility, because his answer was quite specific:

> We would deploy all our resources to get the courts open and to keep them open. We might have to use troops, but we wouldn't use them in place of the courts or the law; we would use them in support of the courts. We have careful plans ready to be put into effect in the event of any emergency requiring federal troops. A team of civilians headed by an assistant attorney general is to be dispatched to any crisis city.

He would direct the activities of the troops, so there would be no danger of undue military influence. We have a book on every city in which an emergency might occur. We have had numerous rehearsals, but fortunately we have had to act only once: we sent a civilian team under [William] Ruckelshaus up to New Haven last year when it looked like the Panther trial demonstration might get out of hand.

Had he sent that team, I asked, in response to a request from the governor? "No," replied Mr. Kleindienst, "we acted on our own initiative but with full cooperation from the local authorities. Let me assure you once again, however, that our object is to support the local civil authorities, not to supplant them."

I asked whether he thought Canada had overreacted to the two kidnappings. He responded with a twinkle:

We conservatives would not have reacted that way. Cool-headed Wall Street types — like Nixon, [John] Mitchell, and me — would never respond emotionally. We would be conservative in invoking extraordinary powers. You liberals, on the other hand, you wait too long before you act; you don't anticipate crises; you worry about upsetting your constituencies. When you finally do act, things have gotten so far out of hand that you have to overreact. That's why liberals are more likely to invoke emergency powers than conservatives. But in fairness to Canada, you have to remember that they don't have the law enforcement machinery that we have. If we had a crisis, we would divert all our existing resources away from nonessential duties and turn them onto the problem at hand. And we would be able to solve it without the need for any emergency powers.

But what if we faced a situation similar to the one that confronted the Canadian government, where those fomenting violence were well known to the authorities, but the absence of admissible evidence made conviction impossible? Wouldn't you be tempted, I asked Mr. Kleindienst, to invoke extraordinary powers of temporary detention in order to break the back of the movement? "We wouldn't have to," he assured me.

There is enough play at the joints of our existing criminal law — enough flexibility — so that if we really felt that we had to pick up the leaders of a violent uprising, we could. We would find something to charge them with and we would be able to hold them that way for a while.

Mr. Kleindienst's last remark reminded me of something the Canadian attorney general, John Turner, had told me during a conference he recently convened to evaluate his country's experience under the War Measures Act: "In a certain sense, it is a credit to the civil liberties of a country that it has to invoke extraordinary powers to cope with a real emergency. Some countries have these powers at their disposal all the time."

But whether a country has to invoke extraordinary powers or whether it already has sufficient powers at its disposal tells us little about the actual condition of liberty within its borders. Every legal system has its "stretch points," its flexible areas capable of expansion and contraction depending on the exigencies of the situation. The "stretch points" in our own system include broad police and prosecutorial discretion; vaguely defined offenses (such as disorderly conduct); inchoate crimes (which may also be vaguely defined, like conspiracy); and denial of pretrial release (which can sometimes result in confinement exceeding a year). Some systems employ such devices as common-law (judge-made) crimes, ex post facto (after the fact) legislation, and emergency powers, to achieve similar results. As Attorney General Turner put it: "When placed against the wall, most governments act more alike than differently; they do what they have to do to survive." There are, nevertheless, important differences in the manner by which governments respond to perceived emergencies. Some will take considerable risks to their security in order to preserve a maximum of liberty; while others will become harshly repressive at the slightest threat — real or imagined — to their security. The true condition of a country's freedom can best be seen by stripping away the legal jargon and focusing on the actual balance it has struck between liberty and security.

The fact that Canada invoked emergency powers, while we seem to be relying on "play at the joints of our existing criminal law," does tell us something important about the different status of constitutional rights and their judicial enforcement in our two countries. The Canadian Bill of Rights is subject to suspension by legislative act; accordingly, extraordinary powers can be invoked quite easily in that country without the fear of judicial disapproval. The American Constitution, on the other hand, has been described by our Supreme Court as "irrepealable law...for rulers and people, equally in war and peace, [which] covers with the shield of its protection all classes of men, at all times under all circumstances."

But are the safeguards of our Constitution as irrepealable as the judicial rhetoric proclaims? Is Mr. Kleindienst correct when he says that under our law a president would not be "allowed" to suspend the Bill of Rights? Would the courts step in and protect a citizen against the unauthorized actions of a high-handed chief executive during a period of national emergency? Neither American history nor current constitutional doctrine answers these questions unambiguously, as a brief recounting of some episodes from past periods of upheaval will demonstrate.

The great president who proclaimed emancipation also issued another, less well-known proclamation that had the effect of virtually suspending the Bill of Rights. A week after the fall of Fort Sumter, in a communiqué authorizing General Winfield Scott to commence the "bombardment" of certain cities in Maryland "if necessary," Abraham Lincoln also empowered the general to suspend the writ of habeas corpus in designated areas, but only "in the extremest necessity." (Habeas corpus, though not a part of the Bill of Rights, is the critical safeguard without which all other constitutional protections would remain largely unenforceable, since its suspension would deny the courts the power to release persons held in violation of other protections.) Shortly after Lincoln issued his "incarceration proclamation," an obscure Marylander named John Merryman, whose loyalties were apparently with the South, was roused from his bed at two in the morning, taken to Fort McHenry, and imprisoned there under military guard. A writ of habeas corpus was sought from the chief justice of the United States, Roger B. Taney — a Lincoln antagonist and author of the infamous Dred Scott decision. Taney's opinion gave Lincoln a failing grade in constitutional law: "I had supposed it to be one of those points in constitutional law upon which there was no difference of opinion," he commented sarcastically, "that the privilege of the writ could not be suspended, except by act of Congress." But though the chief justice ordered him released, Merryman remained confined; the general in charge of the fort simply denied the marshal permission to serve the necessary papers, and Lincoln took no official notice of the opinion (which was personally transmitted to him by order of the Court).

Following this confrontation between the executive and the judiciary, Congress enacted a statute giving President Lincoln even more authority to suspend constitutional safeguards than he had requested. And so, when Lambdin Milligan was arrested in Indiana on October 5, 1864, there was little doubt that the privilege of the writ of habeas corpus had been properly suspended.[1] Not content to detain him, the military authorities decided to try Milligan — a civilian — before a military commission, which promptly sentenced him to hang. By the time the case worked its way up to the Supreme Court, the war was over and — in the words of Justice David Davis — "now that the public safety is assured, this question . . . can be discussed and decided without passion or the admixture of any element not required to form a legal judgment." The Supreme Court held that since the civil courts of Indiana — a loyal state — had been open and "needed no bayonets" to protect them, it had been unconstitutional to try Milligan before a military commission. Recognizing that Milligan was arrested in wartime, when passions run high and "considerations of safety" are deemed all-important, the Court concluded that the framers of our Constitution

> foresaw that troublous times would arise, when rulers and people would become restive under restraint, and seek by sharp and decisive measures to accomplish ends deemed just and proper; and that the principles of constitutional liberty would be in peril, unless established by irrepealable law. . . .
>
> This nation . . . has no right to expect that it will always have wise and humane rulers, sincerely attached to the principles of the Constitution. Wicked men, ambitious of power, with hatred of liberty and contempt of law, may fill the place once occupied by Washington and Lincoln, and if this right [to suspend provisions of the Constitution during the great exigencies of government] is conceded, and the calamities of war again befall us, the dangers to human liberty are frightful to contemplate.

Having delivered itself of this bold rhetoric about "irrepealable law," the Supreme Court then proceeded to suggest that the right to bail could be suspended during emergencies:

> If it was dangerous, in the distracted condition of affairs, to leave Milligan unrestrained of his liberty, . . . the *law* said to arrest him, confine him closely, render him powerless to do further mischief; and then . . . try him according to the course of the common law.[2]

This view was reaffirmed — and strengthened — by Justice Oliver Wendell Holmes in a case growing out of a private war between Colorado coal miners and owners, which led to a declaration of local martial law. In addition to suppressing newspapers, deposing civil magistrates, and closing all saloons, the governor suspended habeas corpus and ordered the arrest of certain "objectionable characters." One of these "characters," a leader of the miners, was detained without bail for two and a half months and sued the governor after his release. Though Holmes need never have reached the legality of the detention, the Civil War veteran went out of his way to justify the governor's action. Employing "logic" for which he surely would have chastised his first-year Harvard law students, Holmes argued that since a governor can order soldiers to "kill persons who resist" efforts to put down a rebellion, it certainly follows that "he may use the milder measure of seizing the bodies of those whom he considers to stand in the way of restoring peace." (This non sequitur would, if taken seriously, justify detention of all persons suspected of felonies, since — under the laws of most states — deadly force can be used against anyone resisting a felony arrest.)

Although Justice Holmes intimated that the Court might not sustain a detention of undue duration, his uncritical legitimation of the governor's exercise of extraordinary power was a clear invitation to abuse. And abuse was not long in coming. Numerous governors invoked the magic phrase "martial law" as a kind of "household remedy" to accomplish such diverse and illegitimate ends as closing a racetrack, manipulating a primary election, keeping a neighborhood segregated, and — most often — settling labor strikes to the advantage of management. It was inevitable that the Supreme Court could not long tolerate such bogus declarations of martial law. The case that finally wore the Court's patience arose in the East Texas oil fields during the early years of the Depression. The governor declared martial law and ordered restrictions on the production of oil in an effort to raise its price. There were no riots or violence; nor were any troops employed. Martial law was invoked simply to accomplish economic ends. The Supreme Court enjoined the governor's action, reasoning that unless it did so "the fiat of a state Governor, and not the Constitution of the United States, would be the supreme law of the land."

That is where the law stood on December 7, 1941, when the Japanese air force bombed Pearl Harbor, throwing Hawaii into turmoil and generating fear of attack in our West Coast cities. Within hours, the governor of Hawaii — at the insistence of the army — declared martial law, suspended habeas corpus, ordered the civil courts closed, and empowered military tribunals to try all criminal cases. The civilian governor handed the reins of government over to the military only after receiving assurances that civilian control would be restored as soon as the immediate emergency was over — within days, or, at most, weeks. Relative calm returned quickly to the islands as the threat of renewed attack dissipated; places of amusement and saloons were permitted to open in February of 1942; and life returned to near normalcy after our victory at Midway removed any realistic threat of invasion. But the military still insisted that the civil courts remain closed and the writ of habeas corpus remain suspended. A considerable battle ensued over the next years between the ousted civilian officials and the governing generals. This battle culminated in a contempt citation issued by a federal judge against the commanding general, followed by an order issued by the general threatening to court-martial the judge if he persisted in issuing writs of habeas corpus. It wasn't until after the war (and the restoration of habeas corpus by the president) that the Supreme Court decided that Congress, in authorizing martial law in Hawaii, had not intended to permit the "supplanting of courts by military tribunals." By that time, thousands of man-days of illegal imprisonment had already been served.[3]

Martial law in Hawaii, with all its abuses, did not include mass detention on racial grounds of the kind employed on our West Coast between 1942 and 1944. The removal and confinement of 110,000 Japanese Americans, though carried out by the army, resulted from intense pressure brought by civilian officials (such as the then attorney general of California, Earl Warren). The story of this shameful episode has been frequently recounted. Today it is publicly defended by almost no one (including even the House Internal Security Committee, which recently called the episode — "at least in hindsight" — "a dark day in our history").

It is important to recall that the Supreme Court, although it did approve the forced removal of Japanese Americans from the West Coast, did not sustain their long-term detention in the camps. The only detention case decided by the Court involved a woman who the government conceded was loyal. That case reached the Court near the end of the war, when plans were already in progress to return the detainees to their homes, since the threat of Japanese invasion had disappeared. It was easy for the Court, therefore, to order the woman's release on the ground that Congress had never explicitly authorized detention of a "citizen who is concededly loyal [and who] presents no problem of espionage or sabotage." "Loyalty is a matter of the mind," said Justice William O. Douglas, "not of race, creed, or color." The import of that opinion is extremely limited, since it is doubtful that we would ever be so foolish as again to detain a group simply on the basis of their race or color. But we might attempt to detain individuals on the basis of their assumed loyalty or propensity to commit acts of sabotage or espionage. Indeed, not long after the last of the Japanese detention camps were dismantled, Congress enacted just such a law.

On the heels of the Communist invasion of South Korea, the Emergency Detention Act of 1950 was introduced by a group of liberal senators (perhaps in a misguided effort to defeat other provisions of the McCarren Act).[4] After devoting fifteen paragraphs to a recitation of the evils of the "world Communist movement," the statute proceeded to empower the attorney general to arrest and detain anyone "as to whom there is a reasonable ground to believe that such person probably will engage in, or probably will conspire with others to engage in, acts of espionage or sabotage." The suspect could be kept in a "place of detention" for an indefinite time, but he was denied such basic constitutional safeguards as trial by jury, bail, confrontation of his accuser, and proof beyond reasonable doubt. This extraordinary measure could be invoked in the event of a presidential declaration of "internal security emergency." But such an emergency may not be declared unless our territory is invaded, Congress declares war, or there is an insurrection in aid of a foreign enemy. Had Congress declared war against North Korea or North Vietnam, as many — including some liberals — urged it to do, then the president could have invoked the Detention Act. He also could have invoked it had he agreed with some congressmen who perceived the urban riots as "insurrections in aid of a foreign enemy."[5] But since there has, in fact, been no presidential declaration of internal security emergency since the enactment of the law, the detention provisions have never been employed.[6]

There was a time, however, when serious thought was given to mass detention of potential saboteurs. It was no less a liberal than former senator Paul Douglas who, in the course of the debate over the Detention Act, made the following statement:

> Mr. Hoover says there are 12,000 ["hard core . . . potential saboteurs and spies"]. In my judgment, if we had a period of national emergency — and I think it is pretty close to being a period of national emergency now — the best thing the country could do would be to "put them on ice," so to speak, treating them nicely, but to take them out of circulation so that they could not commit acts of treason.[7]

Following the passage of the act, the Justice Department established six detention "camps" throughout the country. These camps remained unused and generated little concern until a few years ago, when a writer named Charles R. Allen achieved some prominence by publishing a pamphlet entitled *Concentration Camps, U.S.A.*, which alleged that the Justice Department had a plan — code-named Operation Dragnet — under which it could round up hundreds of thousands of dissidents "overnight." That hysterical document was given considerable credence by the publication of another hysterical document, this one a report by the House Committee on Un-American Activities, entitled *Guerrilla Warfare in the United States*. Among the actions that the report said "could be taken" in the event of a ghetto riot was the invocation of the Emergency Detention Law:

> Acts of overt violence by the guerrillas would mean that they had declared a "state of war" within the country and, therefore, would forfeit their rights as in wartime. The [Detention] Act provides for various detention centers to be operated throughout the country and these might well be utilized for the temporary imprisonment of warring guerrillas.

The report also stated that during a "guerrilla uprising most civil liberties would have to be suspended." It is not surprising therefore that mimeographed copies of this report were widely circulated in black areas (at a cost of up to five dollars a copy) and that a *Washington Post* survey found a "deep and abiding" belief in the black community that massive riots would lead the government to "make a vast indiscriminate sweep down the streets of black ghettos and hustle every man, woman, and child off into a concentration camp."

Another incident which lent some credence to the concentration camp charge was an interview with then deputy attorney general Kleindienst in which he was quoted as saying that demonstrators who "interfered with others . . . should be rounded up and put in a detention camp." On the very day that this charge was categorically denied, Kleindienst wrote a letter to Senator James O. Eastland stating the administration's recommendation that the Detention Law be repealed, because such action would "allay the fears and suspicions — unfounded as they may be — of many of our citizens"; and this benefit "outweighs any potential advantage which the act may provide in a time of internal security emergency."[8]

In 1970 the Senate voted by voice and without debate to repeal the Detention Law, but the House sent the recommendation to the newly named but familiar Committee on Internal Security. Its chairman, Representative Richard H. Ichord, tried to persuade the House that retention of the Detention Act would be in the interests of civil liberties, since the act would not permit a roundup on racial grounds such as that directed against the Japanese.[9] The act was, however, repealed and is no longer on the books. But many other statutes presently on the books authorize the president to employ extraordinary powers during periods of crisis — powers that include the closing or taking over of radio and television stations; the censorship of newspapers; the imposition of travel restrictions on citizens and aliens; the summoning of the "posse comitatus" (the old "posse" of the cowboy movies); the calling out of federal troops; and the expropriation of private property (subject to subsequent reimbursement). Moreover, the president has considerable inherent powers that are said to derive from the nature of his office without regard to congressional authorization.[10]

The power to declare martial law, for example, is not even mentioned in the Constitution. Nor is the scope of that power anywhere defined, as an opinion of the attorney general pointed out in 1857: "The common law authorities and commentators afford no clue to what martial law, as understood in England, really is. . . . In this country, it is still worse." "And what was true [of martial law] in 1857 remains true today," observed Justice Hugo Black in a 1946 opinion. Some commentators have been content to cite Wellington's cynical apothegm that martial law is simply the will of the general; or the equally simple-minded aphorism that "necessity knows no law." The Supreme Court has recognized that "Civil Liberty and this kind of martial law cannot endure together; the antagonism is irreconcilable." (Or, as Groucho Marx might have put it, "Martial law, like military intelligence, is a contradiction in terms.")

While the courts have delivered opinions full of promise and prose about their majestic role during crises and the "irrepealable" nature of our fundamental safeguards, they have acted far more cautiously. And experience teaches us that what courts have in fact done in the past is a far better guide to what we may expect from them in the future than is the rhetoric they have invoked.

What then could we reasonably expect from our courts if any American president during a period of dire emergency were once again to suspend important constitutional safeguards? Our past experiences suggest the following outline: The courts — especially the Supreme Court — will generally not interfere with the executive's handling of a genuine emergency while it still exists. They will employ every technique of judicial avoidance at their disposal to postpone decision until the crisis has passed. (Indeed, though thousands of persons have been unlawfully confined during our various periods of declared emergency, I am aware of no case where the Supreme Court has ever actually ordered anyone's release while the emergency was still in existence.[11]) The likely exceptions to this rule of judicial postponement will be cases of clear abuse where no real emergency can be said to exist, and cases in which delay would result in irrevocable loss of rights, such as those involving the death penalty.[12] Once the emergency has passed, the courts will generally not approve further punishment; they will order the release of all those sentenced to imprisonment or death in violation of ordinary constitutional safeguards. But they will not entertain damage suits for illegal confinement ordered during the course of the emergency.

When these strands are woven together, there emerges an approach to the limits of martial law that was encapsulated by Justice Holmes: martial law is not "for punishment," but rather "by way of precaution, to prevent the exercise of hostile power." This distinction between "punitive" and "preventive" law runs through the cases and has been echoed by many commentators.[13] But no sharp line exists between punishment and prevention, as Blackstone recognized many years ago: "If we consider all human punishment in a large and extended view, we shall find them all rather calculated to prevent future crimes than to expiate the past." Practically speaking, the distinction means simply that the courts will tolerate preventive detention during an emergency but they will not approve the carrying out of any part of a sentence after the emergency has ended.

This prediction of "what courts will do in fact"[14] may not, of course, prove entirely accurate. Important changes have occurred since the end of the Second World War. The Warren Court entered "political thickets" into which previous Courts had been reluctant to tread; and its bold record of recognizing and enforcing fundamental rights will not be undone by the Burger Court. Civil rights organizations have proliferated and are better — though probably not well enough — prepared for their roles in the event of an emergency suspension of civil rights. And, most important, the Vietnam War and other recent events may have divided the country beyond any possibility of full repair; short of the threat of mass destruction, we will probably never again see an emergency that will bring the country together in a unanimous display of solidarity and patriotism such as that which accompanied our entry into the Second World War.

But our historical experience — even when tempered by these recent developments — ought to teach us that we cannot place our entire reliance upon judges to vindicate our liberties in the midst of great national crises. Learned Hand recognized this when he said: "Liberty lies in the hearts of men and women; when it dies there, no constitution, no law, no court can save it." But just how deeply is liberty ingrained in the hearts of American men and women? Can we rely on their "eternal vigilance" to resist suspension of fundamental safeguards during periods of crisis (especially those safeguards designed to protect a small minority)? Our historical experience in this respect is disappointing. When the military took over the governance of Hawaii, few protests were heard from the average citizen.[15] Part of the reason, of course, is that it is in the nature of military rule to discourage dissent; in Hawaii, newspapers were forced to print only what the generals wanted the people to read; and public criticism was punished by court-martial. But there is a subtle, and dangerous, sense in which people — even people whose traditions proclaim liberty — become comfortable with regimentation and authority; they do not necessarily welcome it, but neither are they willing to take risks in order to secure greater freedom. Many Hawaiian businessmen and store owners, for example, resisted the return of civilian authority and even wired the president urging caution in the restoration of habeas corpus. As one businessman commented:

> [We] were a darned sight safer as American citizens under that kind of military control, when the fear of immediate punishment was facing the violation of military law, as against cases dragged along in the courts.

It has been indeed fortunate for the survival of our liberties that there have always been some Americans — often only a small group and sometimes not those directly affected — who have been willing to challenge government high-handedness, even during periods of crisis. Under our constitutional system it takes only a single person challenging the government to create a case or controversy suitable for judicial resolution. Even though the Supreme Court has been reluctant to decide these cases and controversies in the midst of the crisis, it has performed an important historical cleansing function by condemning illegal action after normalcy has been restored. But the courts should do more than issue retrospective *pronunciamentos*. This is not to suggest that justice should remain blind to the existence of a real emergency endangering the survival of the nation. As Justice Arthur Goldberg once wrote: "While the Constitution protects against the invasion of individual rights, it is not a suicide pact." But it is precisely during times of crisis — when the balance between momentary expediency and enduring safeguards often goes askew — that courts can perform their most critical function: to restore and preserve a sense of perspective.

Nor is there any sound reason why the courts should refuse to entertain declaratory actions challenging emergency powers *before* they are invoked in the midst of a crisis. Legal issues can be "discussed and decided without passion" before a crisis as well as after it, and with considerably greater impact. But such anticipatory litigation has been uniformly rejected on the ground that there will be ample opportunity for challenge when the emergency power is invoked. (A constitutional attack on the Emergency Detention Act, for example, has been dismissed on this basis.) In light of the course of avoidance consistently followed by courts during periods of emergency, this "wait for the crunch" argument is indefensible.

In the eternal struggle between liberty and security we have come to expect the executive and legislative branches to champion the latter. The judiciary — with its lifetime tenure, its tradition of independence, and its unique stewardship over our irrepealable Rights — is the institution most able to resist the passing fears and passions of a dangerous moment.

But liberty, like life itself, needs many sources of nutriment to sustain it. It is not a commodity that can be obtained once and for all and then passively held on to. The difficult struggle for liberty must be endured by every new generation and in each new crisis. What Thomas Paine taught us on the eve of our own Revolution remains true today: "Those who expect to reap the blessings of freedom must, like men [and women], undergo the fatigue of supporting it."

---

*The September 11, 2001, terrorist attacks on the United States did, in fact, unite most Americans in a way not seen since World War II. These attacks, and the biological scares that followed, also led many Americans to rethink old values based on new experiences. On October 13, 2001, I published an op-ed article in the* New York Times *entitled "Why Fear National ID Cards?" which helped stimulate a national debate on this and the related issues of what information should be in governmental databases and when government officials should be authorized to demand identification.*

---

# FIFTY

# PREVENTIVE DETENTION OF CITIZENS DURING A NATIONAL EMERGENCY

## A Comparison Between Israel and the United States

*The right not to be imprisoned without proof of a past crime would seem fundamental to any democracy. Yet throughout history, people have been preventively imprisoned during times of emergency in order to assure the safety of the community against anticipated violence. The following chapter, first published in 1971, deals with that phenomenon.*

TIMES OF CRISIS TEST THE DEPTH OF A PEOPLE'S COMMITMENT to civil liberties. Nations whose fundamental laws proclaim freedom during times of normalcy often see these protections virtually erased by the exigencies of external or internal danger.[1]

Israel has not been immune to this phenomenon. It too has departed from fundamental principles of freedom in the name of national security. And world opinion has not ignored Israel's departures from the norms of liberty. Indeed, the comparative level of criticism directed at Israel might lead one to conclude that no nation had ever taken away more liberties with less justification.[2] My thesis is that precisely the opposite is true — that although Israel has suspended some important liberties during recent crises, it has retained far more than any other country faced with comparable dangers. This is not to say that the suspensions have been justified on absolute terms. I myself have been and continue to be critical of some of Israel's policies in this regard. But comparative analysis is essential to a sense of perspective. I propose, therefore, to compare Israel's response to the dangers it faces with that of other countries that have faced comparable dangers, particularly the United States.

Among the most fundamental safeguards of liberty is the requirement that imprisonment be predicated on proof that a past criminal act was committed, rather than on speculation that an individual may be dangerous in the future. It is precisely this safeguard that is typically suspended during periods of crisis. This should not be surprising, since the requirement of a conviction for past proven acts entails the possibility that dangerous persons, or even guilty ones, may go free. Accordingly, no civilized nation confronting serious danger has ever relied exclusively on criminal convictions for past offenses. Every country has introduced, by one means or another, a system of preventive or administrative detention for persons who are thought to be dangerous but who might not be convictable under the conventional criminal law.

The Israeli preventive-detention[3] law permits the imprisonment, without limit of time, of "any person" whose confinement is deemed "necessary or expedient . . . for securing the public safety, the defense of Palestine, the maintenance of public order, or the suppression of mutiny, rebellion or riot."

The Israeli Knesset has never enacted a preventive-detention law. The power to detain derives from a series of emergency defense regulations inherited by Israel from the British Mandatory Government. Ironically, these regulations, originally promulgated in 1937, were directed at the Jewish underground then operating against the British. Many Jewish freedom fighters — including Golda Meir, Moshe Dayan, and others in the present Israeli government — were detained between 1937 and 1948 (as their entries in *Who's Who* proudly proclaim).

During the Mandate period, the Jews bitterly opposed preventive detention. The Federation of Hebrew Lawyers convened a protest convention at which they vowed to do everything they could "to abolish the emergency regulations and restore the elementary rights to the individual." In 1948, however, when Israel was established as a state, the emergency regulations, including preventive detention, remained on the books, to be used sporadically until the Six Day War of 1967 and more extensively after Israel's victory and the resulting occupation.

Many Jews in Israel still oppose preventive detention, even though it is now their government that employs it. The New Left (known in Israel as Siah) has seized on the case of Fawzi al-Asmar as the symbol of what they claim to be political repression of Arab intellectuals. Wherever preventive detention is discussed in Israel, al-Asmar's name is likely to be invoked by its critics.

Having long opposed preventive detention in America,[4] I was greatly troubled when I learned of its use by the Israeli authorities. While in Israel during the summer of 1970, therefore, I decided to try to interview al-Asmar and to learn all I could about why he and the other Israeli Arabs were being detained. When I set out for Damon Prison, I was doubtful whether the authorities would let me talk to him or whether he would be willing to speak to me. I had read accounts of how uncooperative the Israeli authorities were said to be with "snoopers." Moreover, I had called Felicia Langer — a Jewish Communist who represents many detainees — and asked her to arrange an interview. She laughed. "They won't even let me see my clients about legal matters." I had called the Bureau of Prisons, which granted me permission to tour the facility and see the area where the detainees are held, but nothing had been said about interviews.

When I arrived at Damon, I was taken to the special area where the preventive detainees are separately kept. It was a spacious spare courtyard surrounded by three large dormitories and a dining area. The detainees — at that time twenty-three Israeli citizens and seventeen from East Jerusalem — were sitting around in small groups. Most of them were young, in their twenties and thirties. They were not dressed in prison garb (a number were wearing Arab burnooses) and they were not behaving like prisoners. There was no genuflecting before the warden; they made demands, rather than requests. And not a few times I heard remarks prefaced with, "Remember, we're not prisoners."

I walked among the inmates and asked for Fawzi al-Asmar. A tall man emerged, strikingly handsome, with a captivating smile. Looking more mature than his thirty-one years, he emitted an aura of confidence, determination, and honesty. I could tell, both by looking at him and by the way he behaved with the other inmates, that Fawzi al-Asmar is a leader of men.

I told al-Asmar that his name had been given to me by critics of preventive detention and that I wanted to hear his story. He put an arm around my shoulder and led me toward the empty dining hall where we began to talk. The governor of the prison made no objection and even provided me with a private room in which I later spoke to other detainees.

I asked Fawzi al-Asmar why he was being detained. He looked me directly in the eye and said, "Because I am an Arab." But there are 300,000 Israeli Arabs, I observed, and only a few handfuls are in prison; why were you singled out? "Because I express the feelings of the three hundred thousand and that makes me dangerous. There are Jews who share my beliefs, maybe even some who express them better. But they are not dangerous because they are Jews, and no Arab will listen to them. That is why I am being detained, and not Meir Vilner [the Jewish head of Rakah, the radical Communist party]."

I asked him what the Israeli authorities had accused him of when they had detained him thirteen months earlier. He said that they had concocted a story about his being a terrorist organizer. This time I looked straight into his eyes and asked: "Were you a terrorist organizer?" He smiled. "If they could have proved it, they would have brought me to trial."

Did he support Al Fatah? "I support their ideas, but not all of their means." Would he harbor a terrorist fugitive? "None has ever sought refuge with me, and that is the kind of question one must answer with his heart, not his lips. I cannot know what I would do until I hear the knock on the door."

Al-Asmar had few complaints about conditions in the prison. He writes all he wants to — poems, articles, letters — but he has not tried to publish his prison writings. His greatest complaint is that there is no one to talk to in Damon. I asked him if there is any truth to the charge that Israel is using preventive detention against Arab intellectuals. He laughed and said, "If only that were true, at least I would have someone to talk to. Most of those detained are simple people, half of them can't read or write. There used to be a lawyer here and we talked, but he's been freed."

I asked him why Israel was detaining illiterates; surely not for their political activities? Were they terrorists? "No," came his quick reply, "most of them are here as the result of family quarrels and personal vendettas. If two families are feuding in a village, one will sometimes go to the Israelis and make up a story that someone in the other family is working with the Fatah."

I asked how he saw the rest of his life unfolding. Would he remain in detention indefinitely? Did he intend to leave Israel after his release? He told me that he could probably be released whenever he chose to be, that various influential people had offered to intercede on his behalf, but that he did not want "special treatment." No, he would never leave the country. "That's just what Israel wants me to do — go away. But this is my homeland. I would rather write my poetry in Damon than in Paris."

As I was leaving, he told me that he was a man of the pen, not of the lips, and that his views on preventive detention were best expressed in two poems he had just written. I asked to read them. He doubted the authorities would allow that. I asked the governor of the prison, and without having seen the poems, he said that al-Asmar was free to give me any writings he cared to.[5]

Meir Shamgar, the attorney general of Israel, denies that al-Asmar is being detained because he is an Arab. "He is being detained because he is a terrorist leader who would kill innocent people if he were free. Sure he is a poet, but the cloak of a poet can sometimes conceal deadly bombs."

Shamgar, a career legal official who was formerly judge advocate general of the army, knows all there is to know about preventive detention and about terrorism. He has literally been on both sides of the wall. As a young man he was a member of Irgun Zva'i Le'umi (known in the United States as the Irgun and in Israel as Etzel). Under the leadership of master terrorist Menachem Begin (now the head of Gahal, the right-wing party that recently left Golda Meir's government), the Irgun's raison d'être was to make life so miserable for the British that they would leave Palestine. Among their most notorious accomplishments was the blowing up of the English High Command Headquarters in the King David Hotel. Although Begin himself eluded capture, Shamgar was caught and detained without trial by the British under the very same regulation that now has authorized al-Asmar's confinement. Shamgar remained in British detention camps, both in Palestine and in North Africa, for more than four years. (After telling me about his career as a terrorist, Shamgar reminded me, in a tone of humorous warning, that the Emergency Defense Regulations, which have never been altered, still have a provision punishing anyone who has contact with a "member of . . . Irgun Zva'i Le'umi.")

Nor was preventive detention used against Shamgar's comrades-in-arms only by the British. Within weeks after Israel declared its statehood, a half-dozen Irgunites were detained by the new Jewish government in order to head off an insurrection threatened with the arrival of the *Altalena*, a ship packed with weapons earmarked for the Irgun rather than the Haganah (semiofficial Jewish self-defense organization). In the fall of 1948, preventive detention was again used by the Israeli government against another group of Jewish terrorists. Following the brutal murder of Count Folke Bernadotte, about a hundred members of Lohamei Herut Israel (known in the United States as the Stern Gang, and in Israel as Lehi) were detained for a number of months. During the next four years, preventive detention was twice again employed against Jewish groups: first against an ultra-Orthodox religious organization that was allegedly plotting to plant a smoke bomb in the Knesset, and then against leaders of an organization suspected of bombing two embassies.

Since 1953, preventive detention has not been used against any Jewish group. Indeed, between 1953 and 1967 it was used very sparingly; it served primarily as a short-term "holding operation" against suspected spies until a decision could be made as to whether to deport, to try, or to exchange them for Israeli spies.[6] These were years of relative quiet for Israel, during which numerous attempts were made to repeal, or at least to modify, the Emergency Defense Regulations. When Ya'akov Shimshon Shapiro, the incumbent minister of justice, assumed his position in 1966, he convened a committee to study the regulations with an eye toward repeal. (Shapiro had repeatedly expressed disapproval of these laws while in private practice.) The committee was leaning in that direction when the Six Day War forced the government to turn its attention to more pressing concerns.

Israel's victory, accompanied by its occupation of Gaza and the West Bank, brought about an almost immediate increase in terrorist activities. Israeli Arabs, who had been cut off from direct contact with Jordanian Arabs (except through television, which respects no political borders), began to mix freely with Arabs from the West Bank. Indeed, under Israel's "open bridge policy," they were able to establish contact with Arabs from the East Bank as well.

Israel's unwillingness to seal the borders resulted not only in a free exchange of views; it also brought about a traffic in weapons and explosives. Now, for the first time, those Israeli Arabs who had preached terrorism could obtain the material with which to practice it. The Israeli authorities, who had always tolerated advocacy of the most extreme ideas, now had the job of keeping potential terrorists from practicing what they had been preaching.

Among those who had been preaching such measures was the family of Fawzi al-Asmar. Al-Asmar's mother was also a writer famous for her anti-Israeli prose. His brother was recently convicted of being a Syrian spy and sentenced to a term of imprisonment. But what about Fawzi himself? Shamgar arranged for me to meet with the chief of the Shin Bet's Arab section in order to learn some details of the government's case against al-Asmar.

The Shin Bet is Israel's small but highly respected counterintelligence organization, which is responsible for compiling the dossiers on detainees. The chief, whose name I never learned, was a warm and friendly man in his late forties who, like most Israelis of every rank, wore sandals and an open shirt. He explained the procedure employed in building a case for detention. No piece of information is ever relied upon unless it is corroborated by at least two independent sources. "We know about these family quarrels. We don't want to waste our resources on somebody who is the victim of a grudge." He brought out a pile of thick files and laid them on the table. I picked out a few at random for him to go through. He showed me how each important allegation is corroborated in various ways, how each piece of the puzzle is locked into place.

The file on al-Asmar was voluminous and convincing. In every instance where I could, I myself checked the details with independent sources. Here — on the basis of what I was told by various officials and my own investigation — is what I believe to be the truth about Fawzi al-Asmar:

Early last year, the Israeli army caught an Arab attempting to make an illegal crossing over the Jordan. On his person was discovered a number of papers. One was a coded message to a named person in a city on the West Bank. When decoded, the message proved very re-

vealing; it was a detailed series of instructions to the leader of a terrorist group based in that city. The army went to the courier's destination
and discovered an enormous cache of weapons and explosives in the
home of the intended recipient and sixteen of his associates. They
were all subsequently tried, convicted, and sentenced to prison terms.

While this raid was in progress, the search of the courier's effects
continued. Another seemingly innocuous piece of paper was found. It
turned out, however, that this paper contained a message written in invisible ink. This paper, when processed and decoded, sealed al-Asmar's
fate. It was an instruction to a named person to contact one Fawzi al-
Asmar in Lydda about various terrorist activities to be carried out by
"the group that he has under his control." Among the activities described in the message was the assassination of certain individuals.

Despite this information, al-Asmar was not yet detained; he was
placed under surveillance. Over the next weeks, a number of events occurred that made it plain to the Israelis that more stringent measures
would have to be taken: two of those slated for assassination in the
instructions turned up dead (apparently duplicate messages had been
sent with other couriers); the "middle man" who was supposed to deliver the message to al-Asmar was interrogated and said that although
he had never met al-Asmar, he knew from others that he was "very active in the field of sabotage and terrorism"; he also said that but for his
arrest he would have contacted al-Asmar pursuant to the instructions.
Finally, the Shin Bet received corroboration from an Israeli agent who
said that he had heard directly from a Palestinian commander in
Jordan that al-Asmar had been active in assassination and terrorism
since the end of the Six Day War. As a result of all this information,
al-Asmar was detained in Damon Prison, where he remained until his
release in the fall of 1970.

The case of Fawzi al-Asmar puts the problem of preventive detention into sharp focus. If the Israeli information is correct, then
al-Asmar is an extremely dangerous man whose freedom might result
in death and injuries. And the information does seem correct. That the
Arab caught crossing the Jordan was a bona fide courier is evidenced
by the discovered cache and the conviction of the terrorist group; that
the messages found on him were genuine is evidenced by the death of
two of those marked for assassination; that Fawzi was not the innocent
recipient of a message he knew nothing about is evidenced by the

statement of the man who was to contact him and corroborated by the agent's report of his discussion with the commander in Jordan. (It is, of course, possible that the entire file was contrived by the Shin Bet. My own investigation convinces me that this was not done, though I cannot, of course, vouch for the authenticity of every piece of information in the file. I am personally convinced, for whatever that is worth, that Fawzi al-Asmar was the leader of a terrorist group.)

Yet even with this apparently tight web of evidence, it would have been quite impossible, under Israeli law, to charge al-Asmar with a crime and bring him to trial. The courier's document, dramatic as it is, would be inadmissible hearsay; it is merely the statement of an unknown person somewhere in Jordan that al-Asmar was the head of a terrorist group. The statement of the "middle man" would also be inadmissible hearsay, since he knew of al-Asmar's activities from others; in any event, he refused to repeat his statement in open court for fear of his life. (Numerous "collaborators" have, in fact, been killed by Arab terrorists.) The Israeli agent from Jordan could not, quite obviously, be brought into court (even if the power of subpoena extended across the Allenby Bridge).

What, then, are the options available to a democratic society in a case, like this one, where it seems fairly clear that the suspect is indeed a dangerous terrorist but where a criminal trial under the usual rules of evidence is precluded?

One obvious option is to follow the rules wherever they take you. If al-Asmar cannot be tried and convicted under the established rules of evidence, then he must be released no matter how dangerous he is thought to be. This is what we in the United States do — at least in theory — in ordinary criminal cases: if a suspected murderer cannot be convicted because his confession was coerced or because the weapon was discovered unlawfully, he is supposed to be released. Often, however, ways are found to keep the dangerous defendant in confinement despite the absence of a criminal conviction: if he has "homicidal propensities" he may be committed to a mental hospital; if his crime has sexual overtones, he may be confined as a sexual psychopath; even if he must eventually be released, he may be held in pretrial detention for a year or two before his acquittal. It is true, of course, that some suspected murderers are in fact released even though they are thought to be extremely dangerous.

In times of war, however, the United States does not even purport to follow the usual rules of evidence when these rules would lead to the release of suspected spies or saboteurs. During both world wars we had, and still have, special administrative procedures for detaining dangerous persons who could not be convicted of crime under the established rules of evidence. During World War II we used administrative tribunals not only to detain; we actually used them to execute suspected enemy agents.[7] I am not aware of any country in the world that follows the customary rules of evidence during wartime, when those rules would lead to the release of persons who are known to have committed, but who could not be convicted of, serious acts of sabotage, espionage, or terrorism. As one high court correctly observed: "Preventive justice . . . is common to all systems of jurisprudence," especially during times of war or national emergency.[8]

And Israel today is a country at war. Although a cease-fire is currently in effect between Israel and some of the Arab states, Israel is at war with various nations and also with the Palestinian terrorist organizations. The war with the Palestinians is being fought not only on Israel's borders but also in its marketplaces, its cinemas, its bus terminals, and its civilian airplanes. The fear of a bomb planted in a crowded location is ever present. The security guard who looks into the purse of every woman entering the concert hall and the Supersol (supermarket) is a constant reminder of the Palestinian terrorists' boast that every Arab living in Israel is carrying a bomb in his heart and perhaps in his pocket.

It is interesting to compare Israel's reactions to the dangers it faces with the reaction of the United States when it faced dangers following the bombing of Pearl Harbor and the outbreak of World War II.

At that time there were about 110,000 Americans of Japanese ancestry living on the West Coast, of whom 70,000 were American citizens (virtually all of them born here, since residents who emigrated from Japan were ineligible for American citizenship under the racial prohibitions then on our statute books). A virulent anti-Japanese hysteria followed Pearl Harbor. Rumors were circulated that Hawaiians of Japanese ancestry were signaling enemy pilots and submarines, that Japanese Americans had intentionally infiltrated the power and water companies, and that they had formed sabotage and espionage rings numbering in the thousands. In fact, none of these stories proved truc. The records of "the Federal Bureau of Investigation and Army and Navy intelligence indicate that there was not a single instance of espionage or sabotage by a resident of Japanese ancestry before, during, and after World War II."[9] The absence of such activities did not, however, satisfy a hysterical population with deep-rooted racial antagonisms. Indeed, Earl Warren, then attorney general of California, expressed the Alice in Wonderland view that it was the very absence of sabotage that was "the most ominous sign in our whole situation." It convinced him, he said, "that the sabotage . . . the fifth-column activities that we are to get, are timed just like Pearl Harbor," and that the present inaction by the Japanese Americans was designed to lull us "into a false sense of security."[10]

The various intelligence agencies — the FBI and army and navy intelligence — preferred to approach the problem of potential terrorism and espionage "on the basis of the individual, regardless of citizenship, and not on a racial basis." This was what was done with persons of German and Italian extraction on the East Coast. Thousands of aliens "regarded by the Attorney General as dangerous to the national security if permitted to remain at large" were preventively detained on an individual basis. But on the West Coast the prevalent attitude was reflected by General DeWitt, head of the Western Defense Command: "A Jap's a Jap. There is no way to determine their loyalty." Earl Warren agreed: "We believe that when we are dealing with the Caucasian race we have methods that will test their loyalty. . . . But when we deal with the Japanese . . . we cannot form any opinion that we believe to be sound."[11] Accordingly, the decision was made to confine the entire West Coast population of Japanese Americans: 109,650 men, women, and children were put in detention camps, where they remained for nearly the entire war. Virtually no exceptions were made; those detained included veterans of World War I, future soldiers who would die fighting in the famous 442nd Regimental Combat Team (the "Nisei Brigade"), and lifelong members of the American Legion (whose monthly publication advocated "putting American Japanese on some Pacific island").

Liberal opinion in the United States was extremely critical of the detention of the Japanese Americans on racial grounds. Prominent leaders of the American Civil Liberties Union urged President Franklin D. Roosevelt to "constitute a system of hearing boards to test the loyalty" of individual citizens and noncitizens. Those justices of the Supreme Court who dissented from the judicial approval given the exclusion and detention orders criticized the government for not treating "these Japanese-Americans on an individual basis by holding investigations and hearings to separate the loyal from the disloyal as was done in the case of persons of German and Italian ancestry." (Virtually no criticism was ever leveled against the preventive detention of the latter.) Academic criticism centered on our failure to detain Japanese Americans "on the basis of individual suspicion," and also on our unwillingness to adopt a system of graded restrictions — as the English and French did — whereby only the most dangerous were detained and others "were subjected to certain continuing restrictions especially as to their travel."[12]

What liberals in the United States urged that we do with our Japanese citizens is essentially what Israel has done with its Arab citizens. It has made an intensive effort to separate out the potential terrorists from the loyal Arab, or even the "merely disloyal" Arab. "We are not interested in loyalty," I was told by the minister of justice. "We don't care what they believe in their hearts; we care only about what they conceal under their clothing. Let them pray for Arab victory, as long as they don't work for it."

The Israeli authorities have divided their Arab citizens into four categories. The first covers the loyal and "merely disloyal," which includes more than 99 percent of Israel's 300,000 Arab citizens. They are not subject to any significant restrictions on their liberty. They enjoy the rights of citizenship; they may live and travel almost anywhere (including the occupied territories); they may read the various anti-Israel newspapers published in Jerusalem and elsewhere; they may, as a considerable number of them do, belong to the Rakah party, which has three members in the Knesset.[13] The fact that they are Arabs and that Israel is at war with Arabs has not resulted in legal discriminations against them (unless their not being subject to the draft is regarded as discrimination).

The Arab-Israeli is, to be sure, subject to some de facto discrimination. He is stopped more frequently at the roadblocks that the Israeli police routinely set up at the entrance points to every large city. But if his identification is in order — every Israeli, Jew as well as Arab, must carry an identification card — he is politely sent on his way. It is far more difficult for an Arab — even a loyal Arab — to get a job that has any connection with security (a word that has a broad meaning in Israel). And, most unfortunately, it is often difficult for an Arab to find housing in certain parts of the country.

Thus, those Arabs who are not regarded by the security service as potential terrorists, saboteurs, or assassins are not subjected to legal restrictions, even if it is known that their sympathies lie with the enemy. Even those who are regarded as potential terrorists are not all detained. The majority are simply told not to leave their city, town, or village without permission; within that area they are free to move about as they please by night or day. Permission to travel to other cities is routinely granted for business reasons and periodically for family and social reasons.

Those who are regarded as especially dangerous — a few hundred — are subject to further restrictions: they may not leave their homes during the hours of darkness without special permission (a kind of personalized curfew), and they must report daily to the local police station.

Only a tiny portion of potential terrorists — twenty-three Israeli citizens during the summer of 1970, and fifteen at the most recent count in the spring of 1971 — are actually detained. (The number has never been more than about one hundred.) The Israeli authorities claim that every one of those detained has, in fact, been involved in serious terrorist activities and that they could not effectively be prevented from carrying on future terrorism by restrictions less total than actual detention.[14]

If there are only two dozen Israeli citizens who are sufficiently dangerous to be preventively detained, would it not be wiser, I asked an Israeli official, to release them and take the risks of a few additional acts of terrorism? He responded by telling me the story of Leon Kanner.

Leon was a Hebrew University student who had recently emigrated to Israel from his native Uruguay. His family lived on a kibbutz, where they worked in agriculture. Leon shared a small flat in Jerusalem with his friend Edward Joffe, a student who had been twice wounded during the Six Day War. On the weekend of February 21, 1969, the boys were planning a "trip to the hills to pick flowers," as Edward wrote to his parents. On Friday morning, the roommates went together to the Supersol at Jerusalem's busiest intersection to do some shopping for their trip. The store, which is one of the largest in Israel, was crowded with women doing their pre-Sabbath shopping. As the boys approached the meat counter, an explosion ripped through the store. A bomb containing five kilograms of dynamite had been planted in a biscuit can. Both boys were killed instantly. Many women, including a survivor of Auschwitz, were seriously injured. On another Friday — the eve of the Jewish Sabbath seems to be a favorite time for terrorist activities — Al Fatah planted a massive charge of explosives in an automobile in Machane Yehuda, the always-crowded outdoor market in Jerusalem. Twelve shoppers were killed and fifty-two seriously injured.

These are the realities of living in Israel today. They are not rumors, like those used to justify our detention of the Japanese. Every Israeli knows a family that has suffered from terrorism, whether it was the blowing up of the Hebrew University cafeteria, the bomb in the Tel Aviv bus station, or the explosions in the Haifa apartment houses.[15] A decision to release a known terrorist who cannot be brought to trial is viewed as a decision to risk the lives of dozens of civilians. Rightly or wrongly, these are the reasons Israel will not — at least in the most serious handful of cases — follow the usual rules of evidence when these rules lead to release. Indeed, I was surprised that the Israeli population had not demanded detention for more of those under village restriction.[16]

A second obvious option available to a democratic country in a case like al-Asmar's is to change the usual rules of evidence — especially the often anachronistic hearsay rule — so as to allow the introduction of reliable information even if its direct source cannot be produced in court. If hearsay evidence were admissible, a conviction might very well be obtainable against al-Asmar: the invisible-ink document could be introduced if the prosecutor established its authenticity; the statement of the man who was supposed to contact al-Asmar could be admitted without his identity being disclosed; and even the communication from the agent in Jordan might be considered by the judge.

I asked a high-ranking Israeli legal official whether it would not be better to loosen up their hearsay and other evidentiary rules. "We are very proud of our civil liberties," he told me. "It would be absurd to wreck our entire judicial system to accommodate a few wartime security cases." But would you really have to wreck the system, I asked; couldn't you just change some of the rules of evidence? "The rules of evidence lie at the center of our civil liberties, and the right to confront your accuser is the heart of any fair system of evidence. If we created a rule allowing into evidence the invisible-ink message and the agent's report, there would be virtually nothing left to the right of confrontation. I would rather see us act completely lawlessly in a few security cases than a little lawlessly in every case." This official felt strongly enough to say that he would "resign in protest" if Israel ever changed its rules to allow hearsay evidence in the general run of cases.

A third option, and the one adopted by Israel, is to create a separate category of cases entirely outside the judicial system: to handle them administratively, and to apply the flexible rules of evidence traditional in administrative cases. The basic reason Israel opted for this approach is that the mechanism was there, fully blown: the law establishing this system was on the books of Israel, even though it had been inscribed by a British pen.[17] There is no written constitution in Israel under which the regulations could be invalidated, though one Israeli Supreme Court justice, writing in dissent, would have struck down preventive detention as inconsistent with the judicial conscience (a phrase similar to the "shock of conscience test" sometimes applied by our Supreme Court).

The preventive-detention regulation inherited from the British is written in the broadest possible terms. There are no restrictions on military commanders' discretion, no limits on the duration of detention, no rules of evidence, and no judicial review. The regulation does require that there be "one or more advisory committees [whose chairman] shall be a person who holds or has held judicial office or is or has been a senior officer of the government." But the commander is under no legal obligation to follow the advice of the committee.

When the British administered this regulation in Palestine, they did so in the spirit in which it was written. It was a purely arbitrary grant of power to the military, unlimited by narrowing rules or practices. The Israeli government, although it has left the broad language of the regulation unamended, has circumscribed it by a series of carefully drawn rules and established practices. Until now these rules were unpublished and regarded as secret (though lawyers had some idea of what they provided). After numerous requests, I was finally given a copy of them. Among other things, they explicitly remove the power to detain for more than three months from any military commander (as provided in the regulation) and give it solely to the chief of the General Staff. In addition to the advisory committee required by the regulations, the rules establish an internal advisory committee that includes lawyers and professors; no request for a detention order may be made to the chief of staff unless a majority of the committee so votes. Another rule limits any period of detention to six months and requires a complete review at the end of this period. In addition, the advisory committee, which includes a justice of the Supreme Court, is regarded as more than advisory; its advice has never been ignored by the Israeli military authorities in twenty-two years. What is most important, however, is not the language of the regulation or of the narrowing rules; it is the fact — and a fact that is not challenged by Arab or Jewish critics — that the number of Israeli citizens actually detained has been so impressively small.

Despite the fact that so few have been detained, there has been much criticism from students, journalists, leftists, lawyers, and, of course, Arabs. And the criticism has by no means emanated exclusively from the Left. Hans Klinghoffer, the intellectual leader of the right-wing Gahal party, told me that he was unalterably opposed to "this unpardonable exception to the rule of law." "Terrorists must be imprisoned," he declared, "but not by means of legal terrorism." He feared that a population gets used to "special rules of war" and has difficulty living without them even when peace returns. He has tried to enact an Israeli security law to replace "British abomination." Under his proposal the suspected terrorist would be tried by a court, but the rules of evidence would be specially adapted to security cases. Could a person like Fawzi al-Asmar be convicted under his proposal? "Probably yes."

I asked the minister of justice, Ya'akov Shapiro, why he opposed Klinghoffer's proposal. "I do not want to get the courts involved in the business of the military. The only effect would be to legitimate — to impose a judicial imprimatur of lawfulness — on actions which are taken for military necessity but fall outside the rule of law."[18]

I asked Shapiro whether it would not be wiser for Israel to enact its own preventive-detention law to reflect its narrowly circumscribed practices. He preferred to keep things the way they were. "It is one thing for the military to use somebody else's law. It is quite another thing for the Knesset to enact as its own a new preventive-detention law." He told me that he could not vote for a preventive-detention law. "I have seen the inside of a prison, and not as a visitor. I know what it means to be preventively detained. How many ministers of justice do you know who were in jail?" (He described a recent meeting of a committee of distinguished Israeli jurists. "You know that every member of the committee had spent some time in British, German, or Russian jails. People like us could not bring ourselves to vote for an Israeli law of preventive detention.")

I asked the minister how he could speak so sanctimoniously about not wanting to enact a preventive-detention law when he readily enforces the present regulation. He was hurt by my question. "I do not enforce that regulation. I have nothing to do with it. That is a matter between the military authorities and the advisory committee. It is not within my jurisdiction. It is not a matter of law. It is a matter of military necessity."

That kind of argument is not very convincing to New Left critics, the most prominent of whom is a no-nonsense journalist named Amos Kenan, who has long been critical of preventive detention in particular and of Israeli policies toward Arabs in general.

He too had known preventive detention from the other side, having been a member of the Stern Gang as a young man. Kenan had no doubt that most of the Arabs detained were indeed terrorists. He knew, from personal contacts, that numerous Israeli Arabs were working with Al Fatah and with the Popular Front for the Liberation of Palestine. "Before the Six Day War I know that many Israeli Arabs were reporting Israeli troop movements to the Arab government. Our army knew it as well; in fact, they arranged some phony movements with the expectation that they would be reported." I asked him on what he based his information. He told me that he is, and has been for many years, very close to Arab radicals. This began during his days with the Stern Gang, which, he claims, was the "only true anticolonialist army in Palestine. We had no quarrel with the Arabs. We had a common cause with them against the British. I wept bitterly the first time we were attacked by Arabs and had to fight back. I really did regard them as brothers fighting a single enemy." On the eve of the Six Day War, a group of Kenan's Arab friends, confident of Egyptian victory, offered his family refuge from the massacre they expected against the Jews. Kenan politely declined the offer and went to join his reserve unit.

(Virtually no one in Israel, regardless of his political views, declines to serve in Israel's army.)

I asked Kenan whether, in light of his own observations about Arab attitudes and actions, he could really say that Israel was unjustified in detaining the small number of Arabs now in Damon Prison. He told me that this condemnation of preventive detention had to be understood in the context of Israeli-Arab relations over the past twenty years. "Maybe it is needed now. But it might not have been needed if our government had adopted a different policy toward its Arab citizens over the past generation. I could support preventive detention only if I were certain that there had been no other way. But there was another way."

I discussed with him the allegation that people like Fawzi al-Asmar were being detained for their political views. He smiled when I mentioned the poet's name. "I've known Fawzi for a long time. We worked together on many causes. There isn't an honest bone in his body. He's deceitful, he's a parasite, and I think he's a lousy poet. There may be political detainees; Fawzi may even be one of them; but don't believe a word he tells you; don't be taken in by that goddamn smile.

"Fawzi is one of those Arabs," he continued, "who criticize the hell out of Israel whenever she deserves it, but he doesn't have the guts to criticize any Arab government or group, ever. When I ask him why he doesn't, he says that you have to understand that the risks of making such criticism are very great. But that's the goddamn problem with the Palestinian movement. They should take personal risks for their beliefs. The Palestinians will become a real people only after a few of them have been hung for saying what they believe. I'm sorry, but I can't accept a double standard when judging Arabs and Jews."

I asked him whether he himself wasn't employing a double standard by being so vocal in his criticism of Israel's detention practices and so silent about the far more extensive use of preventive detention in Arab countries. His answer was that Israel deserved special criticism because its performance did not match its boasts about human liberty. "In any event, I am an Israeli and therefore I have a special obligation to be critical of my government."

I asked him whether he would advocate releasing the detainees even though he knew that among them were potential terrorists. "Yes," he said sadly, "even if it results in an explosion or two. That's the price we have to pay for our past errors." I asked whether he thought the day would ever come when Jewish critics, like him, would be detained. "I anticipate that happening in your country sooner than mine," he said. "Look at the way you treat your Communists. Ours are elected to the Knesset and practice law."

Felicia Langer is a Communist who practices law in partnership with an Arab Israeli named Ali Rafi. She sees preventive detention as directed primarily against the Communists. "Our people were the first to be detained. That's how I got into this area." (The real reason she got into this area is that there is no tradition in Israel — as there is in the United States — under which leaders of the bar are willing to defend people whose views they despise. Some good Jewish lawyers have represented terrorists in Israel, but most of the cases have, unfortunately, in my view, gone by default to the Communist lawyers.) I asked Langer whether preventive detention was used for political reasons. "Yes, for political reasons against Communists and also as a means of pressure to get Arabs to collaborate." Does it work, I asked? "Not against our people. Not a single Communist has collaborated."

If it is used against political opponents, I asked, why are there no Jews being detained? "It is a racist law, just as in your country the laws are directed against Third World people. Israel is a fascist country, they fight aggressive wars. I am concerned where this is all going to lead. I am concerned not for me but for my seventeen-year-old son, who will be in the army next year." I was surprised. "If your son feels the way you do," I asked, "why doesn't he refuse to fight? That's what the young people are doing in my country." Her answer came automatically. "The party has decided that our children must serve and must try to indoctrinate the troops. My own views are unimportant."

I asked whether the Communist party was against preventive detention in principle or just when it is directed at Communists. She boasted that there are no such laws in Communist countries. I reminded her that thousands of people are detained in Russian jails without trials and that we all know what a Russian trial means. "I am not interested in their practices, only their laws," she said with contempt.

My own academic bias leads me to be at least as interested in actual practices as in written laws. I set out, therefore, to make an independent appraisal of preventive detention in practice. On the basis of my experience, I find it difficult to understand the criticism leveled against

Israel by groups such as Amnesty International and the United Nations Commission on Human Rights, who claim that Israel will not open its doors to their investigatory teams. Almost every door in Israel seemed unlocked; all that was needed was some initiative and, sometimes, a gentle push. The authorities in Israel were aware of my critical attitude toward preventive detention, yet they imposed no restrictions on my activities.

I interviewed numerous Arabs, both in detention and under village restriction. I spoke to their lawyers, to government officials, and to men on the street. I heard both sides of every case. In each instance where I could, I checked these often conflicting versions with third parties or documented records.

My investigation led me to conclude that virtually all of those detained had, in fact, been involved in terrorist activities, that the vast majority could not be tried under Israeli law, and that a considerable number would probably engage in future terrorism if released. Some of the detainees were not bomb throwers themselves; they were recruiters, money raisers, and, like al-Asmar, commanders. Not one of them was a mere politician or a writer without connection to terrorist activities.[19]

Only one detention case troubled me greatly on its facts, perhaps because it involved a lawyer. It deserves recitation because it marks, in my view, the boundary beyond which Israel has not gone in preventively detaining its citizens.

Sabri Jaris is a thirty-one-year-old Arab who began speaking and writing against the Israeli government when he was still a teenage law student at Hebrew University. Until recently, he practiced law in Haifa, sharing office space with an older Arab lawyer active in Rakah and a Jewish lawyer affiliated with Maki (the Jewish Communist party). Jaris divided his time between representing members of the Palestine Liberation Organization charged with terrorism and writing books about the plight of the Israeli Arab.

On February 20, 1971, Jaris found himself in need of a lawyer. He was arrested by the Shin Bet and detained. Preventive detention was no stranger to Jaris. During the last hours of the Six Day War, he, along with a handful of other Arabs who had publicly called for Egyptian victory, was detained for a short time. (Jaris is fond of remarking:

"You know, the Israelis never would have won the war if they hadn't detained me.")

For the first month of detention, Jaris was angry but hopeful of early release. When it did not come, he began to organize the other detainees. He started a hunger strike, which received international publicity; he brought lawsuits challenging the conditions of detention; he sought his own freedom by writ of habeas corpus; he notified his French publisher, who came to Israel with a famous Continental advocate; he stimulated protests by other members of the Israeli bar (Jewish as well as Arab). Three months after his arrest, Jaris was sent home to Haifa.

It was in that city, just a few weeks after his release, that I spoke to Sabri Jaris. His office, which was a third-floor walk-up in the Arab market, was shabby and not even charming. There was no privacy; three large rooms, each with a number of desks, simply adjoined one another without any doors. Loud discussions in Hebrew and Arabic permeated every corner, while a dozen Arab clients, mostly old, waited to speak with one of the lawyers. Jaris invited me into his room and we began our often-interrupted conversation.

Jaris told me, in his soft, fluent English, of his early life in a small Arab village on the Palestinian side of what is now the Israel-Lebanon border. His parents and most of their nine children still live there, and Jaris and his younger brother used to visit them on Christian holidays. During his university years, Jaris became active in various Arab nationalist movements. He was one of the founders of El Ard, an extreme movement that advocated the destruction of Israel. Even before the Six Day War he had been in trouble with the security service. Once he was briefly detained for investigation after a Lebanese Arab caught trying to cross the border illegally had "mentioned his name." For the past eight years, there has been an order outstanding against him that limits his movements outside Haifa without special permission.

I asked him how this restriction affected his life. He told me that it had little or no impact on his professional career, that he could, and does, go anywhere his law practice takes him. His personal life is, however, severely restricted. He told me that he was recently denied permission to attend a friend's wedding and that his visits to his parents' village near the Lebanon border have been limited to certain religious and family occasions. (Twice he has been caught violating these restrictions and fined.)

We talked about his most recent detention. The Shin Bet had received information that Jaris's younger brother had crossed over into Lebanon and joined Al Fatah. They accused Jaris of harboring him on his way to carrying out a terrorist mission, and Jaris denied all knowledge of his brother's activities. He told me with a smile that was both sad and proud: "I think the authorities are right. My brother is working with the Fatah in Lebanon." But he quickly added that he did not harbor or help him. "My brother's activities were the pretext the government has been looking for all along. They detained me because of my political views."

Moving to those views, I asked him what he thought of Al Fatah. "I understand them, I sympathize with the way they are fighting and what they are fighting for." Did he agree with their tactics? "I feel good when I hear that the Fatah have attacked an enemy — that is, an Israeli — army camp. I don't like the idea of bombs for innocent people. But how do you expect them to do otherwise when Israel blows up the houses of innocent people in Hebron?"[20] Would he help a member of the Fatah who sought refuge in his home? "No, I would not give him a place to stay. But neither would I inform the police that he sought refuge. That would be asking too much." Did he regard himself as a loyal citizen of Israel? "I regard myself first and foremost as a Palestinian Arab. Israel was imposed on me. But I have accepted Israeli citizenship and membership in its bar. I have chosen to remain here. I obey the laws, but no more. I would not fight against my brother Arabs, and that is not required of me by Israeli law. I long for Arab victory, but I do not actively work for it." Why did he suppose they released him after three months? "They had no choice. The pressure was too great. World opinion does not tolerate the detention of a lawyer. In the end they were sorry they had started up with me."

I suspect that Jaris may be right: Israeli officials do seem sorry now that they detained him. The case against Sabri Jaris, as told me by government officials and others, was not nearly as compelling as the case against Fawzi al-Asmar. It was the least convincing of the many cases I had investigated.

It seems that Jaris's native village on the Israeli side of the Lebanon border, Fasuta, was a favorite stopping-off place for terrorists entering Israel from the north. One day early this year the Israeli police observed a small truck driving suspiciously fast in the area of Fasuta. After a brief chase the truck crashed into a tree, but the occupants escaped into a wooded area. Inside the truck the police found two large sacks of explosives and detonating devices. They ultimately traced the truck to its owner in Fasuta and were told the driver of the truck was Jarius Jaris, Sabri's younger brother. They also learned from a number of reliable people in the village that Jarius spent both the night before and the night after the truck incident with Sabri (who had traveled from Haifa to Fasuta to meet him).

Within a few days the Shin Bet received a communication from an agent in Lebanon corroborating their information about where Jarius had spent the two nights. They also were told by the agent that Sabri and Jarius had planned further sabotage action in the Haifa area. Sabri was then detained — according to the Israeli authority, not for the purpose of punishing him for harboring a member of Al Fatah, but to prevent him from carrying out further collaborative work with his terrorist brother, who was still at large. The reason Sabri was not brought to trial was because all the evidence against him was obtained from sources that either would not testify (the Fasuta villagers) or could not testify (the agent in Lebanon).

If Jaris was planning future terrorist activities, then why, I asked, was he released after only three months of detention? I was told that something had occurred in May of this year that made it highly unlikely that Jarius Jaris could carry out the planned activities. I asked what this occurrence was, and for the first and only time in my numerous interviews, I was told: "This we cannot tell you." My surmise is that the Israeli authorities have learned that Jaris is no longer a threat and have concluded that Sabri himself, without his brother, does not constitute a sufficient danger to justify his continued detention. Accordingly he was sent back to Haifa, restricted in his travel, but otherwise unhampered in the practice of his profession. In September 1970, Sabri Jaris left Israel and moved to Beirut, Lebanon. The reason given for his departure was that he had "probably done all he could effectively do under the prevailing conditions of repression."

Sabri Jaris's case is disturbing to me. I believe that he probably did harbor his brother as the Shin Bet charges. But that does not purport to be the basis on which he was detained. His future dangerousness was evidenced merely by the uncorroborated report of an agent. Moreover, it did not have the kind of specificity contained in the evidence marshaled against al-Asmar. Finally, if the only fear was that Jaris might collaborate with a given person, namely his brother, then it seems to me that careful surveillance might have been adequate to prevent this eventuality.

It must be remembered, however, that the Sabri Jaris case was not permitted to run its full course. Since his detention ended after three months, it need not have been approved by the internal advisory committee of the chief of staff. Nor did the outside advisory committee or the courts have an opportunity to review its merits. Any one of these might well have decided to release him, as in fact the security people themselves decided to do after ninety days. It must also be remembered that following his release Sabri returned to the active practice of law, despite his various detentions and violations. Consider whether a lawyer in this country would, after Jaris's experience, be permitted to resume his practice unhampered by bar association investigation and discipline.

The case of Sabri Jaris leaves me with two impressions: first, the suspicion that he might have remained in Damon well beyond the three months if he had not been as prominent and vocal as he was, and second, the confidence that this is as far as the Israelis will take preventive detention, and perhaps that they will never again apply it in so questionable a case.

I have attempted, in this article, to present a fair picture of how a democratic society faced with real danger from within and without is coping with the delicate task of balancing the interests of liberty and security. Some critics of Israel, domestic and external, act as if there were no real threat of terrorism — as if the explosions at Machane Yehuda and the Supersol were "Reichstag fires" contrived by the government for the explicit purpose of curtailing liberties. Some Israeli government officials, on the other hand, speak as if there were no restrictions on civil liberties. Neither of these views is correct. Civil liberties have in fact been curtailed in the face of a genuine threat of terrorism. The curtailment has been considerably less than one might have expected, certainly less than one might be led to believe by various organizations such as Amnesty International and the United Nations Commission on Human Rights.

Having attempted to place the problem in context, I am, of course, entitled to my own personal views. I fully understand the arguments in favor of preventive detention as it is presently practiced in Israel; I am convinced that it is not being abused and that every effort in good faith is being made to apply it only to persons who have engaged in terroristic activities and are likely to continue to be so engaged. I am impressed with the tiny number of Israeli citizens actually detained. And I appreciate, of course, the danger that Israel faces from terrorism. Nonetheless, I personally favor repeal of the Emergency Defense Regulations and particularly of the preventive-detention provisions. Nor is there any paradox in understanding the reasons behind a law, in recognizing that it has been fairly applied, and yet, at the same time, in favoring its repeal. Although the potential for abuse has not materialized, abuse is inherent in the nature of detention laws of the kind now on the books in Israel. Such laws, in the words of Justice Robert Jackson, "lie about like a loaded weapon."

If Israel feels that it cannot live with the normal rules of evidence in cases of suspected terrorists, then the Knesset should enact special rules of evidence for a narrowly circumscribed category of cases during carefully defined periods of emergency. All other safeguards should be provided, as in ordinary cases. In the last analysis, such a system might result in the release of some who are now detained. It is in the nature of any judicial system that in order to prevent confinement of the innocent, it must sometimes release the guilty. And those released might engage in acts of terrorism. But risks to safety have always been the price a society must pay for its liberty. Israel knows that well. By detaining only 15 of its 300,000 Arab citizens, Israel today is taking considerable risks. Indeed, what the world must come to realize is that no country throughout recorded history has ever exposed its wartime population to so much risk in the interest of civil liberties.

---

*In 1987 Justice William J. Brennan — perhaps the justice most sensitive to civil liberties — delivered a paper at an international conference in*

*Jerusalem in which he offered the following assessment of Israel's efforts at balancing security and civil liberties:*

> *It may well be Israel, not the United States, that provides the best hope for building a jurisprudence that can protect civil liberties against the demands of national security. For it is Israel that has been facing real and serious threats to its security for the last forty years and seems destined to continue facing such threats in the foreseeable future. The struggle to establish civil liberties against the backdrop of these security threats, while difficult, promises to build bulwarks of liberty that can endure the fears and frenzy of sudden danger — bulwarks to help guarantee that a nation fighting for its survival does not sacrifice those national values that make the fight worthwhile. . . . The nations of the world, faced with sudden threats to their own security, will look to Israel's experience in handling its continuing security crisis, and may well find in that experience the expertise to reject security claims that Israel has exposed as baseless and the courage to preserve the civil liberties that Israel has preserved without detriment to its security. . . .*
>
> *I [would not] be surprised if in the future the protections generally afforded civil liberties during times of world danger owed much to the lessons Israel learns in its struggle to preserve simultaneously the liberties of its citizens and the security of its nation. For in this crucible of danger lies the opportunity to forge a worldwide jurisprudence of civil liberties that can withstand the turbulences of war and crisis. In this way, adversity may yet be the handmaiden of liberty.*[21]

# FIFTY-ONE

# WIRETAPS
# AND NATIONAL-SECURITY
# SURVEILLANCE

---

*The advent of electronic eavesdropping has had a considerable impact on the right of privacy, especially during perceived emergencies. In 1972 I wrote the following article for* Commentary *magazine about the increasing resort to so-called national-security wiretaps.*

---

THE TERM *NATIONAL SECURITY* CONJURES UP THE IMAGE of spies, sabotage, and invasion, but a considerable number of so-called national-security wiretaps are conducted against domestic organizations or individuals who are suspected of activities deemed contrary to the national interest. I know, for example, that such persons as Martin Luther King and Elijah Muhammad and such organizations as the Jewish Defense League and the Black Panther party have been the subject of extended national-security taps. These taps are authorized exclusively by the prosecutorial arm of the government — the attorney general — without the need for a judicial warrant based on probable cause. How many national-security taps and "bugs" are currently in operation, and against what sort of persons, is a well-guarded secret, but bits of information that are slowly emerging raise some disturbing questions.

The case presenting the issue of the constitutionality of warrantless national security taps involves "Pun" Plamondon, an alleged "white panther" standing trial for conspiracy to blow up a CIA office in Ann Arbor, Michigan. Plamondon's lawyer, William Kunstler, filed a pretrial motion asking the government to disclose whether any of the defendant's conversations had been monitored. Motions of this kind are made rather routinely these days in so-called political cases, and — not infrequently — they strike paydirt, as Kunstler's motion did. It elicited an affidavit from the attorney general himself, acknowledging that "Plamondon has participated in conversations which were overheard by government agents," and that no warrant had been obtained. But Attorney General John Mitchell vigorously asserted that the tap — which was on some unnamed person's phone, not on Plamondon's — was legal, since it was "employed to gather information deemed necessary to protect the nation from attempts of domestic organizations to attack and subvert the existing structure of the government."

The lower court disagreed. It described the "sweep of the assertion of the presidential power" to tap without a warrant as "both eloquent and breathtaking," but it declined to "suspend an important principle of the Constitution." It held that "in dealing with the threat of domestic subversion," the warrant requirement of the Fourth Amendment could not be dispensed with. (The lower court did not decide whether a warrantless tap could be authorized to protect the country from "attack, espionage, or sabotage by foes or agents of a *foreign* power," since the government had conceded that the Plamondon tap was not installed for any such "foreign intelligence" purpose.) The court ordered the government to disclose to Plamondon the transcripts of each of his monitored conversations. If this ruling is upheld, Plamondon could be tried and convicted only if the government can prove that neither the indictment nor any of the trial evidence emanated from the tainted tap.

The issue thus presented to the Supreme Court to resolve is a fundamental one, going to the heart of the "separation of powers" on which our government is based. For the executive branch is asserting the power to dispense with an important judicial "check" on its action, namely, the requirement that a judicial officer determine whether there is probable cause on which to issue a warrant. It is somewhat surprising that the Supreme Court has never decided — or even intimated how it would decide — whether national-security wiretaps constitute an exception to the warrant requirement, especially since the practice of warrantless national-security taps is now more than thirty years old.

It was on May 21, 1940, that President Franklin Roosevelt sent to his attorney general the confidential memorandum that is regarded as the baptismal certificate of the national-security wiretap (though, significantly, the term *national-security* was not used). Roosevelt began by expressing his agreement with an early Supreme Court decision that "under ordinary and normal circumstances wiretapping by government agents should not be carried on for the excellent reason that it is almost bound to lead to abuse of civil rights." But these were not ordinary and normal times: America was preparing to enter the war, German and Japanese spy rings were operating on both coasts, and "certain other nations" had been engaged "in preparation for sabotage." Concluding that the Supreme Court had never intended its prohibition on wiretapping to extend "to grave matters involving the defense of the nation," Roosevelt informed the FBI that they were "at liberty to secure information by listening devices directed to the conversations . . . of persons suspected of activities against the government . . . including suspected spies." The president cautioned, however, that these investigations must be limited "to a minimum" and "insofar as possible to aliens."

But governments grow comfortable with special war powers, even when peace returns. And so, after the cessation of hostilities, Attorney General Tom Clark convinced President Harry Truman that "the present troubled period in international affairs, accompanied as it is by an increase in subversive activity here at home," required a continuation of the "investigative measures" authorized by Roosevelt. Nor was Clark content merely with retaining the status quo. Warning that "the country is threatened by a very substantial increase in crime" — an exaggeration typically made by attorney generals requesting additional powers or appropriations — he "reluctantly" requested the president to approve the power to tap "in cases vitally affecting the domestic security" (for that high-sounding phrase, read "organized crime") or "where human life is in jeopardy" (for that, read murder, kidnapping, robbery, arson, burglary, and the sale of narcotics). With Truman's quick concurrence, the narrow exception virtually became the rule. It was President Lyndon Johnson who — at the urging of another Clark (this one, Ramsey, more sensitive to civil liberties) — again narrowed the exception. In doing so, he introduced the current phrase "national security," which falls somewhere between Roosevelt's national "defense" and Truman's "domestic security."

It is not entirely clear why the government needs a national-security exception to the ordinary rules now governing wiretaps. When the exception was first created, there was an absolute prohibition against all wiretapping by federal officials — *with* or *without a warrant.* (The rule was not technically framed in terms of a prohibition on tapping, but rather in terms of a prohibition on all use of such evidence — and its fruits — in federal criminal prosecutions.) Thus, if national-security wiretaps were to be conducted at all, they would have to be authorized under an exception to the ordinary rules. In 1967, however, the Supreme Court said that wiretaps could be conducted — where any kind of criminal conduct was suspected — provided that the government secures a warrant based on probable cause and narrowly limited in time and scope. Under that decision, the FBI may lawfully conduct wiretaps in national-security cases if they secure a warrant. Unwilling to comply with this requirement, the federal government claims that national-security taps are still an exception to the ordinary rules, even though the ordinary rules that gave rise to the national-security exception have now been dramatically changed.

The government, arguing in support of this position before the lower courts, invoked "the inherent power of the president to safeguard the security of the nation"— the "historical power of the sovereign to preserve itself." The government was saying, in effect, that there is no separation of powers — no checks or balances on the executive by the other branches — when the president decides that the security of the nation is involved; the president must be trusted to exercise his power in a constitutional manner, since "the occupant of that office, like the members of the Court, takes a solemn oath to protect and defend the Constitution," and this "carries with it the weightiest presumption that those powers will not be abused." (The attorney general — to whom the president has delegated all authority in these matters — also takes such an oath, but it is not without relevance that the attorney general is the country's top prosecutor; nor is it immaterial that two of the holders of this office during the past ten years have also been presidential campaign managers, intensely involved in partisan politics.) If by some chance these powers were to be abused by the president or his deputies, the argument continues, then the "final significant restraint" lies not with the courts but with the "electorate," which "can reflect its dissatisfaction with the exercise of the power."

This argument — which entirely neglects the countermajoritarian purpose of the Bill of Rights and the anticentralist thrust of the Constitution itself — has been rejected by the Supreme Court over and over again. The classic response was formulated in a case growing out of Lincoln's attempt to limit the judicial power during the Civil War:

> This nation, as experience has proved . . . has no right to expect that it will always have wise and humane rulers, sincerely attached to the Constitution. Wicked men, ambitious of power, with hatred of liberty and contempt of law, may fill the place once occupied by Washington and Lincoln. . . . If our fathers had failed to provide for just such a contingency, they would have been false to the trust reposed in them. They knew — the history of the world had told them — that unlimited power, wherever lodged at such a time, was especially hazardous to freemen.

More recently, the Supreme Court rejected a similar assertion of executive power in the Pentagon Papers case, and it was probably this rejection that led the government to play down the "inherent power" argument in its wiretap brief recently filed in the Supreme Court. Instead, the government is now claiming that warrantless national-security taps were authorized by Congress in the Omnibus Crime Control and Safe Streets Act of 1968.

That act actually provides three separate national exceptions to its otherwise absolute requirement of a warrant before any tap. The first authorizes a forty-eight-hour tap if "an emergency situation exists" with respect to "conspiratorial activities threatening the national security interests," provided that a warrant is immediately sought at the expiration of that period. The government did not act pursuant to that emergency exception in the *Plamondon* case. Nor is it relying on the attack of a foreign enemy or the gathering of foreign intelligence information. The "exception" that is being relied on by the government provides as follows: "Nor shall anything contained in this chapter be deemed to limit the constitutional power of the president if he deems it necessary to protect the United States against the overthrow of the government by force or other lawful means, or against any other clear and present danger to the structure in existence of the government." That provision, however, begs the critical question: What precisely is "the constitutional power of the president" in dealing with domestic threats to the structure and existence of the government? As the lower court observed, the 1968 act was "clearly designed to place Congress in a completely neutral position in the very controversy with which this case is concerned." Moreover, even if Congress had explicitly exempted domestic national-security wiretaps from the warrant requirement of the Fourth Amendment, the constitutionality of that exemption would still have to be decided by the Supreme Court.

In passing on that difficult constitutional question, the Supreme Court might well ponder why the government is so vigorously asserting its right to dispense with warrants in national-security cases. Is it interested merely in preserving its convictions in the few pending cases that might be reversed if warrantless taps, conducted years ago, were held unconstitutional? Or does it have a real — and legitimate — need to tap phones without judicial intervention in this category of cases? There is little doubt that it could secure a warrant in any case in which there were a plausible — even a weak — claim that the national security required a tap. After all, the government may seek its warrant from the magistrate or judge of its choice. In the unlikely event that it were to fail on the first (or even the second) attempt, it could continue until it succeeded.

The government explains its unwillingness to comply with the warrant requirement by suggesting that compliance would pose problems of security, presumably because an indiscreet or corruptible judge or court employee might betray the tap or disclose the identity of a secret informant whose information was used in the warrant application. But the government's wide discretion in selecting the judge before whom it would make the application diminishes the force of this argument. Surely there are some judges whose patriotism and discretion are beyond question in the view of the government. In an extremely delicate case, for example, the government could present the application to the chief justice without even the clerk's being made privy to its contents. Moreover, under existing law, the government need not disclose the name of its informant — even to the judge in secret — in order to secure a warrant. Finally, the government concedes that in the event of a prosecution against anyone whose conversation was overheard, it must disclose the entire tap to a judge in a secret proceeding (as it did in the *Plamondon* case). Now, if the government is willing to trust the discretion of a judge (selected at random) not to disclose the object of a tap before it has occurred, the "indiscreet judge" argument, though vigorously pressed by the government, is obviously a makeweight.

There is a weightier argument against requiring a warrant in national-security cases, but the government has been reluctant to articulate it. A warrant, after all, must be based on probable cause that a crime has been, is being, or is about to be committed. The government would like to be free, however, to conduct certain wiretaps even when probable cause is lacking. For example, the Soviet ambassador engages in no crime when he discusses his country's negotiating position on the Mideast or SALT, but our government would like to — and surely will try to — monitor such conversations (as the Soviet government just as surely tried to monitor similar conversations by our diplomats). If a warrant based on ordinary probable cause were required, the monitoring of this kind of conversation would become legally impossible.

But this argument, which has considerable force in the context of foreign intelligence wiretapping, is wholly inapplicable to the kind of tapping at issue in the case now before the Supreme Court. For the tap in the *Plamondon* case was not installed for the purposes of gathering foreign intelligence; it was installed, in the words of the government, "to protect the national security against the threat posed by individuals and groups within the United States." Put most generously to the government, this means that the tap was directed against American citizens and organizations suspected of engaging in and planning bombings, riots, and other violent activities. All such activities are, of course, illegal and anyone who is planning them — or even talking about planning them — is, under present government thinking, guilty of conspiracy (witness the Berrigan indictment). Surely, in any such case there would be little difficulty in obtaining a warrant. Yet the government insists that it must — and that it will — continue to tap phones without securing the judicial approval that it could so readily get in any plausible case.

If it is true that warrants in national-security cases would be so easy to obtain, then another question — really the converse of the question previously posed — is suggested: Why do civil libertarians press so hard for what appears to be the hollow protection of a warrant secured from a government-selected magistrate? Or to put it another way, Why is the warrant issue viewed as so crucial by both sides?

To understand why civil libertarians feel the way they do about warrants in national-security cases requires a bit of background on the way they view wiretaps in general. To begin with, a great many civil libertarians oppose all wiretapping, even when authorized by warrant. They single out that technique of law enforcement because of its tendency to be indiscriminately overinclusive. As Ramsey Clark has put it: "No technique of law enforcement casts a wider net than electronic surveillance. Blind, it catches everything in the sea of sound but cannot discriminate between fish and fowl." Of course, no technique of law enforcement casts a perfectly narrow net. We do, after all, convict some innocent people; we shoot some fleeing "felons" who turn out to be guiltless bystanders; we preventively detain some defendants who are ultimately acquitted. But we do insist, as we should, that these deprivations be imposed mostly on people who are guilty and only rarely on those who are innocent.

Wiretapping is different. It is a deprivation that falls mostly on the innocent. The ratio of "innocent" monitored conversations to "guilty" monitored conversations is extremely high, especially in national-security cases. This is so for a number of reasons.

National-security taps are often installed on the phones of persons who are conceded to be innocent of any wrongdoing. And even taps installed on the phones of persons who are themselves guilty succeed in picking up the conversations of many innocent callers and recipients of calls. Finally, most of the monitored conversations, even between two guilty persons, involve matters unrelated to any wrongdoing. Moreover, because wiretapping is a clandestine "deprivation," its precise effects are difficult to assess. The behavior of some persons whose conversations are not, in fact, being monitored is significantly affected by the *fear* that their phones are tapped (witness the "debugging" operations recently conducted by various senators and congressmen), while others, whose phones are being tapped, but who do not — and never will — know that their conversations were monitored, are entirely unaffected. Yet despite the pervasiveness of the wiretap and its obvious chilling effect, the government blandly asserts in its brief that "the overhearing of a telephone conversation involves a lesser invasion of privacy than a physical search of a man's home or his person." (This assertion sharply raises the question of whether an administration that values the privacy of conversation and thought less than the privacy of property is the appropriate authority to decide, without any judicial check, that a phone must be tapped for national-security purposes.)

Making national-security taps conditional on a warrant, some civil libertarians argue, would reduce the ratio of innocent to guilty conversations overheard because warrants must be narrowly circumscribed, limited in time and scope, and related to criminal conduct. While recognizing that most magistrates issue wiretap warrants as if they were presents at Christmastime, the civil libertarians contend that there might be some reluctance to issue them in instances where it was plain that the primary motivation was political and that the national-security concern was a pretext. For it is widely assumed by civil libertarians today that a considerable number of domestic national-security wiretaps are conducted primarily for reasons unrelated to genuine national-security concerns. They are thought to be directed against political dissidents — both inside and outside the government — and general troublemakers who could be adequately and lawfully dealt with by the ordinary process of the criminal law. This is not to say that a plausible national-security concern — broadly defined — is lacking in each instance of a tap. It is to say that this concern frequently serves as an *excuse* for a broad surveillance whose primary purpose is either political or conventional law enforcement.

Whether or not the civil libertarians are correct in their assessment of the value of warrants in curbing abuse, their claim that domestic national-security wiretaps have been authorized in highly questionable cases is supported by the evidence currently available. Consider, for example, the tapping of Martin Luther King's telephone (and the electronic "bugging" of his hotel rooms). These warrantless invasions of King's privacy — and the privacy of countless others who conversed with him — have been defended as necessary for the national security. But in what specific sense did the security of this nation depend on the FBI's overhearing King's telephone conversations and eavesdropping on his hotel-room activities? A number of justifications have been offered by those close to Robert Kennedy, who, as attorney general, acceded to J. Edgar Hoover's request to authorize the tap. (No authorization whatsoever was given for the bug in the hotel rooms.)

The Kennedy version goes something like this: two of King's close associates — one a New York lawyer, the other a member of the Southern Christian Leadership Conference staff — were thought to be either Communist agents, party members, or sympathizers. After receiving warning from the Justice Department that associating with these persons might damage the civil rights movement, King dismissed the tainted staff member and initially severed his relationship with the suspected lawyer. But after a while, contact with the lawyer was gradually reestablished. It was this that led Kennedy to authorize Hoover to tap King's home phones and those in his Atlanta and New York offices.

Burke Marshall — Kennedy's respected and civil liberties–minded assistant attorney general — has made the shocking statement that his boss may have "refused too long" to authorize the King national-security tap. "I can't tell you who the man was or what the allegations were," he says, "but I can tell you I think it would not be responsible for an attorney general — in view of the characterizations of what that man was doing and who he was working for — for the attorney general to refuse a tap." He continues, suggestively but mysteriously: "If you take it as being true that there has been an espionage system and that the Bureau has an obligation to do things about that — if you put that all together, I would say you could say he refused too long."

Very well, then, let us "take" all that as "being true." Let us assume the very worst: that the New York lawyer was a real Russian spy, working for and being paid by the KGB. Assume further that his sole job was to influence King in directions favored by the Soviet Union. Assume even further that he was succeeding. Would this justify a national-security tap on King's phone? There is surely no claim that King was being used to further espionage or sabotage activities. He was, after all, engaged primarily in entirely lawful and constitutionally protected activity (even if the activity could hypothetically be shown to have favored the interests of the Soviet Union). He made and received thousands of calls to and from concerned, patriotic, and law-abiding American citizens about matters that were none of the government's business to overhear. He also engaged in — or erroneously believed he was engaged in — a private life, which also was none of the government's business to monitor. His telephone contact with the New York lawyer was an extremely small and sporadic part of his activities (and there is no evidence that he met with *him* in the bugged hotel rooms). Yet the wiretap picked up and recorded *all* the conversations of these phones. Even if the scenario suggested by the Marshall version is accurate, would it not have been more sensible to tap the New York lawyer's phones? (Indeed, since it is technically feasible to monitor and record calls placed only between two specified numbers, it would have been possible to tap and record only those calls placed between King and the suspected lawyer.) It is significant that a former public official as respected and dedicated as Burke Marshall would argue that it would "not be responsible" for an attorney general to have declined, or even delayed, authorization for a warrantless national-security wiretap on the basis of the evidence that he suggested existed. We only rarely have men in positions of power as sensitive and committed to civil liberties as Marshall. If this is what we can expect of a Burke Marshall, what can we expect of the men who generally populate high office?

Another justification offered by some Kennedy intimates is that the tap was authorized, as former attorney general Nicholas Katzenbach put it, "for the protection of Dr. King." Giving the FBI the power to protect King is like giving the cat the power to protect the canary. In fact, it is now widely acknowledged that no sooner did J. Edgar Hoover come up with some damaging information about King — relating to his sex life — than he leaked it to the press. Was this also done to protect King?

It is not difficult to understand what really motivated the King wiretap. The existence of the lawyer in New York provided a plausible — that is perhaps too strong a word — argument that some vague national-security interest was involved. The FBI seized upon this excuse to request authorization to do what they wanted to do for other — completely illegitimate — reasons. It was difficult for the Justice Department to deny the request: what would it look like later on if it did turn out that King was indeed involved with Communists and if Hoover leaked to his congressional or newspaper cronies the fact that Kennedy had stood in the way of an investigation that would have disclosed this? So Kennedy took the least politically risky course. And J. Edgar Hoover got his wiretap.

The King episode does not stand alone in suggesting that the primary reason certain domestic national-security taps are employed has little to do with the genuine needs of national security. The recent case involving Muhammad Ali, which revealed the previously unacknowledged King tap, also disclosed that pervasive taps had been authorized on the phones of Elijah Muhammad, the leader of the Black Muslims.

Here, too, I would speculate that there may have been a plausible national-security interest in a limited aspect of Elijah Muhammad's activity. But the warrantless tap was not limited, as one with a warrant would have to be. It extended to every call to and from Elijah Muhammad's various offices over a considerable period of time. And it picked up conversations relating to political and personal activities that were none of the government's legitimate business (for example, a disclosure that a well-known person's brother had been kicked out of the Nation of Islam for being out with a girl all night).

The phrase "domestic national-security wiretap" is not self-limited or self-defining. It means what history tells us it means. It means what this and previous administrations have defined it to mean. Only if we are given some idea of how it has been used can the people, and the courts, have any intelligent basis for judging whether the alleged need for a domestic national-security exception outweighs its potential for abuse. On the basis of the evidence presently available, I would suggest that if we were to examine all the domestic national-security wiretaps conducted by the FBI, a disturbing picture would emerge. We would find numerous cases where a plausible but narrow national-security concern has been used as an excuse for an improper and pervasive wiretap whose real purpose is political surveillance. Unfortunately, however, there is no way for the citizenry — or even the courts — to examine the logs of all national-security wiretaps. We are left instead with the assurances of people like former attorney general Herbert Brownell that "experience demonstrates that the Federal Bureau of Investigation has never abused the wiretap authority."

But what "experience" is Brownell referring to? To whom has this been "demonstrated"? Certainly not to the public. I, for one, do not feel that we can rely on the self-interested assurances of former Justice Department officials that all is in order. My surmise is that if the Justice Department were to turn over the records of domestic national-security wiretaps in any given year to a nonpartisan group of scholars for study, many abuses of the kind suggested here would emerge. If I am wrong — if an impartial evaluation were to disclose that warrantless domestic national-security taps have been narrowly employed only in cases of immediate, extreme, and irremediable danger to our survival — then there might be grounds for exempting this class of wiretap from the usual constitutional requirements. But neither the people nor the courts can intelligently decide whether this is so until we are given some idea of how such wiretaps have in fact been used. In the meantime, on the basis of what we already know, we have good reason for supposing that "national security" is sometimes invoked as a pretext for political surveillance of an altogether illegitimate kind.

# FIFTY-TWO

# TORTURE OF TERRORISTS

### Is It Necessary to Do—
### and to Lie About?

*If there are two phenomena that invoke horror in the minds of decent people they are surely "terrorism" against innocent civilians and "torture" of incarcerated prisoners. When the latter is used to prevent the former, there is certain to be conflict. I wrote about this conflict in Israel Law Review in 1989.[1]*

IT IS A CONUNDRUM THAT HAS LONG INTRIGUED PHILOSOPHERS, novelists, lawyers, and ordinary citizens: a captured terrorist knows the location of a ticking bomb that threatens hundreds of innocent lives; the only way to prevent the mass murder is to torture the terrorist into disclosing the bomb's location; there is no time for reflection; a decision must be made. Does the noble end of saving innocent lives justify the ignoble means of employing torture?

We know, of course, what all governments would actually do under these conditions of tragic choice: they (or more precisely, some flak-catching underling) would torture with the implicit approval of the powers that be. But could the government *justify* it? Would they write a law expressly *authorizing* such means? Or would they choose what the Landau Commission calls the "way . . . of the hypocrites: they declare that they abide by the rule of law, but turn a blind eye to what goes on beneath the surface."

A second classic conundrum is whether it is ever justifiable to lie: an SS man is hunting Jews; a righteous gentile knows that a Jewish family is hiding in his closet; the SS man asks him if he saw the family; he says yes, and tells him that they escaped into the woods. Only the most per-

verse Kantians would have a problem with such a deliberate lie. Nor would the assessment change if the lie had to be given under oath, even on a Bible. But again, the question is how to justify such lying and generalize such a justification without inviting a situational ethic that is so open-ended that it is no ethic at all.

It is against the background of these intractable dilemmas that the Landau Commission has issued its extraordinary report.[2] The report is extraordinary in that it discusses publicly a series of issues that virtually every government confronts but almost no government discusses officially and openly. For example, in the United States, police perjury is rampant. This fact of life has been recognized by judges,[3] prosecutors,[4] civil libertarians,[5] and the police themselves.[6] And the justifications for it are far less pressing than in Israel, since it is done, for the most part, in ordinary criminal cases, especially drug prosecutions.[7] Yet there has been no official report in any way comparable to the Landau Report for more than half a century in the United States.[8] The problem is similar in other democracies.[9]

The commission also emphasizes that the means employed were designated to elicit only truthful confessions, since in the fight against terrorism, it is counterproductive to elicit false information. This is especially so because the primary goal of the interrogation of terrorist suspects is not to secure convictions but "to collect information about terrorists and their modes of organization and to thwart and prevent the perpetration of terrorist acts whilst they are still in a state of incubation." The apprehension and conviction of terrorists for past acts is, however, also of considerable importance, and indeed the specific problem addressed by the commission — lying at trial about the means of interrogation employed — arises only in the context of criminal prosecutions. But the report assures its readers that the interrogation methods in question here "are as far as East is from West, from the notorious methods of the secret police in certain totalitarian states, where pressure is used to extract false confessions."

Thus, the first action of the General Security Service (GSS) questioned by the report is the use of these "means of pressure" in the interrogation. The second action involved the systematic perjury of GSS interrogators when called to testify at the "trial within a trial" of accused terrorists. "Not to mince our words — they simply lied, thus committing the offense of perjury." Nor was this lying merely episodic:

"False testimony in court soon became an unchallenged norm which was to be the rule for 16 years." Indeed, directions to lie were committed to memoranda, and the interrogators were expressly ordered "to deny carrying out" the methods of pressure actually employed.

There were two reasons offered for the systematic denials. First, truthful testimony would require public disclosure of the means actually used and "the moment such a method is exposed and revealed its efficacy is damaged or completely disappears." The second reason for the lying is typical of criminal cases: the concern that if the truth were told, the confession would be rejected by the court and the guilty criminal freed.

The commission suggests that there are "three ways for solving this grave dilemma between the vital need to preserve the very existence of the state and its citizens, and to maintain its character as a law-abiding State." These are (1) to allow the security service to continue to fight its war against terrorism in "'a twilight zone' which is outside the realm of law" (2) "the . . . way . . . of the hypocrites: they declare that they abide by the rule of law, but turn a blind eye to what goes on beneath the surface"; and (3) "the truthful road of the rule of law," namely, that the "law itself must ensure a proper framework for the activity of the GSS regarding Hostile Terrorist Activity."

It is not surprising that when the choices are put that way, the conclusion necessarily follows that "there is no alternative but to opt for the third way." The real question is whether a legal system can honestly incorporate the extraordinary actions of the GSS without becoming so elastic as to also invite other kinds of abuses.

The commission's answer to this question is problematic. In seeking to rationalize the interrogation methods deemed necessary by the GSS, the commission attaches "great importance" to the legal defense of "necessity." The defense of necessity is essentially a "state of nature" plea. If a person finds himself in an impossible position requiring him to choose between violating the law and preventing a greater harm, such as the taking of innocent life — and he has no time to seek recourse from the proper authorities — society authorizes him to act as if there were no law. In other words, since society has broken its part of the social contract with him, namely, to protect him, it follows that he is not obligated to keep his part of the social contract, namely, to obey the law. Thus, it has been said that "necessity knows no law."

It is ironic, therefore, that in an effort to incorporate the interrogation methods of the GSS into "the law itself," the commission has selected the most lawless of legal doctrines — that of necessity — as the prime candidate for coverage.

The Israeli law of necessity is particularly elastic and open-ended. It provides:

> A person may be exempted from criminal responsibility for any act or omission if he can show that it was done or made in order to avoid consequences which could not otherwise be avoided and which would have inflicted grievous harm or injury on his person, honour or property or on the person or honour of others whom he was bound to protect or on property placed in his charge:
>
> Provided that he did no more than was reasonably necessary for that purpose and that the harm caused by him was not disproportionate to the harm avoided.

The commission acknowledges that this "full exemption from criminal responsibility" reflects the "clash of opposing values: on the one hand, values protected by means of the prohibitions of criminal law, and on the other hand, the duty, grounded in ethical precepts, to protect one's life or bodily integrity or that of others." In other instances of conflict, such as self-defense, the law established rules of action and inaction, refusing to leave the decision solely to the subjective perceptions and priorities of the person claiming the defense, but under the rubric of "necessity," the law "foregoes the attempt to solve the problem only by [means of formal law] . . . and appeals to the sense of legality innate in the conscience of every human being." The problem, of course, is that "every human being" has a different conscience and sense of legality in situations involving the trade-off between law violations and the protection of other values. To make matters worse — far worse — "the course test [of necessity] is what the doer of the deed reasonably believed, and not what the situation actually was."

Even if the mere *public* disclosure of the problem would be dangerous to the security of the state — always a matter of degree, especially in an open democracy like Israel, where the problem will inevitably surface as it did here — there are *secret* options that are far more democratic than the ones employed here. Among these are special cabinet committees or judicial panels authorized to approve special measures under extraordinary circumstances.

Perhaps I am especially skeptical of the claims of "necessity" as an American. If that defense were available in the United States, it would be quickly employed by the likes of Colonel Oliver North, to justify his lying to Congress, and by former president Richard M. Nixon, to justify the break-in at the Democratic National Committee and its subsequent cover-up. Indeed, in the United States, the defense of necessity has been used — abused — by all manner of illegal protesters, ranging from Abbie Hoffman to Amy Carter to antiabortion protesters.

Moving back to Israel, what if Palestinian rock throwers raised the defense of necessity in defense of their "honor or property"? Would the courts be forced to choose — on an entirely political basis — between conflicting claims? Or what if a suspected terrorist decides to resist the "physical pressures" of his interrogators by physical countermeasures designed to protect his honor or person — that is, what if he fights back? Could he defend himself against assault charges by invoking "necessity"?

The point of the necessity defense is to provide a kind of "interstitial legislation" to fill "lacunae" left by legislative and judicial incompleteness. It is not a substitute legislative or judicial process for weighing policy options by state agencies faced with long-term systemic problems.

To demonstrate the inappropriateness and subjectivity of the application of the necessity defense to the problems faced by the GSS, it is interesting to ask why the commission so quickly and forcefully rejected its application to the systematic lying engaged in by the agents. This is what the commission says: "Here the investigator cannot rely on the defense of necessity . . . since perjury is a grave criminal offence and manifestly illegal, above which flies the black flag saying 'forbidden.'"

So held! *Ipse dixit!* But why? The GSS interrogators believed that lying was *as necessary* to their work as applying physical pressure. Both are grave criminal offenses and both are manifestly illegal. The difference surely cannot be that the immediate victims of the illegal physical pressure are suspected Arab terrorists, whereas the immediate victims of the perjury are the judges!

In fact, there are circumstances when a person who lies — or even commits perjury — should and would have the benefit of the necessity defense. For example: A person whose family is secretly being held hostage by escaped criminals is asked by the police for the where-abouts of the criminals; the criminals have threatened to kill his family unless he misdirects the police. He lies. Under these circumstances, his lie would fall within the defense of necessity. The same would be true if the person were called into court and gave the information under oath, while his family was being held under threat of imminent death by the criminals.

But systematic perjury committed over a long period of time should not be excused by necessity, because the systematic perjury is not an emergency response to a nonrecurring state-of-nature situation re-quiring the legislative and judiciary to delegate — in effect — their policy-making authority to the citizen for an ad hoc weighing of choices. This is as true of the systematic long-term policy of physical pressure as it is of the systematic long-term policy of lying.

I am not necessarily suggesting by my criteria that the commission's ultimate conclusion is wrong. I lack the information necessary to reach any definitive assessment of whether the GSS should be allowed to employ physical pressure in the interrogation of some suspected ter-rorists under some circumstances. (I am personally convinced that there are some circumstances — at least in theory — under which ex-traordinary means, including physical pressure, may properly be au-thorized.[10] I am also convinced that these circumstances are present far less frequently than law-enforcement personnel would claim.) My criticism is limited solely to the dangers inherent in using — misusing, in my view — the open-ended "necessity" defense to justify, even retroactively, the conduct of the GSS.

At the very most, its unlawful conduct might have been "excused" rather than "justified." Though this distinction may sound somewhat technical, the entire enterprise of finding a conceptual hook on which to hang the commission's policy judgments is an exercise in technical-ity. Indeed, the very rule of law relies on technical compliance with es-tablished norms. If such technical efforts are to be useful, they should, at least, be technically correct. And finding the conduct of the GSS to be justified, which means desirable, rather than excusable, which means merely understandable, is wrong.

Perhaps the commission adopted this tactic to send a prospective message: until legislation is enacted, the GSS should *continue* to engage in the necessary and justifiable activities in which they engaged *prior* to the report. If this is the message the commission intended to send, it should have done so more candidly. If not, it should have avoided reliance on a legal defense that invites misunderstanding over whether the continued use of "physical pressure" is necessary and thus justified. The great virtue of the Landau Commission Report is that it raised to the surface an important conundrum that few democracies ever openly confront. The vice of the report is that it purports to resolve that conundrum by reference to a legal doctrine that is essentially lawless and undemocratic.

---

*In 1999 the Supreme Court of Israel confronted the issues raised above. The case, in essence, posed the following question: If an arrested terrorist knew the location of a ticking time bomb that was about to explode in a busy intersection but refused to disclose its location, would it be proper to torture the terrorist in order to prevent the bombing and save dozens of lives? The court answered with a qualified no. As the president of the Supreme Court, Aharon Barak, put it: "Although a democracy must often fight with one hand tied behind its back, it nevertheless has the upper hand."*

*If the court had applied a cost-benefit analysis, the issue would be a simple one. The life of one guilty terrorist is surely worth less than the lives of hundreds of innocent citizens. We make that kind of trade-off all the time when we impose capital punishment, when we send soldiers to war, and when we permit the shooting of fleeing felons. Even when we build large hospitals designed to save lives, we know as a matter of actuarial reality that some lives may be lost in the process of construction.*

*Why is this case different? Why have nations that continue to impose the death penalty been so insistent that Israel stop engaging in nonlethal torture designed to save lives? The answer is partly aesthetic. There is something about torture — even torture that does not endanger life — that is harder to accept than the injection of a lethal substance into the vein of a condemned murderer.*

*The Supreme Court of Israel left the security services a tiny window of opportunity in extreme cases. Citing the traditional common-law defense of necessity, the Supreme Court left open the possibility that a member of the security service who honestly believed that rough interrogation was the only means available to save lives in imminent danger could raise this defense. This leaves each individual member of the security services in the position of having to guess how a court would ultimately resolve his case. That is extremely unfair to such investigators. It would have been far better had the court required any investigator who believed that torture was necessary in order to save lives to apply to a judge. The judge would then be in a position either to authorize or refuse to authorize a "torture warrant." Such a procedure would require judges to dirty their hands by authorizing torture warrants or bear the responsibility for failing to do so. Individual interrogators should not have to place their liberty at risk by guessing how a court might ultimately decide a close case. They should be able to get an advance ruling based on the evidence available at the time.*

*Perhaps the legislature will create a procedure for advance judicial scrutiny. This would be akin to the warrant requirement in the Fourth Amendment to the United States Constitution. It is a traditional role for judges to play, since it is the job of the judiciary to balance the needs for security against the imperatives of liberty. Interrogators from the security service are not trained to strike such a delicate balance. Their mission is single-minded: to prevent terrorism. Similarly, the mission of civil liberties lawyers who oppose torture is single-minded: to vindicate the individual rights of suspected terrorists. It is the role of the court to strike the appropriate balance. The Supreme Court of Israel took a giant step in the direction of striking that balance. But it — or the legislature — should take the further step of requiring the judiciary to assume responsibility in individual cases. The essence of a democracy is placing responsibility for difficult choices in a visible and neutral institution like the judiciary.*

*Issues of this sort are likely to arise throughout the world, including in the United States, in the aftermath of the World Trade Center disaster. Had law enforcement officials arrested terrorists boarding one of the airplanes and learned that other planes, then airborne, were headed toward unknown occupied buildings, there would have been an understandable incentive to torture those terrorists in order to learn the identity of the buildings and evacuate them. It is easy to imagine similar future scenarios.*

# FIFTY-THREE

## SAFETY AND CIVIL LIBERTIES NEED NOT BE IN CONFLICT

*I wrote this article immediately after the terrorist attacks of September 11, 2001.*

EXPERIENCE TEACHES THAT MASSIVE TERRORISM AND PRO-tracted warfare invariably alter the balance a democratic society is willing to strike between safety and civil liberties. Already we are hearing strident calls for contraction of such basic rights as privacy and ethnic equality. These calls are answered by equally strident demands that we not tolerate any compromise with liberty.

There will be some compromises. Some have recently been enacted by Congress, and there will be more to come. The question is whether these changes will be sensibly calibrated to maximize our safety while minimizing the contraction of our liberties, or whether the fear of terrorism will merely serve as an excuse for a knee-jerk assault on the already controversial rights of marginalized individuals and groups.

It is imperative in this time of crisis that those who are in charge of our safety and those who see their role as defending our liberty work together as much as possible so as to avoid unnecessary conflict. Just as elected government officials strive for bipartisan cooperation between Republicans and Democrats, so too law enforcement officials and civil libertarians should work together to ensure that every change in the balance between safety and liberty is both necessary and effective.

When the Canadian government invoked the War Measures Act in response to terrorism in the early 1970s, the attorney general of Canada invited leading civil libertarians to work together with government officials in an effort to talk *to* each other in advance rather than *at* each other after the government had unilaterally imposed constraints on civil liberties. This worked tolerably well. Now is the time for our government to invite prominent civil libertarians into the tent to consult with law enforcement officials. Civil libertarians need not be on the other side of government, especially during times of national crisis. We can try to work together to avoid lawsuits and recriminations. Civil libertarians need not fear every change or technological innovation. Indeed, there are technologies and tactics that have the potential to maximize both safety and civil liberties at the same time.

Consider, for example, the divisive issue of racial or ethnic profiling that would target Moslems and Arabs. Such broad-based profiling is both unfair and ineffective. There are technologies in use and on the drawing board which promise both increased fairness and improved efficiency. For example, face-recognition computers focus on those people who are already in the database as the result of specific prior conduct or allegations. This technology will inevitably make mistakes and "recognize" some innocent people, but far fewer than broad-based ethnic profiling. The same is true of computerized profiles based on a large number of factors beyond race and ethnicity, such as travel history, country of origin, prior arrests, and affiliations with violence-prone groups. By narrowing the focus of the profiles, we avoid unfair ethnic stereotypes and improve efficiency, though there will still be inevitable errors of over- and underinclusion.

New approaches are also available for wiretaps and other forms of electronic and computerized eavesdropping. There are technologies now in the works that can identify certain words, phrases, and even concepts, thereby focusing on the most relevant information and the most likely suspects, rather than intruding wholesale on the communications of a large group of people. Roving wiretaps, which follow suspects who keep changing cell phones, are an effective way of trumping the use of technology by sophisticated criminals and are less likely to intrude on the private conversations of innocent citizens.

Even in regard to the most controversial of the current proposals — targeted preemption of known terrorists, including deadly force as a last resort — it can be argued that the goals of both civil libertarians and terrorism prevention can be better served by incapacitating individuals who pose a specific and imminent threat of terrorism than by retaliating against large populations after the fact. The one thing we know about suicide bombers is that they cannot be deterred by threat of retaliation against them. They can be prevented from carrying out their suicide missions only by advance interdiction, including, when necessary, targeted assassination. If narrowly employed — perhaps even based on advance judicial approval when possible — such use of deadly force can save lives both among the intended victims and among the large number of those who would be collaterally killed or injured in any retaliatory attack.

Any change in our fundamental civil liberties should be debated and acknowledged. A civil liberties impact statement should accompany every compromise, as should a sunset provision. New measures will not ensure our safety with absolute certainty. The balances we ultimately strike will contain trade-offs between our liberties and our safety that will not satisfy absolutists within either the law enforcement or the civil liberties camp. But if we work together — if civil libertarians are brought into the tent in advance, rather than playing their traditional role of criticizing from outside the tent only afterward — the beneficiaries will be all Americans who rightly demand both safety and freedom.

# FIFTY-FOUR

# COULD AN ACCUSED TERRORIST RECEIVE A FAIR TRIAL IN AN AMERICAN COURT?

*This article, like the preceding one, was written soon after the World Trade Center disaster.*

AS THE HUNT FOR TERRORISTS CONTINUES IN THE AFTERMATH of the World Trade Center catastrophe, law enforcement officials are assuring the international community that any accused terrorist brought to trial before an American court would receive a fair trial. This assurance is being offered in order to counter suggestions for a trial in front of some kind of international tribunal.

Our own courts have at least one distinct advantage over international tribunals. Every defendant in an American court has the right to trial by jury, whereas international trials are generally conducted in front of judges. And in highly political cases — and any international trial of an alleged global terrorist would be distinctly political — judges are likely to be far less independent than jurors, and more likely to do the bidding of the governments that selected them for the tribunal. Many judges have future judicial and political aspirations, and all judges want to be well regarded among their patriotic peers.

A jury, on the other hand, disperses after completing its singular job of administering justice in a particular case, and the individual jurors return to the prior anonymity of their lives. Government officials can (and do) whisper to judges, but they cannot whisper to jurors, since anything communicated to a juror must be a matter of record. Jurors often refuse to do the bidding of the government, as evidenced by the recent refusal of a New York jury to impose the death penalty on the terrorist it convicted of blowing up an American embassy and killing numerous people. Juries do, of course, make mistakes — perhaps even more often than judges do, but jury mistakes are less likely to be a function of political pressures. Emotions, of course, are extremely high throughout the United States, and a fair jury trial will be much more difficult to ensure, but so will a fair trial before judges. Were I defending an accused terrorist, even after the recent disaster, I would almost certainly prefer a jury trial to a trial before a judge.

The issue of who would actually defend an accused terrorist in front of an American jury raises the most daunting questions regarding the possibility of a fair trial in this country. Within hours of the terrible events of September 11, 2001, my telephone began to ring off the hook. The second question invariably put to me — the first being, Is your family okay? — was whether I would defend the people who did this. It was not so much a question as a plea: "You're not going to defend these bastards, are you?" Even today, people stop me on the streets to urge me not to defend accused terrorists. It seems as if most Americans believe in the right of every defendant to be represented by a zealous lawyer — as an abstract matter. But when it comes to the hard cases, the cases of defendants accused of the most despicable crimes, attitudes change. Americans want to be sure that every accused murderer is represented by a lawyer, as long as that lawyer isn't very good or doesn't try too hard to win! No one complained about Timothy McVeigh's lawyer, because he went through the motions and lost. But millions of Americans were furious at the O. J. Simpson defense team, because we used every procedure and tactic legally available to us. It was only after we won that we began to receive death threats.

The threats have already begun in regard to the World Trade Center case, even before there is a case, and despite the fact that I am not a trial lawyer and have expressed no interest in defending anyone accused of the September 11 terrorism. But threats of this kind will have an impact on those lawyers who may be asked to perform the patriotic duty of defending those who may be accused of those dastardly acts. Yes, it would be a patriotic duty, comparable to the duty performed by prosecutors — or doctors who ministered to the wounded victims. But the defense lawyer's job is far more difficult, controversial, and in some respects hazardous. The lawyers who end up representing accused terrorists — even Osama bin Laden, if we are fortunate enough to bring him to trial — will be vilified and threatened, especially if they provide the kind of zealous advocacy demanded by the Constitution. They will be providing a constitutional service to clients they detest and fear. They will receive no praise for doing their job, especially if they do it well.

This is the great paradox of our legal system. We boast of a process in which the most despised are treated fairly and represented zealously, and yet we condemn those who provide this constitutionally required zealous representation. Unless we begin to understand how inconsistent we are, we will not be true to our claim of providing the fairest trials of any nation in the world.

## CONCLUSION

❋

## OLD RIGHTS
## FOR NEW WRONGS

*Can Our Traditional Rights Continue
to Protect Us in the Age of Biotechnology,
the Internet, and Unpredictable
Future Innovations by Both
Good Guys and Bad Guys?*

THERE IS AN OLD STORY, PROBABLY APOCRYPHAL, ABOUT the patent official, near the end of the nineteenth century, who proposed shutting down the office because he believed that everything that could possibly be invented already had been. At the beginning of the twenty-first century, almost no thinking person holds such a static view of human progress. We live in an age of expanding thought, technology, and innovation. Even a quarter century ago, no one could have contemplated the information or biotechnology revolutions. What was science fiction a decade ago is science reality today and will be anachronism a decade from now. Innovation is moving at so quick a pace that it is difficult for old rights to keep up with new wrongs. Yet unless rights stay ahead of technological innovation, we will become subject to the tyranny of technology.

The genius of our constitutional framers is that they defined most rights with sufficient breadth and flexibility to make them capable of adapting to new realities. A wise Supreme Court justice once cautioned that "we must not read the Bill of Rights as if it were a last will and testament, lest it become one." It is the job of those of us who try to do rights to think ahead, to assume the role of science fiction writers who refuse to limit their horizons to what is, or even to what can currently be contemplated. We must become writers of "rights fiction" so that rights reality will be able to keep up with tomorrow's science realities, which are today's science fiction. This is our challenge, and we must not shrink from it.

Nor are we without models for meeting this challenge. In 1624 one of the greatest jurists in history, Francis Bacon, imagined a world of the future that is not so far from ours. In his *New Atlantis*, Bacon employed science fiction to alert his readers to legal challenges that could be faced by English law in the future. Among his fantasies were airplanes, submarines, and weapons of mass destruction. He also imagined eugenic breeding of human beings as well as medical fountains of youth. Understanding that "knowledge is power" — Bacon coined that expression — he conceived of a state in which "technology obviously required control over individuals and individual freedom."[1] Bacon never finished this book, leaving it to future generations to take up the challenge of inventing new technologies without curtailing individual freedom.

In June of 2001, the United States Supreme Court took up that challenge and decided a controversial case with an eye to the future. The case itself involved the use of a fairly primitive thermal imager, which measures the heat radiating from various parts of a house.[2] The imager was used by the police to detect the presence of high-intensity lamps used to grow marijuana in the home of a man named Danny Lee Kyllo. The question posed by the Court transcended the narrow issue presented by this crude machine and its relatively limited intrusive capabilities. The Court asked broadly what limits there are "upon the power of technology to shrink the realm of guaranteed privacy."

In addressing this question, the Court turned to the future, citing research being done on "a radar-based through-the-wall surveillance system" that "will enable law officers to detect individuals through interior building walls." The Court suggested that the ability to see through walls and other opaque barriers "is a clear, and scientifically feasible, goal of law enforcement research and development." Instead of waiting for this goal to be fully accomplished, the Court stepped in and drew a line in the sand, ruling that the police must secure a warrant based on probable cause before they may employ any "sense-enhancing technology" that is "not in general public use" to obtain "any information regarding the interior of the home that could not otherwise have been obtained without physical [intrusion]." In announcing this rule, a majority of the Supreme Court sought to assure "preservation of that degree of privacy against government that existed when the Fourth Amendment was adopted." The framers of the Constitution could not have imagined this, and other, technological challenges to privacy. Nor could they have contemplated recent technological and biological threats to our safety, especially those posed by weapons of mass destruction in the hands of terrorists and rogue nations. Yet the policies underlying the Fourth Amendment surely mandate a broad if flexible approach to protecting personal privacy.[3] The key is for rights always to remain several steps ahead of technological innovation, in order to ensure that we control technological innovations rather than allowing technology to control us. It is also important for the technologies employed by law enforcement to remain ahead of those employed by terrorists and other criminals. Striking an appropriate balance between safety and liberty in the brave new world of high-tech terrorism and antiterrorism will pose a daunting challenge.

In addition to radar flashlights with Superman-like X-ray vision, consider the rights implications of the following innovations, some already in existence, others on the drawing board, and still others merely in the realm of the feasible:

- A surreptitiously implantable chip making it possible to track its wearer anyplace in the world.
- A similar chip implanted in every human being at birth so as to prevent disappearances, kidnappings, and the hiding of bodies.
- Currency with chips that record transactions, locations, and other data.
- Video surveillance cameras on police cars and policemen that record every arrest, search, and other encounter.
- Video and audio surveillance cameras capable of recording and later accessing virtually all outdoor activity (and some indoor activity).
- Face-recognition machines capable of identifying specific people as they walk down the street or into buildings or airports.
- Drugs that make someone tell the truth about past or contemplated acts.
- Body-scan machines at airports that can see almost anything concealed on and in the body.
- Sophisticated explosives, poisons, and germs that can evade detection by all available technology.
- Black boxes in every car that record speeds, stops, turns, level of alcohol, and can stop the vehicle upon command from law enforcement authorities.
- Completely effective nonlethal incapacitators. (Would police ever have authority to use lethal force?)
- A computer virus capable of tracking and/or destroying classified material improperly possessed on any linked computer.

- Computerized censorship or eavesdropping devices that automatically prevent certain words (ideas? images?) from being printed, transmitted, accessed — or alert the police to the source.
- A completely anonymous Internet incapable of identifying message senders.
- A privately launched satellite space station that serves as the base for information transmission but that is subject to no national or international laws.
- Software capable of copying any voice perfectly and having it say anything.
- Computer-generated images of any human being doing anything.
- Virtual sex machines that permit the user to have sex with a virtual person of his or her choice. (Would Britney Spears have the right to choose who could have virtual sex with "her" image? Would it constitute virtual "adultery"?)
- An "emotion reading" device that could tell one person whether another person wanted to have sex with him or her or wanted to agree to a financial transaction on certain terms.
- Genetic testing that can predict fatal illnesses and when they will strike.
- CAT scans or genetic testing that can predict future violent crimes with a degree of accuracy akin to proof beyond a reasonable doubt.
- Subliminal advertising — commercial and political — capable of changing the minds of viewers without their knowledge.
- Completely accurate public opinion polling that precludes the need for expensive elections.
- A computer that can decide cases fairly based on an evaluation of the facts and the law.
- An injection causing sterility that can be reversed only by another injection requiring a governmentally issued license for childbearing.
- A penile implant that prevents sexual predators from achieving erection, except with a specified partner who has the correct code.

- A brain transplant that transfers not only cells but also memories, biases, temperaments, and behaviors.
- Brain scan lie detectors that can visualize the interior of the human brain.
- Brain electrode implants capable of controlling human behavior.
- Partially bionic, partially human beings composed of human brain cells (or even complete brains) in a robot.
- Partially animal, partially human beings composed of human brain cells (or brains) in an ape's body.
- Genetically improved apes that have more human characteristics, including intellectual and moral qualities.
- Discovery of beings in accessible space who are humanlike to some degree.
- Easy human cloning from hair, fingernail, saliva, or other samples from living or dead persons. (Would individuals have the right not to be cloned? Would individuals have the right to create a fetus in order to obtain a lifesaving organ?)
- Medical breakthrough that extends average life to two hundred years and makes the earth incapable of sustaining its population without mandatory birth limitations — or life-length limits.
- Genetic engineering that would give us the capacity to create all babies as roughly equals (though not identical) in health, beauty, and intelligence.
- A harmless chemical spray that would turn all human skin pigmentation into the same color. (If so, what should that color be: black, brown, white, yellow . . . or blue?)
- A hibernation drug that can put someone to sleep for months or years without taking time off the person's total active life, thereby allowing people to live their lives in interrupted phases or to sleep until a cure is found for a currently fatal disease.
- Discovery of a time-travel device that makes it possible to learn whether Moses received the Ten Commandments, Jesus was resurrected, Muhammad ascended to heaven on his horse, and O. J. Simpson killed his former wife.

- A machine capable of predicting the movement of every molecule — and hence the future.[4]

In considering how old rights relate to potential new wrongs, it is important to have a theory of rights. If rights are the static product of external sources — God, nature, the original intent of the drafters of a constitution — then one must ask metaphysical questions about how the sources *would* have regarded matters that were unimaginable even a few decades ago. The answers to these questions are likely to reflect the disguised biases and hidden agendas of those who claim to hear the voice of God, to understand the message of nature, or to know the intent of our Constitution's drafters. If rights are the dynamic product of democratic processes, informed by the gradual changes of history and experience, then the questions can be debated more honestly, openly, and democratically. The answers may depend in part on the persuasive powers of those who advocate the rights at issue.[5] That is how it must be in a democracy, where the struggle for individual rights never stays won and where every right is always a work in progress. And that is precisely the object of this book and its author's life: to advocate and to do humanly created individual rights — as defined and refined by history and experience — in a world of so many natural and humanly created wrongs.

# NOTES

## INTRODUCTION: A PREFERENCE FOR RIGHTS

1. My approach does not require unanimous or even near-unanimous acceptance of these or any other events as perfect injustice. For example, I recently encountered an eminent professor who actually tried to defend the Crusades. It quickly became apparent that he was abysmally ignorant of the facts concerning the mass slaughter of Jews, Muslims, and heathens, including thousands of babies and children. I can state my view more conditionally: For those who wish to try to prevent a recurrence of events like these, this book contains lessons that can be learned.

2. The essays in this book were written over a thirty-five-year period. The following essays were written especially for this book and/or are published here for the first time: chapters 1, 2, 3, 4, 6, 9, 11, 13, 14, 19, 33, 53, and 54; the introduction to each of the parts; and the conclusion.

3. My views are not presented chronologically but, rather, by subject matter.

## CHAPTER 1: WHERE DO RIGHTS COME FROM?

1. See John Rawls, "The Law of Peoples," in Stephen Shute and Susan Hurley, eds., *On Human Rights: The Oxford Amnesty Lectures* (New York: Basic Books, 1993).

2. In English, the word *law* is used to describe both man-made rules of conduct and the formulas that describe nature. These very different meanings have contributed to some of the confusion regarding "natural law."

3. *Right* also means correct. I use it here in its other meaning: a claim that can be made by an individual against the power of government.

4. The concept of "divine rights" was originally employed as a justification for power, especially the power of kings to rule by virtue of their divine right. Other rights, such as those recognized by Magna Carta, afforded certain classes of people counterveiling powers. Eventually the rights of ordinary people, as against the power of the state, were also acknowledged.

5. Various modifiers other than *individual* are often placed before the word *right* — such as *human, civil, natural, inherent, divine* (or *God-given*), *inalienable* (or *unalienable*). Subtle differences are sometimes conveyed by these modifiers. Another distinction is between "negative rights" and "positive rights." More about that later.

6. As defined in the *Dictionary of Modern Legal Usage*, "Positive law, referring primarily to statutes and regulations, might be defined as coercively implemented law laid down within a particular political community by political superiors, to govern members of the community as distinct from

moral law or law existing in an ideal community or in some nonpolitical community." *Dictionary of Modern Legal Usage*, 2nd ed. (New York: Oxford University Press, 1995), p. 672.

More simply, it may be defined as "law actually and specifically enacted or adopted by proper authority for the government of an organized jural society." *Black's Law Dictionary*, 6th ed. (Saint Paul: West Publishing, 1990), p. 1162.

7. Under a positivist approach, one claim of right may prevail over another, but only if the power to trump also derives from humanly enacted legal authority. In theory, positive law may derive from a God-given legal document, such as the Bible. But the term, as generally used, does not include divine positive law. For example, a federal constitutional right generally supersedes a state constitutional right, because the federal constitution — which was ratified by the states — contains a supremacy clause that grants superior authority to properly exercised federal constitutional rights.

8. There can, of course, be positive law whose claimed source is God. The Jewish Halakah, and its variants in Catholic and Islamic law, are positive law whose claimed source is God. The point is that positive law needs no external source to be valid.

9. This is John Stuart Mill's prescription for what ought to be a universal right. This claim of right has been put colloquially as "Your right to wave your hand ends at the tip of my nose," or more relevantly, "Your right to puff tobacco smoke ends at the entrance to my nostrils."

10. *Lochner v. New York*, 198 U.S. 45, 76 (1905), dissenting opinion.

11. There is significant variation in views among natural-law theorists, but there is general consensus about the central proposition that there are sources beyond the positively enacted human laws that do or should determine the content of rights.

12. See Albert W. Alschuler, *Law Without Values: The Life, Work, and Legacy of Justice Holmes* (Chicago: University of Chicago Press, 2000).

13. Lloyd Weinreb, *Natural Law and Justice* (Cambridge, Mass: Harvard University Press, 1987), p. 99. This formulation obviously oversimplifies an enormously complex body of thinking, but in broad outlines it is accurate.

14. *Boston Globe*, August 25, 2000, sec. A, p. 23.

15. H.L.A. Hart, *Essays in Jurisprudence and Philosophy* (New York: Oxford University Press, 1983), p. 163.

16. God's law has also been cited for the opposites of these evils.

17. This is also the history of human law, as well as other human institutions, but more is to be expected of an infallible God and those who speak on his behalf.

18. In the 2000 presidential election, Senator Joseph Leiberman repeatedly invoked God as the source of American rights, citing our Declaration of Independence. Though I am not an advocate of divine law, a case can be made that Jewish tradition (or at least some renderings of it) supports a human, process-based positive law rather than an externally based natural law. The Pentateuch commands that "justice shall you pursue," suggesting that the quest for justice is an active, continuing process. Then there is the

wonderful story of the rabbis who reject God's own voice as the authoritative source of law and instead look to the process of legal decision making established by the Halakah (see pp. 391–92). The human process — from the Mishnah to the Gemorah to the responsa — continues to this day. In reality, it is far more akin to the common-law process of legal development than to the divine-law process of discovering "revealed" law, though it purports to partake of the latter as well.

19. This is not to suggest that natural law is so reductionistic as to argue that doing "what comes naturally" is always right. But some defenders of natural law come close to arguing that doing what is "unnatural" will always be wrong. My take on the complex relationship between the "is" of human nature and the "oughts" of morality appears on pages 53–55 and 112–20.

20. "The naturalistic fallacy states that it is 'logically impossible for any set of statements of the kind usually called descriptive to entail a statement of the kind usually called evaluative.'" John R. Searle, *Speech Acts: An Essay in the Philosophy of Language* (Cambridge: Cambridge University Press, 1977), p. 132. See, generally, George Edward Moore, *Principia Ethica* (Cambridge: Cambridge University Press, 1960).

21. Cicero, *De senectute* XIX (c. 78 B.C.); Juvenal, *Satires* XIV (A.D. 128); Saint Augustine, *Of Continence* (c. 425); John Florio, *His Firste Fruites* (1578). The word *nature* has many meanings, especially when translated from several different languages. The quotations above are intended merely as illustrative of a range of views on the subject.

22. Blaise Pascal, *Les Pensées*, XXIV (1670); Dante, *De Monarchia* (c. 1313).

23. Baruch Spinoza, *Ethica I* (1677). Nor are the wonders of nature proof of any moral component for those who believe that "the beauty, symmetry, regularity and order seen in the universe are the aspects of a blind, unintelligent nature." Pierre Bayle, *Pensées diverses sur la comète* (1680).

24. The Jewish concept of Tikun Olam — repairing the world — would seem to imply the imperfection of nature and the human obligation of improving on the natural condition of the world. According to a midrash, God needed human beings to complete the ongoing process of creation — to make nature better. The never-ending quest for justice is a reflection of the perfectibility of nature.

25. See T. W. Adorno, *The Authoritarian Personality* (New York: Harper, 1950).

26. Consider Germany, for example, which had a long tradition of liberty — at least among its intelligencia. It then quickly succumbed to Nazism. Among the most influential Nazi supporters were leading intellectuals, artists, lawyers, businessmen, church leaders, and doctors.

27. Put another way, valuing rights may be more "natural" among some elements of society than others, and it is the responsibility of the former to persuade the latter of their importance.

28. Frederick Kidder, *History of the Boston Massacre, March 5, 1770* (Albany, 1870). Reprinted by The Notable Trials Library (New York: Pantheon, 2001).

29. Oliver Wendell Holmes Jr., in *The Common Law* (1881).

30. Kant, *Metaphysische Anfangsgründe der Rechtslehre*, quoted in Rawls, p. 128.

31. Ronald Dworkin, *Taking Rights Seriously* (Cambridge, Mass: Harvard University Press, 1977), pp. 177, xi, 184.

32. "The institution of rights against the Government is not a gift of God, or an ancient ritual, or a national sport." Ibid., p. 198.

33. "The strongbox theory of law is, of course, nonsense." Ibid., p. 216.

34. "The idea of individual rights that these essays defend does not presuppose any ghostly forms." Ibid., p. xi.

35. Ibid., p. 158. In support of an intuition for rights, a colleague has observed that children are always invoking their "rights" in relation to their parents. This is surely true *today* in *America*, but it was just as surely not true in the past and in other places. In fact, the observation supports my view that there is no hardwired intuition for rights and that they are more nurtural than natural. We live today in a culture of rights (see Mary Ann Glendon, *Rights Talk* [New York: Free Press, 1993]), and kids pick up on that culture at a very early age. I know! I have a twelve-year-old.

36. He cites the psychologist Ronald Lang in support of a similar proposition for which I cited Dostoyevsky's Grand Inquisitor, namely, that "a good deal of mental instability in modern societies may be traced to the demand for too much liberty rather than too little." Dworkin, *Taking Rights Seriously*, p. 272.

37. "It remains the judge's duty, even in hard cases, to discover what the rights of the parties are, not to invent new rights retrospectively." Ibid., p. 81.

38. Dworkin also rejects the notion of the "brooding omnipresence in the sky." Though suspicious of "metaphysical natural law, I have avoided that phrase [natural law] because it has, for many people, disqualifying metaphysical associations: they think that natural rights are supposed to be special attributes worn by primitive men like amulets, which they carry into civilization to ward off tyranny." Ibid., p. 176. Dworkin appears to approve of some species of transcendent natural rights based on "the hypothesis that the best political program . . . is one that takes the protection of certain individual choices as fundamental, and not properly subordinated to any goal or duty or combination of these." Ibid., p. 177.

39. Ibid., p. 160. This man-made constructive model is to be contrasted with the kind of natural model that derives from "an objective moral reality," not created by men or societies but rather "discovered by them as they discover laws of physics."

40. Ibid.

41. Ibid., p. 177.

42. In this formulation, Dworkin seems to confuse the utility of *a particular* speech with the utility of freedom of speech *in general.*

43. Ibid., p. 271.

44. Perhaps Dworkin is saying that although *specific* rights must not be subjected to consequentialist tests, the broad concept of a rights-based system must be justified by the consequentialist test that it is "the best political program."

45. Even the claims of some natural-rights advocates rest — at least to some degree — on the implicit consequentialist assumption that the world will be a better place with eternal natural rights than with only amendable positive rights.

46. In fairness to Dworkin, I have been unable to find a single place where he claims to have come up with a comprehensive theory of the origin of rights. The text discussion is based largely on selective quotations, in a variety of contexts, from his masterful book *Taking Rights Seriously*.

47. Dworkin, *Taking Rights Seriously*, p. 190.

48. This approach is entirely consistent with the rhetoric of our Declaration of Independence, which speaks of "unalienable rights" but then says that "to secure these rights," we have governments and laws.

49. If ever our Constitution were to be amended so as to abrogate these "natural rights," we would have to confront the difficult issue of sources and claimed "unalienability." At that point, Dworkin would have the burden of showing why humanly constructed rights, which do not come from God, intuition, or other "ghostly entities," cannot be abrogated by the same humans who constructed (or discovered) them (at least if they could come up with compelling moral arguments).

50. If it became necessary for a government to require every family with extra bedrooms to house a soldier for several months during a period of preparation for a possible war, no one's natural rights would be violated.

51. Even the Supreme Court appears to have recognized the lower status of the grand jury right as compared with, for example, the right to counsel or the privilege against self-incrimination. It "incorporated" the latter rights into the due process clause of the Fourteenth Amendment and applied them to the states as well as to the federal government, while declining to incorporate the grand jury right, thus leaving the states free to adopt other procedures.

52. See Akhil Reed Amar, *The Bill of Rights: Creation and Reconstruction* (New Haven, Conn.: Yale University Press, 2000), and *The Constitution and Criminal Procedure: First Principles* (New Haven, Conn.: Yale University Press, 1998).

53. It should not be surprising, therefore, that the warrant requirement is being considerably watered down by the courts, as we grow further removed from the historical experiences that animated it. But see *Kyllo* v. *United States*, 533 U.S., 121 S. Ct. 2038, 150 L. Ed. 2nd 94, no. 99-8508 (June 11, 2001).

54. The right to a jury trial in civil cases where more than twenty dollars is in dispute surely would not qualify as natural.

55. Even in our country, cities and states have imposed restrictive zoning laws that have diminished the value of private property, without having to pay compensation. In Massachusetts, private citizens may own their own oceanfront beaches. Many citizens are outraged by the denial of access to what they regard as our collective public seashore. Because of the limited amount of oceanfront in Massachusetts, the value of such beaches has skyrocketed to the point that the state could not now afford to buy them at

market value for public use. Were the legislature to enact a law providing a phaseout of private ownership of ocean beaches — say, over a twenty-year period or the lifetime of its present owners — there would surely be a constitutional challenge based on the "taking" clause of the Fifth Amendment. But it would be difficult to make the case for a natural right to future private ownership of ocean beaches or market-value compensation for their taking.

56. Nozick has modified some of the views relating to property that he first expressed in *Anarchy, State, and Utopia* (Oxford, Eng.: Blackwell, 1975). See his *Philosophical Explanations* (Oxford, Eng.: Clarendon, 1981). Nozick is a wonderful example of a brilliantly intuitive philosopher who has combined a priori insights with experiences and history and has modified some of his views with changing experiences.

57. See "Week in Review," *New York Times*, September 24, 2000, p. 7.

58. If the militia must be well regulated, it follows — according to this argument — that the private possession of weapons for use in the militia must also be well regulated.

59. Blackstone includes this right as basic, but many other British colonies, with experiences different from our own, have downgraded this "right." It is not surprising that the written (and unwritten) constitutions of most other nations do not include private gun ownership as among the fundamental rights of citizens. Only Mexico and Switzerland have any "right to bear arms," and in both countries this right is subject to extensive regulation. According to Japanese law, "no one shall possess a firearm or a sword." In most other countries, gun ownership is severely restricted and few citizens own firearms or believe they have any right to do so. This does not necessarily disqualify a given right from being deemed fundamental or even natural, but it surely supports the view that many rights derive from the unique experiences of a people and can hardly be deemed universal.

60. Some Quakers deny it.

61. Even were the Constitution to be amended to specify the right of the pregnant woman to abort her fetus, that amendment — though properly enacted — would not be the law, according to this view. There is even a fringe political party in the United States that calls itself the Natural Law Party.

62. A classic study of abortion concluded that women's attitudes toward the "right to life" versus "the right to choose" are largely a function of their socioeconomic status and life experiences, rather than any abstract commitment to a particular theory of rights. Kristin Luker, *Abortion and the Politics of Motherhood* (Berkeley: University of California Press, 1984). Paul Robinson, writing in the *New York Times Book Review* (May 6, 1984), said that the book "demonstrates that the controversy derives its intensity not from differences of ideology or religion but from the radically antithetical social circumstances of the combatants."

63. James Madison was explicit in his belief that our Constitution "is founded" on "the laws of God."

64. Both former president George Bush and presidential candidate Alan Keyes have suggested that atheists cannot be good citizens, since they do

not accept the statement in the Declaration of Independence that Americans are endowed by "their creator" with rights.

65. Notice that although the Declaration invokes the laws of nature's God, it never mentions the Bible, Christianity, or organized religion. Jefferson, Franklin, and Paine — among others — had great doubts about organized religion but believed in a God of nature. Thomas Paine was a radical anti-Christian who wrote a book trashing the Bible: *The Age of Reason*.

66. Midrashim (singular "midrash") are interpretations of the biblical text by the use of illustrative stories, explanations, commentaries, and other forms of exegesis. See Alan Dershowitz, *The Genesis of Justice* (New York: Warner, 2000).

67. Book of Mormon.

68. See essays by Ernest Fortin in Ernest L. Fortin and J. Brian Benestad, *Classical Christianity and the Political Order* (Lanham, Md.: Rowman and Littlefield, 1996).

69. According to the Internet Encyclopedia of Philosophy, "*Rule utilitarianism* is a formulation of utilitarianism which maintains that a behavioral code or rule is morally right if the consequences of adopting that rule are more favorable than unfavorable to everyone. It is contrasted with *act utilitarianism* which maintains that the morality of each action is to be determined in relation to the favorable or unfavorable consequences that emerge from that action."

70. See Dworkin, *Taking Rights Seriously*.

71. Eugene Genovese, *The Slaveholders' Dilemma* (Columbia: University of South Carolina Press, 1992), p. 38.

72. Ibid., p. 47.

73. Ibid., pp. 27–29.

74. Ibid., pp. 37, 51, 53, 92.

75. M. T. Wheat, *The Progress of Americans; Collateral Proof of Slavery . . .* , 2nd ed. (Louisville, 1862), p. 19.

76. Ibid., pp. 20, 19.

77. Seth Mydans, "He's Not Hairy, He's My Brother," *New York Times*, August 12, 2001.

78. Wheat, *The Progress of Americans*, p. 56.

79. Such healthy cynicism about the honest use of selective arguments to justify a particular practice or result quickly turns into something most sinister when a respected institution, like the United States Supreme Court, is thought to be consciously manipulating arguments in an improper manner. This occurred when a majority of that Court accepted arguments they would normally be expected to reject, in order to help bring about the election of a favored candidate. See Alan Dershowitz, *Supreme Injustice* (New York: Oxford, 2001).

80. Even "the law" is somewhat ambiguous. Various state *statutes* prohibit certain kinds of abortions, but various *constitutional* provisions — federal and state — have been interpreted to entrench a positive-law right to choose abortion, at least under certain circumstances.

81. See note 62 above and Alan Dershowitz, *Contrary to Popular Opinion* (New York: Pharos, 1992), pp. 207–43.

82. For example, it is moral for an army to bomb a legitimate military target even if it is completely predicable that some innocent civilians will be killed. So, too, it may be permissible to execute many guilty murderers even if it is predictable that a small number of falsely convicted innocents will also be executed. See my book *The Genesis of Justice*, chapter 4.

83. As evidence of the nonhumanity of the fetus, they point to the fact that the law does not generally punish abortion as murder.

84. Some approaches to natural law (and its corollary natural rights) presume that there is a correct answer to every moral dilemma. We can discern that answer if only we can properly access the correct source: God, the Bible, the church hierarchy, the Halakah, the Shari'ah, nature, reason, a categorical imperative, a social contract — even a utilitarian calculus. Some advocates of positive law (and its corollary positive rights) also claim that positivism can provide a right answer to every legal conflict. We can discern that answer as well by reference to the correct sources: the Constitution, statutes, common law, international law, treaties, and other accepted legal mandates.

85. Dworkin supposes that "there is often a single right answer to complex questions of law and political morality." *Taking Rights Seriously*, p. 279. But there are surely many such questions that have multiple right and wrong answers.

86. The dispute over the right to life and choice is replicated in the arguments concerning assisted suicide, the death penalty, just war, and other deeply divisive issues growing out of the strong human impulse to "choose life," as the Bible puts it. Scientists prefer to point to the instinct to preserve one's own life and those of one's family members over the lives of strangers.

87. See "Report About English Bill of Rights," *New York Times*, October 2, 2000.

88. George Washington put it this way: "It is now no more that toleration is spoken of as if it was by the indulgence of one class of people, that another enjoyed the exercise of their inherent natural rights." Quoted in Alan Dershowitz, *The Vanishing American Jew* (Boston: Little, Brown, 1997), pp. 144–45.

89. I am not speaking of scientific truth, which may well be singular and uniform, but rather of moral truth, which is not nearly as objective.

## CHAPTER 2: RIGHTS COME FROM WRONGS

1. Among my inspirations for this bottom-up theory of rights is the Book of Genesis, which contains narratives of injustice on which the later rules of justice are built. I elaborate on this approach in my book *The Genesis of Justice*, where I argue that the genesis of justice is in the injustice of Genesis. It may seem ironic to some that one who rejects divine natural law can be inspired by the Bible. But it is precisely because I believe that the magnif-

icent, if imperfect, books of the Bible were written, collected, and edited by humans that I am so inspired about the human capacity to improve upon nature.

2. In his *Discourse on the Constitution and Government of the United States*, published shortly after his death in 1850, John C. Calhoun wrote: "That a state, as a party to the constitutional compact, has the right to secede — acting in the same capacity in which it ratified the Constitution — cannot, with any show of reason, be denied by anyone who regards the Constitution as a compact — if a power should be inserted by the amending power, which would radically change the character of the Constitution or the nature of the system; or if the former should fail to fulfill the ends for which it was established." John C. Calhoun, *Discourse on the Constitution and Government of the United States*, vol. 1 of *Works of John C. Calhoun* (New York: D. Appleton, 1883), p. 301.

# CHAPTER 3: THE CHALLENGE OF RIGHTS BASED ON HUMAN EXPERIENCE

1. Stephen Jay Gould, *Wonderful Life: The Burgess Shale and the Nature of History* (New York: Norton, 1989).

2. Kafka, in my estimation, makes a more powerful case for rights by portraying a world without them than do many positive advocates of rights who seek to demonstrate a utopian world with rights.

3. Alvin H. Rosenfeld and Irving Greenberg, *Confronting the Holocaust: The Impact of Elie Weisel* (Bloomington: Indiana University Press, 1979).

4. But see Alschuler, *Law Without Values*.

5. I do not regard the *forms* of legality as bestowing actual rights, when the outcome was predetermined by the ideology.

6. See, H.L.A. Hart, *Essays*, pp. 72–78. Hart distinguishes between challenging particular law and an entire legal system, such as Nazism, on moral grounds.

7. William Nicholls, *Christian Antisemitism: A History of Hate* (Northvale, N.J.: Jason Aronson, 1993), p. 360. Nicholls goes on:

> The conflicts in question would have been, one presumes, between their duty to God and their duty to the Nazi state. Perhaps, too, he had in mind the casuistic argument that if he did not formally condemn actions against the Jews, Germans who took part could be said to have sinned in ignorance, thus incurring a lesser spiritual penalty.
>
> This is false compassion, apart from its implications for Pius' view of the moral priorities between saving Jews and the mental comfort of his own flock. Moreover, the argument is hardly convincing. Even given the anti-Jewish conditioning we have been describing, no one with a Catholic education could have been wholly in ignorance of the fact that actually killing defenseless Jews, or even taking part in measures leading to that end, was a mortal sin, whatever their duty to the state, and whether or not the pope chose to say so. But this does not remove the pope's responsibility to warn and condemn.

> On his own premises, the pope must have imperilled the eternal salvation of German and East European Catholics far more by his silence than he could have done by speaking, since he failed to direct them away from actions objectively evil beyond measure. Without the moral support of his outspoken condemnation, hundreds of thousands of Catholics gave in and took part in the most evil act of all history, unrebuked by their spiritual leader [pp. 360–61]. See also David Kertzer, *The Vatican's Role in the Rise of Anti-Semitism* (New York: Knopf, 2001).

8. See *New York Times*, November 2, 2000, sec. A, p. 6.

9. Mary Ann Glendon, *A World Made New: Eleanor Roosevelt and the Universal Declaration of Human Rights* (New York: Random House, 2001).

10. Marlise Simons, "Tribunal in the Hague Finds Bosnian Serb Guilty of Genocide," *New York Times*, August 3, 2001; Reuters, "Three Bosnian Muslim Officers Face War Crimes in the Hague," *New York Times*, August 4, 2001.

11. Quoted in Alan Dershowitz, *Chutzpah* (Boston: Little, Brown, 1991), p. 281.

## CHAPTER 4: WHY WE SHOULD PREFER RIGHTS

1. I realize, of course, that even these core rights may come into conflict with each other and that we need mechanisms for resolving or accommodating such conflicts.

2. Most Americans — other than Native Americans and African Americans — have been the beneficiaries of this right, since our ancestors made the decision to leave oppressive lands for this free country.

3. The Greeks and Hebrews pioneered rights on a theoretical basis, but these theories were first put into modern practice in the eighteenth century. And if they were applied more broadly in the twentieth century, they were also denied more horribly.

4. Even this distinction is not as sharp as it may appear. Dworkin, too, ranks rights by reference to what we understand "from our general knowledge of society." Dworkin, *Taking Rights Seriously*, p. 277.

5. Ibid., p. 271.

6. See Howard Gardner, *Intelligence Reframed: Multiple Intelligences for the Twenty-first Century* (New York: Basic Books, 1999), and *Frames of Mind: The Theory of Multiple Intelligences* (New York: Basic Books, 1983).

7. Hart, *Essays*, p. 187.

8. Ibid., p. 54.

9. Alschuler, *Law Without Values*, p. 136.

10. Hart, *Essays*, p. 196. This is, of course, an empirical proposition based on the collective experiences of humankind: without external sources of morality, catastrophe will ensue. And it may well be accurate. It also purports to derive from the nature of human beings: we *need* external sources of morality because without them we will not be able to resist the temptations of freedom.

11. Ibid., p. 198.

12. Ibid., p. 264.

13. Fyodor Dostoyevsky, *The Brothers Karamazov*, quoted in Hart, *Essays*, p. 263.

14. Quoted in Alschuler, *Law Without Values*, p. 136.

15. H.L.A. Hart talks about "the rough seas which the philosophy of political morality is presently crossing between the old faith in utilitarianism and the new faith in rights" (*Essays*, p. 221). He is more cautiously optimistic than I am that hard work by moral philosophers will eventually lead us to the holy grail of a perfect theory of rights with a legitimate source of authority.

16. Or, as George Santayana said, "Those who cannot remember the past are condemned to repeat it."

17. Alschuler, *Law Without Values*, pp. 189–90.

## CHAPTER 5: OUR ENDURING BILL OF RIGHTS

1. Those who did not choose — Native Americans and African slaves — have also had a unique history: of victimization and oppression.

2. I prefer to speak about "original assumptions" rather than "intent," since few were consciously or overtly thought about by the framers.

## CHAPTER 6: A DANGEROUS VOCABULARY OF NEW RIGHTS

1. A victims'-rights amendment has been introduced in Congress on several occasions, but to date it has not been enacted.

## CHAPTER 7: RIGHTS AND INTERESTS

1. The Meares-Kahan essay and other responses can be found in Dan Kahan and Tracey Meares, *Urgent Times* (Boston: Beacon Press, 1999).

## CHAPTER 8: DO GRANDPARENTS HAVE RIGHTS?

1. Apparently he did, and he dissented from the majority decision that struck down the Washington law.

# CHAPTER 9: DO (SHOULD) ANIMALS HAVE RIGHTS?

1. My first professional encounter with animal rights occurred in the unlikely context of a United States Supreme Court argument about the censorship of the film *I Am Curious, Yellow* back in 1967. Chief Justice Warren Burger kept invoking the analogy between consensual sex and bearbaiting (despite the fact that bears do not consent to being baited). See Alan Dershowitz, *The Best Defense* (New York: Random House, 1982), pp. 165–67.

2. Seth Mydans, "He's Not Hairy, He's My Brother," *New York Times*, August 12, 2001.

# CHAPTER 10: RIGHTS IN A WORLD WITHOUT GOD

1. For the complete symposium, see *Harvard Law Review* 112, no. 8 (June 1999).

2. It is to be regretted, perhaps, though understood, that many atheists remained wedded to prior tribal groups. There were Jewish atheists, Catholic atheists, Protestant atheists, Muslim atheists, and other smaller groupings, arguing vigorously over which god *not* to believe in.

    Even prior to the great apocalypse, many thoughtful people understood that their religious "beliefs" and practices were based on myths similar to those of their polytheistic predecessors. But they also saw that religion was important to the lives of many of their friends and that it produced much good — like a placebo taken by one who believes it to be a potent medicine. They were content to regard religion as a pious and harmless fraud. But the great apocalypse demonstrated how dangerous such myths had become, and most citizens began to demand that religion be treated like other irrational belief systems such as astrology, tarot, and voodoo. Soon it became as unfashionable to believe in the supernatural doctrines of formal religion as it was to believe that the earth was flat.

    Even prior to the Great Fundamentalist Wars of the third millennium, some courageous intellectuals began to challenge monotheistic dogma, but they had considerable difficulties in persuading the masses. Part of the reason for their hardship was that certain evil totalitarian regimes had forced atheism on their citizens, thereby associating disbelief in God with tyranny. It became voguish for prudent intellectuals to argue that science (empirical truth) and faith (belief) must be kept separate and that matters of faith should not be judged by scientific criteria. This, too, however, was a myth, because many of the claims of faith — for example, that Moses parted the Red Sea, that Jesus walked on water, and that Muhammad ascended to heaven on a horse — are empirical and historical: they either happened or they were made up. Following the wars, more people began to insist on proof of such claims and concluded that they were fictional.

3. Contemporary historians still cannot solve the intellectual puzzle of why, for more than two thousand years, so many people concluded that belief in

one supernatural being (monotheism) was regarded as an "advance" over belief in many supernatural beings (polytheism).

4. I, too, believe that certain rights should be accepted *by agreement* as inalienable, or at least as not subject to abrogation by a simple majority. This is my preference, and I hope to persuade others to agree with it.

5. As the ancient Talmud rhetorically asked: "Who knows that your blood is redder?" Sanhedrin 74a in I. Epstein, ed., *The Babylonian Talmud*, trans. H. Freedman (London: Soncino Press, 1935), p. 503.

6. In the old days, the prospect of punishment in the afterlife — eternity in hell — could be threatened. Today, of course, few believe in such irrational "ghost stories." Even in the past ages of religions, it is doubtful whether many people actually believed in heaven and hell, because so many sins were committed by "believers." The threat of eternal punishment and reward did not dispense with the need for earthly punishments to deter crimes that were also sins.

7. There may, of course, be moral objections if the penalties necessary to deter the conduct are too harsh or fall too heavily on innocent third parties.

8. It could be argued that elite philosophers or jurists are better suited because of their intellect and education to make such decisions. Many millennia ago, a Greek philosopher named Plato proposed such an elitist theory of decision making. Most democracies have rejected it, concluding instead that representative decision making is preferable. Choosing who should decide the law, too, is ultimately a matter of preference and persuasion. However, the advocates of representative decision making have generally prevailed over time.

9. See, e.g., David Daube, *Collaboration with Tyranny in Rabbinic Law* (London: Oxford University Press, 1965); Marilyn Finkelman, "Self-Defense and Defense of Others in Jewish Law: The *Rodef* Defense," *Wayne Law Review* 33 (1987): 1257. Among the cases — some actual, others hypothetical — considered in the Talmud are the following: an enemy general surrounds a walled city and threatens to kill all of its inhabitants unless they turn over one individual for execution; two people are dying of thirst in the desert with enough water between them to save one but not both; a child, below the age of legal responsibility and thus deemed innocent, threatens the life of another innocent person and can be prevented from killing only by being killed (the filmmaker Alfred Hitchcock presented a variation on this theme in an episode from his television program); and a fetus endangers the life of a pregnant woman who can be saved only by killing the fetus (a variation is that during delivery, the baby endangers the life of the mother, who can be saved only by killing the partially delivered baby).

10. See *Regina v. Dudley and Stephens*, 14 Q.B.D. 273 (1884).

11. Johann Christoph Friedrich von Schiller, *Wallenstein's Camp*, sc. 6 (1798), quoted in *Bartlett's Familiar Quotations*, 16th ed., p. 365.

12. The killing was also premeditated, as are all judicial executions. The official death certificate in a famous death-penalty case during the last century of the second millennium — the Sacco and Vanzetti case, *Commonwealth v. Sacco*, 151 N.E. 839 (Mass. 1926) — listed the cause of death of the defen-

dants as "electric shock judicial homicide." Certificate of death of Bar-
tolomeo Vanzetti (1927) (on file with the Harvard Law School Library).

13. One of my judicial colleagues, whom I will not name, is sometimes referred to as "Necessity," because he too "knows no law."

14. See Sanford H. Kadish and Stephen J. Schulhofer, *Criminal Law and Its
Processes: Cases and Materials*, 6th ed. (Boston: Little, Brown, 1995), pp.
860–80. Surely the death of several people is a greater harm than the death
of one person. But see Nezikin 5 in Epstein, *Babylonian Talmud:* "Whoso-
ever preserves a single soul of Israel [it is] as though he had preserved a
complete world."

15. See Finkelman, "Self-Defense and Defense of Others," 1278–80.

16. Perhaps this decision would be influenced by the tragic reality that so
many of those who created the dilemma — the Nazi murderers — got
away with it.

17. Model Penal Code (commentary, page 10), sec. 3.02 (1962). The necessity
defense has been "anciently woven into the fabric of our culture." Jerome
Hall, *General Principles of Criminal Law*, 2nd ed. (Indianapolis: Bobbs-
Merrill, 1960), p. 416, cited in Laura J. Schulkind, "Applying the Necessity Defense to Civil Disobedience Cases," *New York University Law
Review* 64 (1989): 79, 83 n. 20. It can be found in case law dating as far back
as 1551 in *Reniger v. Fogossa*, 75 Eng. Rep. 1 (K.B. 1551). Arguing that a
captain who docked his ship to avoid a storm would not have to forfeit his
goods as the statute would have required, the court concluded: "A man
may break the words of the law, and yet not break the law itself. . . . And
therefore the words of the law . . . will yield and give way to some acts and
things done against the words of the same laws, and that is, where the
words of them are broken to avoid greater inconvenience, or through necessity." Ibid., 29.

   The *Reniger* court reached even further back to the New Testament example in Matthew 12:3–4 of eating sacred bread or taking another's corn
through necessity of hunger. See Edward B. Arnolds and Norman F. Garland, "The Defense of Necessity in Criminal Law: The Right to Choose
the Lesser Evil," *Journal of Criminal Law and Criminology* 65 (1974): 289,
291 n. 27 (citing *Reniger*). Arnolds and Garland enumerate many other
older (Arnolds and Garland, "Defense of Necessity," 291 nn. 29–34) and
modern (ibid., 291–92 nn. 35–37) English cases that "recognize the general principle of necessity" (ibid., 291) as well as both federal (ibid., 292 nn.
38–44) and state (ibid., 292 nn. 45–50), cases in the United States. The
court system's recognition of the necessity defense is also acknowledged in
casebooks. See, e.g., Kadish and Schulhofer, *Criminal Law and Its Processes*,
pp. 860–80.

18. The necessity defense is part of the Model Penal Code (see sec. 3.02) and
has been incorporated into many state criminal codes; see Lawrence P.
Tiffany and Carl A. Anderson, "Legislating the Necessity Defense in Criminal Law," *Denver Law Journal* 52 (1975): 839 (examining how many states
included the necessity defense when they recodified their criminal statutes).

19. See, e.g., Ky. Rev. Stat. Ann. (Michie 1985), sec. 503.030 (stating that "no
justification can exist . . . for an intentional homicide"); Mo. Rev. Stat.

(1994), sec. 563.026 (stating that "conduct which would otherwise constitute any crime other than a class A felony or murder is justifiable and not
criminal when it is necessary as an emergency measure to avoid an imminent public or private injury"); Wis. Stat. Ann. (West 1997–98), sec.
939.47 (stating that necessity "is a defense to a prosecution . . . except that
if the prosecution is for first-degree intentional homicide, the degree of
the crime is reduced to 2nd-degree intentional homicide"); *Regina v. Pom-
mell*, 2 Crim. App. 607, 608 (1995) (stating that the necessity defense does
not apply to murder and attempted murder), cited in Alan Reed, "Duress
and Provocation as Excuses to Murder: Salutary Lessons from Recent
Anglo-American Jurisprudence," *Florida State University Journal of Trans-
national Law and Policy* 6 (1996): 51, 68 n. 20.

    According to LaFave and Scott:

> Those jurisdictions that limit the necessity defense to crimes other
> than killing face the following conundrum: A person who was pro-
> voked into killing by seeing his wife in bed with another man can have
> the charges reduced from murder to manslaughter if he is deemed to
> have acted as a reasonable man would have acted under a similar
> provocation. But a man who kills one person to save multiple lives
> faces conviction for first-degree murder. Such cases and statutes also
> contradict the general principle found in the Model Penal Code
> commentaries that the defense is available [when] a person intention-
> ally kills one person in order to save two or more.

Wayne R. LaFave and Austin W. Scott Jr., *Substantive Criminal Law* (St.
Paul, Minn.: West, 1986), sec. 5.4, p. 632.

20. As Tiffany and Anderson conclude: "The common law rejection [in *Dudley*] of the defense when the intentional killing of an innocent person was
involved, appears now to be almost universally rejected itself. The most
common statutory approach is to provide, merely, that if the other conditions of the defense are all satisfied, the actor's 'conduct' is justified."
Tiffany and Anderson, "Legislating the Necessity Defense," 860 (foot-
notes omitted).

21. Model Penal Code (commentary, page 14) sec. 3.02. The American Law
Institute continued:

> For, recognizing that the sanctity of life has a supreme place in the hi-
> erarchy of values, it is nonetheless true that conduct that results in
> taking life may promote the very value sought to be protected by the
> law of homicide. Suppose, for example, that the actor makes a breach
> in a dike, knowing that this will inundate a farm, but taking the only
> course available to save a whole town. If he is charged with homicide
> of the inhabitants of the farm house, he can rightly point out that the
> object of the law of homicide is to save life, and that by his conduct he
> has effected a net saving of innocent lives. The life of every individual
> must be taken in such a case to be of equal value and the numerical
> preponderance in the lives saved compared to those sacrificed surely
> should establish legal justification for the act. So too, a mountaineer,
> roped to a companion who has fallen over a precipice, who holds on
> as long as possible but eventually cuts the rope, must certainly be
> granted the defense that he accelerated one death slightly but avoided

the only alternative, the certain death of both. Although the view is not universally held that it is ethically preferable to take one innocent life than to have many lives lost, most persons probably think a net saving of lives is ethically warranted if the choice among lives to be saved is not unfair. Certainly the law should permit such a choice.

Kadish and Schulhofer, *Criminal Law and Its Processes*, pp. 877–78 (quoting Model Penal Code [commentary, pages 14–15] [1985], sec. 3.02).

22. *United States v. Bass*, 404 U.S. 336, 347 (1971) (quoting *Rewis v. United States*, 401 U.S. 808, 812 [1971]) (internal quotation marks omitted). See also *United States v. Lanier*, 520 U.S. 259, 266 (1997) ("The canon of strict construction of criminal statutes, or rule of lenity, ensures fair warning by so resolving ambiguity in a criminal statute as to apply it only to conduct clearly covered"); *Staples v. United States*, 511 U.S. 600, 619 (1994) (noting that under the rule of lenity, an "ambiguous criminal statute" should be "construed in favor of the accused").

23. See *Bouie v. City of Columbia*, 378 U.S. 347, 352–54 (1964).

24. Indeed, it is fair to say that few lawyers get through law school without discussing this conundrum and its numerous variations. Most law students read *Dudley and Stephens* and *United States v. Holmes*, 26 F. Cas. 360 (C.C.E.D. Pa. 1842) (no. 15,383). Many also study the writings of the great twentieth-century philosopher Robert Nozick, who, in 1974, constructed the following prescient hypothetical:

> If someone picks up a third party and throws him at you down at the bottom of a deep well, the third party is innocent and a threat; had he chosen to launch himself at you in that trajectory he would be an aggressor. Even though the falling person would survive his fall onto you, may you use your ray gun to disintegrate the falling body before it crushes and kills you? Libertarian prohibitions are usually formulated so as to forbid using violence on innocent persons. But innocent threats, I think, are another matter to which different principles must apply. Thus, a full theory in this area also must formulate the *different* constraints on response to innocent threats. Further complications concern *innocent shields of threats*, those innocent persons who themselves are nonthreats but who are so situated that they will be damaged by the only means available for stopping the threat. Innocent persons strapped onto the front of the tanks of aggressors so that the tanks cannot be hit without also hitting them are innocent shields of threats. (Some uses of force on people to get at an aggressor do not act upon innocent shields of threats; for example, an aggressor's innocent child who is tortured in order to get the aggressor to stop wasn't *shielding* the parent.) May one knowingly injure innocent shields? *If* one may attack an aggressor and injure an innocent shield, may the innocent shield fight back in self-defense (supposing that he cannot move against or fight the aggressor)? Do we get two persons battling each other in self-defense? Similarly, if you use force against an innocent threat to you, do you thereby become an innocent threat to him, so that he may now justifiably use additional force against you (supposing that he can do this, yet cannot prevent his original threateningness)?

Nozick, *Anarchy, State, and Utopia*, pp. 34–35. Students have also debated the following hypothetical case: A doctor is experimenting with a deadly virus; the virus begins to spread (through no fault of the doctor's); the only way to prevent the spread of the virus is to seal the room from which the doctor is trying to flee, thus dooming him.

25. Justice Frank H. Easterbrook premises his decision largely on the assumption that these defendants implicitly consented to the decision ultimately taken and the conclusion that "society should recognize th[at] agreement." The problem is that consent, even when explicit, has not always been accepted as a defense to willful killing, as evidenced by the ancient case of *People v. Kevorkian*, 527 N.W.2d 714 (Mich. 1994).

26. Indeed, under governing case law, his homicide was even premeditated because premeditation can occur in an instant.

27. There are, however, some who justify using organs of prisoners condemned to death, despite the reality that this might result in more executions for the sole purpose of using the prisoner's organs to save others' lives.

28. As Justice West states:

    There are currently a sizable number of citizens in this country awaiting organ donations, bone marrow replacements, and blood transfusions. The profound scarcity of such organs, bone marrow, and non-contaminated rare blood types is the sad reality that all such patients (as well as those of us who may at any point become such a patient) are forced to endure. That scarcity prompts incomparable anguish among the needy donees, and tortured decisions by medical personnel.

29. See Kadish and Schulhofer, *Criminal Law and Its Processes*, pp. 877–78.

30. Another important indication that our legislature did not intend to include the type of necessity killing under the general prohibition against murder is that it failed to specify an appropriate punishment for this kind of tragic-choice killing. Surely it would be wrong for a judge to be empowered to punish our defendants as severely as a defendant who killed for profit, thrill, or hatred.

## CHAPTER 11: THE RIGHT TO YOUR BODY AFTER DEATH

1. Thomas Hobbes put it somewhat ironically in his *Leviathan* XVII (1651): "The laws of nature, as justice, equity, modesty, mercy and in sum, doing to others as we would be done to, of themselves, without the terror of some power to cause them to be observed, are contrary to our natural passions, that carry us to partiality, pride, revenge and the like."

2. Ivory, unlike food or transplantable organs, is not a necessity. It is a luxury. But for those whose livelihoods depend on securing and selling this luxury, the line between luxury and necessity blurs.

## CHAPTER 13: RIGHTS AS A CHECK
## ON DEMOCRACY

1. *Learned Hand: The Spirit of Liberty*, 3rd ed. (New York: Knopf, 1960), p. 190. "Liberty lies in the hearts of men and women; when it dies there, no constitution, no law, no court can save it; no constitution, no law, no court can even do much to help it. While it lies, it needs no constitution, no law, no court to save it."

2. See John Ely, *Democracy and Distrust: A Theory of Judicial Review* (Cambridge, Mass.: Harvard University Press, 1980).

3. For legal positivists, the amending process demonstrates that even the most basic of rights — such as freedom of speech — is subject to change and that no rights are "unalienable." For some natural-law advocates, amending the First Amendment so as to eliminate freedom of speech would violate our natural rights. For me, I would have to persuade my fellow Americans to oppose such an amendment on the basis of our collective history and experiences regarding censorship.

4. See Amartya Sen, *Development as Freedom* (New York: Knopf, 1999).

5. See Bruce Ackerman, "The Court Packs Itself," *American Prospect* 12, no. 3 (February 12, 2001).

## CHAPTER 14: THE LAW AS MORALITY

1. My discussion of Durkheim's views concerning law and morality derive primarily from Roger Cotterrell's excellent summary in *Émile Durkheim: Law in a Moral Domain* (Stanford, Calif.: Stanford University Press, 1999). As Cotterrell notes, Durkheim "never wrote systematically about legal phenomena and his insights are scattered through many sources." (p. ix) Accordingly, Cotterrell's book — "the first detailed analysis in English of the entirety of Durkheim's legal theory" (p. x) — is an invaluable resource.

2. This would be especially so if the advocate of this universality of a particular right agreed with the general criteria for evaluating the morality of a society. See *Boston Globe*, August 22, 2001, p. A18, for a description of a similar "nineteenth-century custom" among certain Arctic cultures.

3. Jeremy Bentham, *An Introduction to the Principles of Morals and Legislation*, J. H. Burns and H.L.A. Hart, eds. (New York: Oxford University Press, 1996).

4. Cotterrell, *Émile Durkheim*, pp. ix, 17.

5. Ibid., p. 19.

6. Ibid., p. 50.

7. Émile Durkheim and Paul Fauconnet, *Sociology and the Social Sciences* (1903; reprint, 1982), quoted in Cotterrell, *Émile Durkheim*, p. 53.

8. See Dershowitz, *Genesis of Justice*.

9. Advocates of natural law and advocates of positive law are really asking two different questions. Although both appear to be addressing themselves to the sources of law, they use *sources* in different ways. The natural-law advocate, by seeking sources outside of positive law, is really asking about how we *evaluate* existing law. The legal positivist *describes* existing law and seeks its sources in the lawmaking process.

10. Quoted in Cotterrell, *Émile Durkheim*, p. 15

11. Cotterrell, *Émile Durkheim*, p. 57.

12. Ibid.

13. Ibid.

14. Quoted in Hart, *Essays*, pp. 188–90.

15. Cotterrell, *Émile Durkheim*, p. 200.

16. Durkheim saw no sharp line between philosophical and sociological views of morality, since he regarded morality as a function of the particular society rather than as universal or timeless. "As such it is relative, yet not a matter of preference" (ibid., p. 203). H.L.A. Hart took Durkheim's challenge a step further by arguing that "there is, in the very notion of law consisting of general rules, something which prevents us from treating it as if morally it is utterly neutral, without any necessary contact with moral principles" (Hart, *Essays*, p. 81). Yet he acknowledges that a legal system could be moral in its application by being equally applicable to all, while being immoral in its substance.

17. Cotterrell, *Émile Durkheim*, pp. 115–17.

18. This critical capacity is recognized very early in the Jewish religion by the story in Genesis of Abraham's argument with God over the sinners of Sodom. See Dershowitz, *Genesis of Justice*.

19. Cotterrell, *Émile Durkheim*, p. 159.

20. Ibid., p. 164.

## CHAPTER 15: THE MOST FUNDAMENTAL LIMITATION ON STATE POWER

1. John Stuart Mill, *The Subjection of Women* (Philadelphia: Lippincott, 1869).

2. Lawrence Tribe, "The Seat-Belt Law Does Not Intrude on Freedom," *Boston Globe*, March 22, 1986, p. 11.

3. See John Stuart Mill, *On Liberty and Utilitarianism*; with an introduction by Alan M. Dershowitz, (New York: Bantam, 1993), pp. 24–26.

4. John Donne, "Meditation XVII," in *The Norton Anthology of English Literature*, vol. I (New York: M. H. Abrams, 1979), p. 1108.

5. See Mill, *On Liberty*, pp. 24–25.

6. Mill addressed "offenses against decency" (ibid., pp. 108–9), but he contented himself with the conventional distinction between indecent acts done in public and in private.

7. Many feminists demand that johns — occasional consumers of sex for hire — must be prosecuted if prostitutes are prosecuted. For a civil liber-

ties perspective, see Alan M. Dershowitz, *Taking Liberties* (Chicago: Contemporary Books, 1988), pp. 90–92.

8. Mill put it this way: "As soon as any part of a person's conduct affects prejudicially the interest of others, society has jurisdiction over it, and the question whether the general welfare will or will not be promoted by interfering with it, becomes open to discussion." Mill, *On Liberty*, pp. 83–84.

9. Some thinkers have suggested that individuals be allowed to opt out of all social welfare systems by agreeing not to use them even if they were desperate. But would the rest of us really be willing to see an opt-outer suffer without helping him or her? And would a system permitting such opting out be cost-efficient? These questions are beyond the scope of this essay.

10. This is how Brandeis put it:

> But it is hardly conceivable that this court would hold constitutional a statute which punished as a felony the mere voluntary assembly with a society formed to teach that pedestrians had the moral right to cross unenclosed, unposted, waste lands and to advocate their doing so, even if there was imminent danger that advocacy would lead to a trespass. The fact that speech is likely to result in some violence or in destruction of property is not enough to justify its suppression. There must be the probability of serious injury to the State. Among free men, the deterrents ordinarily to be applied to prevent crime are education and punishment for violations of the law, not abridgment of the rights of free speech and assembly.

*Whitney v. California*, 274 U.S. 357 (1927) (Justice Brandeis, concerning).

11. Distinguishing between action and speech will not always be easy, as demonstrated by the trespass case and others — such as the Boston Tea Party, flag burning, and cross burning. But the distinction, even if not subject to a bright line, is essential to any society, like ours, committed to elevating freedom of expression over freedom of action.

## CHAPTER 19: "WHY PORNOGRAPHY?"

1. I represented the defendant and the sentence was vacated.

2. Catherine MacKinnon, *Feminism Unmodified: Discourses on Life and Law* (Cambridge, Mass.: Harvard University Press, 1987), p. 148.

3. Word games are frequently played with the concept of censorship. MacKinnon and Andrea Dworkin eschew that label but would grant the courts power to enjoin publication of pornography at the request of private plaintiffs. As I use *censorship* it would include any governmentally enforced prohibition on publication, whether initiated by private parties or by public officials.

4. The Indianapolis statute drafted by MacKinnon and Dworkin was declared unconstitutional by the United States Court of Appeals in *American Booksellers Association v. Hudnut*, 771 F.2d 323 (1985). The decision was affirmed by the Supreme Court, 106 S.Ct. 1172 (1986).

5. The Meese Commission defined pornography as material that is "predominantly sexually explicit and intended primarily for the purpose of sexual arousal."

6. In his introduction to *Pornography: A Human Tragedy* (Wheaton, Ill.: Tyndale, 1986), a collection of religious essays by Charles Colson, James Dobson, C. Everett Koop, and others, the editor Tom Minnery talks about the "forms of pornography which injure a Judeo-Christian understanding of life." He argues that prohibitions against such pornography should be imposed by persuasion rather than force. Some religious zealots have included "mere nudity" within the meaning of pornography, while critics of mainstream television and motion pictures have argued that "pornographic violence" fills our screens.

7. H. L. Mencken once defined puritanism as "the haunting fear that someone, somewhere, may be happy."

8. *Time* magazine reported on March 30, 1987, that a new genre of pornography — "porn in the feminist style" or "romantic porn" — is now being produced by women for women (and couples). Even Gloria Steinem — who generally supports the MacKinnon-Dworkin approach to pornography — was quoted approvingly: "If this porn is the new erotica that appeals to women, then I think it's terrific." This seems to confirm the observation made by Al Goldstein, editor of *Screw* magazine, about the feminist distinction between pornography and erotica: "If you like it, it's pornography, but if they like it, it's erotica."

9. Nearly everyone — even the most absolute civil libertarians — is prepared to accept some government regulation on public displays of sex. The conflicting right of those citizens who do not wish to be exposed to such material, or to have children exposed to it, is widely accepted as a legitimate basis for "time, place, and manner" limitations that have always been imposed. The real debate, and the one I focus on, concerns the availability of pornography to adults who wish to consume it themselves without thrusting it on others or making it available to children.

10. She argues that "obscenity law prohibits what it sees as immoral, which from a feminist standpoint tends to be relatively harmless" (MacKinnon, *Feminism Unmodified*, p. 152), such as "nudity, excess of candor, arousal or excitement, prurient appeal . . . unnaturalness or perversion" (ibid., p. 175). But she insists that pornography is entirely different from, and far more harmful than, obscenity, because it is "sex forced on real women, so that it can be sold at a profit and forced on other real women." Her historical and epistemological distinction between "pornography" and "obscenity" — which is central to her entire theory — is questioned by Walter Kendrich in his intriguing book *The Secret Museum* (New York: Viking, 1987). Kendrich demonstrates the common origin of both terms and, indeed, their historic and epistemological interchangeability (*Secret Museum*, pp. 13–18).

11. The research falls into several general categories. The laboratory experiments tend to be conducted on undergraduate students who are exposed to pornography and then given an opportunity to "aggress" against men or

women. There are also demographic studies of regions and countries with different laws or degrees of availability of pornography. The studies and their criticisms are summarized in chapter 1 of *The Question of Pornography* (New York: Free Press, 1987).

12. "Harm" is so subjective and conclusory a concept that it is impossible to use it meaningfully as a scientific measure of effects — except, of course, for nondebatable harms such as rape, murder, and so on. Even then, the amount of harm caused would have to be offset by the amount prevented. Thus, for example, if allowing *Hustler* magazine to be published could be shown to have caused three men who would not otherwise have raped to rape, but at the same time caused ten men who would have raped to stay home and masturbate instead, it would be inaccurate to say — without more information — that allowing *Hustler* to be published caused three rapes.

13. Other methodological problems — such as transferring the results of laboratory experiments on college students to a general population in an uncontrolled setting — are satisfactorily addressed in the book (except for the fact that in real life, but not in the laboratory, exposure to explicit sexual imagery is often followed by masturbation). But there is insufficient consideration of the false positive problem as it relates to inferring causation from retrospective studies: i.e., even if a large number of offenders (however defined) were exposed to the offending material (however defined), it may still be true that only a tiny fraction of persons exposed to the material become offenders. And that such a correlation may reflect another factor common to both the consumers and the offenders. Under these circumstances, can it correctly be argued that the offending material "causes" the offenses?

14. The question "Why pornography?" derives from the old joke about Hitler's question to a crowd at a Nazi rally, "Who is causing all of Germany's problems?" A voice from the back shouts out: "The bicycle riders." Hitler asks in surprise, "Why the bicycle riders?" The voice replies: "Why the Jews?"

15. "The clearest effect of the media on violent behavior appears to come from the tendency of some people to imitate recent, specific, newsworthy incidents." James Q. Wilson and Richard J. Herrnstein, *Crime and Human Nature* (New York: Simon and Schuster, 1985), p. 353.

16. The study would, of course, be useful to those committed to eating only kosher foods and to improving their health. They would cut down on chicken fat. But it would not convince a health-conscious atheist to adopt a kosher diet for health reasons.

17. These characteristics derive from the feminist critique of pornography. A similar breakdown could be attempted using a fundamentalist or other critique. I have purposely omitted the evils associated with the photographing of pornographic images — evils such as coercion of models and the use of children, since these evils can be regulated directly by laws prohibiting coercion and use of children, without requiring censorship of the expression.

18. These characteristics, too, derive from the feminist critique and could be expanded to include the religious critique as well as other, more-subtle, attitudinal effects. If pornography is defined to include other than women — e.g., male homosexuality and bestiality — then other effects would be perceived.

19. MacKinnon, apparently anticipating this kind of argument, offers a response that appears to be empirical: "Pornography does not work sexually without hierarchy. If there is no inequality, no violation, no dominance, no force, there is no sexual arousal" (MacKinnon, *Feminism Unmodified*, p. 160). To the extent that this argument purports to be empirical, it is demonstrably false: many men (and women) are sexually aroused by the portrayal of egalitarian, nonviolent explicit sex (see Donnerstein et al., *Question of Pornography*, pp. 38–60). To the extent it purports to be definitional — i.e., it is not *pornography* unless it arouses *because* of its inequality and violence — it supports the argument that sexual explicitness should be eliminated as a component of pornography. But MacKinnon leaves it as the central component of her definition. Indeed, she argues that "escalating explicitness . . . is the aesthetic of pornography" (MacKinnon, *Feminism Unmodified*, p. 150).

20. I include *hard-core* to eliminate explicit portrayals in medical texts, museum art, and other genres of explicit portrayal that are not subject to obscenity prosecutions — at least not yet.

21. Donnerstein et al., *Question of Pornography*, pp. 328, 324. The commission reached the same conclusion about degrading materials: "As with sexually violent material, the extent of the effect of these degrading materials may not turn substantially on the amount of sexual explicitness once a threshold of undeniable sexual content is surpassed" (ibid., p. 335). Indeed, Donnerstein and his colleagues cite a study that compared "Triplex" films — hard-core porn — with "Adult" or "R-rated" videos and found:

    Triple X films depicted more "egalitarian" and "mutual" sexual depictions than adult films. For example, within the adult video it was usually the male who played the more dominant role in sexual scenes. In the Triple X video, on the other hand, males and females were depicted in the dominant role about equally as often. Even when Palys considered who was being dominated, females were more often found in this role in the adult videos than in the Triple X videos (ibid., p. 90).

22. Ibid., p. 112.

23. Nor is the demand for censorship limited to radical feminists and reactionary fundamentalists. There appears to be an increasing demand for censorship from some Jews (of Holocaust denial, Nazi propaganda), some blacks (of Ku Klux Klan marches, negative images in literature), some antiwar activists (of CIA recruiters, promilitary speakers on campus), some environmentalists (of smoking and nuclear energy ads), and others. Once the demands of any group are acceded to, the claims of "ism equity" make it difficult to resist the demands of other groups.

24. As Judge Frank Easterbrook mockingly put the censorship argument in the context of striking down the MacKinnon-Dworkin statute: "We know

what the truth is, yet a free exchange of speech has not driven out falsity, so that we must now prohibit falsity." He concluded that "under the First Amendment, however, there is no such thing as a false idea."

## CHAPTER 20: TELEVISION CENSORSHIP

1. See my book *Taking Liberties*, p. 92.

## CHAPTER 25: UPHOLDING THE WALL OF SEPARATION

1. On February 12, 1991, an appeals court threw out Bakker's sentence, saying that Judge Potter abused his discretion and violated Bakker's due process rights with his remarks at sentencing. "Regrettably, we are left with the apprehension that the imposition of the lengthy prison term here may have reflected on the fact that the court's own sense of religious propriety had somehow been betrayed," Judge Harvie Wilkinson III said in the opinion.

## CHAPTER 27: WHEN THE WALL COMES TUMBLING DOWN

1. See chapter 26, "The Right to Disbelieve."

## CHAPTER 28: LIFE IS NOT A DRAMATIC NARRATIVE

1. Alan M. Dershowitz, *The Advocate's Devil* (London: Headline, 1995), pp. 24–25. This fictional account is based on an actual case I won with the help of this argument. In real life, my son, Elon — then in college and today a film producer — came up with the Chekhov analysis.

2. *Anton Tchekhov: Literary and Theatrical Reminiscences*, ed. and trans. S. S. Koteliansky (London: Routledge, 1927), p. 23.

3. Initially attributed to the ancient Greeks, Cosmos is the idea that everything in the universe, from the motions of the planets to the workings of the human mind, can be explained by science or reason. Philip P. Weiner, ed., *Dictionary of the History of Ideas*, vol. 4 (New York: Scribner, 1973), pp. 46–51.

4. Compare Rabbi Adin Steinsaltz, *The Talmud: The Steinsaltz Edition: A Reference Guide* (New York: Random House, 1989), p. 6. "Points already made are not repeated without reason."

5. See, e.g., Sigmund Freud, *The Interpretation of Dreams*, trans. A. A. Brill (London: Allen and Unwin, 1994), p. 32.

6. See, e.g., Robert Bork, *The Tempting of America* (New York: Free Press, 1990), p. 145. Even a quick reading of some carelessly written, confusing, and even mistaken provisions of our hastily drafted Constitution and Bill of Rights should dispel any notion of divinity in its very human authors. For example, the Seventh Amendment provides for trial by jury in "suits at common law, where the value in controversy shall exceed twenty dollars." I can just imagine the framers looking down at our crowded courts from constitutional heaven and moaning, "Did we say twenty dollars? Damn, we meant the value of twenty dollars taking inflation into account. We didn't want every two-bit case in front of a jury. Why didn't we write it more carefully!"

7. Stephen J. Gould, *Wonderful Life* (New York: Norton, 1989).

8. The "naturalistic fallacy" refers to G. E. Moore's discussion of the analytical flaw whereby a person "is *either* confusing Good with a natural *or* metaphysical property *or* holding it to be identical with such a property or making an inference *based* on such a confusion" (emphasis added). Casmir Levy, "G. E. Moore on the Naturalistic Fallacy," in *G. E. Moore — Essays in Retrospect*, ed. Alice Ambrose and Morris Lazerowitz (London: Allen and Unwin, 1970). Egregious examples of such thinking include statements by Patrick Buchanan that AIDS is "nature's form of retribution" against "unnatural acts" and by Rabbi Eliezer Shach that the Holocaust was caused by Jews' eating pork. Patrick Buchanan, "AIDS Is Retribution," *Newsday*, February 28, 1992; *Star Tribune*, December 28, 1990.

9. Jean-Paul Sartre, *Nausea*, trans. Lloyd Alexander (New York: New Directions, 1964), pp. 39–40.

10. This is not to discount the power of science as a predictive tool in many areas, including human behavior. Among the most difficult predictive tasks, however, is to identify correctly, without too many false positives, which individuals will engage in relatively rare conduct.

11. A production code enforced by the Motion Picture Producers and Distributors of America in the 1930s dictated that "the sympathy of the audience shall never be thrown to the side of crime, wrong doing, evil or sin" (emphasis omitted). Raymond Moley, *The Hays Office* (Indianapolis: Bobbs-Merrill, 1945), pp. 98–99. Since then, movie audiences have grown used to seeing crime always followed by punishment.

12. Another parody is recounted in James Gleick's biography of Richard Feynman:

> He had developed pointed ways of illustrating the slippage that occurred when experimenters allowed themselves to be less than rigorously skeptical or failed to appreciate the power of coincidence. He described a common experience: an experimenter notices a peculiar result after many trials — rats in a maze, for example, turn alternately right, left, right, and left. The experimenter calculates the odds against something so extraordinary and decides it cannot have been an accident. Feynman would say: "I had the most remarkable experience. . . . While coming in here I saw license plate ANZ 912. Calculate for me, please, the odds that of all the license plates . . ." And he

would tell a story from his days in the fraternity at MIT, with a surprise ending.

"I was upstairs typewriting a theme on something about philosophy. And I was completely engrossed, not thinking of anything but the theme, when all of a sudden in a most mysterious fashion there swept through my mind the idea: my grandmother had died. Now of course I exaggerate slightly, as you should in all such stories. I just sort of half got the idea for a minute. . . . Immediately after that the telephone rang downstairs. I remember this distinctly for the reason you will now hear. . . . It was for somebody else. My grandmother was perfectly healthy and there's nothing to it. Now what we have to do is to accumulate a large number of these to fight the few cases when it could happen."

James Gleick, *Genius: The Life and Science of Richard Feynman* (New York: Pantheon, 1992), p. 374.

13. In this chapter I focus on the narrative as traditionally employed in classic literature. The works of Mamet, Beckett, Pirandello, Proust, Robbe-Grillet, Duras, and others often employ narratives that are much more reflective of the randomness of life.

14. Alan Cowell, "German Scholar Unmasked as Former SS Officer," *New York Times,* June 1, 1995.

15. See George Arthur Buttrick et al., eds., *The Interpreter's Bible*, vol. 3 (New York: Abingdon-Cokesbury, 1954), pp. 1196–97.

16. If the concept of "law" begins with human laws of behavior, such as "Thou shalt not murder," one might think that science borrowed this concept of laws and metaphorically applied it to natural phenomena, as with the laws of thermodynamics. In reality, the laws of science predate human laws, and the latter are borrowed from the former. In some languages, there are distinct words for human and scientific "laws."

17. Richard K. Sherwin, "Law Frames: Historical Truth and Narrative Necessity in a Criminal Case," *Stanford Law Review* 27 (1994): 39 (demonstrating the tendency in the legal search for truth to oversimplify complex situations to meet the demands of the modern mind for consistency and certainty).

18. See *State v. White*, 271 N.C. 391, 395; 156 S.E.2d 721, 724 (1967).

19. See "Scientists Deplore Flight from Reason," *New York Times,* June 6, 1995, sec. C, p. 1.

20. See Amos Tversky and Daniel Kahneman, "Judgment under Uncertainty: Heuristics and Biases," *Science* 185 (1974): 1124, reprinted in *Judgment under Uncertainty: Heuristics and Biases*, ed. Daniel Kahneman et al. (Cambridge: Cambridge University Press, 1982).

21. Even Chekhov acknowledges the often-unrealistic nature of his canon:

Shtcheglov-Leontyev blames me for finishing the story with the words, "There's no making out anything in this world." He thinks a writer who is a good psychologist ought to be able to make it out — that is what he is a psychologist for. But I don't agree with him. It is time that writers, especially those who are artists, recognize that there is no making out anything in this world, as once Socrates recognized it, and Voltaire, too. The mob thinks it knows and understands everything; and the more stupid it is the wider it imagines its outlook to be. And if a writer whom the mob believes in has the courage to say that he does not understand anything of what he sees, that alone will be something gained in the realm of thought and a great step in advance.

Anton Chekhov, letter to A. S. Suvorin, May 30, 1888, in *Letters of Anton Chekhov to His Family and Friends*, trans. Constance Garnett (London: Chatto and Windus, 1920), pp. 84, 89.

## CHAPTER 29: CRIME PREVENTION

1. Alan Dershowitz, "Preventive Detention," *New York Review of Books*, March 13, 1969.
2. *Williamson v. United States*, 194 F. 2d 280 (2d Cir. 1950).
3. *Maung Hla Gyaw v. Commissioner*, 1948 Burma Law Reps. 764, 766.
4. William Blackstone, *Commentaries on the Laws of England*, bk. 4, ed. William Lewis (Philadelphia: R. Welsh, 1897), pp. 1649–50.
5. See *Hirabayashi v. United States*, 320 U.S. 81 (1943).
6. 59 U.S.C. sec. 647.
7. *Commonwealth v. Franklin*, 172 Pa. Super. 152; 92 A. 3d 272 (1952).
8. *In re Gault*, 387 U.S. 1, 76.
9. *Commissioner's Committee on Arrests for Investigation* (Washington, D.C.: 1962).
10. Penal Code of California, sec. 647.
11. That there are occasional tragic convictions of innocent men was well documented many years ago in Edwin M. Borchard, *Convicting the Innocent* (New Haven, Conn.: Yale University Press, 1932), and more recently in Jerome Frank and Barbara Frank, *Not Guilty* (London: Gollancz, 1957), but as Borchard observed, there are still "about nine cases of unjust acquittal to one case of unjust conviction" (Borchard, *Convicting the Innocent*, p. 407). And as Frank and Frank warned: "The horrors portrayed in this book, however, should induce no belief that most convicts are guiltless. On the whole our system works fairly and most men in prison are almost surely guilty" (p. 38).
12. E.g., Alan Dershowitz, "The Psychiatrist's Power in Civil Commitment," *Psychology Today* (February 1969): 43.
13. *Baxtrom v. Herald*, 383 U.S. 107 (1966).
14. See Jonas Rappeport, *The Clinical Evaluation of the Dangerousness of the Mentally Ill* (Springfield, Ill.: Thomas, 1967).
15. Tydings would permit confinement if the defendant is charged with any of the following: (1) armed robbery or a related offense, (2) a felony involving serious bodily harm committed while the defendant was out on bail, (3) a felony involving serious bodily harm where the government alleges

that if released he will inflict such harm or pose, because of his prior pattern of conduct, a substantial danger to other persons or to the community.

16. Perhaps the proposed criteria for confinement could first be tested on records of past cases before they are applied — even experimentally — to live defendants. This could be done by giving to judges the past records of defendants, some of whom did and some of whom did not commit crimes while out on bail; they would then be asked to "predict"— or more accurately, postdict — which defendants fall into which category.

## CHAPTER 31: PSYCHIATRY
## IN THE LEGAL PROCESS

1. The mistake-of-fact defense precludes conviction of a person who reasonably believed that what he was doing would not produce a criminal harm. An example would be a person who fired what he reasonably believed was a toy gun.

## CHAPTER 32: MEMORANDUM
## TO JUSTICE GOLDBERG

1. W&M (2 sess) c.2.
2. *Wilkerson v. Utah*, 99 U.S. 130, 135–36 (1878).
3. *In re Kemmler*, 136 U.S. 436, 447 (1890).
4. *O'Neil v. Vermont*, 144 U.S. 323 (1892).
5. Ibid., 399–40.
6. *Weems v. United States*, 217 U.S. 349 (1910).
7. Ibid., 409.
8. The chief justice also said: "Whatever the arguments may be against capital punishment, both on moral grounds and in terms of accomplishing the purposes of punishment — and they are forceful — the death penalty has been employed throughout our history, and, in a day when it is still widely accepted, it cannot be said to violate the constitutional concept of cruelty." *Trop v. Dulles*, 356 U.S. 86, 99 (1958).
9. Justice Felix Frankfurter has implied agreement with this test as well. He said in *Lambert v. California*, 355 U.S. 225, 231 (1957) (dissent), that "cruelly disproportionate relation between what the law requires and the sanction for its disobedience may constitute . . . cruel and unusual punishment."
10. *Robinson v. California*, 370 U.S. 660, 677 (1962).
11. There is one other significant case that was not discussed in the foregoing section: *Louisiana ex rel Francis v. Resweber*, 329 U.S. 459 (1947). The case again dealt with the "cruelty inherent in the method of punishment, not the necessary suffering involved in any method employed to extinguish life

humanely." Ibid., 464. The Court held that the state could execute a murderer whom it had once failed to execute through no fault on its part.

12. See, e.g., *Williams v. New York*, 337 U.S. 241, 249 (1949), "Retribution is no longer the dominant objective of the criminal law."

13. The latest Gallup Poll indicates that 51 percent of those questioned favored capital punishment; 36 percent were opposed; and 13 percent were undecided. The comparable statistics seven years earlier were 68 percent, 25 percent, and 7 percent. *Washington Post*, March 25, 1960, sec. A, p. 23.

14. Jerome Michael and Herbert Wechsler, "A Rationale of the Law of Homicide," *Columbia Law Review* 37 (1937): 701.

15. Norval Morris, "Thoughts on Capital Punishment," *Washington Law Review* 35 (1960): 335.

16. *Royall Commission Report on Capital Punishment* (1953), p. 23.

17. H.L.A. Hart, "Murder and Its Punishment," *N.W. Law Review* 12 (1957): 433, 437.

18. "Such inquiries rarely approach any minimum standards of decent scientific rigor." Francis Allen, "Review," *Stanford Law Review* (1958): 600.

19. Richard Donnelly, "Capital Punishment in Connecticut," *Connecticut Bar Journal* 35 (1961): 39.

20. Hart, "Murder and Its Punishment," 460.

21. *Andres v. United States*, 333 U.S. 740, 752 (1948).

22. *White v. Washington*, 374 P.2d 942 (1963).

23. *Snider v. Cunningham*, 169 Misc. (1963 term).

24. This would also eliminate the presently intolerable situation, recognized by all, whereby the death penalty for sexual crimes is reserved almost exclusively for nonwhites.

25. Alexander M. Bickel, *The Least Dangerous Branch: The Supreme Court at the Bar of Politics* (New York: Bobbs-Merrill, 1962), pp. 242–43.

# CHAPTER 36: UNEQUAL JUSTICE

1. Jerold Auerbach, *Unequal Justice: Lawyers and Social Change in Modern America* (New York: Oxford University Press, 1976).

# CHAPTER 42: THE SOURCE OF JUSTICE IN THE MIND OF A JUSTICE

1. Review of *The Enigma of Felix Frankfurter*, by H. N. Hirsch (New York: Basic Books, 1981), in *New York Times Book Review*, February 22, 1981.

# CHAPTER 43: INSIDE THE
# SANCTUM SANCTORUM

1. Review of *The Court Years: 1939–1975. The Autobiography of William O. Douglas* (New York: Random House, 1980), and *Independent Journey: The Life of William O. Douglas*, by James F. Simon (New York: Harper and Row, 1980), in *New York Times Book Review*, November 2, 1980.
2. Justices Sandra Day O'Connor and Ruth Bader Ginsburg have since been appointed.

# CHAPTER 44: THE JUDGE JUDGED

1. Review of *Hugo Black and the Judicial Revolution*, by Gerald T. Dunne (New York: Simon and Schuster, 1977), in *New York Times Book Review*, April 10, 1977.

# CHAPTER 45: APPRECIATING LIBERTY

1. Review of *The Morality of Consent*, by Alexander M. Bickel (New Haven, Conn.: Yale University Press, 1975), in *New York Times Book Review*, September 21, 1975.
2. On the basis of first-hand experience with affirmative action over many years, I have changed my mind somewhat and come closer to Burke's "flexible, pragmatic recognition of imperfect justice," discussed in the text.
3. In fact, it was the unabashed liberal Justice Douglas who first raised questions about the constitutionality of race-specific affirmative action in *De Funis v. Odegaard*, 416 U.S. 312, 316, 40 L. Ed. 2nd 164, 94 S. Ct. 1704 (1974).

# CHAPTER 46: JUDICIAL REVIEW

1. Ely, *Democracy and Distrust*, p. 87.
2. Ibid., pp. 1–9.
3. Ibid., p. 3.
4. Ibid., p. 13.
5. Ibid., p. 31.
6. Ibid., p. 43.
7. *United States v. Carolene Products Co.*, 304 U.S. 144, 152–53 n. 4 (1938).
8. Ely, *Democracy and Distrust*, p. 103.
9. Ibid., p. 181.
10. See generally Moshe Silberg, "Law and Morals in Jewish Jurisprudence," *Harvard Law Review* 306 (1961): 75.

11. Babylonian Talmud, Baba Mezi'a 59b.

12. *Marbury v. Madison*, 5 U.S. (1 Cranch) 137 (1803).

13. *Stincer v. Kentucky*, 712 S.W.2d 939, 940 (Ky. 1986), rev'd, 107 S.Ct. 2658 (1987).

14. Ibid., 940–41.

15. *Kentucky v. Stincer*, 107 S.Ct. 2658 (1987).

16. Wílliam Bradford Huie, *The Execution of Private Slovik* (New York: Delacorte, 1970).

17. *United States v. Salerno*, 794 F.2d 64 (2d Cir. 1986), rev'd, 107 S.Ct. 2095 (1987).

18. *United States v. Salerno*, 107 S. Ct. 2095, 2101.

19. Ibid., 2103.

## CHAPTER 47: THE CONFIRMATION PROCESS

1. The list consisted of Robert C. Byrd, a senator from West Virginia; Sylvia Bacon, a D.C. judge; Mildred Lillie, a California judge; Charles Clark, a Mississippi judge; Florida judge Paul H. Roney; and Arkansas attorney Herschel H. Friday.

2. *Harris v. New York*, 401 U.S. 222 (1971).

3. *Wyman v. James*, 400 U.S. 309 (1970).

4. In 2000 Rehnquist wrote the court's decision upholding *Miranda* against attack by political conservatives. He relied explicitly on stare decisis. See *Dickerson v. United States*, 530 U.S. (2000).

## CHAPTER 48: THE QUALITY OF JUSTICE

1. Foreword to "The Quality of Justice: In the Lower Criminal Courts of Metropolitan Boston," by Stephen Bing and S. Stephen Rosenfeld, *Criminal Law Bulletin* 7, no. 5 (1971).

## CHAPTER 49: COULD IT HAPPEN HERE?

1. The Constitution specifically authorizes suspension "when in cases of Rebellion or Invasion the public safety may require it," and the Civil War was, of course, a rebellion within the intended meaning of that term.

2. Implicit in the Court's reasoning in *Milligan* is a compelling argument against the constitutionality of pretrial detention during normal times. The Court suggested that it required the suspension of habeas corpus to confine a defendant until trial. The obverse of this would seem to be that, in the absence of such suspension, denial of bail is unconstitutional.

3. The main reason this issue did not reach the Supreme Court earlier was that the Justice Department "mooted" prior cases by releasing the defendants as soon as they filed petitions in the Supreme Court.

   An extreme — and pathetic — example of the inclination of judges to defer decision until after the emergency had passed was provided by a case growing out of the Hawaiian martial rule. In 1944 a circuit court of appeals had approved the military trial of civilians. Two years later Circuit Judge Stephens filed a belated dissenting opinion, saying he had been reluctant to file it while the war was still going on.

4. The senators included Harley Kilgore, Paul Douglas, Hubert Humphrey, Herbert Lehman, Frank Graham, Estes Kefauver, and William Benton.

5. A proposed amendment to the Detention Act would require a "concurrent resolution of the Congress declaring the existence of an insurrection within the United States in support of a foreign enemy."

6. We are now in a state of "national emergency" as a result of President Truman's proclamation of December 16, 1950. The existence of this state has been reaffirmed by subsequent presidents. But we are not in a state of "internal security emergency," which carries very different powers. Other possible states include "extreme emergency," "sufficient emergency," "war or similar emergency," and "public peril."

7. Not all liberal senators supported the detention bill. The late senator William Langer had this to say: "So now it is proposed to have concentration camps in America! We can be absolutely certain that the concentration camps are for only one purpose: namely, to put in them the kind of people those in authority do not like! So we have come to this! Concentration camps!"

   But Senate Majority Leader Scott Lucas observed: "I favor a strong measure. . . . One may talk about concentration camps, one may talk about . . . creating a police state if he desires; but when we are dealing with Communists such as we know exist in this country . . . *there is nothing too drastic to meet that situation.*"

8. My own discussion with Mr. Kleindienst convinced me that he did not — and does not — advocate the use of the Detention Law attributed to him.

9. Ichord's Alice in Wonderland logic assumes that the president would have more power to detain without a congressional act than he would with such an act. What he neglects to mention is that the Supreme Court specifically relied on congressional ratification in sustaining certain aspects, and in disallowing other aspects, of the Japanese relocation. Moreover, the disingenuousness of Ichord's claim for civil liberties is established by the fact that when repeal was considered in committee, he introduced an amendment explicitly saying that repeal should not be construed to limit the president's inherent powers to order detention.

10. In *Youngstown Co. v. Sawyer*, the Supreme Court held the president could not, in the absence of congressional authorization, seize the steel mills during the Korean War, but it did say that Congress could authorize the president to take such action. No presidential declaration of emergency should ever, in my view, be permitted to remain in effect for any substantial time unless Congress ratifies that action (probably by more than a mere majority vote).

11. The Japanese detention case was decided while we were still at war with Japan, but well after the danger of a Japanese invasion had ended. Some lower federal courts did order the release of individuals of German and Italian origin who were detained on the East Coast.

12. In *ex parte Quirin*, the Supreme Court held that German spies captured in the United States could be tried and sentenced to death by a military commission. The Court expedited the hearing in that case "because in our opinion the public interest required that we consider and decide these questions without any avoidable delay." The true dimensions of that scandalous episode in our judicial history are now beginning to emerge in the public record.

13. "[M]artial law properly administered is preventive and not punitive." Frederick Wiener, *A Practical Manual of Martial Law* (Harrisburg, Pa.: Military Service, 1940), cites numerous authorities to the same effect.

14. Holmes defined law as "the prophecies of what the courts will do in fact, and nothing more pretentious."

15. See J. G. Anthony, *Hawaii Under Army Rule* (Stanford, Calif.: Stanford University Press, 1995), pp. 105–108.

# CHAPTER 50: PREVENTIVE DETENTION OF CITIZENS DURING A NATIONAL EMERGENCY

1. See chapter 49, above.

2. See, e.g., *Report of the Special Working Group of Experts* (established under Res. 6 [XXV] of the U.N. Commission on Human Rights) UN Doc. E/CN 4/1016 (1970).

3. The literal translation of the Hebrew term is "administrative detention"; the words *preventive* and *administrative* are used interchangeably when the subject is discussed in English.

4. See, for example, Alan Dershowitz, "Preventing Preventive Detention," *New York Review of Books* (March 31, 1969); Dershowitz, "The Psychiatrist's Power in Civil Commitment," *Psychology Today* (February 1969); and *Hearing on Bail Reform Before the Senate Subcommittee on Constitutional Rights* (January 23, 1969), pp. 172–85 (Dershowitz testimony).

5. Here are translations of the two poems. Al-Asmar has written that he prefers the term *administrative detention* to *preventive detention*, but I can see no significant difference.

**Preventive Detention**
I sit in preventive detention.
The reason is that I am an Arab.
An Arab who has refused to sell his soul,
Who has always striven, sir, for freedom.
An Arab who has protested the suffering of his people,
Who has carried with him the hope for a just peace,
Who has spoken out against death in every corner,
Who has called for — and has lived — a fraternal life.

That is why I sit in preventive detention,
Because I carried on the struggle and because I am an Arab.

**The Way**
I would not despair;
Even though my only way is within a jail,
  Under the sun,
    In the Exile —
I would not despair:
I would not choose but the Right as a realization,
For my right is that we behold the sun,
  Destroy the black tent and the banishment,
  Eat the fruit of the olive,
  Irrigate the vineyard,
  Sing melodies, melodies of love,
    In the quarters of Jaffa and Haifa,
  Sow our green soil with seeds;
Since these rights are mine,
I would not choose but the Right as a refuge.

My way is that we would extend hand to hand,
In order to build a castle of dreams,
Full of flowers,
Without hate,
Without unwise manners,
Since this is my way,
And even if the cost,
Of my adherence to my way,
Is to sacrifice the lids of my eyes,
And my soul,

I would pay,
And would not despair.

6. A recent example of this was provided by the detention of two Algerian security officials who were taken off their airplane at Lod airport, held for a short time, and then released.

7. See *Ex parte Quirin et al.*, 317 U.S. 1 (1942).

8. *Maung Hla Gyaw v. Commissioner*, 1948 Burma Law Reps. 764, 766. Compare, for example, the emergency rules recently put into effect by the Canadian government. The infringement of civil liberties authorized under these laws far exceeds that authorized under the Israeli regulations, yet the threat of terrorism is clearly not as serious in Canada — at least not yet — as in Israel.

9. This is the claim of the Japanese American Citizens League, and I know of no allegations to the contrary.

10. Quoted in Bill Hosokawa, *Nisei: The Quiet Americans* (New York: Norton, 1969), p. 288.

11. Ibid., pp. 287–88.

12. Eugene V. Rostow, "The Japanese-American Cases — a Disaster," *Yale Law Journal* 54 (1945): 489.

13. The day I visited the Knesset it was presided over by the deputy speaker, who is a Christian Arab from Nazareth.

14. It must be pointed out that the 15 detainees mentioned do not include the Arabs from occupied territories or from East Jerusalem. A considerably larger number of Gaza Strip and West Bank Arabs — in the area of 500 — are being held in preventive detention. Following the terrorist hijackings in the summer of 1970, an additional 450 West Bank Arabs were detained for a brief period and then released. Residents of the West Bank are Jordanian, not Israeli, citizens. Under the Geneva Accords, Jordanian law is supposed to govern their conduct. The Jordanian law applicable to the West Bank derives from the very same Emergency Defense Regulations inherited by Israel and explicitly authorizes preventive detention. When the Jordanian government controlled the West Bank, they made extensive use of preventive detention against Palestinian political opponents. During a visit to the West Bank, I was shown a petition, found by the Israeli army during the war, that had been signed by hundreds of Palestinian women whose husbands, sons, and fathers had been preventively detained by the Jordanian government, on "political" grounds. Preventive detention of dangerous members of an occupied population is also authorized by the Geneva Accords. It has been practiced by all occupying armies confronting a hostile population. I have, in this article, limited myself to preventive detention as it is practiced on citizens of Israel; I have not dealt with the occupied territories, which present different considerations, both legal and practical.

15. Indeed, the Dolphin, an excellent fish restaurant in East Jerusalem that is jointly owned by a Jew and an Arab, was blown up shortly after I ate there.

16. The Israeli authorities publicly belittle the damage done by terrorists, claiming that more Israelis die each year from automobile accidents than from terrorist attacks. But anyone who has driven on Israeli roads can take little comfort from that comparison.

17. It was there as a result of the First Law of the State of Israel, under which "the Law that existed in the Land of Israel on the Fifth Day of Iyar 5708 [the last day of the British Mandate] will be in force" unless repealed or inconsistent with subsequent enactments.

18. He reminded me of the observation made by Justice Robert Jackson in the Japanese-American detention cases: "In the very nature of things, military decisions are not susceptible of intelligent judicial appraisal. They . . . are made on information that would often not be admissible and assumptions that could not be proved. . . . Hence courts can never have any real alternative to accepting the mere declaration of the authority that issued the order that it was reasonably necessary from a military viewpoint."

    Jackson went on to conclude that the *judicial approval* of the army order detaining the Japanese was a "far more subtle blow to liberty than the promulgation of the order itself."

19. There has been some suggestion by Israeli authorities that preventive detention might be used against convicted terrorists who have served short prison terms, who are due for release, and who pose a danger of renewed terrorist activities. A change in sentencing practices would seem to be a better way to deal with the recidivistic terrorist.

20. Israel has blown up some houses in which terrorists have hidden, after clearing the houses of all occupants. No inhabitants have ever been hurt in these explosions.

21. William Brennan, "The Quest to Develop a Jurisprudence of Civil Liberties in Times of Security Crisis." Paper delivered in Jerusalem, December 22, 1987. Thanks to Einer Elhauge for bringing this to my attention.

## CHAPTER 52: TORTURE OF TERRORISTS

1. A special edition of *Israel Law Review* in 1989 presented a written symposium on the report of the Landau Commission, which in 1987–89 investigated interrogation practices of Israel's General Security Services.

2. Or at least part of it. A second volume was submitted but not published because of classified information.

3. Judge Irving Younger, a former New York State criminal court judge, once observed that "every lawyer who practices in the criminal courts knows that police perjury is commonplace." Quoted in Dershowitz, *The Best Defense*, p. 51.

4. Indeed, a standard argument currently offered by some prosecutors against Miranda and other exclusionary rules is that these rules increase police perjury.

5. Dershowitz, *The Best Defense*, pp. xxi–xxii, n. 2.

6. Ibid., p. 377.

7. *United States v. Rosner et al.* (S.D. N.Y.), 352 F. Supp. 915 (1972).

8. *Wickersham Commission Report* (publication of the National Commission on Law Observance and Enforcement) (Washington, D.C.: U.S. Government Printing Office, 1931).

9. J. Bishop Jr., "Control of Terrorism and Insurrection: The British Laboratory Experience," *Law and Contemporary Problems* 42 (1978): 140.

10. We do, after all, authorize the use of deadly force to capture escaping prisoners and some suspects.

## CONCLUSION: OLD RIGHTS FOR NEW WRONGS

1. Daniel Coquillette, *Francis Bacon* (Edinburgh, 1992), p 261. Thanks to Professor Coquillette for bringing this to my attention.

2. *Kyllo v. United States*, 533 U.S., 121 S. Ct. 2038, 150 L. Ed. 2nd 94, no. 99-8508 (June 11, 2001).

3. The Fourth Amendment does not use the word "privacy," which was not in common usage at the time of its enactment. Instead it uses the word "secure": "The right of the people to be secure in their persons, houses, papers, and effects, against unreasonable searches and seizures, shall not be

violated . . . ." The very word "secure" suggests a balance between liberty and safety.

4. In *Essai philosophique sur les probabilités* (1814), Pierre Simon Laplace argued that in theory we could predict the future if one knew the positions, directions, and speed of every particle of matter. Werner Heisenberg disputed this.

5. For example, John Rawls's clever formulation of an original position challenges the reader to decide these questions, e.g., whether all babies should be genetically engineered to create rough equality, without knowing whether, in the absence of such imposed equality, the child would be born better or worse than the current average. One criticism of this heuristic test is that it is virtually impossible for the intellectual elite who study Rawls to imagine themselves as intellectually inferior.

# INDEX

ABA. *See* American Bar Association
abortion
  arguments on, 26–28, 103
  criminalization of, 208, 305
  as evil, 189
  and fetal rights, 130
  forced, 113, 115
  and freedom of speech, 180
  and U.S. Supreme Court, 9, 18, 360,
    363–365, 372
  women's right to choose, 55, 67,
    103, 130–131, 176
ABSCAM (Arab scam; FBI sting), 250–
  252, 254, 256, 258
ACLU (American Civil Liberties
  Union), 154, 235, 293–294, 441
Adams, John, 13
Adler, Renata, 148–152
*The Advocate's Devil* (Dershowitz), 224,
  335, 348
affirmative action, 111, 194, 331, 385
African Americans, 74, 194, 339, 349,
  350
  and death penalty, 302–303
  and Jews, 342–343
*The Age of Reason* (Paine), 203
Agnew, Spiro, 108, 158
agnosticism, 89, 214, 215, 217, 328
AIDS (Acquired Immune Deficiency
  Syndrome), 226, 311
airplanes
  shooting down of hijacked, 31, 48n,
    98, 99
  used as bombs, 48n
al-Asmar, Fawzi, 433–435, 437–439,
  444, 446, 448, 450, 452, 454
Al Fatah, 434, 435, 444, 447, 452, 453
Ali, Muhammad, 467
Alien and Sedition laws, 66
Allen, Charles R., 425
Allen, Francis, 286
Alschuler, Albert, 62
*Altalena* (ship), 436
American Bar Association (ABA), 318–
  322, 401
  Code of Professional Responsibility,
  322

  Ethics Committee of, 319–321
  and legal ethics, 320, 322
  response to Watergate of, 322
American Center for Law and Justice,
  325
American Law Institute, 94
*The American Lawyer* (journal), 327
American Public Health Association,
  312
American Revolution, 41, 58, 430
Amnesty International, 450, 455
*Andres v. United States*, 287
animal rights, 23, 24, 82–87
  human-centered approach to, 86–87
animal sacrifice, 10, 82, 85
Anti-Defamation League, 337, 338
anti-Semitism, 178, 193, 385
  and natural law, 10
  and Simpson trial, 334, 336–337,
    340–343
Arabs
  detention of, in Israel, 433–435,
    437–439, 442–443
  Israeli, 436, 442–443, 447, 450, 455
  Jordanian, 436
  Palestinian, 452
  profiling of, 479
  as terrorists, 439, 443, 453
Arafat, Yasir, 337
Aristotle, 40
Armstrong, Scott, 350, 361–363, 365,
  367
Arnold, Thurman, 367
Asian Americans, 303
assassination, 438
  of terrorists, 480
atheism, 89, 214–217
Auerbach, Jerold, 318–322
Augustine, 11
Austin, John, 59
authoritarianism, 12
  religious, 216

Bacon, Francis, 487–488
Baer, Elizabeth, 143
Bakker, Jim, 211
Barak, Aharon, 476